THE FAMILY

THE MANSON GROUP AND ITS AFTERMATH

REVISED
AND UPDATED EDITION

Ed Sanders

A SIGNET BOOK
NEW AMERICAN LIBRARY
A DIVISION OF PENGUIN BOOKS USA INC.

NAL BOOKS ARE AVAILABLE AT QUANTITY DISCOUNTS WHEN USED TO PROMOTE PRODUCTS OR SERVICES. FOR INFORMATION PLEASE WRITE TO PREMIUM MARKETING DIVISION, NEW AMERICAN LIBRARY, 1633 BROADWAY, NEW YORK, NEW YORK 10019.

Copyright © 1971, 1972, 1989 by Ed Sanders

All rights reserved

Published by arrangement with E. P. Dutton.

SIGNET TRADEMARK REG. U.S. PAT. OFF. AND FOREIGN COUNTRIES
REGISTERED TRADEMARK—MARCA REGISTRADA
HECHO EN DRESDEN, TN, U.S.A.

SIGNET, SIGNET CLASSIC, MENTOR, ONYX, PLUME, MERIDIAN and NAL BOOKS are published by New American Library, a division of Penguin Books USA Inc., 1633 Broadway, New York, New York 10019

First Signet Printing, February, 1990

1 2 3 4 5 6 7 8 9

PRINTED IN THE UNITED STATES OF AMERICA

For my friend
Paul Fitzgerald
and
to the memory
of Phil Ochs,
who knew these times,
knew them well

Acknowledgments

For help, advice, and information for the first edition of *The Family,* I would like to thank the following: Tim Sandoval, Vincent Fremont, Phil Ochs, John Carpenter, Andy Wickham, Kathy Torrance, Karen Fleming, Ron Hughes, Mustl, Mark Mayer, Burton Katz, Barry Farrell, Mo Ostin, Mike Ochs, Walter Chappell, Bud Shrake, Warren Hinckle, Andrei and Alice Codrescu, Herbie Cohen, Richard Kaplan, Larry and Toni Larsen; Stan Atkinson, Carl George, Marty Kasindorf, Mary Neiswender, Theo Wilson, Michael McGovern and other reporters who covered the case; the staff at the Tropicana Motel, Glenn Frey for the film stake-out at the Los Angeles Airport, J.D. Souther, Mike Ochs, Hal Scharlatt, Charity Randall, and Carl Brandt. Thanks also to Sgt. Paul Whiteley and other police officers associated with the case. And to those Family associates who gave information, and also the always helpful staff of the Los Angeles Free Press; Art Kunkin, Judy Lewelyn, Sue Marshall, Brian Kirby, Paul and Shirley Eberle, Larry Lipton, Kitty Jay, and others.

For the *Family* update, I would like to thank Maury Terry, Jim Pursell, Ted Gunderson, Doris Tate, Stan Atkinson, Frank Fowles, Buck Gibbens, Paul Whiteley, William Gleason, Steven Kay, Vincent Bugliosi, Daye Shinn, Paul Fitzgerald, Aaron Stovitz, Lt. Quinn of the Los Angeles Sheriff's Office, and those who wish or need to remain nameless. Many thanks also to Larry and Toni Larsen, and the staff of Larry Larsen, Private Investigations; and to Pat Jackson, Rebecca Daniels, Miriam Sanders and Gus Reichbach.

Contents

Section 2

The Murders (July 25, 1969–August 15, 1969)

Section 3

Manson Captured (August 16–December 1, 1969)

Section 4

The Family: The Trials and Aftermath (1970–1989)

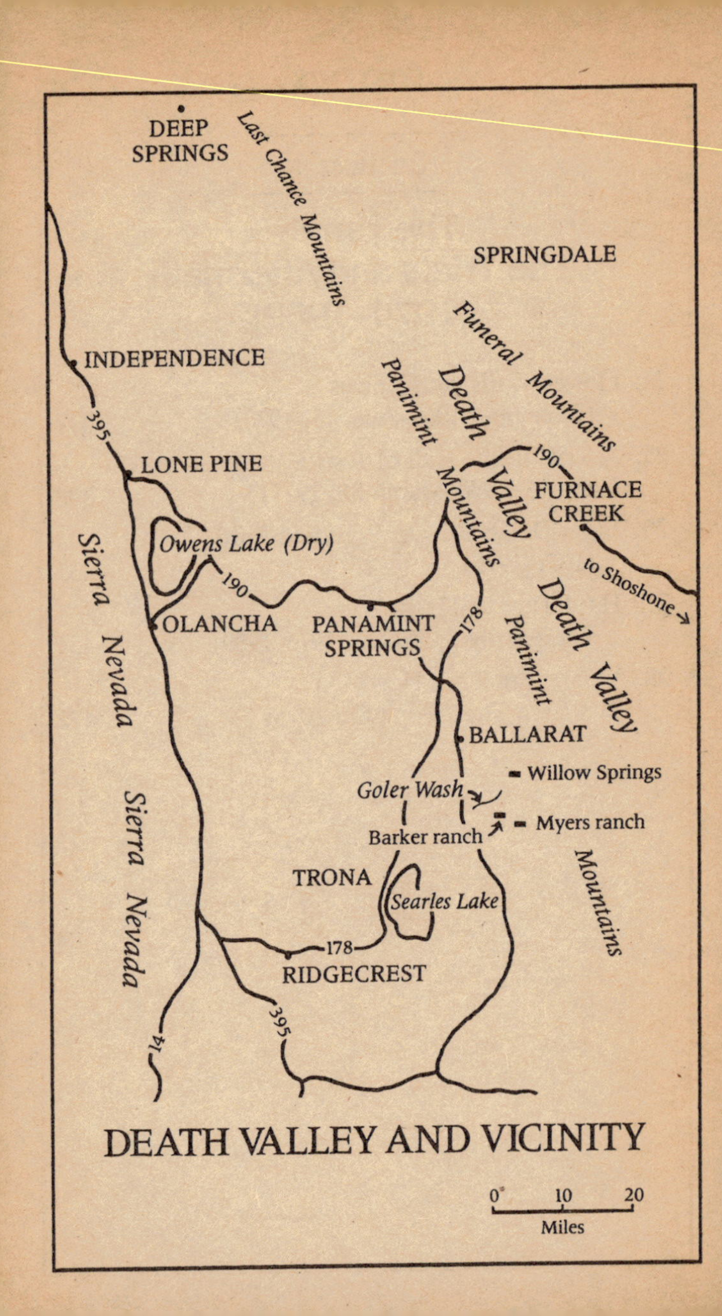
DEEP SPRINGS
Last Chance Mountains
SPRINGDALE
Funeral Mountains
INDEPENDENCE
Panimint
Death
395
LONE PINE
190
Mountains
Valley
FURNACE CREEK
Owens Lake (Dry)
Sierra
190
to Shoshone
Death
OLANCHA
PANAMINT SPRINGS
178
Panimint
Valley
Nevada
BALLARAT
Willow Springs
Goler Wash
Barker ranch
Myers ranch
Sierra
TRONA
Mountains
Searles Lake
Nevada
178
RIDGECREST
395
14
DEATH VALLEY AND VICINITY
0
10
20
Miles

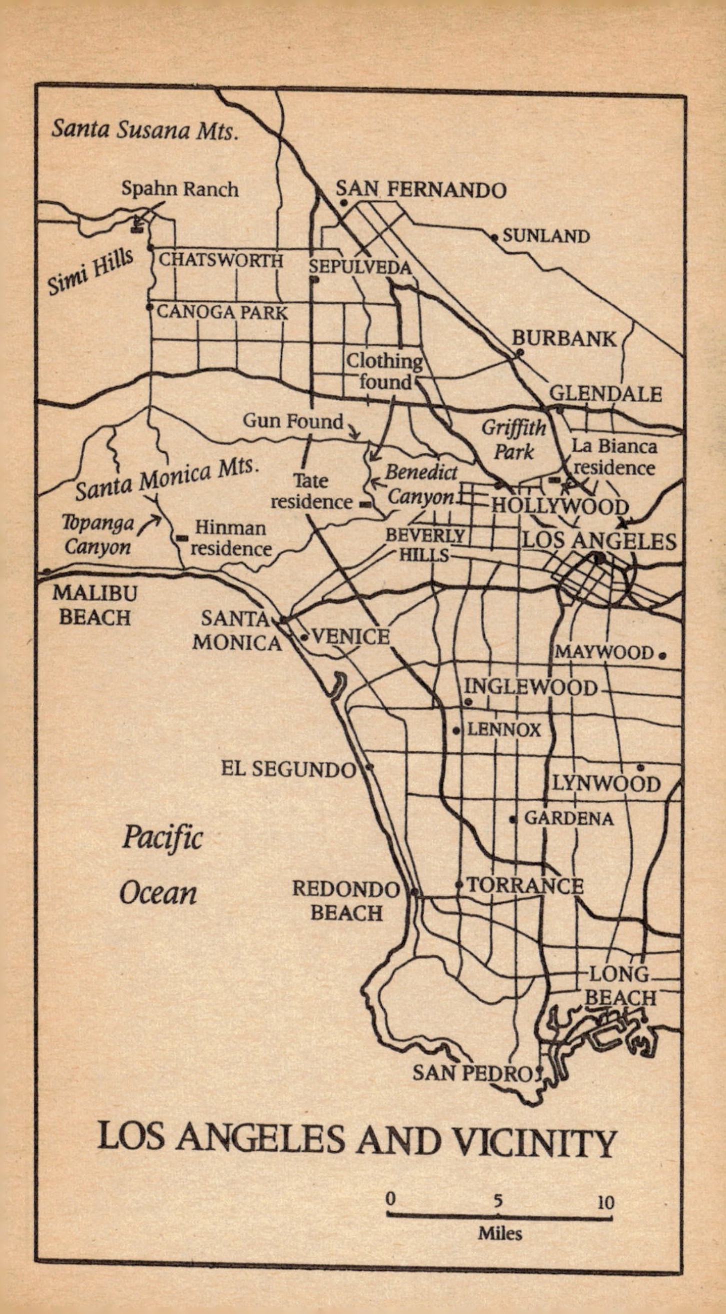
Santa Susana Mts.
Spahn Ranch
SAN FERNANDO
SUNLAND
Simi Hills
CHATSWORTH
SEPULVEDA
CANOGA PARK
BURBANK
Clothing found
GLENDALE
Gun Found
Griffith Park
La Bianca residence
Santa Monica Mts.
Tate residence
Benedict Canyon
HOLLYWOOD
Topanga Canyon
Hinman residence
BEVERLY HILLS
LOS ANGELES
MALIBU BEACH
SANTA MONICA
VENICE
MAYWOOD
INGLEWOOD
LENNOX
EL SEGUNDO
LYNWOOD
GARDENA
Pacific Ocean
REDONDO BEACH
TORRANCE
LONG BEACH
SAN PEDRO
LOS ANGELES AND VICINITY
0
5
10
Miles

Introduction to the Revised and Updated Edition

> One's file, you know, is never quite complete;
> a case is never really closed, even after a century,
> when all the participants are dead.
>
> —Graham Greene,
> *The Third Man*

Twenty years have passed, and I wanted to take another look at this strange, complicated case whose loose ends still dangle, even two decades later.

The first edition of this book told the story of the family from its inception in 1967, after Charles Manson was released from Federal prison, and ended with the arrests for the Tate-LaBianca murders in December of 1969.

This updated edition contains five new chapters that cover the murder trial of 1970 and 1971 and then track the case through two decades of strangeness and turmoil, including Squeaky Fromme's attempt on the life of President Ford. It takes a look at what happened to some of the key players in this crime drama during the ensuing twenty years.

Even though my writing style has changed, I decided not to tamper with the nervy, fact-suffused tone of the 1972 edition. One of the reasons I packed the original chronology with information is that I felt strongly that the full story of these murders had not yet come out and that there might be other murderers out there that had not yet been reeled into justice. I wanted to help the investigation, hoping that someone might come forward with new information to solve some of the mysteries.

And even though an abundance of new information has been uncovered and presented in this new edition, the mystery is still there, the picture still has blank spots, and the file may never get fully closed.

For this new edition I went back to Los Angeles and interviewed a number of people intimately associated with this case, including former prosecutors Vince Bugliosi, Stephen Kay and Aaron Stovitz. I spoke with police officers and others who had investigated the family. I returned to Goler Wash, three hundred miles northwest of Los Angeles, where the key members of the Manson family had their final rendezvous with handcuffs. I interviewed the defense lawyers, I corresponded with Manson and I spent an afternoon with Sharon Tate's mother, Doris Tate, who has become a leader in the victims' rights movement.

For this update, once again I had the great assistance of my friend, ace private investigator Larry Larsen, who had helped in collecting information for the original edition.

I sometimes ponder why two decades ago I became involved with a case that had more loose ends than a fringed tablecloth. I think I became involved chiefly because of my instant perception that this group helped wreck the dream of the 1960s.

I was very active in the 1960s as a poet, musician and political activist. My band, The Fugs, performed regularly in California. We played outdoors for the flower children in Golden Gate Park the very spring that Manson was roaming the Haight. We took part in love-ins and peace demonstrations all over America, and we helped stir up the expectations of a generation for permanent change. I encountered a number of roaming psychedelic buses during those years and had friends who lived on communes. No one had ever mentioned Charles Manson.

I had only heard of his group once before they were indicted for murder. A friend edited an ecology newsletter called *Earth Read-Out*. In late October of 1969 he reprinted a story from the *San Francisco Chronicle* dated October 15, 1969:

> The last survivors of a band of nude and long-haired thieves who ranged over Death Valley in stolen dune buggies have been rounded up, the sheriff's office said

> yesterday. A sheriff's posse, guided by a spotter plane, arrested 27 men and women members of the nomad band in two desert raids. Deputies said eight children, including two babies suffering from malnutrition, were also brought in. Some of the women were completely nude and others wore only bikini bottoms, deputies said. All the adults were booked at Inyo county jail for investigation of charges which included car theft, receiving stolen property and carrying illegal weapons. Six stolen dune buggies were recovered, deputies said.
>
> Deputy Sheriff Jerry Hildreth said the band lived off the land by stealing. He said they traveled in the stolen four-wheel-drive dune buggies and camped in a succession of abandoned mining shacks. The band previously escaped capture by moving only at night and by setting up radio-equipped lookout posts on the mountains, he said. "It was extraordinary the way they covered up their tracks and would make dummy camps to throw us off," Hildreth said. "They gave us a merry chase. . . . This is probably one of the most inaccessible areas in California."

Six weeks after I read those two paragraphs in *Earth Read-Out,* the front pages of newspapers were filled with glaze-eyed pictures of Manson, the accused murderer.

He was depicted all at once as a hippie satanist car thief cult-leader sex-maniac bastard butcher. His followers —a few young men and around twenty girls—were depicted as "Satan's slaves," willing to do anything, anytime, anywhere for him. Out of all the headlines and stories, no consistent set of facts seemed to emerge that explained in any depth how a group of young American citizens could develop into a commune of hackers.

This case had everything—sex, drugs, gore, Hollywood, hints at black magic and hippies. The media went wild. The cameras rolled frantically and the front pages were filled worldwide with a mix of fascination and revulsion. At once Manson's family seemed to wound the best qualities of a generation—its sharing and self-reliance, its music and wild colors, its love of the outdoors and the natural beauty of America, its search for higher standards, its early sense of the need to protect the environment. Could it be that this one group would put a grotesque and hideous capstone upon a decade that had such a powerful and beautiful promise?

Late in 1969 I began to gather data about the family, as a matter of personal curiosity. At first I thought they might have been set up. Then I decided to write a book, thinking it would take about six months, after which I could return to a quiet life of poetry and peace. Almost at once, upon my first flight to Los Angeles, I dipped into a frenzy of continuous day and night activity that would last for a year and a half, resulting in the first edition of this book.

For that year and a half, I wrote down literally everything I heard or saw related to the so-called Manson family. I carried with me at all times a tape recorder and recorded at least a hundred hours of interviews, confrontations and comments. Nothing was too trivial to escape my jotting pen. Often a strange bit of information that seemed to have no meaning would, a year after I received it, turn out to be important.

Over the period of a year I wrote about twenty-five articles for the *Los Angeles Free Press* covering the Manson trial and the ongoing existence of his family of followers. Without the friendship of the staff of the *Free Press*, this book could not have been written, for the *Free Press* office was a zone of sanity where I could escape after a day of gathering insane data about corpses, bloodshed and weirdness.

Part of this book was written in the Hall of Justice in downtown Los Angeles, where I attended some four months of the trial of Susan Atkins, Patricia Krenwinkel, Leslie Van Houten and Charles Manson. I also attended Robert Beausoleil's second trial for the murder of Gary Hinman and numerous court hearings pertaining to other trials and murders involving the family. It was necessary to maintain a considerable correspondence with individuals all over the United States and Europe.

It's difficult to recreate the fear and blood-tinged freakiness that surrounded the Tate-LaBianca trial, a climate of surreality commingled with sleaziness that should have been called what it was—i.e., sursleaze. There were so many death threats from members of the family that finally no one paid much attention to them.

There were problems of a scarier nature that tended to

hamper proper investigation, particularly the problem of the body in the car trunk. Several business friends of Jay Sebring were murdered during the trial. I was trying to locate one of them, a man named Rostau, from whom I wanted some information, when news came in the fall of 1970 that he had been found dead in a car trunk in New York. Another associate was found murdered in Florida around Christmas in 1970. These events caused me to swerve my investigation elsewhere. No book is worth permanent meditation next to a tire.

Nevertheless, I was able finally to amass the story of the family. And now, twenty years later, we have added new chapters, to bring this classic American crime story up to date.

SECTION 1

THE FAMILY

From the Beginning to mid-1969

1

A Poor Risk for Probation

Around July 22, 1955, Charles Manson drove a stolen 1951 Mercury from Bridgeport, Ohio to Los Angeles, bringing with him his seventeen-year-old pregnant wife, Rosalie. All was.

In September he was arrested and pleaded guilty on October 17, 1955. The psychiatric report prepared after Manson's arrest stated that he was a "poor risk for probation" but, on the other hand, it was felt that married life plus incipient fatherhood, which calms down juvenile delinquents everywhere, might put him onto the direct path of the American Way. So on November 7, 1955, Manson was sentenced to five years' probation. Manson had been on parole since May 18, 1954. He was twenty-one years old. He had been in prison since he was sixteen and in various corrective institutions before that since he was thirteen.

After his arrest Manson made the mistake of admitting to the Feds during interrogation that in 1954, the year previous, he had taken a hot auto from the strip-mine area of West Virginia down to Florida.

As a result of this self-snitch, on January 11, 1956, Manson appeared before the Federal Commissioner in Los Angeles regarding a complaint filed in Miami, Florida charging violation of the Dyer Act.

Released on his own recognizance, Manson was told to

return to court on February 15. Shortly thereafter he fled Los Angeles, evidently accompanied by his heavily pregnant wife Rosalie. They drove back home to Appalachia.

On February 29 the chief probation officer in Los Angeles requested the court to issue a bench warrant because Manson had not reported in to his probation officer. He was arrested on March 14, 1956, in Indianapolis, Indiana and transported back to Los Angeles for trial.

In March of 1956 a son Charles, Jr., was born.

On April 23, 1956, Judge Harry C. Westover revoked probation and imposed a three-year federal prison sentence for Manson at Terminal Island Penitentiary in San Pedro, California.

For almost a year during the first part of his Terminal Island sentence, Rosalie, his wife, stuck by him—living with Charles, Jr., the son, and Manson's mother, Kathleen, in Los Angeles. Early in 1957 Rosalie discontinued her visits and according to a Federal probation report, was living with another man, which upset Manson greatly. On May 24, 1957, Manson tried to sneak away from Terminal Island and was indicted under the United States Code Title 18 Section 751, Escape from Federal Custody after Conviction. Manson pleaded guilty on May 27, 1957, and on June 10, 1957 was given a suspended sentence by Federal Judge William Mathes and placed on probation for five years.

Shortly thereafter Manson's West Virginia wife sued for divorce. A summons was served on Manson on July 15 at Terminal Island in San Pedro. Affidavit of final judgment of divorce was filed August 30, 1957. Adios, wife.

Manson served from April 23, 1956, until September 30, 1958: two years, five months, five days of so-called rehabilitation. In prison the young, 125-pound man played on various basketball teams and evidently boxed a bit. He continued his sex life in the only way possible in jail—by hand, by mouth and by buttock.

For two and one-half years Manson was exposed to the endless discussions of schemes and crimes and psychopathy out of the mouths of older, so-called seasoned criminals. At Terminal Island there was a lot of what might be called "pimp talk"—about the devices to be used in controlling a bevy of prostitutes. Charlie listened avidly, according to people interviewed from Terminal Island. A friend who knew him then writes: "We'd rap a lot about whores, especially how to control them. We talked about Main Old Ladies—a pimp's number one girl who controlled all the others; stables—more than one girl working for you; and we talked mostly about how to turn chicks out."

Time passed for young Charlie Manson and "Subject was released from the FCI, TI on 9–30–58 and is on CR till 10–24–58"—noted his federal parole office on October 1, 1958, in what are called chrono notes.

Manson announced that he was going to live with his mother on Harkinson Avenue in Los Angeles. This was the first of twenty addresses Manson would have in this particular year and eight months' stretch of freedom.

The parole office gave him some employment leads. His employment pattern for the following months reads like a struggling novelist's. But Manson was just struggling, working as a bus boy, bartender, frozen-food locker concessionaire, canvasser for freezer sales, service station attendant, TV producer and pimp.

On January 1, 1959, an irate father complained to the Los Angeles police department that Manson was making attempts to turn his daughter Judy out onto the streets to hustle. Manson also ran around with Judy's roommate, a wealthy UCLA student named Flo from Baker, California, who drove a white Triumph.

On May 1, 1959, Manson was caught running from a Ralph's Market in Los Angeles having attempted to forge and cash a stolen government check for $34.50. Earlier in the day he had cashed another stolen check at a Richfield service station. He was to be severely spanked for this. Impounded at the scene of the crime was a blue 1953 Cadillac convertible evidently belonging to Manson's mother.

After the Los Angeles police department had turned Manson over to the federal authorities, the Feds while questioning Manson made the mistake of leaving the forged check lying out in an open dossier. Manson appears to have seized and gobbled down the check when the secret service agents turned their backs for a moment. In any event, the check disappeared and Manson soon begged to go to the bathroom in order to void the contents of his stomach due to gobbled check nausea.

On June 19, 1959, an attractive, according to the parole officer, nineteen-year-old female Caucasian named Candy Stevens visited Manson's parole officer and announced that she was pregnant by Manson and that he and she were going to get married if only the mean old federal authorities wouldn't salt him away. In reality, she was not pregnant but was a strumpet currently working for Manson. In fact, Manson may have been the first to turn her out.

On September 4, 1959, another psychiatric examination was given Manson by the same doctor who had examined him four years previous. The report concluded:

> He does not give the impression of being a mean individual. However, he is very unstable emotionally and very insecure. He tells about his life inside the institutions in such a manner as to indicate that he has gotten most of his satisfactions from institutions. He said that he was captain of various athletic teams and that he made a great effort to entertain other people in the institutions. In my opinion, he is probably a sociopathic personality without psychosis. Unfortunately, he is rapidly becoming an institutionalized individual. However, I certainly cannot recommend him as a good candidate for probation.

Charlie Manson was twenty-four years old.

Manson had a hearing on September 28, 1959, with the young lady Candy beseeching and weeping in court before the judge in behalf of Manson—and the judge relented and suspended sentence of ten years, placing Manson on probation for five.

In November of 1959 Manson met an eighteen-year-old girl from Detroit named Mary Jo who had been suckered out to Los Angeles by a magazine ad for an airline stewardess school. When the girl reached Los Angeles the school turned out to be a fraud and she couldn't get her money back. She talked her parents into letting her remain in Los Angeles and moved into an apartment with a girl friend named Rita.

In late 1959 Manson hooked up with a Tony Cassino

forming something called 3-Star Enterprises, Night Club, Radio and TV promotions, Suite 306, 6871 Franklin, Hollywood. (This address was just a couple of doors away from the apartment where a decade later Manson would gun down the black dope dealer Bernard Crowe.) Manson was president and Tony was VP. Allegedly Manson obtained some money from Detroit Mary Jo for three of his so-called promotions. The reality of 3-Star Enterprises seems to be that Manson was dealing female sex objects out of the Hollywood Roosevelt Hotel.

In October Charlie's mother moved back to West Virginia and alleged that she was going to stay there.

December 4, 1959, Candy Stevens, the girl who cried in court, was arrested in Beverly Hills for prostitution. Manson raised money and bailed her out, but a short time later she was given a jail term. In the meantime, Manson caused pregnancy to occur within that girl from Detroit, Mary Jo.

On December 24, 1959, Christmas Eve, Manson was arrested and was accused of sending a person named Harold in a stolen car with Candy and a girl named Elizabeth to Needles, California in order to deal out bod. He was soon released for lack of evidence. On New Year's Eve Manson was picked up on charges of stealing credit cards but was released on January 4, 1960.

On January 5, 1960, Manson was summoned to court as a witness regarding theft of American Express and Bank of America credit cards. Things were heating up for the young Manson, "this weak, tricky youth"—as his parole officer called him. The FBI began an intensive investigation of Manson, and February 15, 1960, was the last date that Manson reported in to his parole officer.

On February 20, 1960, the pregnant Mary Jo from Detroit became very ill. Her pregnancy became ectopic—i.e., the fetus was growing in the Fallopian tube, a serious condition—and the girl began to bleed and was taken to a hospital. Manson called the girl's father, an insurance executive in Detroit, who flew immediately to Los Angeles where he was met at the Los Angeles International Airport by Manson and Mary Jo's roommate Rita. On the way back Manson announced that he didn't have a driver's license and that he was a federal parolee. Mary Jo's father, according to a Federal probation report, was shocked at the sudden flash that his daughter had been knocked up by a convict.

Mary Jo seesawed through her crisis, then quickly recovered. Her father hustled her away to a private recuperation home. Manson somehow found her phone number and began to call her. Mary Jo told her father that she was deeply in love with Manson. The girl's father began to snoop around Hollywood and discovered a few people who alleged that Manson had been doing a bit of pimping. To quote the parole officer's report of that era, the father was "sick with the thought that this subject planned to have his daughter and Rita work for him." Then to the father's horror, he discovered that the man his daughter loved, on the very night that Manson had taken Mary Jo to the hospital in serious condition, this man Manson had seduced Mary Jo's roommate Rita.

On February 29, 1959, the father visited Manson's federal parole officer to complain. The father, a skilled insurance investigator already, had really burned up the roads getting the data on Manson. He was angered over Manson's refusal to hand over Mary Jo's luggage. The father even had tried to get the Pasadena police to arrest Manson, but they refused.

In the afternoon after seeing the parole officer, the irate father drove to Manson's rooming house in Pasadena and found that Manson had abandoned the pad but not Mary Jo's luggage which Charlie took with him. Father was horrified to find semi-nude girlie photos left behind. A police officer neighbor in the rooming house described Manson as a "sex maniac" and hinted that Manson may have been taking beaver photos for sale out of state.

It was all over for Manson. The machinery of justice began to gobble up his trail.

In April of 1960 Candy Stevens snitched to a federal grand jury and on April 27, 1960, an indictment was handed down charging Manson with violation of Title 18 Section 2421, Transportation of Women in Interstate Commerce for Purposes of Prostitution. Evidently he himself transported the young ladies, Candy and Elizabeth, on December 12, 1959, from Needles, California to Lordsburg, New Mexico in a stolen Triumph convertible.

On petition of the federal parole office, Judge Mathes

revoked parole on the previous check forgery charge. On May 23, 1960, bond was set at $10,000. On June 1, 1960, a week after the issuance of the bench warrant for his arrest, Charlie was picked up in Laredo, Texas, evidently on a separate matter, charged with violation of the Mann Act, aka (also known as) White Slave Act. A few days later, on June 16, Manson was returned to authorities in Los Angeles.

On June 23, 1960, Judge William Mathes sentenced Manson to serve ten years at McNeil Island Federal Penitentiary in the state of Washington. On July 10, 1960, the federal pimp charges were dropped but Manson had already been sentenced for parole violation.

Manson had been free for one year, eight months and two days. He appealed the ten-year sentence and remained about a year in Los Angeles County Jail on the top floors of the Hall of Justice where a decade later he would be tried for murder.

In June of 1961 he gave up after losing a court appeal, and allowed himself to be shipped to McNeil Island Penitentiary.

In December of 1963 Manson's mother, evidently remarried and living in Spokane, Washington, wrote a letter to Judge Mathes offering to put up her house as security for Manson's release. The judge had his clerk write her back that after ninety days the judge had no jurisdiction to alter terms of sentencing.

For most of the 1960's Manson sat in jail. Through the tumult of the various liberation movements outside in America, through riots, through assassinations, the beginning of Vietnam, peace rallies, sexual liberation, rock and roll, the Beatles For Sale, the Beach Boys, napalm, Hare Krishna, and the growing refusal of women to be victimized—a movement of which he had little awareness—through all this sat Manson monitoring reality through magazines and hearsay conversation.

It was while counting the days at McNeil Island that Manson began studying magic, warlockry, hypnotism, astral projection, Masonic lore, scientology, ego games, subliminal motivation, music and perhaps Rosicrucianism.

Especially hypnotism and subliminal motivation. He seemed determined to use it to effect control over others, to his benefit.

One prison mate of Manson at McNeil Island recalls vividly the great Charlie Manson Headphones Caper.

Utilizing the prison radio station, Manson planted what his cell partner called "posthypnotic suggestions" in all the prisoners at McNeil Island Penitentiary.

Each prisoner had access to the station by means of headphones hanging on the bunk beds in the cells. Manson set up a clandestine scheme whereby the radio station would broadcast messages at 3 A.M. over the earphones. The message or instruction was repeated over and over.

The prisoners were required to hang their headsets at night on the bedsteads so that the messages were picked up by the sleepers but were not loud enough to attract the guards.

The story continues that McNeil Island had a basketball team that rarely won any games. Manson beamed messages to the sleeping inmates urging them to get out and to root for the McNeil Island team.

Charlie then placed bets with the zealous new fans that the opposing teams would win and quickly won himself two hundred packs of cigarettes, the medium of exchange in U.S. prisons.

Another was the applause caper: he planted suggestions over the earphones that everyone should keep applauding for Manson when he sang at a particular prison talent contest. Manson won the contest earphones-down, evidently receiving a standing ovation of some duration.

Of irony, Manson seems to have become a protégé in prison of prohibition gangster Alvin Karpis, a member of the evil Ma Barker gang, which left fourteen victims dead.

Alvin "Old Creepy" Karpis taught Charlie to play the steel guitar and seems to have been a general counselor to the young man, although when interviewed after Manson's arrest, Karpis said that he had considered Manson the last man on earth "to go into the mass murder business."

"Charlie was hooked on this new thing called 'scientology,' " says Karpis. "He figured it would enable him to do anything or be anything. Maybe he was right. The kid tried to sell a lot of other cons on scientology but got strictly nowhere."

Scientology is a reincarnationist religion that claims to train individuals to experience past lives, to leave their bodies—i.e., "exteriorize"—and to achieve great power and immortality, among other things. Manson learned about scientology from one Lanier Ramer, from Gene Deaton and from Jerry Milman, who was Manson's roommate at McNeil Island Penitentiary.

Lanier Ramer, according to Manson's followers, had been active in the study of scientology and had become a Doctor of Scientology, an early rank in the movement, now abolished.

Ramer broke away from scientology and formed his own group. He was apprehended for armed holdup and was sent to McNeil Island.

Manson has told a jail house visitor that he received 150 sessions of "processing" in jail, evidently from Lanier Ramer.

Manson has contended that he learned scientology methods very quickly because his "mind wasn't programmed." But Manson was not a "product" of scientology in any way; he merely borrowed a few ideas from it. The scientologists call it "squirrelling"—that is, borrowing and mutating scientology practices or methods.

Manson picked up a fair number of scientology phrases, neologisms and practices which he put to his own use when he began to reorganize the minds of his young followers.

Phrases like "to mock up" and "cease to exist" and "to come to Now" and the concept of "putting up pictures" all seem to have their origin in Manson's McNeil Island sessions with Lanier Ramer.

Manson also studied Masonic lore and picked up some knowledge of Masonic hand signals (which later he would flash to judges during court appearances).

He evidently learned something about scientology recognition signals also. Later, in the era of creepy crawlie, Manson would develop his own complex system of hand and body signals—really a whole language of chopnotation—among his followers.

For someone so unskilled in reading and writing, Manson took a high interest in certain books on hypnotism and psychiatry. According to a friend, he was interested particularly in a book called *Transactional Analysis* by Dr. Eric Berne, the author of *Games People Play*. Charlie, ever the proselytizer, urged his friends to read his discovered books.

From his study of *Transactional Analysis,* Manson may have developed his perverse doctrine of Child Mind. Certainly he borrowed lots of ideas from the pioneer work in group therapy.

He had a friend, one Marvin White, who appears to have been released from McNeil Island and then to have made arrangements to mail Charlie books on black magic and related subjects.

Another book that helped provide a theoretical basis for Manson's family was *Stranger in a Strange Land* by Robert Heinlein, the story of a power-hungry telepathic Martian roaming the earth with a harem and a quenchless sexual thirst while proselytizing for a new religious movement. Initially, Manson borrowed a lot of terminology and ideas from this book—not, hopefully, including the ritual cannibalism described therein.

Manson was, however, to identify with the hero of the book, one Valentine Michael Smith (Manson's first follower's child was named Valentine Michael Manson)—a person who, in the course of building a religious movement, took to killing or "discorporating" his enemies. Smith, in the book, ultimately was beaten to death by an angry mob and ascended to the Sky.

To this day Manson's followers hold water-sharing ceremonies where Manson, in jail, magically takes a long-distance hit off a glass of water which is being stared at by a circle of sitting adepts.

What he seems to have known most intimately though was the Bible, which he was able to quote at great length.

Singing and songwriting began to occupy his time also. The idea of becoming a performer seemed to interest him. Manson at some point appears to have been allowed to own a guitar. "A Mexican taught me the guitar," Manson has written. One young lady who owned a boutique in the Silverlake area of Los Angeles remembered Charlie, after he was released from jail, coming to her shop with his guitar and singing her "beautiful love songs in Spanish"—songs probably learned in jail.

The Beatles attracted Manson's consciousness early in their career, even during the Wanna Hold Your Hand mania of 1963–64.

Alvin Karpis of the Barker Gang remembers it: "He

was constantly telling people he could come on like the Beatles, if he got the chance. Kept asking me to fix him up with high-power men like Frankie Carbo and Dave Beck; anyone who could book him into the big time when he got out."

After five years at McNeil Island, several friends of Manson, "prison lawyers"—prisoners with legal expertise—worked out a legal maneuver whereby on June 29, 1966, Charlie was transferred from McNeil Island, Washington, to Terminal Island prison in San Pedro, California near Los Angeles. Probably it was felt that he stood a better chance of early release at Terminal Island.

At Terminal Island Manson really began to prepare for operation superstar. He spent the better part of a year there. Friends remember him as being fanatically dedicated to music and singing.

One person, Phil Kaufman, in jail on a federal marijuana charge, was impressed by Manson's musical abilities and offered him certaln connections on the outside whenever Manson should be set free. Kaufman gave Manson the name of a person at Universal Studios in Hollywood where Manson, in late '67, would record his songs.

Manson made many friends during this last seven years in prison. Some cellmates say that Manson planned all along to collect an army of outcasts operating "beneath the awareness" of the mother culture. Others say he was an out-and-out creep, but a few remember him with affection and seem almost dazed that he became the leader of a kill-coven.

But it is safe to say that when he was released, he had a chance. A complex, long-term tragedy had been punching Charles Manson in the face all his life. But now in the year 1967, love had caught the attention of war-crazed America and the streets were paved with acceptance for a troubadour and a peripatetic collector of walking wounded war children.

2

Out of the Slams

With thirty-five dollars and a suitcase full of "clothes," Manson walked out of jail on March 21, 1967, after serving six years and nine months of punishment. He was thirty-two and a half years old.

The legend is that Manson actually tried to reenter the prison, or balked at leaving the front gate. Once on the street, however, he began two and a half years of ceaseless wandering.

At first, Charlie walked around and rode buses in Los Angeles for about three days after leaving Terminal Island. Then he went north to Berkeley to visit some friends he had met in prison.

Manson was anxious to impress as a minstrel/wandering singer. He spent time at the University of California Berkeley campus with his guitar.

Guitar in hand, he began to scrounge around the streets of Berkeley. One spring day he was sitting and singing in the open-air mall near Sather Gate on the University of California campus when he met slim, red-haired Mary Brunner of Eau Claire, Wisconsin, a recent graduate of the University of Wisconsin who was working at the library at the University of California. Also working in Berkeley then, at the University of California Art Museum, was Abigail Folger, heiress to the Folger Coffee Company fortune.

Right away Manson and Brunner became friends and evidently he moved into her apartment with her.

As a federal parolee, Manson was required to keep close contact with a federal parole officer, informing the officer of his whereabouts, employments and activities. Manson was assigned to a federal parole officer, a man named Roger Smith, who befriended him. Charlie was heavily into using many Heinleinian words like Grok and Thou Art God and Share Water and other Strange Land terminology, so Manson and the girls renamed Roger Smith "Jubal," after the fatherly protector Jubal Harshaw in the novel *Stranger in a Strange Land.*

Parolees are supposed to find gainful employment so Manson sought or was offered work as an entertainer. He actually played at a club in San Francisco's tenderloin district. He also may have played a club in North Beach. His parole officer says he was offered a job in Canada to sing.

It is nearly impossible to follow the peripatetics of Manson in early 1967 because he began his roaming at once and who indeed really can remember the specifics of a given week in early 1967?

Manson made definite attempts to locate his mother, Kathleen. He secured permission from his federal parole officer to travel out of state several times. Once he went north to Washington in search of her. Another time, east to West Virginia.

A young redhead named Lynne Fromme joined Mary Brunner as addition number two to the inner circle of ladies. She was picked up near the beach in Venice, California where Charlie coaxed her off a curbside as she was sitting, crying. Legend has it that she had just been thrown out of her father's pad in Redondo Beach following a quarrel.

She was initiated. "I am the god of fuck," she later claimed he said after they first made out.

For a while in the spring and summer of 1967, Manson and the girls lived at 636 Cole in Haight Ashbury, reportedly with a beautiful ex-nun named Mary Ann. Manson wandered the streets of the Haight, meandering among the flower children. A sixteen-year-old flower waif, perhaps a boy, perhaps a girl, it doesn't matter, homeless and alone, offered Charlie his or her friendship. It was amazing, to the man who'd spent his youth in jail, that this young boy was sleeping in Golden Gate Park located near Haight-Ashbury.

There are hundreds of anecdotes floating around about Manson in the Haight—a lot of which are glorified. The reality was that he was a glib grubby little man with a guitar scrounging for young girls using mysticism and guru babble, a time-honored tactic on the Haight.

According to Manson, he became a sort of hostel-keeper for runaways. At the start, he ran into a runaway girl whom he put up at a friend's house and as he was walking out of his friend's house he found still another young girl with flowers in her hair who became his housekeeper.

When Manson first took acid the story goes that it changed his life in that he went into a heavy stations-of-the-cross trip where he experienced the crucifixion of Jesus Christ—a common enough LSD experience but one that he really grooved with since it gave form to his chaos. Charlie Manson, the Son of Man, you dig.

The essence of the Jesus rap for the family was that Jesus and his original followers were much like Charlie and the girls. For this is what they believed about Jesus: that ninety years after Christ, priestly creeps killed off the loving sensual-sexual Christians, thus annihilating the original Christian impulse; and substituted for the original their own black-robed sexless death-breaths.

On the Haight, Manson encountered the entire collection of subcultural currents that had been building up in the United States during the previous decade. Acid music. Dope. Sexual freedom. Turn on, tune in, drop out. The politics of free. Peace rallies. Provos. Guerrilla theater. Communes. Long hair. The concept of the underground superstar. Astrology. The occult. Underground newspapers. Crash pads. Dayglo art.

At a Grateful Dead concert at the Avalon Ballroom Manson curled up into a fetal position right on the dance floor while the strobe lights blinked him into a trance.

He seemed to be a familiar figure on the Haight. He claims to have hung around with the Diggers as they distributed their daily food in Panhandle Park. He may have even stayed a while in a house behind the Digger crash pad on Waller Street. This Waller Street house, later, in the era of psychedelic satanism, was to be renamed The Devil House.

Charlie had a tremendous effect on many he met. Open. An incredible talent for using one part of a personality against another. For spotting weaknesses—for creating confusion and appearing therein as a source of leadership. He had a quick, glib but seemingly complicated answer for everything. Even though he told everyone to do their own thing, to be themselves, his own personal magnetism, combined with a constant process of selection, attracted those who thirsted for a leader. Control was what Charles was into all along, in spite of the claims of liberation and freedom.

"I'm a very positive force. I'm a very positive field. I collect negatives," he later told a lawyer friend.

He was always quick to point out his early years of ugliness, rejection, jail and poverty. In a scene right out of Hardy's *Mayor of Casterbridge,* Manson claims his mother once sold him for a pitcher of beer. Now he could have his own flower-power universe. He was terribly insecure, and the praise from his followers was no solace.

Mary Brunner kept her job at the library, and her address in Berkeley was the one given to Manson's parole officer. Manson liked to wander around with his guitar. His method of travel from the Haight to Berkeley and back was hitchhiking. In July of 1967 he was picked up by a man named the Rev. Dean Morehouse, who took him home to San Jose, where he met his wife and fourteen-year-old daughter, Ruth Ann aka Ouish. Manson's tale of meeting Morehouse, told to a lawyer during his later trial for murder, was that Rev. Morehouse, driving a pickup truck, picked Charlie up and kicked off a friendship of great duration. Until Morehouse a year or so later would be sent to prison for forking over LSD to a thirteen-year-old girl.

Manson admired a piano at the Morehouse home, and the reverend gave it to him. Manson spotted a Volkswagen van in Morehouse's neighborhood and made a deal to trade the piano for it. Morehouse brought the piano over in his truck, and Manson owned a 1961 microbus bearing the license plate CSY 087.

At the end of July 1967 the troupe traveled to the

Mendocino coast north of Frisco where Mary Brunner became pregnant.

The pregnancy of Mary Brunner seems to be the only verifiable instance during the history of the family of a pregnancy caused by Manson. Which is strange. Because if one calculates, with data supplied by Manson intimates, an average of three orgasms a day for a total of something like three thousand fornications in two and a half years, one would expect a greater number of pregnancies.

On July 28, 1967, Manson was arrested in Mendocino County for trying to come to the aid of a runaway being apprehended by the police. The runaway was Ouish, the daughter of Reverend and Mrs. Morehouse, whom Manson had enticed into joining his voyage. The parents had sent the fuzz after him, and he received a suspended sentence.

One almost had to live there to understand the frenzy that engulfed the Haight-Ashbury district of San Francisco in the spring and summer of 1967. The word was out all over America to come to San Francisco for love and flowers. California was flooded with what *The New York Times* labeled hippies.

But all over the United States, in hundreds of cities, in the spring and summer of 1967, there were love-ins, be-ins, share-ins and flowers. However, once again, as in the beat generation of the late 1950's, the nerve center was San Francisco. Potentially, flower-power was one of the most powerful forces of change ever seen in recent history. Through the work of the San Francisco Diggers, the Free Clinic in San Francisco, the San Francisco music scene, the *San Francisco Oracle,* its underground newspaper of that time—through these enterprises and others, things came into focus in San Francisco. It was a noble experiment. It was the politics of Free. The Diggers served free food in Panhandle Park each day. The Haight-Ashbury Medical Clinic gave free medical care. There were outdoor free concerts held all the time in the park. People lived and loved in the streets and parks. It was Free. There were no rules. But there was a weakness: from the standpoint of vulnerability the flower movement was like a valley of thousands of plump white rabbits surrounded by wounded coyotes. Sure, the "leaders" were tough, some of them geniuses and great poets. But the acid-dropping middle-class children from Des Moines were rabbits.

The Haight attracted vicious criminals who grew long hair. Bikers tried to take over the LSD market with crude sadistic tactics. Bad dope was sold by acne-faced methedrine punks. Satanists and satanist-rapist death-freaks flooded the whirling crash pads. People began getting ripped off in the parks. There was racial trouble. Puke was sold as salvation. Ugliness was.

And Manson took his children away from it. Because by the end of the summer of flowers, the streets of the Haight were griseous and filthy, psychedelic weirdburger stands were springing up in mutant profusion. As Charlie roamed up and down the California coast, he warned all the hitchhikers and runaways he met not to go to the Haight.

Two jail buddies of Charlie from Terminal Island lived with Charlie on the Haight during the summer of love, 1967. One of them was the legendary Danny M., a skilled counterfeiter. Family members would brag that Danny's twenty-dollar bills were 96 percent perfect, on the average, whereas the U.S. Treasury's were only 94 percent on the simulacral scale.

These guys were mean and rough-tough but when they came under Charlie's influence—just like a wind that blows first one way then another—they grew their hair long and began to groove with flower-power.

One anecdote from the summer of love deals with the ritual of the Golden Gate gun-drop. It goes that at the end of the summer Charlie and the flower girls were set to hit the bricks and roam the void. His dear friends, the two ex-cons, one of whom was the 96-percent-perfect twenty-dollar-bill counterfeiter, evidently were going to remain behind. Charlie asked the guys for the guns he knew they had. He received the weapons, wrapped them up in a cloth, held some sort of ceremony over them, then carried them to Golden Gate Bridge where he dropped the cloth-wrapped guns into San Francisco Bay several hundred feet below.

At the end of the summer of love the group set out to roam the coastal highways.

They survived by odd jobs and cleaning service stations, anything. Another legend swift growing was of Charles Manson the master panhandler. He could get things with ease. He would walk up to a house and people would seem to give him things, the legend being that it was because of his Christ vibes.

Sometime, perhaps in August '67, Charlie and Lynn Fromme aka Squeaky and Mary Brunner acquired a residence at 705 Bath Street in Santa Barbara, California, 334 miles south of San Francisco.

On or around September 8, 1967, Charlie, Lynn and Mary Brunner visited a former jail buddy named Greene who had an apartment in Manhattan Beach near Los Angeles. Visiting Greene also was one Patricia Krenwinkel, a lonely, searching girl from Los Angeles with an endocrine problem—an excess of bodily hair. She was the girl, as her early diaries note, that the men seemed to neglect at the high school dances.

Patricia Krenwinkel of Inglewood, California was eighteen years old, a former Sunday school teacher and a Bible freak—she would really get into the acid Bibleland of Manson, quoting and counterquoting with abandon from the scriptures.

Patricia Krenwinkel was living with her sister Charlene in an apartment in Manhattan Beach, and while the girls drove the microbus north Manson remained with Miss Krenwinkel at Manhattan Beach for four days.

Then Squeaky and Mary returned. Patricia Krenwinkel had been unhappily employed as a process clerk for the Insurance Company of North America. On the night of September 12, 1967, she abandoned her car in a service station to become a clerk in the stable of Charles Manson. Most popular accounts of the Manson story are careful to note that Krenwinkel dared to leave behind uncollected her final paycheck from the Insurance Company of North America. The point being, indeed, what true American would abandon a paycheck?

Patricia Krenwinkel was able to present to the budding family—then known, of course, only as "Charles' girls" besides her soul, the gift of gifts: a valid Chevron credit card backed by her father who loved her enough to pay the bills. Also she gave a telephone credit card number.

They drove north through Santa Barbara to San Francisco, financed by Patricia Krenwinkel's father's credit card. Then on September 15, 1967, they proceeded into Oregon. The Volkswagen van spent two weeks shuttling back and forth between Washington and Oregon, spending a considerable time in the Seattle area. One of the purposes of this trip in the northwest probably was to locate Charlie's lost mother.

It was on this trip north that Manson et al. met a twenty-five-year-old man from Monroe, Louisiana named Bruce Davis, soon to be a prime male follower of Manson. Davis had been the editor of his high school yearbook in Kingston, Tennessee, had attended the University of Tennessee for three years, then had gone through a series of odd jobs until November of 1966, when he dropped down from America and became a transient undergrounder.

On October 1, 1967, the microbus passed through Carson City, Nevada, on the way to San Francisco. The group spent about ten days in the San Francisco-Berkeley area, then hit the bricks, proceeding toward Sacramento where they stayed for a couple of weeks, possibly at the Sacramento residence of the beautiful ex-nun Mary Ann, with whom they had stayed in the summer of flowers.

On October 6, 1967, residents of the Haight held a funeral for Hippie, son of Media, in Buena Vista Park in San Francisco. It was more than symbolic, for it marked the end of a noble experiment and the beginning of the era of pig.

Invitations were sent out reading as follows:

FUNERAL NOTICE
HIPPIE
Haight-Ashbury District
of this city,
Hippie, devoted son
of
Mass Media
Friends are invited
to attend services
beginning at sunrise,
October 6, 1967
at
Buena Vista Park

Manson's group was growing. There were too many to sleep, much less grope, comfortably in the Volkswagen. And winter was oozing onward.

So the opportunity arose to acquire a school bus for their further travels.

It was Ken Kesey and his band of Merry Pranksters, including the wonderful Neal Cassady, who popularized in 1964–65 the concept of the traveling school bus, painted and decorated artistically, full of decorous wanderers.

It was they who experimented in group acid trips and, more importantly, group mystical experiences under LSD. They were into filmmaking during wandering. Kesey's group, however, was essentially good.

Manson took up the brave history of the roaming school bus. This one was painted black, with a goat's head painted upon it by Bob Beausoleil, and this one sailed the sea from the island of flowers toward the island of axes and torture.

It was in Sacramento where they seem to have traded the Volkswagen bus as down payment for an old yellow school bus, large enough to hold the growing youth-pack. Manson claims also to have used money won playing cards in Nevada on one of the van roams. He says they got the bus from a Dutch guy. There was a problem, the Dutch man told them—the bus had been pulled from the bottom of a river with dead children in it. It was haunted. Oo-ee-oo.

On October 16, 1967, at the Stewart E. Miller Standard Chevron station in Sacramento, they outfitted the school bus with a thirty-nine-dollar battery and two sets of 825–20 tires costing $216.20.

They removed the seats from the back of the bus to create an area in which to live. On top of the bus they built a large rectangular storage compartment. Inside the bus, as time oozed by, they emplaced an icebox, a stereo set, a floating coffee table suspended by wires and pillows aplenty. Gradually the walls became painted with Early Acid-American Dayglo whirlings of color. God's eyes, peacock feathers and musical instruments gave the dopemobile cheer. At first, the bus remained school yellow in color, but the police began to stop them for violation of laws governing school buses. At a beach somewhere they acquired a quantity of black spray paint and some bikers sprayed the bus, even the windows, black. They meant to paint the bus with white letters, "Hollywood Productions," but a French girl did the painting and spelled it as she pronounced it, "Holywood Productions."

The scam was to come on like a roving film crew—to avoid the obvious problems that a thirty-three-year-old man with a bus-load of mini-skirted teenage girls might pose, particularly to the police.

In November, Manson's parole supervision was transferred from San Francisco to the Los Angeles office indicating that he intended to shift his base of operations to southern California. Around November 7 or 8, 1967, Manson drove to San Francisco where he met a pretty young female named Susan Atkins, who was living in a house at the corner of Oak and Lyon in Hashbury. She'd been living there, she recalls, with some dope dealers. The singer Janis Joplin lived nearby, and Atkins liked to sit on the front porch and listen to Janis practice. Several other young women in the house also went forth in the thrill bus. One of them was Ella, probably the one known as Yeller, who would later help get the group ensconced in the L.A. mansion of Beach Boy Dennis Wilson.

Susan Atkins was an impressionable nineteen-year-old from San Jose, Cailfornia with a background of strife and bad news. There was fighting and drinking aplenty at home. Her mother died of cancer when Susan was thirteen and Susan led her church choir in a religious serenade outside her dying mother's bedroom window. After the death of Susan's mother, Mr. Atkins had to sell their house to pay the medical bills for the high cost of dying of cancer.

When Susan was fifteen she quit school and then, a year later, in 1964, she headed for San Francisco, where she remained.

In 1966 she was a waitress, living alone, so to speak, in a hotel in San Francisco. She met a couple of men who were into armed robbery.

In August of 1966, when she was eighteen, Sue met a human named Al Sund in San Francisco. Al and another human, Clint Talioferro, took Susan along on a trip north in a stolen Buick Riviera to Salem, Oregon.

They hid in the woods when they learned the fuzz were

after them, snuffing food from other campers—just ordinary outlaws in the wilderness.

On September 12, 1966, she was arrested by the Oregon State Police. She languished in the slams for three months till December of 1966 when she was placed on two years' probation. She hit the trail, returning to San Francisco where she worked as a waitress, a knocker-trembler at a topless bar, and as a domestic on Muir Beach.

She returned to San Francisco, resuming a career as a topless dancer and cocktail waitress. She took LSD and began to experiment with life styles. She had a succession of men friends who used her. Then she met God.

The day before she met Manson she told a social worker she was hot to pursue a career in dancing. When they met, Manson sang songs to her and accompanied her to her apartment where they lay naked together. He asked her to pretend he was her father while they made love. She did. Later she claimed that it was the most ennobling experience of her nineteen years.

The story goes that after this initial encounter, Manson went back to Sacramento and brought to San Francisco the newly bedecked school bus.

He scooped up his waifs, preparing to travel south.

He asked Susan if she was ready to accompany them. Yes, she was. Later he blessed Susan Atkins with a new name, Sadie Mae Glutz.

Around November 10, 1967, Susan Atkins checked in with her probation office in San Francisco all excited about some roaming preacher named Charlie. She did not know his last name. Susan stated that there were seven girls, two of whom were pregnant, who were going to accompany this Charlie on a trip to Los Angeles and on to Florida.

The probation officer was unenthusiastic about the venture. Forthwith the official fired off a letter to Oregon authorities requesting that Miss Atkins be hauled into court for a revocation of probation hearing. But Sadie/Susan was already in the bus whizzing down 101.

Through credit card data, it is known that on November 10, Manson called Universal Studios in North Hollywood, seemingly to arrange for a recording session to kick off operation superstar.

There was a man at Universal Studios in Los Angeles named Gary Stromberg who was a close friend of Manson's jail pal, Phil Kaufman. Through Kaufman, Manson met or contacted Stromberg and a routine was arranged whereby Manson would record a session or so for Universal Records, the company evidently agreeing to pay for the recording costs.

Down the coastline toward an appointment with fame drove the bus. They stopped in San Jose and visited the skeptical Rev. and Mrs. Morehouse and let their fourteen-year-old daughter, Ruth Ann, know how to find them. She followed them right away, joining the M pack for a three-year ride. Three days after Manson had lured his defiant daughter to L.A., Morehouse, traveling with the man who'd given Manson the original Volkswagen microbus, located Manson near Los Angeles and was prepared to kick ass.

"I'm just doing to her what you want to do"—was what Manson is supposed to have said to the raging father. Charlie also slipped him some LSD. Morehouse's wife, subsequently divorced, was amazed at the effect that Manson had on her husband during that trip to get Ruth back. Ruth stayed with Charlie but Dean returned to San Jose a changed man. He had left foaming with anger; he returned a near-convert to the Way of the Bus.

On November 12, 1967, Manson was thirty-three years old.

After his perception of himself as Jesus during the acid trip at the Grateful Dead concert, Manson began subtly to ply one of the greatest scams in cultdom, the "I am Jesus" scam, but in 1967 it had to be plied with care. One method, since he attracted superstitious and spiritist types anyway, was to embed himself in supposed miracles under circumstances of perceptions bent by hallucinogens. One such event—what one could call the Parable of the Beam-Dried Biker—seems to have occurred on this first trip in the black bus down to L.A. The hard-core family was in the bus, including the recently scarfed-up Susan Atkins. There was what Manson called a biker in the bus, and he was freaking out.

Manson stood up and told the biker to lie down and die. He yelled in a voice startlingly loud. The dope-bent minds perceived the biker to start choking and gagging.

Manson kept yelling and, so the parable goeth, the biker shrank, the "meat fell off his bones," and green smoke issued upward. Whoa! thought M, as the vision of prison hit his mind, causing him to stop. He reversed the input and began an incantation that brought the beam-dried biker back to musculature and life. It was a parable told and retold.

The family stopped for a couple of days in Santa Barbara, then drove to Universal Studios in North Hollywood for a recording session. Manson recorded only one three-hour session for Universal Records, then hit the breeze, off to the Mojave Desert though Mr. Stromberg was eager to record more sessions with this barefoot little minstrel. Manson says he was popular at Universal and "had the run" of the place. He was invited to help a group of writers prepare a film script for Universal Studios.

Charlie Manson, biblical quote-freak and living Christ figure, was hired as a "technical advisor" off of whom the writers were to bounce ideas. The writers and potential producer, M says, came up with the "what-if" story of Christ returning as a black man in the South. The white Southerners, of course, would be the drool-lipped Romans. It was a concept that M, himself one of the 1,000 Jesuses of acidland, would not accept, and so his role of advisor was terminated.

Universal never made the Jesus as a Black Man movie because the executives higher up couldn't buy the concept. Working on this Jesus project may have made a strong impression on Manson. Indeed the idea of a Second Coming with the current money-waving Christians starring as the jaded Romans soon to join the rubble of history lay heavily in his later lectures.

Submission was always a key factor in Manson's rap horde. Once during the idea flagpole sessions for the film, Charlie and the twenty-year-old callipygian Squeaky aka Lynn Fromme performed a reciprocal foot smooch, she bending down to kiss his feet and he hers.

All through 1967 and '68 foot kissing, mutual submission and love were very much in vogue with the M brigade. It wasn't until 1969 that Charlie got into kissing people's feet after he shot them.

Manson has made some extravagant claims about his activities during the time at Universal Studios, claiming, for instance, to have made it with a number of stars. "I could authenticate experiences with some of those in Hollywood," he wrote in his autobiography, "that would make the sexual practices I enjoyed look pure and innocent."

Right around the time that Manson was making that demo tape at Universal, Roman Polanski was shooting and completing *Rosemary's Baby,* living in a mansion on Ocean Front in Santa Monica, just off the Pacific Coast Highway. Soon he would return to London for the world premiere of the satanic epic, and he and Sharon Tate would marry.

The family stayed for about a week in the Los Angeles area, then hit the road. They took a swing up into the Mojave Desert, then back to Los Angeles on November 26, 1967. The next day they were in Santa Barbara, then they went to San Francisco, and then back across the state, across the Mojave Desert, then to Las Vegas, Nevada where they spent four days in early December. They passed through Arizona and New Mexico and arrived in El Paso, Texas on December 6, 1967. They backtracked into New Mexico for about a week then went into the deep South, into Mississippi and Alabama. Patricia Krenwinkel visited her mother in Mobile, Alabama on December 14, 1967. The black flower bus drove back to Los Angeles, arriving about December 19, 1967. They stayed for four days in Topanga Canyon, then left for Arizona. Out, demon, out.

Topanga Canyon winds and twists up from Topanga Beach on the Pacific Ocean to a high point overlooking the San Fernando Valley. There is a creek that runs its pleasant boulder-strewn and cabin-sited way down the Topanga Canyon into the Pacific. Following along the creek is Topanga Boulevard, which runs from the ocean up over the top of Topanga into the San Fernando Valley and north a few miles in a straight line to Santa Susanna Pass Road, the home of Helter Skelter.

Woody Guthrie once lived in the canyon and his cabin still stands. In spite of the mutant condition of Los Angeles, the canyon maintains a form of rustic beauty and its inhabitants are among the most knowledgeable to be encountered anywhere.

It was in the Topanga Canyon-Malibu Canyon area in

November and December 1967 that the family was to establish itself in Los Angeles. It became necessary—because of the hordes of adepts—to put down roots, to park near a friendly house, to set up tent encampments, to spread out.

While Manson made his initial attempts to record his songs at Universal Studios, he made his base camp at a secluded house at the mouth of Topanga Canyon near the Pacific Coast Highway. It was located behind the Raft Restaurant on Topanga Canyon Lane. This place was called the Spiral Staircase, after its spiral staircase at the entrance. The house had slid off its foundation and rested askew, and apparently its first floor had a creek flowing through it. It was fairly large, and according to Manson there were windows that opened out onto the hill in back and doors that opened upon a twenty-five-foot drop straight down into the creek. It has since been torn down, but then it was a temple of dope, fucking and homage to strange gods.

It was at the Spiral Staircase that Manson, by his own admission, had his first meeting with the So-Cal variety of devil worshipers and satanists. Manson met the owner of the Spiral Staircase in San Francisco. "She was a trippy broad, about forty-five years old," Manson describes her, "who experimented with everything. When I met her, she was pumped up about devil worship and satanic activities."

He says she gave him complete crash privileges. For a few months, the Spiral Staircase became a scrounge-lounge for the family. They parked the bus there between peregrinations and were exposed, according to Manson, to all sorts of blood-drinkers and ritualists. Of course, many other types of people congregated at the spiral house, including an occasional starlet driving a Rolls-Royce.

At one "light show party" at the Spiral Staircase one Robert K. Beausoleil, a young twenty-year-old actor-musician from Santa Barbara, wearing a pointed beard and smoking a hand-carved skull pipe, arrived and found Charlie and the girls singing together. He joined in and began playing along with Charlie. A few days later, Charlie, wearing an old tweed jacket, a tweed cap and a walking stick, came to see Beausoleil then living at Gary

Hinman's house. Hinman was a thirty-year-old music teacher from Colorado with a Master's degree in Sociology.

Beausoleil was a young man who possessed some skill in music and songwriting and more than a passing interest in devil worship and magic. In 1967 he was associated with famed author and weir-warped filmmaker Kenneth Anger in San Francisco. Beausoleil evidently lived with Anger in an old house in San Francisco called the Russian Embassy, where Anger introduced him to the universe of magic, not to mention the cruelty-streaked universe of Aleister Crowley. Anger was involved in making an occult movie called *Lucifer Rising* in which Beausoleil played the role of Lucifer. At that time Beausoleil has said that he was on an all-meat diet and believed himself to be the devil. Beausoleil was the lead guitarist and sitarist for The Magick Powerhouse of Oz, an eleven-piece rock ensemble formed by Kenneth Anger to perform the music for *Lucifer Rising*.

On September 21, 1967, the Magick Powerhouse of Oz played at a gathering at the Straight Theater on Haight Street to celebrate the so-called Equinox of the Gods. The film *Lucifer Rising* was supposed to be nearly completed so the night was one of celebration. Anger filmed the event that night but Beausoleil remembered later that Mr. Anger flipped out during the proceedings and smashed a priceless caduceus-headed cane that had once belonged the king of sex-magic himself, Aleister Crowley.

Things went awry between Beausoleil and his mentor Kenneth Anger shortly thereafter. Beausoleil seems to have ripped off Anger's automobile, some camera equipment and, more importantly, some of the footage of *Lucifer Rising*. Then he split. Beausoleil claims that he only took what already belonged to him.

The rip-off may have occurred in late October 1967 when Kenneth Anger, during the famed Exorcism and March on the Pentagon, was in Washington, D.C. conducting a notable magic ritual beneath a flat-bed truck parked in front of the Pentagon.

While various Diggers and exorcists were standing atop the flat-bed truck screeching "Out Demons Out," Anger, bare from the waist up, revealing what appeared to be a tattoo of Lucifer upon his chest, burned a picture of the devil within a consecrated pentagram, shouting oaths and hissing as he flashed a magic ring at inquiring reporters thrusting microphones at him hunched down in the gravel.

When he discovered that Beausoleil had ripped him off, Anger thereupon fashioned a locket, the face of which bore the likeness of Bob Beausoleil. The obverse contained the likeness of a toad, with the inscription "Bob Beausoleil—who was turned into a toad by Kenneth Anger."

Beausoleil moved down to Topanga Canyon in the fall of '67 following his break with Anger. He became friends with Gary Hinman. When he met Manson, Beausoleil and a girl friend Laurie were living at Hinman's small hillside house at 964 Old Topanga Canyon Road. Hinman had a tendency to allow people in transit to use his home for temporary crashing, and several times members of the family would cop zzz's there.

Beausoleil and Charles Manson would have a difficult relationship since Beausoleil had his group of girls and Charlie his group. There was a bit of friction between the two because of Charlie's Second Coming hangup. Beausoleil would tend to keep himself separate and that was a sin. There were striking similarities in the two. But only Manson had the Rommeloid passion for the fine details of government.

Another convert, Dianne Lake, a red-haired, fourteen-year-old with hip parents, met Charlie and the girls at the Spiral Staircase house of flickers. Dianne and her parents had been living in the Los Angeles area with the Hog Farm, an important seed commune later to roam the continents as a world peace brigade. Somehow, the fourteen-year-old Dianne was impressed enough to join up with the family bus. Squeaky and Patricia Krenwinkel asked her if she wanted to accompany them to the desert and off she went. In fit time, Miss Lake was renamed Snake, evidently in tribute to the transverse ophidian wiggles she made during intercourse.

Dianne Lake's parents both highly valued their daughter's freedom to develop on her own. They allowed Dianne to travel with the family, although later Mrs. Lake would visit the Spahn ranch to try to reclaim her daughter, only to be rebuffed, according to Dianne, by one of Charlie's chief disciples, Squeaky. The story has it that the mistress of the Spiral Staircase house apologized to

Snake's parents when she left with the Manson dope-bus. After all, Snake was fourteen and Manson was thirty-three.

But the bus was very persuasive. There is general agreement that the family was neat, orderly and extremely clean in physical appearance, during these early days prior to snuff. So Diane's parents, just like Ruth-Ann Morehouse's, let their daughter do her thing.

On December 22 the family took the barely pubescent Snake Lake touring through Arizona and the deserts of New Mexico. Five days later, on December 27, 1967, the bus broke down near Winslow, Arizona and had to be towed to a Chevron station. Some people hitched back to Topanga Canyon, and after repairs the bus itself proceeded back to Los Angeles where the family would stay, more or less, for three and a half months until early April of 1968.

The people of the black bus lived in a profusion and confusion of places in Topanga Canyon. One night one place, one night another—but the numbers were growing. They proceeded to try to settle in various abandoned homes and canyon crash camps, but they kept having to move. For a few weeks they parked their bus at The Spiral Staircase.

Strange doors opened to the floweroids. There was no telling where a man with a black bus full of girls might end up for the night—in a cave or castle, by a hot springs in the wilderness or by a heated pool in the Malibu hills. Doors opened all over Los Angeles to Charles Manson and the family.

The police in Malibu became aware of Manson. They saw the bus parked at the Spiral Staircase on Topanga Canyon Lane behind the Raft Restaurant. They noted that the family was doing odd jobs for various residents in the Malibu-Topanga area.

In December of 1967 the Beatles released their album *Magical Mystery Tour* and their corresponding movie. The Beatles to the rescue. This seems to be the first Beatles album from which Manson drew philosophical guidance. The whole black bus trip came to be called "The Magical Mystery Tour." They were into such a trip of mystic transformation that the family evidently believed that there was an archetypal core personality in each human that could be discovered through acid-zap, mind-moil, role-playing, bunch-punching, magic, blasting-the-past and commune-ism. This was the Magical Mystery Tour.

For most of the early part of 1968 the family stayed in the Los Angeles area. They continued to spew out in quick trips here and there. In early 1968, evidently on such a voyage, Susan Denise Atkins, aka Sadie Glutz, was made pregnant by a human named Bluestein in New Mexico.

In February 1968, through a service attendant named Jerry, Manson met a lady named Melba Kronkite who owned a luxurious ranch in the hills between Malibu and Topanga Canyons, near the old Malibu sheriff's substation. Evidently the lady had been wealthy but had fallen into impecunious times. She was amazed at the brigade and became a close friend. Unmentionable and secret were the encounters around her heated Malibu pool. She became so friendly with the family that she was used as a character reference when family members got busted later on.

Off and on the family would visit Malibu Melba. They worked for her. Manson claims to have given her some money. Manson also gave to Melba a 1967 Ford Mustang which a New Yorker named Michael, divesting himself of worldly goods, had given to Manson.

Mrs. Kronkite had huge stables and an exercise track on her property. Once the family (like Heracles cleaning Augean stables) spent a week cleaning an incredible mountain of horse dooky from several hundred stalls in her stables.

Sometime in February '68 Manson and crew were left temporarily homeless. After his stay with Gary Hinman, Robert Beausoleil had moved into his own house on a steep hillside at 19844 Horseshoe Lane, above Fernwood Pacific Road in Topanga. This property was a citadel of porn, consisting of a burnt-out basement dwelling, below which lay a crude swimming pool. Beausoleil said, "Sure, come on up and live here," so a gypsy tent scene was set up down the hillside and the family filled the pool with archeological refuse for reporters to pick over later during research for books. They stayed at the Horseshoe Lane property for about six weeks and this seems to be the first known time they got into making movies—or, as they say, allowing people with cameras to film their activities.

Around this time the family added to itself Brenda McCann of Malibu and one Little Patty aka Madeline Cottage aka Shirley Amanda McCoy aka Linda Baldwin. Both girls would cling to the thrill until the end, one and a half years later. Also oozing into the acid mosaic at this time was a lovely girl named Ella Beth Sinder aka Ella Bailey aka Yeller, whom a biker named Danny De Carlo describes as a slim shapely Greta Garbo type.

Various others, gone now, and nameless, lived with the family. There are a hundred or so whose names are known but who flitted away into the void. This account deals with those who passed the process of selection and remained with the family.

Manson seemed to seek out encounters with the children or relatives of entertainment personalities. In Los Angeles famous sons and daughters often form close associations with one another. This was okay with Manson in that, like one of his beloved coyotes stalking a nestling, he zeroed in on the fame children in order to scarf up free credit cards, money, hospitality, fame-grope, connections and, most important, acceptance and adulation.

While the family was camped on Horseshoe Lane, Bob Beausoleil and Manson formed a six-piece electric rock band called The Milky Way. Manson played guitar and Beausoleil was on guitar and bass clarinet. The Milky Way was short-lived, though it did have one weekend of public performance.

While The Milky Way was rehearsing one day, a man from the Topanga Corral, a country and western night club in Topanga Canyon, came to hear the group and thought they were "tight" so he hired them for a weekend gig.

During the weekend the group was fired. When asked why, Beausoleil said that the group was too far out, that the potheads came to the club but not enough beer drinkers. Adios Milky Way.

Sometime in late March of '68, the family traded houses with someone living on the other side of Topanga Canyon at the top of Summit Trail and High Vale Trail. The dwelling lay above a maze of trails in the woods. There they parked the black bus and set up camp.

Manson's jail friend, Phil Kaufman, was released from prison in March. A couple of weeks later he went out to Topanga to check out the family. Kaufman stayed around for a while but found theocracy a bit overbearing, though he remained a "sympathetic cousin."

Phil Kaufman had a friend named Harold True who came out to Topanga to visit him in March '68. Harold True lived in an opulent house located at 3267 Waverly Drive near the Silver Lake area of Los Angeles. Next door to True's house was a home owned by the family of Leno and Rosemary LaBianca at 3301 Waverly Drive.

Harold True met Manson and the family through Kaufman. Before True moved out of his Waverly house in August '68, Manson visited Waverly Drive four or five times during the summer, sleeping over twice. True himself went out that spring to Topanga approximately ten times to check out the lair of dope-grope.

Danny M., the ace counterfeiter from the summer of love, drove onto the set bearing some fresh sheets of twenties, just off the press. Charlie talked him into printing up some i.d.'s and driver's licenses for the family. Danny, according to Topanga gossip, later went into business in Woodland Hills, got caught and was sent to jail.

On April Fools eve, President Lyndon Johnson abdicated, announcing he would not seek another term in office.

The next day, April 1, 1968, in the woodsides of Topanga, Valentine Michael Manson was born to Mary Theresa Brunner in the shack on Summit Trail. To relax during the birth she filled her lungs with dope. She was attended by her friends.

On the night Mary gave birth, Sandy Good, twenty-four-year-old daughter of a San Diego stockbroker, flew down from San Francisco with a friend in a private plane, rented a car and sped toward the family. Charlie drew her aside and they clinked bodies near the High Vale bus camp. She marveled out loud after they made love at Charlie's continuing permarigid condition. Boy, other girls didn't know what they were missing.

Although a bright, well-read college graduate who was

active in civil rights causes, Sandy was ready to submit herself. It became an item of gossip among her friends back in San Francisco that she had "joined somebody's harem." Sandy was also to acquire great skill at coaxing money from her wealthy father, a skill ever cherished by Manson.

One Paul Watkins, a short, sixteen-year-old baby-faced drifting dropout, became another addition to the family's lair on Summit Trail. He was wandering through the hills and spotted the black bus and six naked girls. Needless to say it was paradise to the young boy Watkins, soon dubbed Little Paul, evidently a name chosen by the girls.

That night everybody took LSD and experienced a group encounter involving indiscriminate apertural-appendage conjugation. It can be seen that LSD was the wafer. Conceivably, the family provided the first instance where a man, believed to be Christ, ever dispensed LSD as a sacrament, before an act of group sexual psychodrama and after a garbage run.

In early April, a few days after Mary Brunner gave birth, the Magical Mystery Tour decided to leave Topanga Canyon. They were around twenty in number, maintaining the four girls to one guy ratio that was pretty constant throughout the history of the family.

Citizens in the area remember how the heat from the fuzz was severe in the Topanga and Malibu Canyon areas in early 1968, a year of great unrest everywhere in the United States. And Manson and his friends received their share. Arrests, particularly for stupid laws regarding marijuana, create hatred. It had to be a factor in the family's switch from flowers to knives. And then there was also the baleful hate-spell cast by the war.

The Vietnam war lay like a curse upon America in 1968. In March, unknown to millions, Calley and friends creepy-crawled a village called My Lai and blew off the head of a white-robed Buddhist monk stooped to his knees in prayer. Such was the curse.

On April 14, 1968, a drifting racist hick, probably under contract, snuffed Martin Luther King in Memphis, Tennessee.

The Panthers had been calling the police pigs for some time. The Hog Farm's main force, a gentle leader named Wavy Gravy, proposed to run a porcine animal for President. The idea caught on. The Yippies, preparing to pull aside the bandages placed atop the unattended sickness of the Democratic presidential convention, adopted the piggie-for-President proposal. Pig was born.

Somewhere in England, probably in the summer of '68, one George Harrison of the Beatles wrote a song called "Piggies." Nobody had heard the song yet, but it was there, to be released in December 1968. Pigs appeared in ecology ads on television, gobbling garbage at the beach. Respected citizens, long accustomed to calling the police fuzz or cops, switched to pig.

Sometimes happy, sometimes blue, Sergeant Charlie's dope-troupe wandered up the coastline.

They camped for a while on the beach at Leo Carillo State Park, setting up tents.

Bruce Davis, whom the family had encountered some months previous, perhaps in Washington state, showed up on a motorcycle about this time and became an avid member. Bruce Davis began to listen so carefully to Manson's speeches on religion and philosophy that he could repeat them word for word with an easy exactness, even imitating Manson's voice. Observers in the canyon, however, noted that when Charlie was around, Davis talked in his own Tennessee dialect.

They broke camp at Leo Carillo Beach sometime around the second week of April '68, and drove further north up the coast to a wooded area near Oxnard, California in Ventura County. This was the location of the great Oxnard bust, which occurred on April 21. The black bus got caught or broke down in a ditch so the family evidently set up camp in nearby woods. Ventura County sheriff's deputies stopped to investigate and were shocked to find a bunch of nude hippies sauntering in the woods.

Charlie and Sadie and several others were arrested, evidently for possessing those homemade driver's licenses from the counterfeiter. The next day each was fined ten dollars. Mary Brunner also was arrested, as a result of felonious breast-feeding in a ditch. Family legend has it that the police were upset over the casual and shameless public feeding of Pooh Bear aka Valentine Michael Manson.

The Oxnard bust made the second page of the *Los Angeles Herald Examiner*, something about "Nude Hippies Found in Woods"; and, of course, the local radio stations made mention of it in the latest up-to-the-minute news bulletins.

After the arrests in the Oxnard ditch, the family drove back to the encampment on Summit Trail in Topanga Canyon. There they dwelled for a few days until around May 2, 1968, when police raided and arrested a bunch of them, including Manson, Sandy Good, Snake, and Patricia Krenwinkel, for possession of marijuana. They were held in jail for a couple of days, then they were released. The charges were eventually dropped.

This seems to be the time that musician Gary Hinman bailed Snake and Sandy out of the slams and then they accompanied Hinman to his house for a couple of days of rest and rehabilitation. At that time Kinman's house on Old Topanga Canyon Road was one of the few semi-crash pads in the canyon housing young transients. Hinman never entirely would "die in his mind" and join the family but was one of those "sympathetic cousins." Until they made a poster with his blood.

Around May 6, 1968, the black bus drove for the first time to the scroungy, dilapidated Spahn Movie Ranch in Chatsworth, California. The family went to consult with a person named John, a friend of Sandy Good, who occupied the so-called "back house," a corroded, wooden building removed about a half mile down a bumpy dirt trail from the main Western movie set.

Manson came back a few days later and convinced Spahn to let him move in with a few friends. They would help with the fifty or sixty horses that were rented out to day trippers and Manson offered his girls to cook and take care of the elderly Mr. Spahn, who was nearly blind. George Spahn said they could live down a draw in what were known as the outlaw shacks. Shortly thereafter, the black bus filled with about twenty people, mostly young girls, plus Pooh Bear, Manson's son with Mary Brunner, and they drove down to the outlaw shacks. Manson had most of his pack sink down in the seats of the black bus so as not to be seen.

John had an arrangement with the then eighty-one-year-old George Spahn to pay for his rent by keeping in repair the various Spahn Ranch automobiles and trucks.

They stayed about four days while John helped to

repair the black bus. Manson continued to give. He sent a couple of the girls out with a credit card to purchase some retreads for an old Chrysler belonging to one Richard Kaplan, from whom Manson was going to secure possession of the back ranch house of the Spahn Movie Ranch.

Around this time, Bob Beausoleil was acting in an X-rated hat-in-lap film called *Ramrodder* shot near Happy Trail in Topanga Canyon.

Beausoleil had been working at a restaurant, since snuffed by fire, called the Topanga Kitchen, located at the Topanga Shopping Center. The producers of *Ramrodder* offered him a job at a dollar per hour building sets for the flick. Beausoleil accepted and began to live in a tepee at the movie location with his girl friend Gail.

While shooting the movie, Beausoleil met a girl named Cathy Share aka Gypsy aka Manon Minette aka etc. who was acting also in the movie. Beausoleil played the foreboding part of an Indian who murdered and tortured a white man who had sexually assaulted an Indian girl.

Gypsy, Gail and Bob became inseparable and lived together in the tepee on the movie set. Gypsy, playing Earth Mother, became part of a two-girls-one-guy triangle which was to serve as a model for nighttime deportment in the family.

Beausoleil was a fierce person in the canyon, with a hooded falcon on his shoulder and a huge black dog. Like Manson, he gave off the dual love-hate vibes. Beausoleil evidently had a grope scene with the wife of the producer of *Ramrodder* and had to split. He struck his tepee camp, scarfed up Gypsy into his group and went to live again at Gary Hinman's house for a few days.

After a while he went to the Spahn Ranch and got employment there, such as it was, for a few days, then Beausoleil and his followers drove north to the San Francisco area, driving an old Dodge powerwagon that George Spahn gave them.

Meanwhile, the Manson group had left the Spahn Ranch, traveling north in the black bus to San Francisco and to Mendocino County before returning to Los Angeles. They seem to have spent a few days back in Topanga Canyon, parked by the Spiral Staircase.

Around this time, the family discovered big-time rock and roll. A bunch of them moved into a luxurious home on Sunset Boulevard belonging to Dennis Wilson, a member of the Beach Boys, an enormously successful singing group of that era that had sold tens of millions of albums to fans around the globe. Their 1967 single "Good Vibrations" had helped set the tone of the time.

Wilson, drummer and singer for the Beach Boys, was living on a three-acre estate at 14400 Sunset Boulevard, with manicured grounds and a swimming pool reportedly shaped like the state of California. The wood-paneled house had once been a hunting lodge owned by Will Rogers.

Dennis Wilson had picked up two Mansonites, Patricia Krenwinkel and Yeller aka Ella Bailey, the Garboesque beauty who had left San Francisco the previous fall with Susan Atkins in the black bus. Wilson brought the damozels to his house on Sunset Boulevard for a couple of hours, and then not long thereafter, returning from a recording session at 3 A.M., Wilson discovered the black Hollywood Productions bus outside and Manson and about twenty nubile caressing females in his living room. A friendship developed, and Manson's group underwent a multimonth mooch on Wilson's resources that drained him of about $100,000.

On Sunset Boulevard Manson plugged into the restless world of successful rock musicians and continued his adventures inside the interlocking circles of young sons and daughters of figures in the motion picture and music industries. It was a sociopath's paradise. Like a dowser's wand, the little hypnosis addict homed in on two American symbols:

A. The Beach Boys—America's perfect singing group with their clear excellent high harmonies and their enormously popular songs about surfing, hot rods, good vibrations and fun, and

B. Terry Melcher—son of virginity incarnadine.

Terry Melcher was born Terry Jordan on February 8, 1942. Doris Day, at the time, was a singer with Les Brown and his Band of Renown. She was married to a musician named Al Jordan. After his parents were divorced, he was raised in Cincinnati by his maternal grandmother.

D.D.'s third husband Marty Melcher adopted Terry. He attended Beverly Hills High School, class of 1960. For a year he attended Principia Preparatory School in Clayton, Mo. Melcher attempted to become a singer himself but after a short atonal period wound up producing groups for Columbia Records. He produced some of The Byrds' early and excellent records and then recorded the hype-ridden Paul Revere and the Raiders, a group from Washington that was quite successful in the late 1960's.

In 1966 he rented a secluded L.A. house at 10050 Cielo Drive and was living there with the actress Candice Bergen when he met Manson in the summer of 1968 at Dennis Wilson's home. Melcher's stepfather, Martin, had died in April of 1968 and Terry had been coexecutor of the estate, which though nominally wealthy in hotels, oil and real estate, was discovered to have been left in chaos. Terry Melcher was also the nominal head of his mother's upcoming comedy series for CBS, plus various music-publishing and TV enterprises. Untangling his stepfather's business affairs was to occupy much of his time during the months Manson relentlessly sought his assistance in becoming a star.

Manson also met Gregg Jakobson, a songwriter and talent scout in the employ of Melcher. Jakobson was to become quite intimate with the family. He recorded Manson singing several times and was privy to non-lethal affairs for several years.

Manson was singing when Melcher first met Manson and the girls. Manson went to Melcher's home several times and even on occasion borrowed Melcher's Jaguar. On one occasion when Melcher visited Dennis Wilson, Dennis and Gregg drove Melcher home to 10050 Cielo Drive while Manson sat in the back of the Rolls-Royce singing and strumming the guitar.

Dean Morehouse, the white-haired former minister, arrived in Los Angeles, evidently still trying to regain possession of his fourteen-year-old flowering daughter, RuthAnn. He sought help from people at the Wilson residence in gaining back RuthAnn but was unsuccessful. Somehow he too began to live with the family at Wilson's estate. Morehouse lived in the guest house and secured some sort of employment from Manson and Dennis Wilson as the gardener and groundskeeper.

The rest of the Morehouse story is acid. Dean became the most devout of Charlie's occult changelings. He was to become an obsequious embarrassment to Manson because Morehouse himself went on a Jesus-identity trip under LSD. And how many Jesuses can one cult contain? Morehouse became a daily dope gobbler, his thin white hair growing long, declaring himself both the Christ and the devil as he made himself happy at the parties that summer at Melcher's home and Wilson's residence.

Dean was such an apostle of lysergic acid that once in the mountains before he broke up with his wife he dropped a few tabs on the sly into her orange juice, leaving her alone in the wilderness to have her own trip. Thanks a lot, Dean.

Morehouse brought with him a young man from Texas named Brooks Posten, a musician who would later create family legend by being able, on command, to put himself into a trance. Posten forked over to Manson a credit card belonging to his mother which was used extensively in family travels in 1968.

Posten too grew quickly to believe Manson was Jesus. He stayed most of the summer with the family at Wilson's house, helping Dean Morehouse with the "gardening."

Manson's greatest work of magic, however, was the transformation of Charles Denton Watson. When they met Watson in the spring of 1968 at Dennis Wilson's house, Watson was a swinger dating a stewardess from Chicago. The family was proud that it could create a change in Tex Watson, the holder to this day of a Texas high hurdles track and field record. Watson dressed mod. He looked mod. He had a wig shop. He was strictly now. Soon he would become the now of Charlie.

Tex Watson was born in Copeville, Texas on December 2, 1946. He lived a normal life for a boy growing up in the agricultural cotton-raising areas of central Texas. People in Copeville remember him riding his bicycle, working in the cotton fields, helping his father at the family grocery store-gas station in Copeville. They were stunned that he had turned into a murderer.

He wore a flat top and modified duck-tails in high

school in Farmersville, Texas where he was an ace high hurdler and a star halfback.

For a couple of years he attended North Texas State College where he studied Business Administration and joined a fraternity. He was an American.

Watson dropped out of college after 1966 and in early 1967 moved to Los Angeles. He attended college for a semester or so in Los Angeles in 1967, then dropped out again. He lived at residences on Glendale Boulevard, Wonderland Road, Dracena and North Larrabee—a street famed for dope-dealing.

Before Manson, he began to work as a wig dealer, opening a hair store called Crown Wig Creations Ltd. at the mouth of Benedict Canyon. He and a buddy from Denton, Texas were in partnership. The shop was located at 9499 Santa Monica Boulevard, near Beverly Hills.

At the time he met Manson, Watson seems to have been living at a beachhouse at 18162 Pacific Coast Highway. He drove an elegant 1935 Dodge pickup truck.

Among three billion possibilities, Watson chose to become Charlie. "I am Charlie and Charlie is me," went a tune of the day. They were his replicas. Watson has complained that he actually thought he *was* Charlie. He even used Manson's name. Once in Mendocino County he signed Manson's name when buying gas with Terry Melcher's credit card.

Tests at the University of Southern California Neuropsychiatric Institute later showed that during his trip in Manson void, Watson's IQ dropped thirty points, probably through use of drugs like telache or belladonna. If the Kremlin or the Pentagon ever formulates the robopathic secret of M, the world's in trouble.

The Wilson house was a great address to use with his parole officer. In fact, Manson used the Sunset Boulevard address on his I.D. long after he moved out of the place. Manson was really cooking in his Jesus image—kissing feet and granting immortality as never before. "Are you ready to die?" he'd say, and if the answer were yes, he'd say: "Then live forever."

He was always finding places for people to crash. He'd send Squeaky with a carload of sleepy crashers out to

Topanga Canyon or to the Spahn Ranch to find beds for the night.

Wilson possessed a rock star's booty: two Ferraris, a Rolls-Royce, a house in Benedict Canyon, a fabulous rock-star wardrobe, a boat equipped with radar. He was rich.

The girls went on garbage runs in the Rolls-Royce. It must have looked weird to see them loading the discarded supermarket produce into the back seat.

But Dennis Wilson let it happen. Once during that summer, he took Snake, Lynn and Ouish with him when the Beach Boys performed at a music festival in Colorado. Later, during a Beach Boys' English tour, in an interview with a rock magazine called *Rave* he would call Charles Manson "The Wizard" and said that Manson would probably issue an album on Brothers Records, a label owned by the Beach Boys. Manson brought Robert Beausoleil out to Wilson's house for a swim at the palatial pool after meeting him in Topanga Canyon one day.

It was strictly a locust scene as far as Wilson's personal property was concerned because the family evidently managed to give away the substance of Wilson's immediate wealth in the course of two or three months. But it was the era of the Maharishi and transcendental meditation, so Wilson seemed to groove with Manson's millenarian material detachment and later came to live, *pro tempore,* in a state of "poverty" himself, when he moved later on into a penurious one-room basement apartment at Gregg Jakobson's house on North Beverly Glen Drive.

It was summer 1968 at the Wilson estate when it first became apparent that Manson had some sort of prostate problem. Part of the legend eagerly spread abroad by the family then was that Charlie made love seven times a day: once before and once after each meal or snack and once in the middle of the night, when he awakened with desire. Each new girl shared with Manson an extensive multihour lovemaking session using the picture-me-as-your-father routine plus lots of perv. And perv is what the L.A. music scene eats for breakfast. The word must have gotten around. It could be called an exhaustion grope. It seems that Charlie felt that it was only after the first three or four hours that the sex really got good—

when the woman "gave up," lost her ego entirely, then the act was of the Soul. And it was true. Out of many, many oral depositions taken from ladies in the Los Angeles area, there was only one who claimed that Manson waxed unable in eros.

Most girls thought Manson was very young, even in his early twenties. Which was okay with Charlie, because his scene really was prepubescent girls. They couldn't get young enough.

But he didn't fool everybody. His face when seen inches away revealed incipient biological phasing.

"His face seemed very young but close up he was wrinkled," recalled one lady friend of 1969.

3

Sleazo Inputs

People remember that Sadie particularly was eager for people they encountered to go to Los Angeles "to meet Charlie." Everything oozed past. Sometime, probably in late May '68, Charlie made a decision to send a scouting expedition north to Mendocino County in the black bus to look for a permanent place to settle. Susan Atkins aka Sadie Glutz was the leader of the journey and driver of the bus.

Charlie, buttressed by a chosen core of followers, stayed behind for fun and games at the Wilson house. Malibu Brenda, Sandy Good, Ouish, Squeaky Fromme and Snake Lake were the girls picked by Charlie to keep close at hand during those easy months on Sunset.

Before going north to Mendocino, Susan Atkins's group resided temporarily at a commune at 532 Clayton a couple of doors up the hill from the Haight-Ashbury Free Medical Clinic. Mary Brunner's seven- or eight-week-old baby, Pooh Bear, was treated for a yeast infection at the Free Clinic.

The bus bearing the family, without Manson, attracted considerable sympathy. There had been that pattern of harassment from the police and the idiotic marijuana arrests. And the girls were eager proselytizers, according to observers. They were zealous, these girls, and when they resided in Mendocino became known as the Witches of Mendocino.

The officials of the Haight-Ashbury Clinic certainly had already heard of them since Manson's former federal parole officer, Roger Smith, had left the parole scene and in January of 1968 had established a drug counseling treatment program associated with the Haight-Ashbury Medical Clinic.

The clinic was housed in a three- or four-story house just off Panhandle Park on Clayton Street. Several of the staff of the clinic began to spend time observing the group. Al Rose, the administrative head of the clinic, gathered data on the girls when they were placed in a Mendocino jail and later visited them when they were at the Spahn Ranch. He and Dr. David Smith, the medical director, later wrote a formal paper entitled "The Group Marriage Commune: A Case Study" about the family of 1968, which was published replete with footnotes and scientific terminology in the November 1970 issue of the *Journal of Psychedelic Drugs,* a slick but interesting publication analyzing the so-called drug culture.

The Haight-Ashbury Free Clinic had opened just prior to flower-power in late 1966. It struggled bravely to survive through 1967 when it treated the countless children.

Once in 1967 it closed briefly for lack of funds but soon re-opened. The need to be perpetuated meant becoming chummy with the foundations to get grants to continue its deserved existence. Also, in previous years, the rock and roll groups of San Francisco occasionally performed benefits to aid the Free Clinic.

To focus briefly on the Free Clinic: There had been a mild furor in the papers during the spring of 1968 over a benefit rock and roll concert the Free Clinic was proposing to present on Easter Sunday, April 15, at the prestigious Palace of Fine Arts in San Francisco. The affair would raise a needed twelve or thirteen thousand dollars for the clinic.

Big Brother and the Holding Company, featuring Janis Joplin, and Quicksilver Messenger Service were scheduled to play at the benefit. Certain San Franciscans complained that the elegant Palace of Fine Arts should not be used for an affair featuring rock and roll especially if it was to benefit clap-suffused hippie slime. They won and at the last minute the concert had to be moved to the Carousel Ballroom.

It was sometime in the spring or summer of 1968 when Mrs. Inez Folger, the mother of Abigail Folger, began to help the Haight-Ashbury Medical Clinic. She worked as a volunteer aiding Dr. David Smith's drug treatment program. Mrs. Folger helped the clinic receive a grant from the Bothin Foundation and $25,000 from the Merrill Trust, according to a high official at the clinic. She held several fund-raising parties during the year she worked at the clinic. Abigail Folger, as well as Colonel and Mrs. Tate, attended one such benefit party given by Mr. and Mrs. Folger and it appears that one or more members of Manson's family, perhaps Manson himself, attended that fund-raising cocktail party.

At least one official at the clinic recalled that fund-raising party on the day when he read in the newspapers that Manson was arrested for the murders.

Sometime in the first two weeks of June, the girls drove north of San Francisco into Mendocino County looking for a home. They lived for a while in a commune-type house located off Route 128 near Philo, northwest of Ukiah, in dope country.

A little while after midnight on June 21, 1968, one Mrs. Rosenthal of Booneville, California phoned the resident deputy sheriff of Mendocino County and requested that an officer be sent to her house because someone had given some dope to her 17-year-old son. When the police arrived they found young Allen Rosenthal speaking of his legs as if, in fact, they were snakes and he was having color hallucinations.

He told the police that the Witches of Mendocino of the Philo "hippie" house had laid a small blue tab of dope on him.

That night the sheriff's deputies raided the hippie lair occupied by five females (the Witches of Mendocino), three males and an infant, Pooh Bear. The police searched the house and surroundings and in a woodshed next to the house came up with a small film can containing cannabis and also a plastic bag with some blue kernels of acid inside. They caught the commies with dope. Arrested were Ella Beth Sinder aka Yeller, Mary Brunner, Patricia Krenwinkel, Sadie Glutz, someone named Mary

Ann Scott, Robert Bomse, Peter Kornbuth and Eugene Nagel plus the eleven-week-old Valentine Michael Manson aka Pooh Bear.

After the arrest one of the girls phoned Dennis Wilson's house down in Los Angeles to tell Charlie about the bust.

The next day, June 22, 1968, Sadie Mae Glutz et al. were charged with violation of Section 11910 of the California Health and Safety Code, possession of a dangerous drug with a prior conviction, Section 11913 of the California Health and Safety Code, felonious implacement of dope into the mouth of a minor, and Section 11530, possession of the herb marijuana.

Katie was booked under the name of Katherine Smith. Evidently Mary Brunner was afraid that she would be the one to be convicted so they told the police that the young Sunstone Hawk aka Pooh Bear was Katie's baby because they thought Katie had a good chance of getting off. And the girls were afraid that the state would take Pooh Bear away when they found out that Mary Brunner had recently been arrested for felonious breast-feeding in a ditch down in Oxnard, California.

Naturally, the girls were unable to raise bail. Pooh Bear was taken away from his mother and placed in a foster home. Mr. and Mrs. Roger Smith of the Free Clinic were somehow chosen to serve as foster parents for the child.

It was discovered, horror of horrors, that not only had the baby no birth certificate, but that it had not been circumcised. Both were accomplished in rapid time.

So the girls languished in jail until at a hearing on July 2 some of the charges were dropped but the Witches of Mendocino were rearrested right in court on what was designated as "an amended complaint." The girls continued to be held in jail.

While the Witches of Mendocino remained incarcerated up north, Manson spent most of his time in June and July '68 in Los Angeles.

The small misogynist was busy dominating women and making contacts.

One of his greatest tricks was talking his followers into the worship of infant consciousness. Somehow, the infant was the ideal. Children were not cursed by the Culture but acted spontaneously, from the Soul. It must be remembered that the family believed in reincarnation and in the possibility of monitoring past lives. So the child was the sum culmination of the life-chain of evolution.

Charlie encouraged childbirth. Rubbers, pills, i.u.d.'s, diaphragms and, Lord forbid, vasectomy were not allowed. Women, according to the Manson hype, had no souls but were super-aware slaves whose duties were to whelp and to serve men. Ironically, there were actually very few pregnancies in the family, a fact, according to Sandy Good, that used to upset Charlie.

In a place where twenty women love one man the attention paid each one by the man becomes an issue. Manson had a quick mind and maintained an intimate disarming relationship with each of his followers—and somehow satisfied them all.

As a flip-side of the jealousy question, Manson had the greatest scam of all. He'd tell the girls that if they really loved him they'd go out and bring him back a girl prettier and younger than they were—and he got away with it. He seemed really to dote upon short, skinny masochistic redheads with superstitious minds. And he loved to find kids who'd been stomped on by their parents.

They came and went. "If you fit in, you can stay" was the formula and some of them did their damndest to fit in.

This is the image his followers would present the world.

But Manson's life wasn't merely spent compiling a harem and gearing for stardom.

There was another Manson, a Manson with years of connections with a seamier side of Los Angeles. Manson seems to have maintained contacts with criminal types for years. It will be remembered that he came to Los Angeles in 1955 and operated in Los Angeles throughout his fourteen-year career in California as prisoner, pimp, bartender, forger and robber and then as minstrel and guru.

Manson was a guy that claimed thousands of friends. For instance, there was a person named Pete who lived in Sacramento with whom in late 1967 the family visited for several days during their wanderings. Pete and Manson evidently had worked together at a bar in Malibu in 1958. He kept up his friendships.

Manson used to hang out on the Sunset Strip using the name Chuck Summers. There were a bunch of sleazo bars and cafés on or near the Sunset Strip with names like the Galaxy Club, Omnibus and The Melody Room that Chuck Summers frequented in 1968. Bikers, prostitutes, petty criminals and porn models flocked to these clubs.

The Galaxy Club was a favorite of Chuck Summers. Manson, as Summers, used to come around in the mornings according to the club manager of that era. The manager was also a stage hypnotist who later opened something called the Hollywood Hypnotism Center. He and Manson used to talk about hypnotism. The Galaxy Club was located up the street from the Whiskey A Go-Go. Manson probably met the bike club, Jokers Out of Hell, at the Galaxy. Some of Manson's lesser-known girl friends, with names like Mouse and Venus, were also frequenters of these establishments.

Sunset Strip seems to be where Manson first made contact with the satanic variety of bike groups, with names like The Satan Slaves, The Jokers Out of Hell, The Straight Satans, The Coffin Makers and other snuff-oriented groups of young men. It is undeniable that an increasing contact with some of these clubs with hellish names would create great violent "reflections" in Manson. With some of the groups like Straight Satans and particularly The Satan Slaves Manson had deep associations during the following year of violence.

There had been a year of flowers. But sometime in the summer or spring of 1968 a change occurred in the family. Into the mix of flowers, sex, nomad-community walked Satan, devil-worship and violence. Perhaps it was the will to change—the need to maintain that magnetism—that caused Charlie to groove with gore.

Something happened. After all, Patricia Krenwinkel didn't just jump upon command, aroused from sleep, and drive to the Polanski residence, as some would like to think, because of sex, drugs and communes.

It was a continuing claim of Manson that he was merely a reflection of those around him, that he was "dead in the head" and therefore acted from the Soul. There is no doubt that he borrowed his ideas from plenty of sources.

He was ever the avid listener and he prided himself on a vast range of weird information.

But what was it that caused Manson's death-trip? The factors that seem to have fed the violent freak-out shall be termed here sleazo inputs.

Gazing about Los Angeles it is possible to discern quite a few death-trip groups that must have provided powerful sleazo inputs into Manson and his so-called family. In the Los Angeles area, groups exist which specialize in creating zombi-minded followers. These groups have degrees of initiation and discipleship; they use indoctrination techniques sometimes very similar to hypnosis; they amplify occult paranoia within the mind of the adept; and sometimes they use certain drugs in association with indoctrination to create a web of weird belief in which to entrap the occult obeyer.

The structure of these groups is fascist, with all power draining to the top leaders of the cult—usually one or two autocratic power-hungry punks who get off behind ach tung! and obedience.

One uptight occult group, certainly a sleazo input, and one whose leader is said, in California police reports, to have met members of Manson's family, is described by a report prepared by the Anglican Church as presenting "two faces to the world. One is that of a pious respectability and the other is that of self-indulgent depravity." This group venerates a variety of gods, including Satan and Christ. It represents the essence of oo-ee-oo. Manson and some of his followers met leaders of this satanic society at the Spiral Staircase house in Topanga Canyon in late 1967.

Manson later wrote about the groups he met at the Spiral Staircase: "Each time I returned, I would observe and listen to all of the practices and rituals of the different groups that visited the place. I'm not into sacrificing some animal or drinking its blood to get a better charge out of sex. Nor am I into chaining someone and whipping them to get my kicks like some of those people were.

"The day we first drove up, we were innocent children in comparison to some of those we saw during our visits there. In looking back, I think I can honestly say our philosophy—fun and games, love and sex, peaceful friendship for everyone—began changing into the madness that eventually engulfed us in that house."

Another sleazo input group was headed by a woman worshipped by the sect and believed by them to be a reincarnation of the Greek goddess Circe who, as the reader recalls, in the poem "The Odyssey" pulled a metamorphosis job on Odysseus' crewmen, turning them into swine by means of weird drugs. This Circe group had as adepts, according to reports, members of the Satan Slaves bike club, a club which had contact with Manson and his "church." Circe was thought to be red-haired and to be English.

Educated in prison and nearly illiterate—an extremely slow reader—Manson was guru-oriented when it came to his education. That is, he received a lot of his information in the form of lectures from friends.

Manson's flower-power guru, for instance, was a well-known figure in the Los Angeles to San Francisco underground communal society of 1967. Manson was seen traveling throughout the state in the company of this individual. If he had retained his guru's advice, things would have been safer later on in California—but there was no redemption for this product of bad jails and sick heritage.

It will be remembered that even before Manson left federal prison, the punk concepts of black magic had been rooted in his schemes. He has stated that he met so-called devil worshipers while in jail and it is known that friends were mailing him books in jail on the so-called black arts.

According to Dean Morehouse, Manson and crew had contact as early as mid-summer 1967 in north Mendocino County, above San Francisco, with a group of "Devil's Disciples." This group of devilists later set up headquarters in the San Francisco area, according to a close family associate.

Robert Beausoleil, who later would murder Gary Hinman, had extensive contact with a devil-worshiping cult operating in San Francisco in 1966 and 1967. Due to their close association it may have been the devil scene that Manson joined.

An individual who claimed to have been involved in the same San Francisco devil cult as Manson in 1968 claimed that Manson's guru within the cult was one Father P. "This death cult was lead by a strange fiery man of about forty-five," the ex-cult member wrote. "They called him Father P . . . the 66th. Father P claimed that, amongst many things, he had a M.D., a Ph.D., and also that he was a magician. There was talk around the ashram that Father P had been chased out of North Carolina for setting fire to the town church, expelled from pre-Castro Cuba and had recently returned from Damascus, Syria.

"The Devil House people said it was a religious order, and it went under many ancient names, one of them being the Companions of Life, another one being the Final Church of Judgement. . . . The Final Church is the name Manson chose for the church he would eventually found." So wrote the former member.

Around the middle of 1968, Manson began to say that he was both Christ and Satan or Christ and the Devil. It has already been noted that Manson's family considered itself like the early Christians—or what they considered the early Christians to be: sexually communal and living outside the social structure. To this they added belief in reincarnation, astral projection and various rituals of blood. Manson, in his Final Church of whatever, was the Christ/Satan figure. His vision was chilling. He wanted to set up a multi-city structure of religious cells of followers. And probably did.

But it was sick. In a lengthy interview with the Los Angeles District Attorney, one of Susan Atkins' cellmates told on October 5, 1970, what Atkins related to her about family blood slurping: "She described to me that on various occasions Charlie would put himself on a cross. And that a girl would kneel at the foot of the cross and that he would moan, cry out as though he was being crucified, and that they also would sacrifice animals and drink their blood as a fertility rite." Oo-ee-oo.

One family witness said that they were into wearing black hoods during some of their ritual weirdness. He recounted a semi-amusing incident of stalking the Spahn Movie Ranch with a friend late at night dressed in black attire and black hoods to see if they could force a breach in the family's sentry system.

By early June 1968, according to Dean Morehouse,

Manson had already developed plans for sending out followers to set up "churches." Said Morehouse in an interview: "I got the idea Charlie was dividing up the world among these people to go and do their thing in but I just never got—he never let me in on anything more—a lot of things Charlie never let me in on."

Manson even had one follower or associate who was on the way to Australia, as of June 1968, to set up a chapter of The Final Church or whatever it was called. Morehouse was asked what the human "setting up" the church in Australia was supposed to do there. Morehouse replied: "He was going to do whatever Charlie was doing. Charlie always encouraged me to go ahead and organize—I was going to organize a church—He was always wanting me to do it—and outline a program that I could do, you know. Like you get people, a small group—and, get them through their hangups to get them turned on, and just send males out, two by two, in VW buses or something. Just let 'em go out and turn people on. Then they could go up and down the highways—or hit some other town and set up a center there. Send some more on to the next place and do the same thing. Just keep going."

Morehouse finally began to organize a Mansonland church but it was interrupted in late 1968–early 1969 by a lengthy jail sentence.

In late summer 1968, Manson would begin to have dealings with a bike club in San Jose, California, a few miles south of San Francisco, named the Gypsy Jokers. Some Gypsy Jokers, according to California police, had been recruited into the service of a well-known international occult society as early as 1967. These biker recruits, according to the police, were referred to by said international society as Agents of Satan. This society had been recruiting and setting up cells in the United States since around 1966 and was active in California in the ensuing years.

It is a group of devil worshipers operating in remote mountain areas of northern and southern California that provides the most pukish data regarding the probable sacrificial nature of the occult life of the family.

An individual caught having eaten the heart of a human victim and charged with murder, has told of a satan-devil organization which operated during 1967–1970 in the Santa Cruz mountains south of San Francisco and in the Santa Ana mountains south of Los Angeles. Hematophagy, cannibalism and other barbarous activities were practiced by the group. Pages could be uglified depicting the grim activities of this cult, but the reader will be spared.

The cult had a specialized terminology and exercised its rituals according to timetables based on stellar superstition. The leader of the cult bore the title the Grand Chingon or Head Chingon or Head Devil. Manson himself was called by several of his followers, The Grand Chingon, in this writer's presence. It has been learned that the Santa Cruz Chingon was not Manson (because Manson was in jail for murder when the cult was still operating) but was someone else, an older person with a crew of "slaves" to do his sick bid.

The cult, according to the informant, was sometimes known as the Four P Movement, devoted to the "total worship of evil." It held out-of-door ceremonies with portable crematorium, dragon festooned wooden altar, portable "morgue table," six-bladed sacrificial knife and other devices. They killed humans and burnt them. It was a sick set.

Meanwhile it was June 1968 and Manson was just getting his illness together, preparing his church of the devil.

And while the family was scrounging on the strip and singing and kissing feet at 14400 Sunset Boulevard, just a couple of miles away to the northeast, Sharon and Roman Polanski were moving into a house at 1600 Summit Ridge Drive located in the hilly fameland above Beverly Hills.

4

The Polanskis

"Characters and utmost fear are the most important things in cinema."

—Roman Polanski

Sharon Tate was born on January 24, 1943, in Dallas, Texas. Her father was a career army officer and the family subsequently lived in various parts of Europe and the United States. Her family entered her in a Tiny Tots beauty contest in Dallas and she won. As she grew older her parents continued to move, living in San Francisco, Washington state, Washington, D.C. etc. She was Miss Autorama in Richmond, Washington.

Her family moved to Verona, Italy where she attended something called Vicenza American High School. She was Homecoming Queen and Queen of the Senior Prom. How many tens of thousands of American girls crowned queen of the prom have hungered for Hollywood? When she was living with her family in Verona, Italy, she met Eli Wallach, Susan Strasberg and Richard Beymer who were shooting a movie there.

Mr. Beymer encouraged Miss Tate with the old "you ought to be in pictures" and it seems to have led to her resolve to become an actress.

Her father was transferred back to the United States and the Tate family was stationed in San Pedro, California, just a few miles from Hollywood. From San Pedro, she made her move. She used to hitchhike to the various movie studios where the soft-voiced eager Miss Tate was known as the girl from San Pedro.

There is one memorable interview about her start in Hollywood that she gave on the set of a movie about vampires, *The Fearless Vampire Killers*. She said: "I used to hitchhike in Los Angeles to all the studios because I couldn't afford the cab fare. The men were so generous, especially the truck drivers; they all gave me lifts. My first experience was doing TV commercials.

"I convinced Daddy that I'd be safe in Hollywood."

Miss Tate acquired an agent, Hal Gefsky, and in due order began to make automobile and cigar commercials. In 1963, when she was twenty years old, her agent sent her to New York to audition for a bit part in *Petticoat Junction,* a CBS-TV series in preparation and produced by one Martin Ransohoff and his company, Filmways.

Ransohoff arrived on the set, checked out the beautiful young girl, then called her over. According to columnist Lloyd Shearer, in a London newspaper story, Ransohoff spoke to Sharon these formuletic words:

"Sweetie, I'm going to make you a star." With the emphasis on the *I'm*.

Mr. Ransohoff was the producer, also, of a yuk-yuk TV comedy series called *The Beverly Hillbillies*. Not since Troy II-a, known in archeological circles as the Slob Culture, had there been anything like *The Beverly Hillbillies*. Ransohoff signed Sharon to a seven-year contract. For two and a half years he kept her as his own. Like a beautiful date-palm, she was watered into stardom. She was given singing and dancing and acting lessons. She was given tiny training roles, wearing wigs, in *The Beverly Hillbillies, Petticoat Junction,* plus several films produced by Ransohoff, including *The Americanization of Emily* and *The Sandpiper.*

She spent a considerable amount of time in the Big Sur area of California, a beautiful coastal region she grew to love. She stayed there with Ransohoff while he filmed *The Sandpiper* starring Elizabeth Taylor.

Sometime in 1963 Jay Sebring, hair stylist for male movie stars, met Sharon Tate in a Hollywood restaurant. They became friends and lovers quickly and sometime later became engaged to be married. Jay Sebring was an eager, successful entrepreneur, rapidly establishing himself as the king of the haircut.

If you are a public performer, you pay a lot of attention to your face and hair—that's all there is to it. You do. In many cases, the face and hair of a talent is just about all he has to donate to his career. Sebring had a way that commanded the respect of many of the famed and wealthy of Hollywood. He was almost a magician at keeping hair from disappearing down the shower drain. And he came along in fit time to aid the transition in hair styles from Marine Corps to mod.

Right around the time they met, Sebring purchased a remarkable home in Benedict Canyon where he lived until his death. Sebring's house at 9860 Easton Drive had a certain grim fame in that it was once the hideaway of actress Jean Harlow and it was there Harlow's husband Paul Bern snuffed himself with a bullet in 1932.

After two years of preparation, the starlet was ready. In late 1965 Ransohoff gave her her first "major" role opposite David Niven and Deborah Kerr in the movie *13* aka *Eye of the Devil,* the story of a hooded religious sect which worshipped the devil and committed sacrificial murders.

The movie was made in London. Jay Sebring came to London and they lived together in an apartment at Eaton Square, but pressures of his own career caused him to return to Los Angeles.

When Ransohoff made *Eye of the Devil* in London, the company hired an English magician called Alex Saunders, the so-called "King of the Witches," as technical advisor. Alex Saunders aka the High Priest Verbius claims that Aleister Crowley tattooed him as a tenth birthday present. He claims to have initiated and trained people in two hundred covens of witches in the British Isles. He also claims that he became a friend of Sharon Tate on the set of the devil movie. Before filming ended, Saunders claims he initiated Miss Tate into Witchcraft. He has photos purporting to show Miss Tate standing within a consecrated magic circle.

In early 1966 Martin Ransohoff hired one Roman Polanski to direct a film written by Polanski called, at various times, *The Fearless Vampire Killers* or *Dance of the Vampires* or *Pardon Me, But Your Fangs Are in My Neck,* or something. Mr. Ransohoff was eager for Sharon

Tate to be in the flick so he made arrangements for Roman Polanski and Sharon to meet.

A number of Polanski films, notably *Knife in the Water, Cul-de-Sac* and *Repulsion,* had achieved great success. *Repulsion* has the grim distinction of being one of the most horrifying films ever made.

Roman Polanski was born Raymond Polanski in Paris of Polish parents on August 18, 1933. In 1936 his family traveled back to Poland and settled in Krakow, where the sleazebag spirit of Hitlerism terrorized his earliest years.

When war broke out, his mother took Roman and his sister Annette to Warsaw. There were constant air raids and shortages of food. His mother scavenged in the street. They stood in line for water. There were dead animals in the street and bombed-out buildings. Then his father joined the family in Warsaw and they all returned to Krakow.

They were forced to move into a walled ghetto where they had to wear armbands with blue stars of David on them. It was scream city. His father's typewriter was confiscated. One day Roman saw the Germans marching a group of women down the street. One old woman couldn't keep up, and Roman saw a soldier shoot her. There were weekly open-air propaganda films where they would periodically flash the words *Jews = lice = typhus* on the screen. His father made arrangements for Roman to live with a family if he and his mother were taken away. His mother, part Jewish, was taken away and died in the concentration camp. Roman wanted to be with his father and returned to the ghetto and was somehow allowed back in. He had returned right in the middle of a raid. He searched for his father at his grandmother's apartment, but it was empty and wrecked.

The Krakow ghetto was liquidated March 13, 1943. Just before dawn, his father took him to a hidden spot behind the SS guardhouse and snipped the barbed wire. Roman went to the home where his father had arranged for him to stay, but it was locked. He returned to the ghetto to see a column of prisoners being marched out, his father among them. He tried to get near his father, who, in desperation, hissed, "Shove off." He stopped, turned away and departed. This rejection may have saved his life. How could the young boy running from the liquidation ever have dreamed that thirty years later a man with a swastika on his forehead in the rich state of California would be sitting in prison for engineering the murder of his future wife?

From childhood, movies became a refuge to him. When he was still very young, he became an actor and a moviemaker. He attended the Polish State Film College in Lodz, Poland, for five years, and while there met Wojtek Frykowski.

His earliest works were short, bleak, Beckettoid films. In 1960 Polanski went to France for eighteen months, where he directed and acted in *The Fat and the Lean.* In 1961 he divorced his wife, Polish actress Barbara Lass. He asked Samuel Beckett if he could make a film of *Waiting for Godot,* but Beckett turned him down on the grounds that it had been created for the stage alone. Polanski's friend Wojtek Frykowski invested 45,000 zlotys in his next short, *Mammals.* His next film was the feature-length *Knife in the Water,* which made him fairly famous in the West.

Knife in the Water won the Venice Film Festival Critics Award in 1962. In 1964, when it finally arrived in America, it was nominated for an Oscar as best foreign film.

In 1963 he went to Holland where he directed an episode for a movie entitled *The Best Swindles in the World.* He also that year co-wrote the scenario for *Do You Like Women?* which is a movie about a "society of cannibals" in Paris who like to cook and eat pretty girls. Oo-ee-oo. *Fade in electronic soundtrack from* Rosemary's Baby.

In the early '60s, Roman Polanski collaborated with Gérard Brach and turned out scripts for three movies: *Repulsion, The Fearless Vampire Killers* and *Cul-de-Sac.* Producer Gene Gutowski, an admirer of *Knife in the Water,* brought Polanski to England where in 1965 he made his first film in English, *Repulsion.*

Repulsion is the story of a beautiful manicurist, played by Catherine Deneuve, who suffers horrific violent hallucinations and winds up hacking and pummeling two male acquaintances to death. *Repulsion,* horribile dictu, was a success and Polanski was able to raise the money to make

Cul-de-Sac, a story of murder and weirdness in a seaside castle.

Polanski gained a reputation as a meticulous and thorough craftsman. The success of his blood-suffused movies and his obvious skill attracted Martin Ransohoff, who agreed to produce Polanski's script *The Fearless Vampire Killers* for MGM. In it, Sharon Tate would play a vampire.

One story always told is that on the night Roman and Sharon met they were alone in an apartment together. Mr. Polanski excused himself and left the room. Then he crept up behind the unsuspecting Miss Tate wearing a Frankenstein mask and pulled a boo! scene, throwing her into hysterics.

Vampire Killers is a comedy about a university professor and his servant, played by Roman Polanski, who travel into Transylvania to brick out a castle full of vampires. Sharon Tate played Sarah, an innkeeper's daughter who is abducted to castle neck-suck by the head vampire. There she is turned into a vampire herself. Etc. On the set of *The Fearless Vampire Killers,* she posed for publicity pictures, flashing her vampire incisors, shiny and fanglike.

In April of 1966 Jay Sebring complained to friends that he'd been bird-dogged by Roman Polanski, who seemed to have scooped the lovely Sharon Tate into his life. Sebring traveled to London and returned in the early summer of 1966, announcing that it was all over between him and Sharon.

Her public statements during that time regarding her breakup with Jay Sebring were almost self-deprecating.

"Before Roman I guess I was in love with Jay. It was a fine relationship but the truth is I was no good for Jay. I'm not organized. I'm too flighty. Jay needs a wife and at 23 I'm not ready for wifehood. I still have to live, and Roman is trying to show me how."

Sharon returned from England in 1966 to play a role in *Don't Make Waves,* with Tony Curtis and Claudia Cardinale. During this stage in her career her father, Lieutenant Colonel Paul Tate, was doing his thing in Vietnam, capping a career in army intelligence.

In the March 1967 issue of *Playboy* magazine there appeared a photo series called "The Tate Gallery" featuring Sharon with bared bosom, shot by Roman Polanski.

In '67 Sharon Tate gained notice for her role as Jennifer in the movie *Valley of the Dolls*. Jennifer was a young starlet who commits suicide in the flick.

Somewhere in the chronology, Martin Ransohoff, the producer of *The Beverly Hillbillies,* and Polanski had a feud over *The Fearless Vampire Killers*. Mr. Ransohoff cut footage out of the film before its release in the United States. This film-cut caused Polanski to demand that his name be stricken from the movie's credits. Ransohoff also bought U.S. rights to *Cul-de-Sac* and altered the movie extensively, angering Polanski. Sharon subsequently severed relationships with Mr. Ransohoff, reportedly purchasing her contract back for $175,000.

His continued triumph made it possible for Polanski to become the first filmmaker from a so-called Iron Curtain country to direct a picture in Hollywood. Lucky Roman.

The head of Paramount Pictures offered Polanski the opportunity to direct and write the screenplay for *Rosemary's Baby,* a novel by Ira Levin. *Rosemary's Baby,* a saga of satanic chauvinism, is a story about the big-league affluent hail-Satan crowd and their evident success in getting Satan to make pregnant an innocent female victim, played by Mia Farrow.

Mr. Polanski flew to Hollywood and stayed up all one night reading the galleys of the book, and the deal was made. Veteran moviemaker William Castle produced the film.

The studio wanted Mia Farrow to play the lead so Polanski was shown reels of the TV series *Peyton Place* wherein Miss Farrow acted, and he okayed her role in *Rosemary's Baby.* The Polanskis and Miss Farrow, according to most accounts, became close friends.

Rosemary's Baby had a shooting schedule of around 56 days. There were around 10 days spent filming in New York at the elegant Dakota apartments off Central Park West. The Dakota was transformed into a lair of Satan during the filming. Editing and dubbing evidently were done in Los Angeles, occupying the latter part of 1967.

Jay Sebring and the Polanskis maintained a friendly relationship. Some friends claim that Sebring still loved Sharon. While *Rosemary's Baby* was being created, some of Polanski's friends threw a party at Sebring's house on

Easton Drive. Evidently the party was a mock-up magical mass where guests wore white robes. One English journalist was invited and blindfolded, whereafter Jay, robed in white, offered him, hopefully in jest, the choice of two antique goblets, one containing wine, one containing rat poison.

San Francisco satanist Anton La Vey was a "consultant" for *Rosemary's Baby*. La Vey played the role of the devil in the movie. There are rumors that the real-life black-mass freaks were angered with Polanski for making such a movie. At the completion of the film, the cast gave Polanski an engraved 45-caliber Colt revolver, perhaps as a bit of amuletic humor because of the grumblings of the hail-Satan crowd. *Rosemary's Baby* has been called the greatest advertisement for satanism ever concocted. And Los Angeles possesses more than one lady moon-yodeler who claims to have given birth to children of the devil.

On January 20, 1968, following the completion of *Rosemary's Baby*, Sharon Marie Tate and Roman Polanski were married in London. He was attired in what the press described as "Edwardian finery," she in a white minidress. They retired to Roman's mews house off Belgrave Square. The world premiere of *Rosemary's Baby* was held in London, and it became obvious that the film was a smash success.

Polanski and his bride returned to Los Angeles, where the owner of their rented mansion on Ocean Front wanted it back. They moved into a fourth-floor kitchen apartment at the groovy Chateau Marmont on Sunset Boulevard at the curve by the big showbiz sign. With the success of the film, Polanski was a popular man—the cooers and backscratchers, as usual, attending the man of the hour. The Polanskis were part of an energetic, liberal group of actors and actresses and businessmen at the height of Hollywood success. They were all airline nomads, always packing, always on the move, but always working and planning.

Both admitted in print that they tried LSD. Polanski was bummered by it but his wife said, "It opened the world to me," although she was hesitant to trip again.

In May of 1968, Roman was a juror at the Cannes Film

Festival. At the same time, the students of France revolted and nearly toppled the government. Polanski was against cancelling the festival, but events roiled it to a close.

On June 5, 1968, Roman and Sharon and friends dined with Robert Kennedy at a beach house in Malibu. After dinner, Senator Kennedy was driven to the Ambassador Hotel where he was shot.

June 15, 1968, was the date of the West Coast premiere of *Rosemary's Baby*. "Pray for Rosemary's Baby" was the legend in the newspaper ads. The film was so popular in Los Angeles that extra showings were added to the theater's schedule. It opened in San Francisco on June 19, where it began a smash engagement. The film was on the track to a ten- to twenty-million-dollar gross.

Mr. Polanski's screenplay was nominated for an Academy Award. Mia Farrow received the Best Actress award at a film festival in Rio de Janeiro. Ruth Gordon received an Oscar for Best Supporting Actress for her role in the film.

In the summer of 1968, Sharon Tate and Dean Martin and Elke Sommers starred together in a movie called *The Wrecking Crew*. In June of that year, Roman Polanski rented a house at 1600 Summit Ridge Drive in the Hollywood Hills. The house was owned by young actress Patty Duke with whom Sharon had become friends during the filming of *Valley of the Dolls*. The Polanskis hired a housekeeper named Winifred Chapman, who worked for them during the following year, first on Summit Ridge and then on Cielo Drive. It was she who was picked by fate to discover the tragedy.

Sharon and Roman gave a housewarming party to celebrate their new rented house on Summit Ridge Drive. There was a strange occurrence at the party, according to a friend of Sharon Tate, involving Roman Polanski and some vicious dogs from down the hill.

The Polanskis had agreed to take care of Patty Duke's sheep dog while they rented the house. The sheep dog had the habit of running away. On the night of the party, the sheep dog bounded away down the hill, in the direction of the old John Barrymore mansion located at 1301 Summit Ridge Drive.

Polanski went after the dog and somewhere down the hill seems to have encountered a group of vicious Alsatian dogs belonging to a group of English occultists who were in America to promote the end of the world. Mr. Polanski got locked in a garage, evidently to try to escape the demi-wolves of the cult's dog pack. He had to batter himself out of the garage.

5

The Spahn Movie Ranch (1968)

Sometime that summer of '68 Manson recorded his songs at the recording studio located in the home of head Beach Boy, Brian Wilson, Dennis Wilson's brother and the producer of their albums. In Los Angeles, it was a heavy status symbol among the nouveau chart-toppers to have a fully equipped recording studio in their homes.

In April of 1968 Brian Wilson had moved to a house on Bellagio Road in Bel Air, which formerly had belonged to the creator of Tarzan, Edgar Rice Burroughs. A fully professional studio was constructed for Mr. Wilson. Brothers Records, the new Beach Boys label on Capitol Records, had as its premise that individual Beach Boys could discover new acts and record them, so Dennis began bringing M to the Beach Boys' office on North Ivar in L.A. and introducing him around. Arrangements were made for Manson to record at night in the studio set up in Brian Wilson's house on Bellagio. M apparently brought a half dozen girls to the sessions for a total of around two or three nights and six or eight songs.

Brian's wife, Marilyn, didn't dig Manson and the femmes fatales, feeling they might give the children diseases, so there was much use of Lysol in the bathroom at their departure.

It was around this time that Manson began to reveal himself to Hollywood as a knife nut. There was one incident, Gregg Jakobson recalls, when M pulled a knife on Wilson, held it to his throat and said, "What would you do if I killed you?" Wilson reportedly just shrugged and said, "Do it!" and M lowered the blade.

Stephen Despar was an electronics whiz who built the Beach Boys' fully equipped studio in Brian Wilson's house. He was the engineer stuck with recording M and was also witness to M's knife nuttery. After a couple of days of recording, Manson pulled out the blade and would flash it around while talking. Mr. Despar got in touch with the Beach Boys' manager, and further sessions were called off.

One of Dennis Wilson's friends, a very young girl named Croxey, said M came to the Will Rogers mansion at 14400 Sunset Boulevard once, looking for Dennis, and wanted to make out. She refused, and Manson pulled out a knife and said, "You know I could cut you up in little pieces." She ran out of the house and down the road to the Coast Highway and then went back to confront him. Manson then put down the knife and split. She realized later how Clotho, Lachesis and Atropos, the Fates, might have been closer to snipping her threads than she had realized.

The Beach Boys, as is common in many rock groups, were quarreling, so Manson claims that he wrote a philosophical song for them to heal their schisms. The song was called, believe it or not, "Cease to Exist" and it was put on the album that the Beach Boys were then working on. It has subsequently been a key family song. It was the song Gypsy was singing when first this writer encountered the family.

The key words of the song "Cease to Exist," were changed by Wilson to "Cease to Resist," as if the song had to do with sexual submission. The title was also changed to "Never Learn Not to Love." The song was given a full Beach Boys' production job with those excellent back-up harmonies. Nevertheless, it was upsetting to Manson, who hated more than anything for someone to tamper with his words.

When the song was released on the B-side of a Beach Boys' single, it did not sell so well. Manson believed the song would have been a smash if they'd left the words intact. As payment for the song Manson evidently got some cash and a BSA motorcycle which he gave to Little Paul.

Tex seems to have been the one to hang out at Terry Melcher's house that summer of 1968. Tex and the former minister, Dean Morehouse. Dean Morehouse was a familiar sight at the parties at Melcher's house where he was well known as a dirty old man.

Manson has said that he was at the Cielo Drive house about five times and that he used to wheel around Melcher's Jaguar.

Rudy Altobelli, Terry Melcher's landlord at the house at 10050 Cielo Drive, was a successful show business talent manager. He testified at Manson's murder trial how Terry and Gregg Jakobson were always talking about Manson and his philosophy. They were anxious for Altobelli to meet Manson, perhaps having in mind that Altobelli might guide Charlie's career. That summer Altobelli met Manson at a party at Wilson's residence on Sunset Boulevard. He listened to a tape of Charlie singing.

"They talked to me on many occasions about Manson. They wanted Dean to come and talk to me." Altobelli expressly expressed to Gregg and Dennis and Terry that he didn't want to be philosophized by Manson and his group. "They were telling me about his philosophy and his way of living and how groovy it was." But Altobelli didn't dig it and was not interested in managing Manson and his crowd.

John Phillips of the Mamas and Papas recording group was approached. Says he: "Terry Melcher and Dennis Wilson and the people who were living with Manson at Dennis Wilson's house used to call me all the time, you know, and say come on over, it's incredible. I'd just shudder every time. I'd say no, I think I'll pass."

Others say that Manson and some of the family in fact met Phillips, not a hard task to accomplish actually, and one witness claimed that Manson's blue bus was parked for a while in the fall of '68 at Phillips' house on Bel Air Road.

Things got weird for Manson on Sunset Boulevard. The family, like the hairy locusts they later admired in the Book of Revelation, had pretty much devoured the scene. Dennis Wilson's fabulous rock and roll wardrobe became community property and Manson gave away Dennis Wilson's gold records, which are given to a group whenever an album grosses over a million dollars in sales. One gold record wound up in the possession of the lady who owned the Barker Ranch in Death Valley. Another gold record wound up in the hands of George Spahn's brother. This was evidently distressing to Wilson.

Around August 1, Dennis Wilson and Gregg Jakobson abandoned ship and moved to a house near the beach on Pacific Coast Highway. They left the house on Sunset open for anybody who wanted to crash, according to Jakobson.

Shortly thereafter, Dennis Wilson's manager threw Manson and crew off the Sunset Boulevard property.

Off and on throughout that fall, people showed up at the Sunset Boulevard crash-estate to pick up belongings left there. New owners purchased that property and hired a guard to defend the house and grounds from crashers in the night.

Sometime around the first week of August, homeless Charlie drove to the Spahn Ranch and asked the people who were living at the back ranch area at the time if it was okay for the family to use the outlaw shacks nearby. The so-called outlaw shacks, small movable huts looking like tornado-devastated motel units from the 1920's, were located near the back ranch. These shacks were evidently used as props during the heyday of the good guys versus the bad guys kind of movies shot at the ranch. Several of the residents were reluctant to let Manson stay but it was agreed to let Charlie and the guys and gals stay "for a few days," as one person remembers. The possibility of gourmet garbage, family cooking, housekeepers and the use of the family credit cards weighed heavily in the decisions to let the brigade remain. John, the previous occupant of the back ranch, had moved out but the family knew the people who had moved in. They stayed this time at the Spahn Ranch about two and a half months.

After a couple of days at the outlaw shacks near the back ranch, Charlie, backed up by some of his silent harem waifs, approached blind George Spahn and conned Spahn into letting the family stay for a while at the front ranch on the Western set itself. They spent the first few days living in the wooden barred jail.

The deal that Charlie worked out was that the family was to cook, bale hay, help rent horses, help keep the barn, corral and grounds clean. Ultimately Charlie set up a near-nude geriatrics care squad for the elderly owner, cowboy-hatted George Spahn.

There were sixty or so horses to tend, many of them headed for the Jello factory, that were rented out for about three dollars an hour to weekenders. On the ranch, almost like a mental affliction, were thousands and thousands of Spahn Ranch horse flies which were a devouring menace, especially to vulnerable love-makers.

George Spahn had bought the ranch in 1948. It had once belonged to silent movie actor William S. Hart.

Spahn's eyesight was failing over the years as he pursued a career owning the movie ranch and renting out horses to high school classes, etc. He had a long-time associate named Ruby Pearl who managed his ranch affairs. Ruby, according to family gossip, was a former animal trainer and dancer. She was in her late forties during the Manson era when she was seen overseeing the activities wearing a cowboy hat and riding clothes. With the family she had a wavering relationship because the family at all costs wanted to keep on George's good side. Ruby Pearl had George's ear and was constantly observing what the family was up to, except at night when she went home. Which was okay with the family, because night is when it *was*.

Ruby Pearl is rumored to have a great autograph book containing the signatures of all kinds of entertainment figures who have visited the Spahn Ranch over the years.

The Spahn Movie Ranch, as it was called, was located at 12000 Santa Susanna Pass Road, running west of the northernmost section of Topanga Boulevard in the northwest of the San Fernando Valley.

The ranch was located midpoint between the wilderness and the city so that it was at the same time a thirty-five-minute ride to Sharon Tate's living room and also a fifteen-minute dune-buggy ride out into the wilderness of Devil Canyon into the Santa Susanna Mountains. It was also located in heavy dope traffic country. The communes of the northwest San Fernando Valley at that time were warehouses for the L.A. dope trade just as on the outskirts of any big city there are wholesale grocery and merchandise terminals.

The Spahn Ranch was situated just in front of a creek which cuts down from the northwest and oozes and trickles down along Santa Susanna Pass Road behind the Spahn Ranch. There are waterfalls in the creek which were the bathing spa of Helter Skelter. The Spahn Ranch is backed up by bouldery hills which climb sharply north and south. It is Grade B Western movie turf from the 1950s. The ghosts of Tim Holt and the Durango Kid yodel in the mountain crags.

The Western set, where movies were made, was located just off Santa Susanna Pass Road. It was a ramshackle collection of buildings in a straight row. A boardwalk extended the length of the set. Sleazy awnings held up by crooked posts ran the length of the mockup cowboy main street. There was a mockup restaurant called the Rock City Café; a jailhouse with wooden-barred cell; the Long Horn Saloon complete with mirrors and room-length bar and juke box; a carriage house full of old carriages; an undertaking parlor and several other buildings including George Spahn's small house which lay perpendicular to the right of the movie set. All these were built in the manner of a Kansas town of the early America. A dirt driveway connected the movie set with the reality of Santa Susanna Pass Road. Painted movie props often were strewn about, leaning against the haystack or corral.

It was fantasy land. But the era of the formula Western was over, and the ranch needed horse rentals to keep it going. On holiday weekends the ranch sometimes took up to $1000. In the case of the Spahn Ranch, an occasional beaver movie, TV commercial, sci-fi or monster movie brought in additional amounts of money.

Across the road from the Spahn Ranch was a bouldered, hilly area called the Garden of the Gods. And in a slit which ran for miles up into Santa Susanna Mountains were Devil Canyon and Ybarra Canyon, which would come to be a favorite helter-skelter haunt of the family. There were several little ranches in the area. In the Garden of the Gods was something called Wonderland Movie Ranch where, after Manson got arrested for murder, the owners kept a caged jaguar in the front yard for protection from the family.

At the Spahn Ranch, the salary for the ranch hands was food, a place to sleep and a pack of cigarettes a day. Some of the ranch hands, like Randy Starr, worked as stunt men in films. Randy Starr specialized in neck drags, horse falls and various gravity-defying stunts and fancied himself a performer of high quality. Others worked the rodeo circuit. Some like Larry Cravens were attempting to be stunt men. Murder-fated Shorty Shea was a Spahn Ranch stunt man and actor who eagerly pursued a career in the movies until they killed him. The stunt men used the Spahn Ranch as a business address.

The family met a sixteen-year-old Spahn ranch hand from Simi, California, Steve Grogan aka Clem aka Scramblehead, who crashed Wilson's red Mercedes into a barn near the Spahn Ranch, trying to see how fast he could take a curve. After crunching up and down the hills of Santa Susanna Pass, the uninsured $21,000 machine was abandoned.

Clem, who lived with his parents nearby, became one of Charlie's righthand men. He was able to copy Charlie's guitar style almost exactly and even copied Manson's voice. Clem was later sentenced to life imprisonment for decapitating Shorty Shea, the stunt man.

Manson met a young muscular Panamanian ranch hand named Juan Flynn who had been working for the Spahn Ranch since 1967 after he had fought in Vietnam. Juan Flynn would have a great effect on Manson because of Flynn's excruciating bloody battle experiences. Under the influence of LSD Juan Flynn would relive the Vietnam blood bath and scream and shriek describing in shocking detail sitting three days trapped in a trench beneath the blown-up bodies of his comrades.

On a typical day at dawn George Spahn arose and clanged the Spahn Ranch dinner bell, whereupon the hippie horse wranglers awoke to feed the horses and put them out to pasture. They gobbled breakfast and then saddled horses in preparation for possible rentals. Some were positioned in the front to guide the riders down the various riding trails. Then they had to clean the stalls and prepare the oats and hay for the horses.

The story is told how some of the family, evidently as

part of the program to experience everything, reveled in horse excrement. They walked barefoot as they cleaned the dilapidated Spahn Ranch barn, shovels in hand, grokking the fullness of the green horsemush between thelr toes.

The family, after staying in the jailhouse barn, quickly branched out to the Long Branch saloon and the nearby Rock City Café, a mockup restaurant. These buildings shared the same boardwalk as the movie set. Charlie set up an "office" in a small building that lay on the extreme east of the Western set, a building which during the era known as Helter Skelter, became a repository for weapons.

Like a Dayglo mosaic, the family began to spread out over the woods and streams and fantasyland buildings of the Spahn Ranch. They built lean-tos, they set up tents in remote clearings in the woods. Manson would roam about supervising the construction. "All my women are witches and I'm the Devil," he told one of the people at the back ranch house.

Evidently they fashioned occult items for the decoration of the ranch. For instance, one person recalled seeing in a gulch by the back ranch a steer skull residing atop a stake, the skull painted with arcane emblems. Manson's very own tent was painted with an occult host of eyeballs, sun symbols and loony-tune scrawls.

The ranch hands were meat eaters but the family was more or less vegetarian, and usually ate communally in a large circle with communal bowls passed around counterclockwise. After dinner, dope was brought forth and Manson would whip out his guitar and lead the singing.

The bulk of the choff was garbage. Part of the "rent" the family paid at the ranch was the preparation of food. To the west of the Spahn Ranch, in Simi Valley, and to the east in Chatsworth, and in fact all over the San Fernando Valley, the family made daily garbage runs. At the San Fernando Valley supermarkets they throw away fruits and vegetables that in the slums of New York would be sold as Grade A.

Even the car the killers would drive to the various murders, Johnnie Schwartz's 1957 yellow Ford, would have the back seats removed in order to receive more readily fruit crates full of throw-away food.

For instance, several miles away from the Spahn Ranch,

at the edge of the concrete loading platform in back of the Market Basket supermarket in Chatsworth, lay two four by four by six-foot salmon-colored wheeled garbage bins. On a typical day, the bin on the left was packed solid with wooden crates tossed askew, cardboard boxes, celery, lettuce, display melons, slightly mutant bell peppers, corn husks, pink unripe tomatoes, raggedy squashed balls of lettuce. In the right bin were hunks of fatty tissues cut from the steaks of dead cows, old peach boxes and pink-brown wavy blobs of suet. To test the edibility of much of it the only known test was the sniff test.

And there was no hesitance on the part of the soul-driven girls to get down and grovel in the gunge of large bins of rotting animal and vegetable matter in order to sort out the good from the less good.

The girls were in to using their witchiness even in preparing for the daily garbage run when they would "get a picture" in their minds as to what store would have the best gourmet garbage. That is, they would scan the void with witch-rays to locate the location of the most food-filled bins. Then they would drive there.

There were always parts of movies being shot at the Spahn Ranch. The karma of the Marlboro man cigarette commercials, some of which were made at the Spahn Ranch, must have lingered on. So they played games, the family. They played, believe it or not, Cowboy and Indians, Mexican knife fighters, flatlanders versus the hill people, Charlie Manson as Mexican bad-ass raping the stockbroker's daughter from San Diego. Be what you don't want to be; free your mind.

These games were part of the so-called Magical Mystery Tour. They were carried out like encounter group games designed to liberate the psyche. The master game was to find the real personality amid the maze of traits handed down through reincarnation and the traits given by parents and society. Whatever role the person "got stuck in" in his various game-roles, that was his real archetypal personality. Charlie called it "getting stuck in one part." Paul Watkins, for instance, got "stuck" in the part of playing the Apostle Paul—and also an entity called "daddy's boy."

Manson, over the years, has taken a more cynical attitude about his relationship with his followers at the

Spahn Ranch. He said he would "play around with the kids at the ranch" and pick up a beat-up old truck at the Spahn Ranch and drive to Dennis Wilson's house all dirty. He would shower, don a few expensive clothes, grab up some money and head out for a few laughs in the luxury hills.

One girl, named Roberta, who left the group shortly thereafter, said this about Manson in the summer of 1968: "He was very beautiful in many ways and gave out lots of love." They were always hugging and kissing and making love. Ceaseless was the lovemaking. And with the remote, seemingly safe fantasyland location of the Spahn Ranch, the word really went out and people began to flock in.

Like any other youth movement, the greatest number of recruits appeared in summertime. Charlie was upset at the throngs appearing at the ranch so he threw matches to see who split.

Recalled Roberta: "Charlie was uptight cause so many people came down to the ranch, so he was doing the thing about . . . like how many of us would stay. . . . He took matches and he threw them out . . . and the direction . . ." would evidently determine who would stay or leave. "It meant that a certain amount of girls would leave and boys would stay."

Charlie would imitate someone's facial expressions if he didn't like them around. Or worse, he would sing songs about them. The girls, with that trump card that men fear, would cut them off of the grope list.

And then there was the gorilla problem for Charlie—guys kept coming around merely for the sex. Some of the girls like Ella and Sadie, who liked to hang out on Sunset Strip downtown, were always bringing home what Charlie termed "gorillas"—guys who did not fit in.

One of the girls (Manson always accused Sadie) brought in the vehement Vietnamese clap to the ranch in summer '68. It got so bad that Charlie had to bring in a doctor to wipe it out. Juan Flynn had such a bad case of it that it took three months to clear it up.

Books were banned by Manson, the semi-illiterate prophet of doom. Manson was heedless of Revelation 1:3—"Blessed is he that readeth." But that didn't stop him from getting the girls to read to the hairy-chested pasha, books such as *Siddhartha* and, of course, the Bible.

Charlie also deprecated what he called "black slave music" and wouldn't allow Jimi Hendrix records to be played. This did not prevent Charlie from trying to sing like Nat King Cole during some of his recording sessions and from borrowing blues riffs and chord progressions for his songs.

Charlie impressed everybody with his drum-playing ability. He was "mean at the drums" according to Richard Kaplan. But his sense of pitch seemed fallible. "Let me hear a note, man," was often heard during pauses to tune, during "family jams." "It is a test of enlightenment how far you are into the drums," Charlie told Richard Kaplan.

Not only books and Jimi Hendrix records but even glasses were put on the nicht list. Charlie did not believe that George Spahn was blind. In fact, that was one of Charlie's raps: about how George was conditioned by his former wife over the years so that he slowly became blind, evidently through some sort of shrewing on the part of the wife. In fact, Charlie did not cooperate with any form of ocular disease. Mary Brunner was supposed to have possessed as many as fourteen pairs of glasses, according to Danny De Carlo, but these were banned by Charlie. No glasses.

Charlie was also out to impress with his power over animals. Picking up snakes and zapping them with the stare, allowing the Spahn Ranch horse flies to land on his mouth and swarm upon his lips. The girls claimed he conjured them not to bite him.

Later on, it was always amazing to see unconcerned family members with horse flies on their lips—horse flies that can really chomp into a lip, should they decide it.

But Charlie hankered to obtain the remote back ranch for his growing family of friends. The back ranch was a ramshackle dive consisting mainly of one large room with a stone fireplace and a large five by eight multi-paned window. The back ranch was powered by a clandestine tapping of county power lines. And for water it had the rather yucky creek water from a homemade dam created upstream. A small water pump pumped the water to a tank up on the hillside. From the hillside, a green plastic water hose brought water to the bathroom, and another green water hose stretched across the living room into the kitchen.

Like any edge-of-desert location, the Spahn Ranch seemed to gather rusty ancient hulks of various pieces of automotive and industrial equipment. It was cluttered, dusty, creepy, tarpapered, metal-roofed, rusty-posted, broken-windowed, tawdry, tarnished ramshackle plexus of buildings that Charlie saw to overrun with his hemp horde. But it was remote and more importantly it was run by a weak, confused old blind man who was beleaguered on all sides by relatives and associates, some seeking to burn him, and all delivering advice gratis.

Manson finally ran the people out of the back ranch and took over.

A biker from Topanga that some of the family probably met downtown at the Galaxy Club, gave Richard Kaplan some LSD which turned out to be p-c-p animal tranquilizers, or steam, as it is known in dope-land. It is a weird and mind-zapping drug. Kaplan, freaked out on the steam, stumbled into Charlie's office at the end of the boardwalk and found Charlie and the torrid twenty listening to a tape of guess who, singing. Charlie then took him on a tour of the family camp and asked him if he would fork over the back ranch to the family because Charlie sorely needed it. Charlie offered to trade his witchy painted tent for it. So, tranced on dope, Kaplan gave up the ranch. That night the family had an orgy of celebration when they moved from the Western set down the trail to the back ranch. To this day, Kaplan possesses the witch tent as a Manson-mania relic first class.

As befits book-haters, the family burnt all his books including his magical library and the young man fondly remembers seeing his books on alchemy and Nietzsche's *Beyond Good and Evil* going up into flames in the back ranch stone fireplace.

Meanwhile, back up north in Mendocino County, the witch girls were finally released on August 16, 1968, on their own recognizance after fifty-five days in the slams. Charlie sent Brenda and Squeaky north to Ukiah to bring the rest of the recently freed girls back to the Spahn Ranch. Eagerly they fixed up the back ranch so that the girls released would have a place to prepare themselves for upcoming court dates, which were to occur several weeks later in early September. When Brenda and the girls were driving the black bus back they passed through San Jose where the bus broke down, leaving people stranded.

Somewhere around August 20 or so, Bob Beausoleil, traveling with his girls in northern California, called the Spahn Ranch. There was something afoul with the pink ownership slip to the truck George Spahn had given him so he called to clear the matter up. It was then that Beausoleil was told the bus had broken down in San Jose.

In June of 1968 an eighteen-year-old girl named Leslie Van Houten was living with some girl friends at the Kalen Ranch near Victorville and Apple Valley, California. Along came Bob Beausoleil, who freaked the group with his throwing of knives. He scooped up Leslie Van Houten, leaving in a 1962 blue Volkswagen offed from Leslie's roommate's stepfather. Later the VW was dewired and dumped in San Francisco.

Throughout the summer, Gail and beautiful Gypsy the Magna Mater embodiment and Leslie and Beausoleil and two unknown female Caucasians from San Francisco drove in the environs of northern California in the old black Dodge powerwagon formerly belonging to George Spahn.

Born in Cedar Rapids, Iowa, Leslie Van Houten had been the freshman class treasurer at Monrovia High School in California. She was in the Job's Daughters service organization and was active in her church choir. She was mystically inclined, became involved in the Self Realization Fellowship, became a dropout, met Beausoleil and slowly became enmeshed in the agreements and submissions and mutations that led to murder.

When Beausoleil called the Spahn Ranch around August 20 and learned that the black bus had broken down in San Jose, he drove to the rescue. Beausoleil and friends went to San Jose and towed the broken bus to a plum orchard. Data regarding events are confused at this point. Beausoleil evidently secured a new bus for the family, abandoning the old one. The new bus also was painted black.

After Beausoleil and the girls drove to the place where the family was stranded, in San Jose, there occurred some sort of jealousy squabble among Beausoleil's girl friends so he was forced to cut loose Gypsy and Leslie from his thrill pack. "About one in a hundred of the girls I'd make love to we'd go through our changes and I'd add her to the pack," he said. Little Paul and Gypsy and Leslie then drove to the Spahn Ranch from San Jose.

While the family was still in San Jose, a schoolteacher named Joan Wildbush aka Juanita picked up four hitchhikers, T. J. Walleman aka T.J. the Terrible, Tex Watson, Ella Sinder and Clem aka Scramblehead, while she was driving her shiny new 1968 Dodge van near Palo Alto, California; or so she said later to the police. She was a schoolteacher on a summer vacation, an eager young lady of Rubenesque frame. She took the four to San Jose where evidently she was persuaded to drive down to the Spahn Ranch to meet Charlie. Juanita was, in the language of police reports, a female Caucasian, height five foot four inches, blond/blue, weight 150 pounds, d.o.b. 1-21-44.

Manson must have singed her soul with the love beams during one of those all-day love sessions because Manson drew her forthwith into the fold of the followers. She withdrew $11,000 from a trust fund which was set up by her father, a New Jersey lawyer, and turned it over to Satan. The family was overjoyed.

Around this time in South Topanga Canyon Manson located a great new bus, a 1956 White or GMC school bus owned by a lady in South Topanga Canyon named Mitzi. They saw the school bus one day when Manson and Kaplan and Ouish were whizzing through the canyon on an errand. The price was $600. Manson used some of the newly acquired Juanita booty to pay for the bus.

The family painted the bus light green in color and began to outfit it for possible trips.

Dean Morehouse recalled seeing Tex and Mary Brunner driving to 10050 Cielo Drive in the new green bus, looking for Terry Melcher, but he wasn't at home.

Another input into the mind of Manson was provided by a religious cult, The Fountain of the World, located west of the Spahn Ranch in Box Canyon near the Santa Susanna fire department. He was very impressed with the Fountain and spent a lot of time visiting it.

The Fountain of the World, a religious sect dedicated

to "peace through Love and Service" or so the sign on the hill above the cult corner reads, was an apocalyptic Christian cult that held public meetings every Saturday night. Several of the Spahn ranch hands, including Shorty Shea, were associated with The Fountain of the World. Ranch hands would attend the Fountain's religious meetings and group song sessions. Manson and the family occasionally attended these meetings. A black guy named John was involved in the leadership of The Fountain of the World and Manson several times hungered to take the place over. The cult members wore robes and practiced celibacy. Charlie assigned some of the girls to try to seduce the priests of the order, evidently to no avail.

The Fountain was formed by a holy man named Krishna Venta who died by violence. The family grooved with the violent history of the Fountain. The religious retreat occupied subterranean chambers and caves wherein they did their thing. As the cult progressed, dissension ensued and parties unknown blew up the founder, Krishna Venta, and nine of his followers—with forty pieces of dynamite placed in the catacombs. This occurred on 12-10-58, whereafter the Fountain struggled onward and was still thriving when Manson discovered it.

Charlie seems to have gotten the idea for his crucifixion ceremony from The Fountain of the World. There was a large rock at The Fountain of the World that looked remarkably like a huge skull. At the top of the "skull" was a wooden upright cross. Fountain members, so one is told, were wont to strap themselves up on the cross for penitential meditation sessions. Far out.

Not far from the Spahn Ranch the family discovered an almost secret clearing guarded by a natural surrounding wall of large boulders. On one side of the clearing was a hill, The Hill of Martyrdom. For upon this hilly boulder-shrouded secret clearing was performed perhaps the world's first outdoor LSD crucifixion ceremony.

There they snuffed Charlie, in role as Jesus, strapping (not nailing) him to an actual rustic cross, while others, acting as tormenters and apostles, jeered or weeped. One chosen female was Mother Mary cloaked and weeping at the foot of the cross.

Then they fucked, evidently after some form of resurrection service.

In August of 1968 part of the family spent about a week living at The Fountain of the World. There is talk that Manson gave about $2,000 of the money given to the family by Juanita to the Fountain.

At some point in its development, the family—particularly the girls—began to say "Amen Amen" whenever Charlie spoke, as if his words were divine.

Manson began to formulate obedience tests for his followers as when he once told Sadie Glutz during a meal to go get him a coconut, even if she had to go clear to Rio. She executed an about-face and she trotted off to Rio. However, after a few steps he called her back. Another time at a meeting at The Fountain of the World, when he was trying to impress the Fountain members with the obeisance of his followers, he instructed Little Paul to go spend a week on the cross—which Little Paul darted off to do but the Wizard showed mercy and called him back.

On August 20, 1968, the very pregnant Sadie Mae Glutz aka Susan Denise Atkins had a hearing in the Mendocino County Supreme Court and pleaded guilty to the 11530 H. and S. possession of pot charge. She was ordered to reappear in court on August 30 for sentencing, pending a probation report ordered by the court. An arrangement was made whereby Susan (Sadie) agreed to cop out to the pot charge and to take that guilt upon herself and Mary Brunner decided to take the acid charge so that the others then would go free.

Sadie managed to pull off a charm job on the deputy probation officer up there, one David Mandel, because he wrote a sympathetic probation report which might be called the damaged soul document. It concludes, "Your Honor, it is our opinion that incarceration for this defendant would be of little or no use to society or to herself.

"Even while she was still a minor, she was well on her way to a career of minor confidence-style operations, high styled prostitution and prostitution of herself in the more general sense, as an object of entertainment and vicarious satisfaction for other damaged souls."

The Witches of Mendocino were able to spend only a couple of days at the Spahn Ranch before they had to go to their dope trials.

Around the last part of August the girls prepared to

drive north to the Mendocino County trials from the Spahn Ranch in the new green and white family bus. They drove up the coast highway through Big Sur to Mendocino County. Sadie was the driver of the bus.

On August 30, 1968, in Mendocino County Superior Court in Ukiah, California Sadie Mae Glutz was found guilty by reason of plea of guilty on violation of Section 11530 of the California Health and Safety Code aka pot bust. And the pronouncement of sentence of sixty days in the slams was suspended and she was placed on three years' probation.

Evidently she waited around until the others had their trials on September 6, 1968. On that day Mary Therese Bunner aka Mother Mary pleaded guilty to Section 11910 of the Health and Safety Code aka LSD bust and Judge Robert Winslow sentenced her to sixty days in jail with time credited already served. Though Mary Brunner also had a favorable probation report, she was carted away to jail.

The rest of the defendants, Susan Scott aka Stephanie Rowe, Katherine Patricia Smith aka Patricia Krenwinkel aka Katie and Ella Bailey aka Ella Sinder, beat the rap in Department Number 1 in Mendocino County Superior Court before Judge Winslow. Another human, one Robert Bomse, was convicted for possession of the herb.

This exercise in justice, the smashing of a cabal of hippie witches, cost the county of Mendocino considerable money. The fees for the court-appointed lawyers alone cost the taxpayers $2,999.50.

After the court hearing on September 6, 1968, Susan Atkins aka Sadie Glutz and the girls drove back down and spent a few days visiting San Jose. Susan was heavily gravid, the child due in about six weeks. Susan's father contends that Manson and Susan and several of the family spent a few days there, staying at his house. Quite a few family members also were scrounging around in San Jose in September of 1968.

One day in September '68, Manson came to Dennis Wilson's Malibu Beach house and Charlie told him and Gregg Jakobson in the style of a psychedelic Billy Graham that it was the hour of decision. It was time for them to join, or not to join. You were with him or against him.

He wanted Jakobson and Wilson to choose. The family was with them, but were they?

Tex Watson of Copeville, Texas, the former sports editor for his high school yearbook, joined the family forever that fall. He gave up his wig shop on Santa Monica Boulevard and he gave to Manson his 1935 Dodge pickup truck.

Manson met quite a few interesting people at Wilson's beachhouse. One was a wealthy young lady named Charlene Cafritz. Mrs. Cafritz took some motion pictures of Manson and various of the girls at Wilson's house. Later in the fall Manson visited her for two weeks at a luxury ranch in Reno, Nevada, about which more later.

While Manson was in San Jose during those days after the Mendocino trials, he ran into a man named Patterson, evidently an employee of a local underground newspaper. Manson told Mr. Patterson an interesting anecdote that gave tribute to Manson's trigger temper.

Manson told Patterson, in fact astounded Patterson—because Manson seemed so much a part of flower power—that one time a few months previous Manson had chased a father and his daughter down a street with a knife in his hand prepared to cut them up and that Manson ascribed this homicidal urge to a toothache where the poison from the inflamed tooth had seeped into his brain.

A leather shop opened up by Victor Wild was located in the head shop area near San Jose State College. Wild made "leathers," i.e., leather pants and jackets, for the bike clubs. Members of the Gypsy Jokers began to hang around the leather shop. One Gypsy Joker was interested in one of the girls associated with the shop and connections with the club sprouted.

Brother Ely aka Wild became so involved, in fact, with them that he was "flying the patch" of the Gypsy Jokers, i.e., wearing a jacket bearing the club's emblem, according to the San Francisco police department.

The Manson family stayed with some of the Gypsy Jokers in San Jose. Charlie told one Straight Satan that the family stayed in several houses that September belonging to the Gypsy Jokers. Later the family had Victor Wild make some leather outfits for Manson and Watson, etc.

The Gypsy Jokers were extremely violence-prone. They

were among the elite of the 1 percenter bike clubs. According to his onetime friends, Wild liked to watch the violence committed by the group.

The Gypsy Jokers lived in the world of aliases, using such names as Theo, Dago, Dirty Doug, Gypsy Jack, the Thumper, Frenchy, Big Rich. Included in the group were a terminal cancer sufferer who decided to die freaky and a one-legged person named Garbage Can who had a shotgun built into his wooden leg. In September of 1968, on the Labor Day "run" to Mendocino County, Brother Ely went along and observed with dispassion according to a witness a violent sadistic "turnout," which is biker terminology for a violent gang rape. Only this girl was nearly killed—punched, slugged, gagging and puking with mouth rape, while four men held her down, punching her in the face whenever she wouldn't obey. Later, they picked her up, put her clothes on and dumped her at a road near the location of the biker frolics.

In August of 1968, Brother Ely and his girl friend casually watched some members of the Gypsy Jokers slam a car door repeatedly upon the head of a middle-aged man who had called one of the bikers a punk in an obscure bar in San Jose.

In December of '68 police shot and killed a member of the Jokers while twenty or thirty of the club were burning down a house on Sunnyvale Road in San Jose.

There was an interesting article which appeared in a Berkeley newspaper authored by a person named Blaine. The article purported to tell of the involvement of Charles Manson in a "death-cult" in the summer and fall of 1968 which operated out of the notorious Waller Street Devil House in the Haight district. The Devil House, it will be recalled, was formerly, during the era of flower-power, a crash-house run by the Diggers. Manson claimed to have lived there briefly.

In any case, the story is internally consistent enough with known facts to be recounted here, numbered from one to thirty.

This is what Blaine alleges:

1. He first heard of Manson in 1964 when he was a prisoner in the U.S. Medical Center, where a guy named Richard was sent, transferred from McNeil Island Federal Penitentiary in Washington. Richard had been a

gobblemate of Manson, but alleged that after Manson spurned his affections, Richard tried to kill himself, an act for which he was sent to the U.S. Medical Center.

2. Blaine met this Richard in the Medical Center prison library where Richard allegedly babbled a lot about his "lost lover" Charles Manson—referred to evidently by name and as a convict from West Virginia. Blaine remembered that Richard said this about Manson: "Charles will be a great man some day." Why? "Because he knows all about magic."

3. Blaine, after release from prison, went to the Haight-Ashbury love scene in 1967. He met Manson in the I-Thou coffee shop in 1967, not knowing who he was. He talked with Manson, Manson mentioning that he, Manson, just got out of the slams. Blaine claims then to have discovered, in the course of the conversation, that Manson was Richard's lost lover, so to speak. Manson evidently said that now he was into girls, allegedly saying: "Boys aren't where it's at. Out here it has to be girls. You can control girls easier than boys." And "Hey, I know where all that's at. And it's this way: two scorpions together would only sting one another to death." A person named Sam Tela was also involved in this conversation at the I-Thou coffee house. Manson left the shop and the two didn't meet for about a year.

4. Blaine and Manson met again in summer-fall 1968, again on the Haight.

5. Blaine claims to have become involved in a "death-cult" called The Companions of Life. "The Final Church is the name Manson chose for the church he eventually founded," Blaine wrote. The church was operating in the Waller Street Ashram or Devil House.

6. Cult members would talk about Manson, saying that he was living down in L.A. on a "movie lot"—evidently the Spahn Ranch.

7. The cult evidently was led by one Father P. the 66th (666?) aka Carl who claimed to be an M.D. and Ph.D. and a magician, and wore a mustache and was said to have been expelled from pre-Castro Cuba, to have set fire to some church in North Carolina for which he was run out of town, and to have recently returned from Damascus, Syria.

8. The cult was homosexual. There was a "crash room"

where girls could sleep but women could not venture into the adyta or inner rooms of the homo-thanatos cult.

9. Manson supposedly showed up at a "medieval trial" in late summer 1968 wherein it was to be decided whether or not to put to death a former cult member named Sadyi for "committing crimes against Haight-Ashbury, against nature and for crimes against Pussycat." They accused him of (1) cursing the Haight, (2) consorting with a woman, (3) causing a demon to enter the body of Father P.'s kept cult-boy, Pussycat.

10. They said, in regard to Pussycat, that Sadyi, after leaving the cult, had re-entered the cult house one night and somehow caused a demon to possess the body of Pussycat. So, evidently, part of the ceremony required trying to drive the demon of Sadyi out of Pussycat. Poor Pussycat.

11. Manson showed up with a female Caucasian, maybe Sadie Atkins-Glutz, who had to remain in the "crash room" and could not come into the trial room. A man named Smith, a former college teacher, allegedly alleged to Blaine that Manson had been called in "to sit in" on the trial, since Manson himself had been a magical understudy of Father P. Evidently Manson was forgiven his interest in young ladies, as long as he did not bring them before the holy of holies.

12. Charlie talked about being his "own master soon." Charlie sat next to a person referred to as D.K., upon a mattress.

13. Father P., to begin the trial, donned a brown tunic and prepared his religious relics, for purification.

14. Pussycat began to fight, calling Father P. an arsonist, so that they tied Pussycat, a twenty-year-old youth, hand and foot and gagged him.

15. Father P. then started running around the room screaming: "I'm God! I'm Satan! I'm Jesus!" while Pussycat on the floor was moaning behind his gag.

16. Father P. proclaimed him, Pussycat, again possessed by Sadyi so he, Father P., sent Manson and D.K. out to steal holy water from a nearby church.

17. Blaine and Smith stood guard over the trussed cult-lad while they went for the holy water.

18. Manson and D.K. returned and Father P. sprinkled the holy water on Pussycat's face.

19. Pussycat calmed down. Father P. motioned for them to untie Pussycat, but as soon as the gag was off, Pussycat began to scream. So Manson and Father P. retied Pussycat.

20. Father P. then supposedly ran to the altar, seized a large wooden "stolen" crucifix and began to beat Pussycat across the face with it.

21. Blaine then claims to have run to his microbus and grabbed a small tape recorder and carried it within the ashram to record the ceremonies, secretly.

22. Pussycat was yelling, "Help! Police!"

23. Father P. threatened to retie the gag, kicking the trussed victim.

24. Evidently it really got freaky for a while, where they got into plans to sacrifice the lad. "If you must die, Sadyi will die with you," Father P. said, allegedly.

25. D.K. got a stake and began to carve it, saying: "He must die."

26. People came to the door, stopping the action inside. Father P. then tried to remove the influence of Sadyi from the lad: "Sadyi, go away or I will take your body and destroy it with great pain. I will bury it piece by piece and I will chop it up in little pieces." Evidently he would also have had to destroy Pussycat.

27. Blaine alleges that Manson left the next day to drive back to the Spahn Ranch in the hot bus.

28. Blaine says that Father P. went down to L.A. subsequently, to see Manson.

29. Blaine alleges that later, after the death of a member of the Final Church, he, Blaine, drove Father P. and Pussycat down to the Topanga Çanyon area and dropped Father and Pussycat off.

30. And as for Sadyi and his pregnant wife, they picked up on the bummer vibes and left the Haight, so at least part of the story has a happy ending. Oe-ee-oo.

The Manson Family seems to have oozed back to Los Angeles where they spent the latter part of September and October occupying the Spahn Ranch. The old black bus, the Love Bus, Charlie gave to a person named John, that friend of Sandy Good who at one time had rented the back ranch. John gave Charlie in return a pickup truck. John took the black bus and drove it to a commune called the Commune of the Sacred Heart in Oregon.

As for Beausoleil, in the early fall he and his girl-friend-wife Gail spent time in Santa Cruz, then went to Santa Barbara where Beausoleil traded his truck for a boat in which he began to live in Santa Barbara harbor. Gail split and went back to San Francisco while Beausoleil remained, living in his houseboat. Later, Manson came to the houseboat, according to Beausoleil, and asked him to come away and help to prepare the music for a record album. This he did.

Sometime in early October during a group acid trip, the family members began to fight and growl and whip one another and tried to throw each other into the burning fireplace. Further family legend has it that they finally succeeded in throwing one another into the flames and even threw a cat into the flames but the soul was so strong among them that no one got burned.

On October 7, 1968, Susan Atkins aka Sadie gave birth at the back ranch to a premature baby boy whom she named, by the eyebrow of Ra, Zezo Ze-ce Zadfrak aka Zezo. When Sadie announced to the happy family that she was about to give birth, she recalls Manson was angry, and he reminded her it was not due for several more weeks. Instead, Manson commanded her to go boil him some water so he could shave. She prepared the water and set up the shaving mirror for him in the bathroom, and then the baby came. Even with labor coming on, Charlie proceeded to shave, thus giving a lesson in cool and calm to his idolators. This was almost like a koan to the family, this "breaking the fear force," as they termed it.

It was a breech delivery. When first the arm and then the body of little Zezo emerged from the laboring mother, Manson, according to legend, seized the moment by halting the singing, tearing from his Spanish guitar a string and tying off the umbilical cord with it.

Evidently the family sang songs to relax the atmosphere as Sadie gave birth. The family had a particular form of relaxation mantra which they sang during times of tension. This relaxation mantra was added by the Beach Boys as a coda to "Cease to Exist/Resist" during the fadeout at the end of the song.

The week following, Tex Watson and kourephile Dean Morehouse drove to Ukiah in Terry Melcher's Jaguar to pick up Mary Brunner's baby, Pooh Bear aka Valentine Michael Manson. There is an area of silence around the matter because of uptight individuals, but it is known that producer Terry Melcher allowed family members to use his Jaguar and his Standard Oil credit card. The family ran up a large bill on his credit card using it for their important travels.

Mrs. Roger Smith, as will be remembered, had been appointed as foster parent for Pooh Bear during Mary Brunner's trouble with the law in Mendocino. Her husband had been Manson's parole officer and was then operating a drug abuse program for the Haight-Ashbury Free Clinic Annex.

On the day Tex and Dean drove to Mendocino, Mrs. Smith brought the baby to Ukiah evidently for a custody hearing, to give it back to its mother.

6

Death Valley (1968)

Sometime in the evening of October 13, 1968, two ladies, Clida Delaney and Nancy Warren, were beaten and strangled to death with thirty-six leather thongs about six miles south of Ukiah, California on U.S. Highway 101. The thongs were left tied around the necks of the victims.

Mrs. Warren was eight months pregnant and the wife of a Highway Patrol officer. Mrs. Delaney was her sixty-four-year-old grandmother who operated an antique store next to a house trailer where she lived.

This double homocide is mentioned because it is the first of a series of unsolved murders that occurred strangely enough when various family members were in the vicinity of the killings. Two of those convicted to die for the so-called Tate-LaBianca murders were in Ukiah, California for hearings of some sort the afternoon of these two hideous events, according to Officer Bob Richardson of the Mendocino County sheriff's office.

Two days after the murders in Ukiah, the family left the Spahn Ranch. Manson decided to take a trip all of a sudden to "Grandma's place" in Death Valley, California.

With the usual satins and silks and pillows and Arabian tapestries, they fixed up the new bus in the style of Manson Moorish.

The family had learned of the place in Death Valley in

the remote vastnesses of the wilderness from one Cathy Myers aka Cathy Gillies aka Pattay Sue Jardin. Cathy Gillies had been raised on a ranch or piece of patented mining land located high in the bordering mountains of the Death Valley National Monument. The ranch was known as the Meyers Ranch after Cathy's grandparents who still own the property. The Myers Ranch was located about a quarter mile east of the Barker Ranch in Goler Wash. Goler Wash, formerly a gold mining area but now an unused wasteland, is a narrow treacherous slit in the Panamint Mountains that connects the Panamint Valley to the west with the hilly high desert area near the Myers Ranch to the northeast. She had met Manson at a ranch in Topanga Canyon and was highly tuned in to the Los Angeles music scene where she had been an ardent Buffalo Springfield groupie.

The green bus traveled somewhere for a few days, then drove to Grandma's place in Death Valley, arriving around Halloween. They proceeded north several hundred miles to a small desert town called Trona, a town plagued by crusty fallout from a potash plant. Trona is located a few miles south of the Death Valley National Monument. From Trona they proceeded north on Highway 28 about twenty miles to a long thin salt lake where they turned right and crossed over the salt lake to the Ballarat ghost town, the home of the only retail food source in the area, the Ballarat General Store.

The ghost town Ballarat—a mining settlement from the late 1800's—serves as a supply center for the local miners who still search avidly for gold. It lies on the edge of a thin, twenty-five mile salt lake at the junction of Ballarat Road and Wingate Road, two roads of the bumpity-bump variety. Having driven up the west side of the salt lake, the bus drove south on the east side of the salt lake of mushy selenite, a good salt source protected by law against encroachment or mining.

It is fourteen miles on Wingate Road from Ballarat to the slim mouth of famed Goler Wash. The bus passed an old Spanish arrastre, a burro-driven ore-munching machine from the previous centuries, but now little more than a rusted metal shaft jabbed up from the hill void.

In the distance, on the left as the bus headed south, up

against the Panamint mountainside, lay the Cecil R. mine, a little man-made greed gouge in the hillside. The bus bounced past South Park Canyon, then past Redlands Canyon and then Redlands camp where Harry Briggs' Schultag Mine is located.

The salt lake ends about ten miles south from the Ballarat General Store and several miles south of the lake's ending is a white pole stuck in the dirt on the right side of the road, which marks the almost hidden access road to Goler Wash.

There the bus hung a left and began the humpity-bump climb east toward the narrow mouth of Goler Wash and the dry waterfalls which mark the way into the Myers-Barker Ranch area.

The road at that point is impassable to normal conveyance, especially to an old bus full of hippie wanderers. The road up Goler Wash used to be the main road between Las Vegas and the Panamint Valley during the heyday of the Goler Wash gold strikes early in the twentieth century. But devastating floods in the winter of 1941 washed out the road leaving a series of sheer waterfalls. According to the local miners, Cathy Myers' grandfather dynamited the falls so as to allow at least some sort of conveyance to pass up and down the Goler Wash road.

The bus drove past the rusty hulk of a Model T Ford and the old rear window lying near it in the dust until it reached the first waterfall where it burnt out one of its brakes and was backed down and abandoned.

The family walked the seven and a half miles from the beginning of the waterfalls to the Myers Ranch, up the long, very narrow, steeply cliffed gash in the mountain where barrel cacti stick out from each cliffside like big green fingers.

Immediately the family hikers encountered the first dry waterfall. Climbing up it they reached a second waterfall and crossed a big curve to the right and encountered the third waterfall. Then, grabbing a boomerang curve to the left they came to the treacherous fourth Goler Wash waterfall, then the fifth, sixth and seventh. Then they had to hang along some sort of sheer cliff. After that it's merely two or three miles of rollercoaster creekbed travel, whereupon they arrived in the vicinity of the Barker and Myers Ranches.

In the journey up Goler Wash there are several cabins in which travelers may stay. All cabins in the area are always kept open. There is the Newman cabin, which is the first cabin to be encountered upon coming up the wash. There is something called the Lotus Mine, which is owned by Warner Brothers, of all people, on which there are two houses and a mine shaft perched up on the mountainside.

After about five miles, the road forked at Sourdough Springs. The left fork proceeds up north over Mengel Pass in the direction of Death Valley. And the fork straight ahead leads directly first to the Barker and then the Myers Ranches. The Barker Ranch consists of two small cabins and a third larger main ranch building. The Barker mine itself exists further down Goler Wash high up on a precipice which is reached only by risky footpath. Scrap iron junkies have long since hauled away the cable and metal for the hopper and the mine car which lowered the ore down to the wash.

Proceeding further east on Goler Wash they encountered the Myers Ranch, which is a well-kept series of buildings, including the ranch house, a trailer and several outbuildings. The watered ground grows all kinds of wild fruits, grapes and wild vegetables. The plants are watered by a spring shafted into the hillside. They stayed for a couple of days at the Myers Ranch but were unable to secure permission from Myers' grandmother to remain so the family established headquarters at the dilapidated Barker Ranch just a quarter mile west of the Myers Ranch down Goler Wash.

A gentleman named Ballarat Bob, a local miner, had been prospecting out of the Barker Ranch for about three and a half years and was more or less in charge of the upkeep of the place. Ballarat Bob trained several wild burros for use in his prospecting expeditions. Shortly after the family arrived at the Barker Ranch, around Halloween 1968, Ballarat Bob showed up with a friend and found nude hippies ensconced in his pad. But there was nothing much he could do about it because this remote area was never patrolled by the police.

The Barker Ranch is encircled by a fence. Inside the fence is deposited forty or fifty years of desert detritus. There were several old collapsed trucks, a chicken coop, plus, upon the hill in back, an old pear-shaped concrete swimming pool.

There was part of an old mining-ball grinder on the property, the body of an old World War II plane, wing tanks and bits of ejected cockpits. There was a huge tire which Ballarat Bob used to drag the wash with in order to make it a more serviceable entrance road. Constant use of Goler Wash, especially by dune buggies, sometimes made it impossible to negotiate the wash even with four-wheel drive because the spinning tires would throw all the gravel out, exposing the boulders.

The main Barker ranch house is an L-shaped building with a kitchen equipped with stove and refrigerator. The electricity was not working at the time. A generator was necessary to supply electricity because the remote ranch is fifty miles from the nearest power lines. There was a concrete bathtub and shower and a small medicine cabinet over the lavatory. Beneath was the twenty-two-inch cabinet in which Manson would be found hiding a year later. There was Ballarat Bob's bedroom in the main ranch house and a haven of mattresses to accommodate the family.

The only transportation they had was Juanita's Dodge camper and a jeep belonging to Gregg Jakobson that Dennis Wilson had given them.

It was a paradise for Manson. He could do anything in this wilderness where park rangers so seldom patrolled. It was as remote as Xtul, Mexico.

Manson became friendly with the gold prospectors who continually comb the Death Valley highlands looking for the Mommie Mine. Manson would pick up rocks from various quartz veins and show them to the prospectors. In Death Valley there are a few younger miners, some of whom smoke pot and some have long hair. It is strange on a summer night in a prospector's camp to hear conversation about rock music and gold mining and minerals and the Grateful Dead. Some of the older miners also knew Manson and they asked him the locations of the various places where Manson had found promising rocks. Manson has said that he showed some miners the sites of possible mining claims and that they had offered him percentages of any gold profits therefrom.

In Hopi Indian legend there was a myth called the Emergence from the Third World wherein there was a reference to a large underground world from which the Hopi nation emerged to dwell on Earth's surface. Manson believed that there was some geological possibility for the existence of The Hole.

Sometime in the fall of 1968, Manson grew zealous about The Hole. He thought The Hole was a large underground city where he could live with his family and escape from the profligacies of the mother culture. "I found a hole in the desert that goes down into a river that runs north underground, and I call it a bottomless pit because where could a river be going north underground? You could even put a boat on it. So I covered it up and I hid it. I called it . . . The Devil's Hole."

It is not known who or what inspired him to believe that a subterranean paradise was waiting for him and his followers. Perhaps it was a vision on an acid trip. Who knows? There evidently have been claims made in the past that there is a huge city-sized cave under Death Valley fed by the underground Amargosa River.

Death Valley, the claim goes, is a geological "graben" developed along formations that could conceivably house a large open underground area. But not certainly a place with chocolate fountains and food-trees and a race of people already living there, as they came to believe.

The family claimed even into 1970 that there are places on the edge of Death Valley where there are openings to the Amargosa River. The family would go out on Hole patrol to try to find hidden openings to The Hole because they felt there was some sort of occult conspiracy to keep secret the entrance to their paradise. Manson seems to have claimed that he had personal access to The Hole and was able to go down there, or so he got his followers to believe.

One such entrance to The Hole was thought to be the so-called Devil's Hole in the northwest triangular corner of the Death Valley National Monument where the monument extends briefly into Nevada. Devil's Hole, fenced off from potential visitors, is a baleful pit full of water, and inhabited by blind fish according to the family. A couple of skin divers had drowned several years previous trying to touch bottom.

For anyone interested, to get to Devil's Hole you proceed to Death Valley on Route 127. Then drive north to a town called Death Valley Junction. Hang a right there and proceed to Ash Meadows Rancho. Then grab a northish county road across the California-Nevada line to The Hole. Manson considered that this Devil's Hole was the key to *The* Hole.

For three days, abject and humble, at the edge of The Hole, Manson meditated and contemplated the meaning of this bottomless well-pit. Then it dawned on him that the water in Devil's Hole must be the door or the blocking mechanism preventing entrance to the Underworld, so that, were the water sucked out, the Golden Hole of chocolate fountains would be revealed.

He consulted a pumping company to see about pumping The Hole dry and supposedly received a bid for the job of $33,000.

Manson received, on the metaphysical plane, further guarantees of the existence of such a hole in key passages of Revelation. Wasn't the world hip to references to locusts proceeding from the bottomless pit—the *puteum abyssi*—as foretold in Chapter 9 of the Book of Revelation?

There was a new persona developing for Charlie: The Devil from the bottomless pit beneath Death Valley. Oo-ee-oo.

Sometime in the desert that fall Manson undertook a prolonged nude meditation period in the high desert chill, discovering death. Indeed it was a legend among Manson's followers that he experienced his "final death" when he picked up a live rattlesnake in Death Valley National Monument. Paul Watkins tells how he and Charlie encountered a rattler one day and Charlie persuaded Watkins to sit right down in front of him, beam it out with a snake.

In his wilderness revelation, Manson seems to have suffered a typical experience that thousands have encountered, say, on psilocybin: that of the experience of submission to Death.

Charlie always talked about a final flash he received while meditating in the desert:

"Once I was walking in the desert and I had a revelation. I'd walked about forty-five miles and that is a lot of miles to walk in the desert. The sun was beating down on me and I was afraid because I wasn't willing to accept death. My tongue swoll up and I could hardly breathe. I collapsed in the sand.

"I looked at the ground and I saw this rock out of the corner of my eye. And I remember thinking in this insane way as I looked at it, 'Well, this is as good a place as any to die.' "

Then he started to laugh. "I began laughing like an insane man. I was so happy." Then he got up "with ease" and walked ten miles forthwith and reached safety.

Manson developed in Death Valley a great fondness for the coyote, the predator's predator. Nothing is more vicious and overbearing in the pursuit of varieties of food than the coyote.

He began to applaud a state of mind called here coyotenoia. Here is the basic Manson quote on coyotenoia: "Christ on the cross, the coyote in the desert—it's the same thing, man. The coyote is beautiful. He moves through the desert delicately, aware of everything, looking around. He hears every sound, smells every smell, sees everything that moves. He's always in a state of total paranoia and total paranoia is total awareness. You can learn from the coyote just like you learn from a child. A baby is born into the world in a state of fear. Total paranoia and awareness. . . ."

Gregg Jakobson wanted back his jeep that Wilson had given to Manson. So on November 24, 1968, Jakobson and Dennis Wilson drove to Death Valley to retrieve the jeep. Jakobson's jeep was broken down somewhere in the vastness of Goler Wash so they towed it out to Trona to be fixed, taking Manson with them. While driving in Goler Wash, Jakobson ran over a spider, which made Manson angry. Better a human, he contended, than a spider.

Jakobson and Wilson took Manson with them out of Death Valley to L.A. perhaps to celebrate the impending release of the song written by Manson.

Two weeks later Jakobson returned to Goler Wash in a motorcycle to visit and broke his bike on the treacherous terrain. So he went back to Trona, picked up his jeep which had just been repaired and threw his motorcycle in the back and went back to Los Angeles.

On December 8, 1968, Capitol Records released the Beach Boys' single, "Bluebirds over the Mountain" B-sided with "Never Learn Not to Love (Cease to Exist)." Charlie Manson was on the charts for the one and only time, although his name wasn't listed on publishing credits, and the single only soared to sixty-one.

A more important event occurred, however, on December 7, 1968. Capitol Records released the white-jacketed Beatles double album containing among the thirty songs such gems of snuff as "Sexy Sadie," "Rocky Raccoon," "Blackbird," "Revolution 9" and "Helter Skelter"—all found by Manson to foretell his conquest of the World.

Manson felt able to twist and interpret the lyrics and production of these Beatles' songs as if they were holy writ. After Wilson and Jakobson took Manson out of Death Valley in late November 1968, Manson seems to have stayed on Topanga Lane at the mouth of Topanga Canyon by the ruins of The Spiral Staircase.

The Spiral Staircase house where Manson and crew had stayed a year previous had subsequently been demolished. Manson was living in a blue bus parked by the ruins.

Manson was seen at a Thanksgiving dinner at Layne Wooten's house in Topanga Canyon on November 28, 1968.

In early December 1968, Manson sent ace-acidassin Bruce Davis on a trip to England where he spent around five months.

Little Paul described it as being a go-to-Rio-and-get-me-a-coconut scene where Manson told Davis to take a trip around the world and report back. Whatever the case, Bruce Davis, with two traveling companions, journeyed to England by way of North Africa.

There is also a story flitting about that Davis took a collection of 500 silver dollars over to England to sell.

People that have intimate knowledge of the Tate-LaBianca case will see an interesting possibility if, in fact, Davis did transport the silver to Great Britain.

In London, Davis approached the Church of Scientology to pursue courses of study. He was employed by the Church of Scientology for a short time, working in their mail room. The Church of Scientology fired Davis after a couple of weeks when he wouldn't stop using drugs, they say.

Davis stayed on in London for a few months where, according to a prominent Los Angeles homicide officer, he became familiar with a very vehement wing of the Fraternity of Lucifer—as the parent world wide satanic organization is sometimes known. Members of this church of satanists in London had been in San Francisco and Los Angeles while Manson himself had been forming his own Final Church.

This occult group's leaders had scoured the world for years looking for groups already set up with which to make liaisons. In Toronto, for instance, they would make contact and live with a cult that was involved in beating a young girl to death in 1967 during a demon-exorcism ceremony.

Manson and crew fell prey to this satan hustle because they, and Manson in particular, had no humanistic values to fall back upon. His mother was sent to jail when he was very young for armed robbery. His father drifted off into the void. Later his mother reclaimed him, but turned him over to juvenile authorities even before he was a teenager. He had nothing. He grew up into a life of crime much as if he had been born in the nineteenth century in India into a Thuggee family and had been destined from the start to become initiated into the grim murderous life of the Thugs.

And the curse moved onward, for Manson's son, Mark, as he was known in his hometown in eastern Ohio, was himself killed by a shotgun blast during a knife fight that occurred just before Manson himself was sent to Death Row for the Tate-LaBianca murders.

Groups with nefarious purposes but with desire to recruit new fodder have to use a front that does not give away their real purposes and scare away new troops. A secret devil society might set up a dummy group—say with a name like "The Human Institute for Occult Touch-Dupe"—then they might run advertisements in the over- and underground press, announcing esoteric classes in psychological therapy. Then line up the marks. Manson's rock group, the Milky Way, seems to have performed at such a front organization's headquarters in Los Angeles.

God knows he used encounter group techniques—only flipping those good intentions around toward the promotion of Christ-Devil schizophrenia. A devious promoter of devil-worship can show strong upward mobility among the mentally sick. What a group of leeches. These leech-class satanists are very hesitant to let the truth out about their proclivities but in remote canyons by eery night, with sentries and attack dogs patrolling, the rot-minded users of losers can commit their crimes in safety.

And there is terrific fear among various so-called white magic outfits in California regarding the blood-letting satanists. There was one group of satanoids whose "membership" pin was found near the gravesite of a decapitated goat in Topanga Canyon—said goat's head having been used in a ceremony. The mere sight of this satanic pin, a small gold-based depiction of the goat of satan, was enough to cause visible alarm and warnings of possible doom from several members of less ferocious religious societies that were interviewed in the course of researching this book.

The devil society that Manson joined considered the whole of creation and the working of the human mind as the Devil. "Thought is the invention of the devil," as he later told a famed singer. It was a racist outfit that hated blacks. It adored Hitler, and especially the swastika. Manson is very fond of the swastika, adorning letters with it and sometimes drawing it on the forehead and heart area of pictures of the devil.

The human from the devil cult who was caught and charged with murder after a heart meal has a swastika tattooed on one hand, and various tattoos of occult significance, the meaning of which he will not reveal. This person's girl friend possessed a tattoo of a swastika on her chest. He claimed to be fond of carving swastikas on the chests of his victims.

This head devil uses his young adepts as henchmen and revels vicariously when they roam out to do their work. One follower was evidently visited in jail (after he was charged with murder) by the Grand Chingon of Santa Cruz and congratulated on the wonderful job he had done is dispatching a victim. He claimed to have been ordered: "I was told I had to take war pills, reds, and she must be sacrificed."

In the outdoor sacrificial rituals, he claimed that this group set up a wooden altar with a "thousand dragons" on it—evidently meaning a carved shrine with beast motifs. The group also had a portable "wooden morgue table with a trough" upon which evidently the human was placed or tied.

The instrument of execution was a set of six knives welded into a football-shaped holder. The welded knives were of varying lengths so when the death-ball was lowered upon the altar, the longer knives at one end of the instrument entered the stomach first and subsequently the two shorter knives at the other end entered the heart last, and thus the Evil-worshipers did their evil. The heart was eaten by the ritualists.

He further claimed that the society possessed a portable crematorium with which they burned their captured prey, evidently for purposes of disposal.

The witness spoke of attending sacrifices where two types of people attended, one a group of younger people about forty in number; the other group being older and about fifteen in number.

Strangely enough at least one sacrifice conducted by the head Devil or Chingon in the Santa Cruz mountains was alleged to have been willing—a young woman done in by the group near Boulder Creek, south of the city, around the first week of November, 1968.

The witness stated that the activities of the cult were later held around the O'Neil park area in the Santa Ana Mountains. One person, in a ritual there, put up a terrific struggle before being dispatched by the head Devil.

Also involved in the Grand Chingon cult, was the ritual dispatching of canines, an activity also practiced, according to Susan Atkins, by the program-people of that other Chingon, C. Manson. Beginning in June 1968, officials in the San Jose—Santa Cruz—Los Gatos, California areas began to find bodies of exsanguinated dogs, many of which had their skins removed when found. The director of the Santa Cruz Animal Shelter said, "whoever is doing this is a real expert with a knife. The skin is cut away without even marking the flesh. The really strange thing is that these dogs have been drained of blood."

Later when L.A. sheriff's officers were digging for the body of Spahn Ranch stunt man, Shorty Shea, at a remote campsite used by the family on the Spahn Ranch property, they found a mass cache of animal bones—many of them chicken—a rather weird discovery for a vegetarian organization like the family.

Another person belonging to one of these satanic organizations was captured by the police near Big Sur. Caught, he uttered a classic sentence to his arresting officer: "I have a problem—I am a cannibal." This person was recruited by the cult near a campus in Wyoming, where he participated in blood-drinking ceremonies, and was indoctrinated and brought into activities of the home punks in California.

When captured, he turned over a human finger-bone from his leather pouch and told the officer where to find the body, heart removed and devoured, of his latest victim killed only three days previous.

One day shortly after a hideous multiple beach murder in California, where a witness reported seeing a caped, hooded procession of humans chanting as they advanced down a beach hill toward the victims, one of the Manson family was overheard talking excitedly about it during the luncheon recess at the Tate-LaBianca trial. She said it was the work of "Maxwell's Silver Hammer." Ugh.

Why is this happening and where are the arrests? Police departments, bound by jurisdictional hassles and stringent rules of procedure, have had difficulty collecting precise intelligence regarding cultic snuffers. A good satanist, wily, intelligent and without moral or ethical restraints is hard to catch.

In the nineteenth century, it took Sir William Sleeman, the head of the investigation into the activities of the bands of Kali-worshiping Thugs in India, many years to break up the organization. There was great public apathy at the time. The Thugs, with their oaths of secrecy, their secret robbery-murders, their religious ceremonies to the bloodthirsty deity known as Kali—it was too much to accept.

The people, bent down with disasters, profit and loss, simply did not want to believe that a group of individuals, bound by weird rituals, would kill and rob and torture people as part of a religious order, in this case for the goddess Kali.

7

From Death Valley to Canoga Park

Wojtek Frykowski and Roman Polanski met while Roman was attending the film school in Lodz. Frykowski had a degree in chemistry. He served as an assistant on several of Polanski's productions, and had helped finance Polanski's short, *Mammals*.

He had married twice, once to the well-known writer Angeski Osiecka. He had a son, Bartyk Frykowski, who was around thirteen at his father's death. Frykowski was an educated, intelligent man who formed part of an energetic circle of artists and intellectuals, some of whom defected to the West.

Sometime in the latter half of 1967 Mr. Frykowski split from Poland and moved to Paris, where Roman Polanski encountered him and gave him some financial help and encouragement.

Polish writers and intellectuals who have fled the confining atmosphere of the homeland help each other considerably. They keep in touch, aid one another's careers and even celebrate Polish holidays together.

In early 1968 it was arranged that Wojtek Frykowski come to the United States to live. He was diligent in his study of the American language and kept daily notebooks learning the nuances of American-speak. He was interested in poetry and evidently was writing verse during his stay in America. He was viewed by his writer friends such as novelist Jerzy Kosinski as a perceptive critic of their work.

Sometime in January of 1968 Mr. Frykowski met Abigail Folger at a party in New York City. Miss Folger was born in 1943 and was raised in the closed tradition of San Francisco society. A talented pianist, she was also interested in art and painting. She was educated at the Catalina School for Girls in Carmel, California and at Radcliffe College. After graduation from Radcliffe, she did graduate work at Harvard.

Her father was the chairman of the board of the Folger Coffee Company, now a subsidiary of Procter and Gamble. Miss Folger's private fortune was extensive. A close friend estimates that her personal income after taxes was around $130,000 per year.

In 1967 she was employed by the University of California Art Museum in Berkeley. In the fall of 1967, Miss Folger came to live in New York City. After working for a magazine she worked for one of the best avant-garde bookstores in the world, the Gotham Book Mart on Forty-seventh Street.

Miss Folger met Jerzy Kosinski at a party when she was working at the Gotham Book Mart. Subsequently, Mr. Kosinski introduced her to Wojtek Frykowski. They were both fluent in French and he was eager to learn the American language.

In the fall of 1968 Abigail Folger and Wojtek Frykowski drove a Drive-a-Car across the United States to the West Coast. They moved into a house at 2447 Woodstock in Los Angeles, a residence located off Mulholland in the Hollywood Hills. Across the street on Mulholland lived Cass Elliott, of the Mamas and Papas.

Miss Folger was involved in the struggle for racial equality. She worked as a volunteer social worker for the Los Angeles County Welfare Department from sometime in fall 1968 till March 31, 1969. Her place of employment was south central Los Angeles, where evidently she aided black ghetto children.

In Los Angeles, Miss Folger and Wojtek Frykowski stepped into the world of movie actors and actresses, friends of Sharon and Roman. They also acquired friends of their own, including friends of Charles Manson and the family.

Miss Folger's money attracted people. More than one aspiring film producer approached her to contribute money to film projects. She met hair tycoon Jay Sebring and he persuaded her to invest in his empire of barber shops and hair-care products. Through Mr. Sebring, they met others in the interlocking circles of film-fame.

In late December 1968, Miss Folger made arrangements to purchase around $3500 worth of stock in Sebring International.

In December of 1968 Charlie and three girls drove in an old Studebaker to an exclusive dude ranch near Reno, Nevada where they spent two weeks as guests of Charlene Cafritz, whom Manson had met the previous summer at Dennis Wilson's beach home. Mrs. Cafritz was in Reno logging enough time to get a divorce.

Manson seems to have had a great effect on the young lady in terms of material detachment. As a result of her divorce settlement, the lady was left with a fortune in excess of two million dollars. This sum she spent in something like ten months, aided in early phases of her spend-frenzy by guess who.

Sometime toward the end of December, a friend named Warnick drove the young divorcée back to Los Angeles from Reno. In January '69 Mrs. Cafritz visited New York, where she spent $92,000 during that month.

At one point, Manson told the young lady that he wanted a blue Fleetwood Cadillac. The young lady erred and purchased instead a fire-engine-red Cadillac and he told her to take it back. She also evidently purchased a number of thoroughbred horses which Charlie gave away for her.

She bought him a number of items, including a chain saw which he gave to some people who were cutting wood for a livelihood and even a quantity of fly spray to help snuff the huge horde of Spahn Ranch horse flies.

Mrs. Cafritz took numerous motion pictures of Manson and the family in Reno which no one seems to want to discuss. Mrs. Cafriz was a friend of Sharon Tate and Terry Melcher and a number of others associated with the oncoming tragedy.

There is great confusion about where certain family members were living in the late '68 and early '69. They seem to have been scattered here and there, some in Death Valley, some in Topanga Canyon, one or more with the Process in England, and some in Laurel Canyon in the Hollywood Hills.

One former Manson family associate claims that a group of four to six family members lived on Laurel Canyon Boulevard in the log cabin house once owned by cowboy-actor Tom Mix. They lived there for a few weeks, in late 1968, in a cave-like hollow in back of the residence.

At the end of the year there was a savage, hideous murder in the Hollywood Hills of a young girl who may have been associated with the family.

Marina Elizabeth Habe, seventeen years old, was home for a vacation from the University of Hawaii, where she was a student. On Sunday, December 29, she had a date with John Hornburg, age twenty-two and an old family friend. Later that night Eloise Hart, her mother, at 3:30 A.M. heard noises in the driveway of their home. She looked through the window and saw a man standing beside Marina's red sports car. A black sedan was in the driveway, Mrs. Hart remembered.

The man said "go"; he got into the sedan and drove quickly away. There seemed to be two people in the car. John Hornburg told the police this: "That among other things they visited a club on the Sunset Strip; that after their evening Miss Habe returned with him to his parents' home, changed from evening dress into capri pants, a white turtleneck sweater, brown coat and drove home in her car."

She was found on New Year's Day in thick underbrush off Mulholland Drive, 100 feet west of Bowmont Drive. Only maniacs could have wreaked such hatred upon a human. Contusions in eyes, slashes in throat and heart, burns inflicted, raped, nude, except for a shoe. According to one former family associate, Marina Habe was known by members of the family.

Manson seems to have attended a New Year's Eve party thrown for the cast of *Hair* by John and Michelle Phillips at their home in Bel Air.

Manson returned to Death Valley in January 1969. Early in January 1969 Little Paul Watkins led a deputation into Las Vegas, Nevada from the Barker Ranch in order to trade Juanita's red Dodge van, which was unsuited for traversing the wilderness terrain, for a 1953 four-wheel drive International Scout jeep.

While Watkins and Juanita were in Los Angeles Charlie was having the green and white bus towed out of the mouth of Goler Wash by a local fireman to have a brake shoe fixed. They had learned of a long, looping route of a couple of hundred miles which would lead them into the Barker Ranch from the north. So Charlie drove the bus full of nascent creepy crawlers north through Emigrant Pass and around Stovepipe Wells, up around the Tucky Mountain area and down the middle of Death Valley where they stopped off at the small town of Shoshone. The townspeople remembered them with some amazement at the thought that anyone could drive a school bus into the wilderness.

Out of Shoshone the bus drove west past vast pile-hills that looked like giant oblong loaves of millions of huge burnt match heads. They drove past Salisbury Pass, Jubilee Pass to the dry Armagosa River. They drove past Ashford Mills and turned left going northwest on the first gravel road passing a sign "Warning: Road Not Patrolled Daily." (Gurdjíeff said not to trust maps of wilderness roads.) One's map of Inyo County indicates that the turn-off is east of Ashford Mills whereas in reality the turnoff is west of the Mills. Although by now the road may have been changed, for a road in those voidal stands is whatever the county road grader creates in his quarterly scraping of the roads.

From the Death Valley floor, the bus climbed up a long ribbon leading up the east side of the Panamint Mountains.

The bus made another left at the Wingate Jeep Trail past a sign "Warm Springs, 4 miles, Anvil Springs, 18 miles."

The bus was, from that point on, as it oozed into the

mountains, inside the Death Valley National Monument, passing a sign with white letters on a black background: "Firearms prohibited."

"Charlie could drive like a mother fucker," Clem commented when he was crossing the same road a year and a half later. It was on this trek over the wilderness down to the Barker Ranch that several miracles were alleged to have been performed by Charles Manson.

The green and white bus had to go over unbelievably bumpy and twisting creek-bed roads. At one point they broke a wheel. They ripped the bottom of the bus. Clem claimed that Charlie levitated the bus over a creek crag. And the girls, naturally, often had to bridge road pits with rocks and planks.

Gradually, as the road headed up into Warm Springs Valley, it began to coincide with the creek bed. Four miles in lay a cluster of talc mines, huge mounds of baby powder on the hillside. At the warm water springs, the bus passed a cluster of trees, gasoline pump and trailers for the miners.

The road got worse immediately as the bus passed the talc mines, evidently because the trucks hauling the talc to market used the road out rather than the road in toward Mengel Pass, so only prospectors and campers used the road which passed the black and white Striped Butte.

Bounce bounce was the experience for the family as it entered the strewn chaos. The road forked and the sign, "Jeep Road—Butte Valley" pointed to the left. To the right the road curved around to more talc mines. Packs of wild burros roamed the Striped Butte Valley and coyotes prowled openly, their thin noses rising above the greasewood bushes.

The bus rose from the high valley floor over Mengel Pass somehow, and then bumped another five miles or so down sacred Goler Wash to the Barker Ranch. There they dwelled.

Somehow, as of a miracle, the bus arrived at the Barker Ranch where to this day, its engine removed, it reposes at an angle facing Ballarat Bob's chicken coop. Upon its back fender some sardonic individual had placed a red and white sticker saying, "America. Love it or leave it."

Meanwhile, in sacred Goler Wash, things started getting brrr in the high desert. A chill swept upon nudism. Winter was creeping in.

Manson left to find more suitable habitats, taking "quite a few people with him"—as Brooks Posten recounted it.

Apparently there was a housing problem in early 1969. Something was preventing their return to the Spahn Ranch.

Susan Atkins spent some time living at a house on the Buchanan Ranch in Topanga Canyon. She lived with a man named Rory. This may have been the time when Manson threw Sadie-Susan out of the family and took baby Zezo Ze-ce Zadfrak away from her.

Friends of Sadie at the Buchanan Ranch were scheming how she might reacquire Zezo. It was interesting that, according to observers, Sadie was actively putting Manson down and asserting her independence. Until one day Manson appeared at the top of a ridge above Sadie and yelled "Sadie!" motioning her to come, whereupon Sadie Glutz immediately returned to the family.

Manson rented a house and small guest house at 21019 Gresham in Canoga Park, California, in the San Fernando Valley, not too far from the Spahn Ranch. This house was dubbed the Yellow Submarine because of its color. It was there that Manson lunged toward his bifurcated goals—becoming a star and putting together the proper equipment so that he could return with his followers to the desert. For this he needed things like electric generators, oodles of dune buggies, and money.

Money he decided to acquire through drugs, theft and mooching. "Within three or four weeks of moving into the Yellow Submarine," he writes in his autobiography, "it had become a concert hall for musicians, a porno studio for kinky producers, a dope pad, a thieves lair, a place to dismantle stolen cars and just about everything but a whorehouse."

The thieves lair-stolen dune buggy aspect of it he tried to keep from Terry Melcher and Dennis Wilson, from either or both of whom he was expecting a record deal.

21019 Gresham is a red-roofed house with columned porch and a small little green "guest house" behind it. To the left are some horse stalls or stables behind a double garage.

Down the dirt road toward Devonshire Street are the

Island Village apartments where various associates of Manson lived.

Cutting down San Fernando Valley from the hills to the north is Brown Canyon wash, more like a huge paved storm sewer. This wash ran just to the west of the house on Gresham, and Manson used to drive his dune buggy down the wash to the Gresham house from the Devil Canyon area, the home of Helter Skelter.

Because Manson allegedly was living in the Death Valley Hills, his federal parole supervision was shifted from Los Angeles to San Bernardino. On January 17, 1969, Manson's new federal parole officer attempted to pay him a visit in Death Valley. He got as far as the Ballarat General Store and there he learned from an old miner that he would have to walk seven miles up the waterfalls if he wanted to visit the family camp. No thanks.

After a week or so at the Canoga Park house on Gresham Street, Manson sent a squad up to the Barker Ranch to remove the rest of the family. These people were left behind at the Barker Ranch to take care of things: Brooks, Juanita and Gypsy the violinist.

A week later, the International Scout jeep, for which Juanita and Watkins had traded her Dodge camper in Las Vegas, arrived in Goler Wash to pick up the remaining three and took them to the house on Gresham Street in Canoga Park.

From around February 1 to 20, 1969, they all stayed at the sleazo cottage on Gresham.

Specific inputs to specific activities of the group at this time are scant but there are ample depositions concerning the famous "Death Mockup Party" that occurred at the house on Gresham Street on the day that Brooks, T.J., Juanita and others returned from the desert in the new jeep.

That was the time that the people arrived from the desert, attired in leather, tanned and trim of form. And they were all sitting around "mocking up stuff," postulating the event of their own death so as to experience it mentally. Sound like fun?

A part of the group was stoned and was sitting in the middle of the room. They had begun to write a song and had left off the project. Charlie was sitting in the midst of the gathering and the topic was the ever-present subject of snuff. Charlie said, "Die," so all lay down and pretended they were dead. Bo started screaming "Charlie" —and then "O-h-h-h-h-h!" Paul Watkins testified to the following concerning this famous party: "I was listening to Charlie say die." Watkins testified that he tried to think of a way to die but he couldn't so when Charlie said, "Die," Watkins lay down and "acted like I was dead." Everybody else did and Bo was screaming and Charlie was sitting in the middle of the room moving his fingers, talking about the confusion in the air, how fine it was.

Evidently Brooks Posten was able to go into a trance on command and Charlie commanded him to die. So he died. He went into a trance that lasted three or by some accounts five days. As he lay wasting on a couch in the living room the girls would clean up after his natural functions and even Charlie would try to pull him out of it but he couldn't. So on the fifth day, lo! Charlie commanded that his very own sacred embroidered gray corduroy vest be placed beneath Brooks as a symbolic diaper. Horrified with the prospect of Jesus' very own vest being used as a diaper, Brooks revivified himself from his trance. Or so it is told.

During this three-week stay at the house on Gresham occurred the famous Manson gobble-miracle. Zonked on lysergic acid, Manson was being blown by a hysteria-prone young adept named Bo. Bo was a small masochistic girl with thyroid eyes and long black hair, one of Charlie's favorite pain-targets.

The legend continues that during the gobble the girl went nuts and, all in one incision, bit in twain Manson's virility. Then, through the miracle of magic, Manson, they claim, at once healed his tragic amputation and continued onward.

Meanwhile back in the Hollywood of reflections, on February 18, 1969, Charles Manson checked in with his parole officer and announced that he was living in Los Angeles. His parole supervision then was changed back from the San Bernardino office to Los Angeles. He told his parole officer that when the snow melted in the high mountains, he would be returning to the wilderness.

Also, on February 18, 1969, a DC-3 "Gamblers' Special" loaded up with a drunk pilot and thirty-five gamblers crashed into the snows of Mt. Whitney near Bishop, California. According to the tale, the plane remained buried in deep snow until summer when the snow melted. The plane and dead occupants were located but supposedly all valuables and cash had been stripped from the gamblers, booty valued at a quarter of a million dollars or so.

The finger of blame has pointed naturally at Manson and his dune buggy battalion. One defected family member says, though it is hard to believe, that pieces of the crashed airplane were used by the family to adorn their dune buggies.

Around February 20, 1969, Charlie sent a force back to Death Valley consisting of Brooks, Juanita, T.J., Bo, Mary Brunner and a female Caucasian named Sherri, probably Simi Valley Sherri.

There were heavy rains in Goler Wash during these days, causing a flash flood, and the water rose up to the ranch buildings. Shortly after the floods, Sherri and Juanita and others went into Shoshone, California and perhaps to Las Vegas to get supplies. On the way back they stopped in Shoshone, where occurred the notorious dope-smoke involving the local deputy sheriff's daughter.

The Inyo County sheriff's deputy stationed in Shoshone, California lived in a trailer camp near the town. The deputy had a teenage stepdaughter. She seems to have become friendly with members of the family. When Sherri and the others came through the town, they stopped at the trailer and were entertaining themselves visiting the deputy sheriff's young daughter. Little Paul remembers the event like this: "She was up there in the bushes with the family, smoking a joint and the sheriff comes up and asked, 'What are you doing?' His stepdaughter replied, 'Oh, smoking a joint, Daddy.' " Waxing furious, the deputy went into action. He sent his stepdaughter away forthwith to live with relatives and then mounted a raid against the Barker Ranch, the alleged dope source.

Somebody called Charlie down in Los Angeles and he immediately sent a big van up to the Barker Ranch and took everybody out except Juanita and Brooks, who were ordered to pretend to be married. Evidently the thinking was that appearing as a married couple would ward off any form of arrest.

Sure enough, the deputy and another deputy and some

Death Valley National Park Rangers came to the Barker Ranch asking about marijuana. No, no, they didn't know anything about marijuana. So they beat the bust.

Juanita and Brooks had enough food for a one-meal-a-day scene for two weeks. When the rest of the family left they told Juanita and Brooks that they would send for them shortly. Manson et al. were not to return to Death Valley for six months, until after the murders.

8

Helter Skelter

Around the first of March 1969, two miners named Paul Crockett and Bob Berry arrived at the Barker Ranch to find Brooks Posten and Juanita living there, following the marijuana raid. Bob Berry had visited the Barker Ranch area the preceding autumn and evidently had enjoyed himself. Crockett, an articulate gentleman in his fifties filled with the lore of scientology, left his home in Carlsbad, New Mexico to come to Goler Wash for the purpose of discovering gold.

In the ensuing weeks, Bob Berry and Juanita began to have an affair, culminating in their marriage and her leaving the clutches of Manson.

Bob Berry and Paul Crockett began to stay in the small tar-roofed cabin to the left of the main Barker Ranch house. The two began to scour old mining sites in the Panamint Mountains, Wingate Wash and south into Dora Canyon, in order to hook into the mother lode. By night Berry and Crockett would sit and chat with Brooks and Juanita, and later Paul Watkins when he returned from Los Angeles. One thing that struck the miner/metaphysician, Paul Crockett, was the enormous fear that Paul Watkins and Juanita and Brooks had for this mysterious Charlie.

It came to pass that Paul Crockett hired, for board, Brooks Posten to help haul ore down from the hillsides.

It is common for miners to engage someone to bring weekly shipments of supplies via jeep to their claims or their camps from supply depots such as the Ballarat General Store. Crockett upped his food order to accommodate the thin young trance-prone Texan Posten.

They would go out by day to inspect old mine sites, old diggings and outcroppings, hauling ore samples back down to the ranch when they returned at dusk. They would crunch up the samples in a rock-breaking machine that could chew the mineral into forty pieces per cubic inch. Then they would pan the gold out to see how much was in the samples.

Sometime in the spring Little Paul Watkins traveled to Death Valley where he visited Juanita and Brooks and met Crockett. Little Paul returned to the Spahn Ranch to announce the horrible news that "scientologists" had taken over the Barker Ranch—news which triggered off a fearful reaction within the family.

Watkins persuaded Charlie to let him go back up to the Barker Ranch, perhaps to keep an eye on the so-called scientologists, looking for the mother lode. Several times during these spring months of 1969, Manson and the others tried to drive up to the Barker Ranch, but it always seemed that something went wrong. Witch-beams were thwarting them? Or were the so-called scientologists keeping the family away? Paul Crockett certainly didn't do anything to dispel this illusion that he was preventing the family from coming up there by means of his mental powers. In fact, he was promoting the idea that he could establish a magical warp to prevent Manson from returning to harm those remaining in Death Valley. The family seems to have begun to believe that occult beams and powers were attempting to prevent them from returning to holy Devil's Hole. Even Manson, ever a beam-phobe, evidently held some belief in Crockett's power.

Paul Watkins, so he claims, decided at the advent of various murderous schemes to get out of the family. So he placed himself in the tutelage of Paul Crockett: "He [Crockett] knows how Charlie set up his whole thing and I went to Paul, 'Paul, help me out of this!' Blam! Just, like, I was hung right up in it. And using processing, and looking at what is, I was able to be free from it. But old Clem, Sandy, Lynn and Gypsy, there ain't no way they can get free from that. I mean they could snuff Charlie out, and they're still stuck to him."

"Is the power that great that held you there?" he was asked.

"It's by agreement," he replied. "You see I can't do anything to you without your agreement, without your saying it's okay. But to someone who's so asleep, and so unconscious, they'll agree to anything—" Then it's a different story.

"I got unhooked from the family with just a few simple words. I got Charlie to agree to a few things and then just walked right out."

Once that spring Sadie and a member of the Straight Satans motorcycle club tried to go up to the Barker Ranch and met with failure. Another time, Charlie Manson himself, the Devil, loaded up the GMC truck and trailer with two dune buggies, but the truck broke down not far from the Spahn Ranch and the mission was aborted. So the legend grew that this guy Crockett up there was using freak-beams to prevent the family from returning to the Barker Ranch.

By the middle of January 1969, the new Beatles' white double album had already grossed twenty-two million dollars in the United State alone. The white double album was the first cultural instruction from the Beatles since the album *Magical Mystery Tour* a year previous. Even its all white cover was symbolic to the family—all white, dig it?

Something freaked Manson out in early 1961 enough for him to prepare for the end of Western civilization. He had already talked about an impending Armageddon of some sort but he had always preached "submission is a gift, give it to your brother." This is, walk humble beneath the violence.

Along oozed Helter Skelter.

Manson had a hypnotic rap about how the modern blacks were arming themselves, how he, Manson, had talked to blacks in prison and he had learned of heavy arms caches here and there.

He had a way of stirring up paranoia that was legendary. Goose bumps shivered the back of the arms during his whispered superstitious lectures on karma and imminent doom. With language as flawed as a president's announcing an invasion of a South Asian country, he announced that the blacks would rise up, kill a few million whites, take over the reins of government.

Then, the story continues, after forty or fifty years the blacks would turn the government over to Manson when they supposedly found themselves unfit to run the world. Oo-ee-oo.

It was the pig Christian wealthy Americans that were going to get cut. He, Christ, he, Devil, was going to pull off the Second Coming. "Now it's the pigs' turn to go up on the cross," he would say.

On a metaphysical plane, Manson linked the impending Helter Skelter with the concept of The Hole. For inside this mystic Hole in Death Valley, Manson and his family would live and dwell while the blacks and the whites in the cities would fight to a bloody end and then the blacks would take over.

From The City in The Hole, Manson would make forays to sack cities with his hairy locusts of the Abyss. And the blacks, through their "super awareness"—in the words of the family—would know that Charlie was where it was at, and nod him into the power.

On a higher level, if *higher* is any word to be used, Manson taught that the family bringing the seven holes on the seven planes into alignment would be the ones to squirt through to the other side of the universe. And The Hole was to be the magic paradise—magic, because where else can you find subterranean chocolate fountains?

He even over-dubbed a weirdo exegesis atop the chapters and verses of the Book of Revelation, to back up his claims.

The dune buggies were the horses of Helter Skelter with those "breastplates of fire," described in the Book of Revelation of St. John the Divine, Chapter 9. And the Beatles, unknown to them, were the "four angels" who would wreak death upon a third part of mankind. And Manson found a scriptural basis for announcing that the Beatles were destined to have a fifth member or "angel"—the angel of the bottomless pit, otherwise known as guess who.

One of Manson's favorite passages from Revelation 9 was: "Neither repented they of their murders, nor of their sorceries, nor of their fornication, nor of their thefts"—words he would quote over and over again, preparing his worshipers to kill. And did not the family have "hair as the hair of women, and their teeth were as the teeth of lions"?

And was not Manson the king of the pit?

"And they had a king over them, which is the angel of the bottomless pit, whose name in the Hebrew tongue is Abaddon, but in the Greek tongue hath his name Apollyon." When they translated the Bible from Latin to English, the translators left out another name in the text besides Abaddon and Apollyon, for the angel of the bottomless pit. The name in Latin is Exterminans.

Exterminans—what a word to sum up Charles Manson.

The correlations that Manson found between the Book of Revelation and the Beatles and his own crazies could be continued in moonfire profusion but the reader will be spared.

Manson began to listen to the song "Helter Skelter" off the new Beatles' album with earphones and somehow, as of a miracle, he began to hear the Beatles whispering to him urging him to call them in London. It is unfortunate that Manson evidently did not know that a helter skelter is a slide in an English amusement park.

The girls say that at one point Manson placed a long-distance phone call to London to try to talk to the Beatles. There is no doubt that the song "Helter Skelter" on the white Beatles double album is a masterful, insistent, rock and roll number—and it is very weird sounding, especially the long final section which fades out twice at the end, sounding like a universal march of wrecked maniacs.

"Charlie, Charlie, send us a telegram" was what he thought lay beneath the noise plexus of the composition "Revolution 9." It was felt that if one were to listen closely on headphones, one could hear the Beatles softly whispering just that. As it is, so be it.

"Rise! Rise! Rise!" Charlie would scream during the playing of "Revolution 9" (which Manson associated with Revelation, Chapter 9). Later they wrote *Rise* in blood on the LaBiancas' wall.

It is necessary to listen to the Beatles white double album to understand what Manson was hearing and seeking to hear. The album, as a whole, is of confusing quality. It has flashes of the usual Beatle brilliance but it was produced at a time that the Beatles were locked in bitter quarrels and it is reflected in the album.

The album has the song "Piggies," of course, and, more creepily, a song called "Happiness Is a Warm Gun." Other songs like "Blackbird," "Rocky Raccoon," etc., were interpreted strictly as racist doom-songs.

The song "Sexie Sadie" must have sent Susan Atkins aka Sadie Mae Glutz, into spasms of happiness. "Sexy Sadie, you came along to turn everybody on," the song croons, and "Sexy Sadie, you broke the rules, you laid it down for all to see."

While the family was still at the house in Canoga Park, Manson began to encourage members of various motorcycle clubs to hang out with the family. The two gangs closest to the family were motorcycle groups with the initials S.S., the Satan Slaves and the Straight Satans. He wanted the bikers to join in his group to supply a needed military wing.

The family was also associated with the Jokers Out of Hell, a group whose members were into the occult and one of whom had a record store in Santa Monica. According to people interviewed, the Jokers had houses in the San Fernando Valley near family headquarters.

Manson used his girls to entice the motorcycle riders to hang around the family. He would order a girl to strip and suck. Forthwith the zippers zipped and the mini skirt hit the ground. The bikers loved it. Manson also set his followers to work on the bikers in terms of material possessions. They would peel the wristwatches from the biker's arms while one girl would coo in his ear, "You don't need time. What's time?" And sometimes a biker would try to move into the ranch with a wife and the girls would say, "Why do you need an old lady?" and they would deprecate the "old lady's" jealousy.

Manson put on a whole public relations project to attract the bikers. He loaned them money. They were encouraged to fix and park their bikes there, and after the family had reacquired the Spahn Ranch, there were plenty of horses to ride and girl-objects and there was always food. Bands of brigands always have flocked on the edges of desert wilderness. The deserts ringing L.A. carry on this distinction, with rip-offs, clandestine shipments of dope and stolen automotive parts, and weird magic ceremonies abounding.

In many ways the Manson family became like a bike club: the incredible male chauvinism, the outlaw attitude, the "death-trip," the satanism, the rituals. The new girls of the family even wore ownership ankle chains like some bike club mamas.

The bikers are famous for their elaborate funerals with single-file lines of motorcycles forming the funeral procession. The woman's "colors"—her club garb—are often buried with the colors of "her man" in the grave. Sometimes there are mourning periods for the woman, with periodic observances at the graveside such as pouring wine on the ground.

One Straight Satan who lived with the family for a while was a tall handsome man named Joe. Joe came to the family's house on Gresham Street looking for directions to a house he was going to rent. So enticed was he by the family, particularly Sexy Sadie, that he stayed on. He had a girl friend who was hooked on reds at the time.

Joe the Straight Satan fulfilled an important role in the helter-skelter preparations: he was the architect of the secret escape route to Death Valley.

Joe's stay with the family cost him about $2600. He gave up his watch, a revolver, a microbus and even his motorcycle to the common kitty. He lived with the family on Gresham Street for about a month, at the Hollowberry Hill Ranch of Satan for a couple of weeks, and then at the Spahn Ranch till Mother's Day, 1969.

A short, black-haired mustached Straight Satan named Danny De Carlo had the longest and strongest known relationship of any of the bikers with Manson.

In March, Danny De Carlo came around to fix a bike. Charlie invited him to stay, proffering an endless supply of women. De Carlo was soon dubbed, by the girls, Donkey Dick Dan due to abundance in down-scope.

A lot of the Straight Satans spent passing time at the various houses in which the Mansonists lived. The Satans had those colorful aliases like Droopy, Dirty Old Man, 86 George, Stickman, Philadelphia John and others.

De Carlo was born in Canada and had been in the U.S. since the early '50s. He had served in the United States Coast Guard. His father owned a machine shop in

Inglewood. In August of 1965 Danny De Carlo, his brother Laurence and a couple of others were busted for smuggling dope at the Mexican border coming back from Tijuana. He was given a five-year sentence which he was still appealing when he came to live with the family.

De Carlo had a son Dennis, over a year old, the same age as Pooh Bear. Dennis was handed over to be raised at the Spahn Ranch creepy-crawl nursery.

De Carlo was one of the first "gun-freaks" to be associated with Manson. De Carlo worshiped guns. He is an authority on many kinds of rifles and firearms.

After the family had conned themselves back onto the Spahn Movie Ranch, he quickly set up a small munitions factory in the "Undertaker's Parlor" on the Western ranch set. The undertaker's parlor was renamed the gun room. It was from the gun room that they sallied forth to murder.

The gun room had equipment for making four or five different types of bullets. It was a repository for all kinds of knives and bayonets. De Carlo slept there and parked his bike there. Among De Carlo's weapons were a 303 British Enfield, a .22 caliber rifle, a .20 gauge shotgun, a .30 caliber carbine, a .12 gauge riot gun, an M-1 carbine and a submachine gun (a spizer MP 40 SH). De Carlo obtained one machine gun from a gun collector in a Hollywood rock and roll group.

De Carlo and various of the Straight Satans used to visit the house occupied by the rock group. The gun collector in the band was on an LSD Spirit of Nonviolence trip and decided to throw away his machine gun so he gave it to Donkey Dan.

Manson and the family really put down alcohol so there was a conflict with some of the bikers, notorious juicers, especially De Carlo. The girls used to get miffed also at Danny listening to black jazz programs on the radio. They were horrified by the Afrosheen commercials. "They thought we were listening to 105 [on his radio dial], listening to jazz was . . . eh . . . was plastic," he said. It offended their Okie-Aryan racism.

Anxious though Manson was to please the bikers, not all of them passed the race test. For instance, Joe of the Straight Satans once brought a guy to the ranch that was one-half Indian, a guy named Sammy. Charlie would not allow him to make it with the girls. A person named Mark who was only one-quarter Indian was not allowed commerce with the Aryans at the Spahn Ranch.

In conjunction with plans for Helter Skelter, Manson began to work on an escape route to Death Valley. He wanted to forge a secret trail over the Santa Susanna Mountains and over the Mojave Desert so he could travel with his chosen band when the blacks were sacking the L.A. Civic Center, clear to Death Valley without crossing a major highway.

He decided to begin to build a fleet of helter-skelter dune buggies with which to transport the family back and forth from the Spahn Ranch to Death Valley, up into the Santa Susanna Mountains by means of Devil Canyon and across the Mojave Desert.

From his experience in the rough terrain of Death Valley, Manson decided that dune buggies were the vehicles for his mobile snuff squad. They were great for outrunning cops in the abyss. They were light enough so that two or three of the gore groupies could lift them over boulders and precipices. Motorcycles, on the other hand, were scorned as being inadequate in the wilderness.

But dune buggies, ah sacred dune buggies—they were like battleships. He would later outfit dune buggies with huge gas tanks giving them a 1000-mile assault field. They put machine-gun mounts on them and Manson's command dune buggy was fixed so that it could be slept in. There could be food dune buggies, ammunition dune buggies, dope-supply dune buggies, etc.

Manson met a young man whose family owned the Steele Ranch on the other side of Santa Susanna Pass Road from the Spahn Ranch. There was a series of dirt fire roads that connected the Steele Ranch with Devil Canyon. So it came to pass, as it is/so be it, that the Steele Ranch was chosen as the beginning of the Armageddon trail.

Manson kept cutting the locks on the gates and substituting his own so finally the foreman just gave him duplicate keys. There was an old World War II weapons carrier and a water truck at the Steele Ranch that Manson coveted for his helter-skelter hardware. For the first time the family was into gathering possessions.

At first, Manson actually bought units for his flotilla of

dune buggy assault vehicles. Later they would steal Porsches and strip off the bodies to make buggies. On March 6, 1969, Charlie, Bill Vance and Little Patti moved into the Butler Buggy Shop on Topanga Canyon Boulevard near the Spahn Ranch. Charlie had a big thick roll of hundred-dollar bills and purchased two rail-job dune buggies for $1300.

The Butler Buggy Shop was owned by two brothers, one a Los Angeles police officer.

The family subsequently had quite an interesting relationship with the Buggy Shop, as did the Satan Slaves who, according to police reports, claimed that they got free Volkswagen parts from the shop. The L.A. sheriff raided the Spahn Ranch and seized some dune buggies that were purchased with money stolen by Linda Kasabian.

Anyway, to pay for the first two dune buggies, Charlie forged and cashed a $700 check which had come in for Juanita from an insurance company. The other $600 came from some stock that slim blonde Sandy Good sold.

One day late in March, a member of the Satan Slaves named Joey C. arrived at the Gresham Street house looking for a place to live. Manson asked him where he had been living and he replied that he had been staying at a large house out west on Mulholland in the remote Malibu Hills near Agoura. The place had about ten bedrooms and a swimming pool and the owner was evidently away. The house was further noteworthy in that a descendant of the outlaw Jesse James lived next door.

Since the owner was gone—a fact that created possibilities—Manson pulled tent pegs and moved the family to the Malibu mansion, where they overran the place for about two weeks.

It was from the ten-room Malibu house that they plotted a helter-skelter escape route down through the fire roads to the sea.

Joe of the Straight Satans knew the fire roads in the area from serving on the county work gangs when incarcerated. In Los Angeles County there are several work camps where prisoners work on fire roads and fire prevention because of the high incidence of fires in the mountains surrounding the city.

Somehow the family obtained keys or a master key to the fire roads in the area.

While the family was at the Satan Slaves' house in Agoura, Joe charted a helter-skelter freak-road from the house in Agoura down to the sea. All they had to do was clear out about a hundred feet of brush and the road was perfect.

Patricia Krenwinkel purchased a couple of hundred dollars' worth of United States topographical maps of the mountainous area between the Spahn Ranch and Death Valley, in order to plot the master helter-skelter escape course. They plotted supply-cache locations along the way. They laid out all the various topographical maps one day in the driveway and taped them together so that all of southern California from sacred Goler Wash to Malibu Beach was one.

These helter-skelter maps later were found buried in Death Valley.

Most of the plotting was done by map although they did check out some of the trails with the buggies. But, according to the person who plotted the helter-skelter snuff-route, the family never did travel the route all the way to Death Valley.

In all its glory, the helter-skelter escape trail led from Malibu Beach up Castro Fire Trail to the Hollowberry Hill Ranch in Agoura. From Agoura it led by fire road and creek bed to the Steele Ranch, north of the Spahn Ranch. From there it sliced up Devil Canyon and oozed across the Mojave Desert and on to sacred Goler Wash, crossing only two major highways (Highway 99 and the Antelope Freeway) on the way.

There is a rumor that Manson or someone in the family stole a half-track from an auto salvage lot in Chatsworth near the Spahn Ranch which was used, and perhaps burned out, in digging part of the helter-skelter escape road over the Santa Susanna Mountains.

There was one heavy problem facing Helter Skelter. By early 1969, the West Valley Station of the Los Angeles sheriff's department had in use Bell-65 two-man helicopters with powerful searchlights installed that could light up a city block from 1000 feet in the air.

Manson had various plans to deal with these helicopters. One was to attack the helicopter with magic. Another method was to thwart the helicopters at night by taping the headlights of the dune-buggy battalion with black tape, leaving only a small slit in the tape to allow a thin ray of light to escape, hopefully undetectable from the air.

Manson added a murderous ingredient to the concept of Helter Skelter—that is, the possibility of a trigger that would set it off. Manson somehow came to believe that the big race war would begin with blacks murdering some white families in their homes.

"The karma is turning," he said, meaning that "to complete the karma of the world," such a collision was inevitable.

Helter Skelter was a dream project for ambulatory schizophrenics. There was something in it for everybody. Those who had had creepy childhoods looked upon Helter Skelter as a means of "saving the children." Others had a more racist point of view in that Charlie put up a picture of a white elite ultimately ruling over a black population.

People who liked violence looked upon Helter Skelter as a chance to engage in warfare. People into robbery and chase dug it for its plunder and looting. End-of-the-world freaks could really rejoice in Helter Skelter.

It was the Satan Slaves—that secretive aloof motorcycle club with occult proclivities that lived and operated in the Malibu-Topanga Canyon areas—which seemed to have provided another impulse for family violence. The previous year, members of the Satan Slaves club had been seen at a Ku Klux Klan rally in the valley, complaining that black people were scarfing up welfare benefits that belonged to good white folk like the Slaves, according to a reporter who attended the rally.

They hung out sometimes in Hollywood. The Satan Slaves used to come into the Compleat Enchanter, a shop on Los Palmas, to purchase medallions.

Manson got into studying what would cause group freak-outs. Around this time a biker came to the Ranch and showed Charlie a plant called telache, believed to be belladonna. Charlie tried it and was in a coma for three days. They collected leaves and stewed them, placing the coffee colored brew in water jugs. This was to be dropped into water reservoirs. Anybody who was stupid enough to try belladonna in the beatnik belladonna craze of the early 1960's, will understand how grim telache was.

Danny De Carlo remembered it vividly: "It drives you insane where they see little people and goofy things like that and you bang your head against the wall. It drives you mad. They had jugs of this stuff because the girls would take all the leaves and they put them in water and boil them and it comes out a coffee color—brown and really rank tasting stuff."

Manson even planned robbery through the use of telache. The theory was to sneak into a house where a party was going on and put belladonna into the water.

Again, De Carlo: "All their drinks were going to have belladonna in it and right away—going to drive them nuts. While they're in there going through all these contortions and don't know what the hell is happening to them, they [the family] just walk on in and take what they want to take and do anything they want to do and just sneak on out."

Manson used to talk about pouring LSD into the L.A. water supply. They believed mass acid use would cause citywide violence.

Around this time Charlie and the girls made a pornographic movie by the swimming pool at 2600 Nicholas Canyon Road in the hills above Malibu. The owner of the property, Mrs. Gibson, after receiving numerous complaints from her neighbors, inspected her house in the company of her lawyer and found a bloody machete which police say Manson used during the filmmaking to slash somebody's arm.

After a couple of weeks living at that mansion on Mulholland near Kannan, the family talked 82-year-old George Spahn into letting them return to live at the Spahn Movie Ranch.

They stole an intercom from the swank Kannan Ranch house and some other items which they stored in back of the Spahn trash dump, the site of the upcoming dune-buggy assembly line.

9

Donner Pass

While the family was still at the house on Gresham Street in early 1969, an old jail buddy of Manson began to hang around. His name was William Joseph Vansickle aka Bill Vance aka William R. Cole aka David Hamic (a name Vance borrowed from his nephew) aka Duane Schwarm. To the family he was Bill Vance and he became in the family structure sort of a Minister of Rip-off.

According to gossip, Vance was the former light-heavyweight boxing champion at Brushy Mountain Penitentiary. He was thirty-four years old, tall, with a broken nose and several teeth missing.

Vance seems to have taken residence in an apartment building on Gresham Street near the family. As the months passed, Vance came to lead a crack team of forgers and second-story men operating out of the Spahn Ranch.

Here is Paul Watkins of the family giving forth on Vance:

"When I first met Bill Vance, we were living in the Canoga house. We just came from the Barker Ranch for a while because it was getting cold up there in the desert; and Bill was a friend of Charlie.

"Bill started coming around and we turned him onto acid. He had some heavy trips with us. One night we just sat around and started eating. Every hour we'd eat a tab and get a little higher.

"And so Bill started staying around. Except that he had this thing about stealing. He just l-o-v-e-d to steal. Really, he had a demon in him that couldn't do nothin' but rob; even if he had all the things he wanted, he'd still have to go out and rob some."

Paul Watkins said that Bill Vance once owned something called the Topanga Stables in Topanga Canyon and that he had an interest in forming a dope-gobbling church so that psychedelics could be used legally as a religious sacrament.

Bill Vance was always coming on with a "money trip." At one point, he was going to set up Joe and Danny De Carlo with a motorcycle repair shop in Venice, California. Another great Vance scheme was the topless dancer caper.

Bob Beausoleil had met Mr. Jack Gerard, the head of the Gerard Theatrical Agency, a company specializing in supplying actors and actresses for porno movies and topless dancers for night clubs in the Los Angeles area. The agency was also a retail outlet for G-strings and dancing apparel. Beausoleil went to work for the Gerard Agency. Among his duties was delivering station wagons full of topless dancers to various clubs each night.

The Gerard Theatrical Agency was located up the hill from the Whiskey A Go-Go at 8949 Sunset Boulevard on the Sunset Strip. On March 23, 1969, Beausoleil signed a songwriting contract with the Gerard Agency. Beausoleil had a copy of the key to the front door of the Gerard Agency and was allowed to use the tape-recording equipment there to produce a demo tape of his songs.

When Beausoleil began talking about the Gerard Agency, Bill Vance became convinced, and Manson also became convinced, that it would be possible to send some of the girls from the ranch to the Gerard Agency to apply for jobs as topless dancers. Bill Vance agreed to act as the "agent" for the girls. He got all dressed up in a suit and tie, and the girls old enough to have I.D. got dolled up in high heels and costumes thought befitting topless dancers. Charlie thought that each girl would make about $200 per week, and he figured that with ten girls working and turning the money over to the family, of course, that there'd be about $2000 a week coming in.

Part of the plan for escaping during Helter Skelter

required the purchase of a very expensive gold rope that cost about three dollars a foot, and Charlie wanted a truck equipped with a winch and thousands of feet of this golden rope in order to dangle the family down into the Hopi hole during the end of the world. It was thought that ten topless skelterettes working full time would quickly pay for the world-end rope. Oo-ee-oo.

Joe of the Straight Satans took Vance and a gang of prospective nude dancers off to the Gerard Agency. He picked them up after the caper at Ben Blue's Coffee Shop on the strip.

Sexy Sadie Glutz was so changed by lipstick and makeup that the people hardly recognized her. They set up an appointment with a lady at the Gerard Agency who interviewed the girls. Mr. Gerard himself then showed up, and because some of the girls had diminutive breasts Gerard evidently wanted to give silicone injections to them, in order to produce the ponderous, jiggly quality sought in topless dancers. No thanks.

During the spring of 1969, Bob Beausoleil was cultivating Dennis Wilson, Melcher and Gregg Jakobson, with hopes of furthering his own musical career. Jakobson went twice to the Gerard Agency to listen to Beausoleil's tapes.

In April, Beausoleil lived for about a week at Dennis Wilson's and Gregg Jakobson's house on North Beverly Glen. There Beausoleil met and later lived with a slender red-haired seventeen-year-old girl named Kitty Lutesinger.

Beausoleil and Kitty then lived for a couple of weeks at the Lutesinger Ranch owned by her parents on Devonshire Boulevard not far from Spahn Ranch. Kitty became pregnant and then in late May 1969 they moved to Laurel Canyon for a few weeks, then to the Spahn Ranch just in time to take part in hell breaking loose.

Meanwhile, back at 10050 Cielo Drive, Terry Melcher and Candy Bergan began to move their belongings out over the holidays, and in January of 1969 they settled into his mother's beachhouse at 22126 Malibu Beach Road.

While the house on Cielo Drive was empty, Gregg Jakobson arranged for Dean Morehouse to stay there briefly. Tex Watson visited Morehouse a number of times while he was at Cielo Drive.

* * *

On February 12, 1969, the Polanskis entered into a lease arrangement with the owner of the three-and-a-half acre property at 10050 Cielo Drive, Mr. Rudy Altobelli, the show biz manager whom Melcher and Wilson had tried to interest in the Charlie Manson superstar project. Altobelli himself lived on the property in a smaller "caretaker's" house located about 150 feet away from the main residence.

On February 15, they moved into the house. The rent for the year's lease was $1200 a month, which seemed to be a bit of a rip-off, especially since the house had only three bedrooms, although it was well lit by night and fully serviced by landscapers and groundskeepers.

There was that elegant loneliness of the location, high in Benedict Canyon, hidden in the wooded hillside. There was also a swimming pool and that huge two-story living room with an overhanging loft edged by a white railing.

The rent was made more palatable by the fact that, according to dear friends, Paramount Pictures was picking up the tab. Roman Polanski was going to put his offices in the apartment above the garage.

On March 15, 1969, Polanski threw a catered housewarming party at 10050 Cielo Drive. There was a brawl of sorts at the party involving uninvited friends of Wojtek Frykowski and Abigail Folger, friends whom they met evidently through Cass Elliott, the singer. Elliott lived near Folger and Frykowski's house on Woodstock Road.

Someone named Pic Dawson stepped on Sharon's agent's foot and jostling occurred. Humans named Tom Harrigan, Ben Carruthers and Billy Doyle sided with Pic Dawson in the hassle. Roman Polanski got angry and threw Dawson and friends out of the party.

All through the following summer, however, the four mentioned above were frequent house guests at the Polanski residence, while Mr. and Mrs. Polanski were working in Europe.

According to a story told by reporters in the hallways outside the Manson trial, a story allegedly emanating from the producer of *The Love Machine,* Nancy Sinatra was a guest at the party and she grew incensed over the open dope-smoking. She requested that her escort take her away from the party forthwith. As they left, walking past a white wrought-iron settee on the elegant lawn, they noticed Warren Beatty and Jane Fonda and Roger Vadim sitting and talking together.

After Miss Sinatra and escort left the grounds and began to walk down the hill to their car, they encountered a group of long-haired hippies who asked them, "Where's the party?" They motioned back up the hill, and to this day they have wondered if the hordes of Helter Skelter were pointed thus into the Cielo Drive estate.

In his autobiography, John Phillips, the leader of the Mamas and the Papas, describes a midsized orgy (only five people) he says occurred among himself, his wife and a pair of extremely famous Hollywood stars after the Polanski housewarming party. This commingling, he writes, occurred in Malibu at the home of a well-known movie director, also apparently a participant.

The next day, March 16, Shahrokh Hatami, Sharon's photographer, and Sharon drove Roman to the airport, for a flight to Rio de Janeiro where Mia Farrow was given an award for her role in *Rosemary's Baby*.

After the Rio de Janeiro film festival, Roman Polanski was off to London to work on a movie script for United Artists called *Day of the Dolphins*—a spy tale involving dolphins who learn to speak. He was also slated to produce and direct the movie, probably through Cadre Productions, a company he co-owned with his good friend, Gene Gutowski.

Sharon was off to Rome where she made a film called *Twelve Plus One Chairs* with Vittorio Gassman. Additional scenes were filmed in London later on in the summer.

Even though they were to be gone for four months, the Polanskis decided not to put their belongings in storage but to keep their house open and get someone to stay there and care for the dogs, etc.

A young Englishman, Michael Sarne, the director of the motion pictures *Joanna* and *Myra Breckenridge*, was going to stay in the Polanski residence, but just prior to Roman Polanski's departure for Rio, he decided to rent a Malibu beachhouse instead.

Wojtek Frykowski volunteered then to stay at the Polanski residence for the spring and summer. Polanski agreed that Wojtek could move in, provided that Miss Folger stay there also.

The owner of the Polanski residence, Mr. Altobelli, planned to spend the summer in Europe. One day he picked up an eighteen-year-old hitchhiker from Lancaster, Ohio named William Garretson. Altobelli hired Garretson to serve as caretaker for the property while he was away in Europe. Garretson was given the "guest house" or caretaker's house on the property as his residence during employment. He was paid a whopping thirty-five dollars a week.

Garretson's duties included taking care of Terry Melcher's twenty-six cats, which Melcher evidently left behind for a while at the house. He also took care of Saperstein (Sharon's Yorkshire terrier) and, later, Abigail Folger's Dalmatian, plus Rudy Altobelli's hostile Weimaraner, Christopher, a dog that loved to bark and even to bite. Also on the care list was Altobelli's green singing finch. He was to keep an eye on the property, but not to fraternize, and he was to man the phone at the guest house.

On March 23, 1969, in the afternoon, Manson showed up at the front door of the Polanski residence at 10050 Cielo Drive.

Hatami answered the door. Shahrokh Hatami was occupied at the time, or so he testified, in filming Miss Tate as she was packing for her trip to Rome the following day. Hatami was making the film supposedly as part of a private-life TV documentary on movie actresses.

Why was the five-foot six-inch hairy-chested person with a woman tattooed on each arm named Charles Manson knocking at the front door of Sharon Tate's house?

Hatami testified at the trial that Manson wanted to know where "somebody" lived—referring to Terry Melcher. Hatami directed him to the caretaker's guest house on the other side of the pool, where Rudy Altobelli lived. While Manson was near the porch, Sharon Tate came to the door to ask who it was.

Manson went back to the guest cottage, but Mr. Altobelli was not there. That evening, however, Manson returned and knocked on Mr. Altobelli's door. In the big house, at that moment, Sharon, Jay Sebring, Abigail Folger and

Wojtek Frykowski—Manson's future murder victims—were having dinner.

Rudy Altobelli was packing to leave. He was going to fly to Rome the next day with Sharon Tate. Altobelli was taking a shower when Manson came to the screened porch.

Altobelli told the court later that his dogs, among their barks, bark two types of bark: people barks and animal barks—so he must have heard people-woofing.

He answered the door, clad in a towel, wet from the shower.

Altobelli testified that the purpose of Manson's visit was to find out where Terry Melcher was living, even though Melcher had moved off of Cielo Drive almost four months previous.

Manson started to introduce himself according to Altobelli, but Mr. Altobelli said to him, "I know who you are, Charlie."

Altobelli supposedly told Manson that he did not know the whereabouts of the executive producer of the Doris Day Show, Terry Melcher.

Since Gregg Jakobson, a close friend of Melcher's, testified at Manson's trial that they were recording Manson while the family was still at the house on Gresham Street, it is hard to believe that Manson didn't know that Melcher had moved out to his mother's beachhouse. The family was living at the house on Gresham up till right around the time that Manson visited the Polanski residence. It is known that Manson made an appointment with Melcher for Melcher to visit the Gresham Street house and he didn't show up, miffing Manson.

The visit of Manson to Cielo Drive is stlll mysterious.

The next day on the plane to Rome, Altobelli and Sharon had a conversation about Manson.

On March 24, 1969, back in sleazo-ville, it was time for a little statutory rape. Two unknown male Caucasians, driving a shiny new convertible, managed to coax a seventeen-year-old girl from Reseda, California into the car as she walked along a Chatsworth street, about two miles from the Spahn Ranch. With the jail bait snared, they whizzed off to a sleazy ranch house west of Topanga Canyon Boulevard. Possibly they took the girl to the back house of the Spahn Ranch because the girl told the police that the house was a distance from the road. When she arrived, it was weirdness. The event is best described by the police report.

> Victim states that this was the strangest place she had ever seen in her life; 20-25 people sitting, standing, lounging around in a living room; men, women, girls, boys and even children; strobe lights were going off and on; things hanging from the walls, everything psychedelic; some were on the floor plunking on some types of musical instruments; and that they were all drinking out of a dirty looking jug and smoking something.

"Where am I?" asked the Reseda flower.

"This is where it is," replied an unknown female Caucasian.

Evidently the entrapped girl became hungry and some girl from the family offered her some corn flakes but, according to family custom, the lady offered the flakes first to a dog named Tom, then she could eat them—for the dogs always ate first, before the women, according to family table manners.

They introduced the young girl to Charlie. He took her out in private to explain the game to her and, according to the girl, raped her in an automobile and then pulled up his pants and went back into the house to sing to the assembly. Later the young girl had someone drive her to a liquor store in Chatsworth for some cigarettes and she ran away to her parents, who were loath to press charges, because of the publicity, you know, and Manson got away with it.

Mr. Polanski's career as writer and director and businessman was speeding along. As of April 1969, an original screenplay written by Polanski titled *A Day at the Beach* had completed filming in Copenhagen by Cadre Productions. Adapted from a Dutch novel by Heer Heresma, the film was directed by a young Moroccan director, Simon Hesera.

And there was more.

When he went to Europe in early April of 1969, in addition to his United Artists project, Roman Polanski was working on two original screenplays evidently for Paramount Pictures.

One, a film of the life of Paganini, was to be written in collaboration with the author who wrote *L'Avventura.*

The other film, in collaboration with Ivan Moffat, was to be called *The Donner Pass,* a tale of pioneers turned temporary cannibals in the Squaw Valley disaster winter of 1851.

In an interview with Joseph Gelmis in early 1969, Polanski said, "The film is the story of people going from Illinois to California. At that time, there were only seven hundred Americans in California. So these travelers were going to this paradise and they were stranded in the snow in the Sierras in very early winter. Most of them died. The few that survived were accused afterwards of cannibalism."

"Cannibalism?" the interviewer asked, as if in surprise.

"Yes, yes, I know, I know. But it has nothing to do with any of my earlier pictures. What makes you think I am obsessed by the bizarre?"

On April 1, 1969, Wojtek Frykowski and Abigail Folger moved into 10050 Cielo Drive.

10

The Spahn Movie Ranch (April–June 1969)

According to Danny De Carlo, it was red-haired and eager Squeaky Fromme who persuaded George Spahn to allow the family to return to the Spahn Ranch en masse. The date of the return to the Spahn Ranch was sometime in the early days of April 1969.

Part of Charlie's master plan was to get George to sign the ranch over to Squeaky when he died. After all, George *was* eighty-two years old at the time, and Squeaky was assigned a permanent position in Spahn's saddle-filled house.

It was not outside the realm of possibility that Manson might have wound up owning a movie ranch. For, to this day, Spahn is eager to have the family ladies around him. And, according to numerous interviews with observers, he had no hesitance, say once a week or so, to get after it with girls sixty-five years younger than he.

Ruby Pearl, George Spahn's long-time associate, was still there, but somehow Manson seemed to overun the ranch, as he had the previous summer. The family always had a fragile relationship with Spahn's family, but in spite of what any of the stunt men or his own family would whisper into Spahn's ear, Manson had the ace of love.

There was always some hassle with Jim, George Spahn's son. Often he wanted to run the hippie freaks off the set. And, in turn, the girls were sorely hostile to him because he castrated the horses. Meanwhile Manson kept the house on Gresham in Canoga Park till May when they were evicted for nonpayment of rent. There he maintained his own private stash of eight girls. No other male was allowed in the house according to a next door neighbor.

Manson seems even to have become involved in the fiscal operations of the ranch. That spring, Spahn needed money to pay his property taxes and Manson, according to De Carlo, helped him with around $3000.

RuthAnn Morehouse aka Ouish was arrested and placed into Juvenile Hall. She was released into the custody of George Spahn, who served evidently as her foster parent. We shall have to pause here for an oo-ee-oo.

Ouish had matured to the elderly age of fifteen. She began to work behind the "register" in the office by the corral, collecting money from horse renters. This is an example of Manson's control of the scene.

When they first moved back to the Spahn Ranch they spent a lot of effort to try to convert the Longhorn Saloon into a "music hall" or a night club. Charlie persuaded George Spahn that it was going to bring in the business. Later Manson told a lawyer that he opened the saloon merely to give the girls something to do.

The girls remember the "music hall" caper as a magnet which attracted the local youth from the San Fernando Valley area in droves.

At the far right end of the Saloon there was a stage with guitar amplifiers and a sound system and drums, suitable for a whole band. There was a rock-stocked juke box in the corner. The ceiling was hung with white and orange parachutes. On the left side was a long bar where they served free popcorn, chips, soda, coffee and dope. On the floor were spread rugs and mattresses for conjunction. These Spahn Ranch helter-skelter teen-hops attracted a lot of heat from the cops, who came to visit the ranch more and more frequently regarding young runaways.

The triumph of the Longhorn Saloon was a mural painted in Dayglo and black-light colors, the fresco of Helter Skelter. In the painting there was depicted a mountain and the desert and Goler Wash. A personification, evidently the Angel of Helter Skelter, was depicted coming out of heaven, or the sky, to save. At the bottom of the mural were the words: "Helter Skelter, Goler Wash and Death Valley." Nearby on a table there was a jug with a notation: "Donations for Helter Skelter"—created by Ouish.

After several weeks the enterprise was snuffed by the police. George Spahn was handed a $1500 citation for operating a night club without a license. Adios Helter Skelter A Go-Go.

Manson had as many interests as a corporation executive. As the spring changed into summer of this year of murder, the pressures, most of which he himself created, mounted from every corner. There was no escape.

One source of pressure upon Manson was the Transcontinental Development Corporation, which avidly sought to purchase the Spahn Ranch in order to build a resort complex for German Americans. They began to purchase property around the Spahn Ranch and they were attempting to work on Spahn, himself of German ancestry, to sell out.

Spahn's family, of course, was eager to close the deal because of the profits to be reaped from the sale. Naturally the Transcontinental Development Corporation would immediately tear down such an asymmetrical eyesore as the Spahn Ranch and run off the hippie slime.

Things were pretty much the same at the Spahn Ranch as they had been the previous year, at least physically so.

In the hidden gullies and remote woody areas of the Spahn Ranch nudity was the order of dress. Only when on the front movie set itself, which was only about a hundred feet from the traffic on Santa Susanna Pass Road, was some body-covering required.

There were the same odorous toilets by George's house. There was a shower that broke down often. An auxiliary shower was the eight-foot waterfall down the creek behind the ranch.

Directly above the waterfall was a cave where occasionally some of the family slept and camped out.

There were a number of vans and old house trailers located in back of the movie set where people slept.

The whole ranch was heavily strewn with sleeping bags and lots of mattresses to aid instant gratification. There may have been a tendency to go to bed early because the longer at night people waited to crash the further away from the ranch they would have to roam to find a mattress.

The bikers, many attired in the grease-suffused leathers with Hitlerian medallions, some with *l-o-v-e* tattooed on one set of knuckles and *h-a-t-e* on the other, provided freedom-training for some of the girls who were afraid of them. Gypsy supposedly at first was extremely hesitant to have affairs with the Satans but grew to love it.

"The motorcycle gangs would come out there and he would tell a girl, 'Take your clothes off,' and she would take her clothes off and he would just give the girl to any of the motorcycle guys there that wanted to screw her," remembered Sunshine Pierce.

As said before, Danny De Carlo of the Straight Satans set up residence in the Undertaker's Parlor, renamed the gun room because of the small arsenal De Carlo owned. De Carlo was a reprobate and never did fit in with the scheme as Manson saw it.

What Manson did see was that De Carlo used to be president of his bike club and that, through De Carlo, they might be able to latch onto the Straight Satans and get them to be the family's brown shirts. But it never really worked out that way, because the theme of the Spahn Ranch was leisure. The family became masters at "hanging out"—that skill evinced outside drugstores in small towns everywhere.

The bikers would fit right in, drunk, carousing and taking their bikes apart at leisure. De Carlo and the bikers would cash in Coke bottles and buy wine and Manson would complain. De Carlo also grew a pot plant named Elmer up by the waterfall. Elmer was one of the least powerful pot plants ever grown, but has acquired a certain fame in that it was about the only gentle symbol at the ranch during that summer of death.

There were literally hundreds of ordinary L.A. people who visited the Spahn Ranch once in a while, just to hang out.

One "starlet" who had performed in a Grade B cheapo-cheapo movie filmed at the Spahn Ranch kept coming back every weekend.

At once, upon her arrival, somebody would haul her onto a mattress or into the bushes and slip her clothes off.

"Every time I come here I get raped," she complained.

A few of the bikers were offered bit parts in commercials and movie segs shot at the ranch. The relationship between the family and moviemakers, a hush-hush paranoid bribe-suffused area in the Manson saga, will be discussed later.

A gentleman who worked for a church in L.A. collected oodles of leftovers from the Van de Kamp's bakery in Los Angeles and used to drive up to the Spahn Ranch to give the families all sorts of pies and cakes and pastries. Sexy Sadie and Joe would take the extra pastries down to Venice or Santa Monica, to give them out to derelicts and hippies on the streets.

A word must be said about meat-fits. Sadie Mae Glutz was prone to meat-fits. The vegetarian diet at the Spahn Ranch was difficult to follow for some. Sadie occasionally would rush off to a restaurant somewhere and order a steak, the need was so great. Danny De Carlo and Joe, of the Straight Satans, also would go off once a week to Venice for a top sirloin meal.

There was one enormous difference at the Spahn Ranch compared to the previous year when the family first showed up. Murder replaced mind-games as the favorite conversational subject.

"They talked about killing all the time," recalled a young man who lived at the nearby Steele Ranch.

For a long time Charlie had been saying, "There is no good, there is no evil," but now he was saying things like "You can't kill kill," and "If you're willing to be killed, you should be willing to kill," and "It's the pigs' turn to go up on the cross."

He began to talk about murder and carnage so openly that it was almost like a self-fulfilling prophecy.

Sometime that spring Manson acquired his "magic sword." It was a homemade two-foot sword with a knuckle-guard that wounded a lot of people. A Straight Satan named George Knowl gave the magic sword to Charlie. Charlie, one day, just asked for it after he had paid a traffic ticket for Knowl down in Simi, California.

It became like Manson's ceremonial sword. As violence overwhelmed him, Manson would be seen jumping around on the ranch boardwalk slashing and jabbing the air with the sword.

During the filming of one of the family movies, Manson supposedly hacked someone's arm with it. God knows what flesh the sword cut.

It cut Gary Hinman's ear in two. It may have been carried into the LaBianca house. It was stuck into a metal "scabbard" on Manson's command dune buggy as he patrolled Devil Canyon.

After the murders the Straight Satans raided the ranch to get the sword. Perhaps they had heard hints about the deeds done with the weapon.

Manson made a deliberate decision to begin to kill. His series of raps, ever added to, like the repertoire of a night-club act, shifting and changing, pointed toward butcher.

Juan Flynn, the tall Panamanian ranch hand who'd worked for George since 1967 and who had been to Vietnam and had lived through horrible slaughter, counseled Charlie against starting to kill.

According to Paul Watkins, when Charlie began to talk about killing, Juan would say, "It's just like smoking cigarettes, Charlie; once you start, you just keep wanting to do it."

As the family got freakier and freakier, doors began to slam in their faces. They began to hate rich people, the piggies, they called them, of Brentwood and Bel Air and Benedict Canyon. One of Manson's favorite raps was built around a rural pig-slaughter. Those who have been unfortunate enough to have witnessed it will know how a pig is tied up and hung by its hind feet, de-skinned and then riped open and innards removed. This is precisely what Manson preached for the so-called pigs of Brentwood. And this is probably the purpose for which Watson carried that forty-three foot piece of rope into the Polanski residence. The origin of the so-called list of famous people to be killed may date from these early months of 1969 when violence overwhelmed the Spahn Ranch.

The family and the bikers began to race motorcycles and dune buggies around at night. Neighbors complained and Manson told one of them to shut up or he'd burn their houses down.

Spahn evidently complained to the police about the late night sound of the motors. It was scaring the horses and alarming the neighbors. A couple of sheriff's deputies came to investigate and to prepare a field investigation report. After they left, George told Manson that the police wanted him to run the family off the property. Manson went into one of his triggered rages. He screamed and yelled. He accused George of being an ingrate, of actually being able to see.

He supposedly flashed a knife in front of George Spahn's eyes to make him blink. He ordered a girl to strip in front of Spahn. No blink.

Then there was silence, and, depending on which family member is telling the tale, there was a grope-scene in the room in front of Spahn.

Manson then, according to legend, said, "I love you, George," and split.

In the spring or early in 1969, Patricia Krenwinkel bought ten or fifteen deer hides with some gift money that somebody, perhaps Sandy Good, obtained from daddy. From these skins, the girls attempted to make buckskin outfits for the men of the family. Snake and Ouish and Gypsy and the others started cutting and sewing the buckskins, but they were not sewing them correctly, so that the project was taken from their hands. Manson evidently took the skins and hides to one Victor Wild, also known as Brother Ely, a member of an occult society Manson had encountered in late 1967 in Topanga. Wild owned a leather shop in Santa Barbara where the buckskin outfits for the men were completed. Manson was wearing his buckskins when finally arrested in Death Valley on Aleister Crowley's birthday.

Because of the heavy war between the Hell's Angels and the Gypsy Jokers, Brother Ely had been forced to move his leather shop to Santa Barbara from San Jose. There, in Goleta, just north of Santa Barbara, he began to prosper.

In the middle of April of 1969, a young Texan named Charles Pierce aka Sunshine was hanging out on the Sunset Strip when he met Ella Sinder aka Yeller and Sadie. Charles Pierce was a young man from Midland, Texas who had come to California in order to surf and hang out in the sun and just enjoy himself. Sadie and Ella persuaded Charles "Sunshine" Pierce to visit the Spahn Ranch, where Sunshine gave up everything—his money, his i.d. and his silver 1968 Plymouth Roadrunner, which Manson gladly received and used for a while, and then gave it away to Randy Starr.

Just before Neil Armstrong jumped down onto the moon in July, repossession agents from Texas took the Roadrunner back to the auto company. But while the family had it, they used it. The Roadrunner was really the only good, sturdy car at the Spahn Ranch at the time, so they used it a lot for various dope dealings.

"We was running dope down from San Francisco and Los Angeles, selling it on the street corners—" said Sunshine.

Manson had one famous incident with the new Roadrunner where he challenged a bunch of cops to a race.

About eleven o'clock one night, Charlie, T.J. the Terrible, Sadie and Ella went out in Sunshine Pierce's Plymouth Roadrunner to cop a few thrills. On Topanga Canyon Boulevard they challenged a cop to a race and sped off.

Danny De Carlo tells it like this: "Nobody outdrove Charlie. He, one night, got loaded on acid, and Ella, I think Sadie was there, . . . they went down to just antagonize the police . . . and he outran four cars. Finally, he pulled over and he just stopped, and they did not know what the hell to make out of this guy, so they stopped 'way behind him and he jumped out of the car and he says: 'Come on, come on after me,' then jumped back into the car and took off again."

Ultimately the police caught them and they held Manson for several days but finally set him free.

Sunshine Pierce, as did all new recruits, received the usual Manson lecture series on Helter Skelter, The Hole, there is no good/no evil, everything belongs to everybody therefore let's steal, etc. Gradually as he gained trust, Pierce was allowed to partake in various criminal capers.

Sunshine Pierce said that one of Manson's dune-buggy fantasies was to kidnap schoolgirls after they got off their school bus in rural areas. They would scout out the area to see where the girls got off the bus and then snatch them up and take them to the desert hideout.

Guys like Sunshine Pierce and Joe and others left the Spahn Ranch partly because they found themselves slowly becoming one of those "program people" that Manson talked about. And who on earth really wants to become a zombie.

There were quite a few arrests for Grand Theft-Auto in April of 1969, charges however which were dropped. Leslie Van Houten aka Leslie Sankston and Stephanie Rowe aka Jane Doe 44 were among those arrested.

On April 23, 1969, Charles Watson, still dressed in a mod fashion, according to his mug shot taken at the time, was stopped by the Los Angeles police department on a charge of being drunk on drugs. Officer Escalente rolled Watson's fingerprints, a grim event for Watson, since it was the set of prints that the police would use to link him to his fingerprints on the Polanski front door.

On April 25, 1969, Bruce Davis, sent to London by Manson five months previous, passed through Heathrow Airport in London, bound for the United States.

In early May, just before Mother's Day, Mr. Davis of Monroe, Louisiana arrived at the Spahn Ranch and threw himself avidly into the crime schemes. Davis developed a novel scheme, or thought he had done so, for getting free gas for the dune buggies. He wanted to drive up into the mountains to the edge of the desert to the location of the gas transmission lines. Then he wanted to tap the lines and put barrels there to collect a permanent supply of gasoline for Mission World Snuff. Sneers met this proposal from at least one biker, because it was either natural gas or raw petroleum—not gasoline. But Manson and Bruce Davis were convinced, so they tried it anyway, even hauling a few stolen fire-department water barrels up Devil Canyon for the purpose of collecting the gas.

In spite of preparations for the end of the world, or Helter Skelter, Charles Manson still found time to make attempts at becoming a superstar.

Beausoleil went to Frank Zappa, the brilliant composer and producer, and wanted Zappa to come to the ranch to hear the music. Beausoleil said that the family was building a tunnel to the Mojave Desert, or something. Zappa, to whom the freak-flocks always flock, did not have the time or desire to handle the "act," however.

Gypsy Share, the former child violin prodigy, arranged for Paul Rothschild, the producer of The Doors, to hear the family music, with no evident success. Gypsy had connections in the business, having once lived with the composer of the hit country and western song, "Don't Sell My Daddy No More Wine."

Gregg Jakobson and Dennis Wilson arranged for Charlie to record at a studio in Santa Monica, in Westwood, not far from the Mormon Temple. This studio was owned by a gentleman named George Wilder, whose attitude was "Where's the mon?" and was worried lest Charlie should burn him for the session money. Charlie got angry and walked out of the studio and left behind what Jakobson described as: "Two or three amplifiers, two electric guitars, an acoustic guitar and some other instruments." Manson managed to record about twelve songs or so, enough for an album. He spontaneously composed two new songs at the recording session. Some of the girls were there to provide choral backup, as was Bob Beausoleil. Dennis Wilson of the Beach Boys, Gregg Jakobson and Terry Melcher were on hand to grok the set.

It was at this recording session that Manson really freaked Melcher out with a little spontaneous guitar vamp. During a break, Charlie was strumming his guitar, scat-singing behind the strumming with apparently nonsense syllables—digh-tu-dai, deigh-du-doi, di-tew-deigh, etc. —and gradually the scat-song came clearer, until die-tew-dai, die-tu-day, die-today became die today die today die today.

In May or June of 1969, during an English tour, Dennis Wiison told an English rock magazine about Manson, in an interview. Wilson called him the Wizard and said that the Beach Boys' record label would probably release an album of Manson.

After Jakobson and Melcher and Wilson had recorded Manson, they talked several times out at Melcher's Malibu house about what to do with this enormous talent of the universe. Jakobson was pushing the potential of a documentary movie about Charlie and his commune, but Melcher, the president of Arwin Productions and Daywin Music Publishing Company besides being the executive producer of the Doris Day Show, needed persuasion. Jakobson was eager for Melcher to serve as "producer and financer" of the flick.

It was the visual impact of the family that would "sell" them to the public, it was thought.

For instance, Jakobson was totally impressed by Charlie Manson's dancing ability. Says he: "When Charlie danced, everyone else left the floor. He was like fire, a raw explosion, a mechanical toy that suddenly went crazy." Now if they could just capture that on film. And then there was the whole visual "beauty" of the family as they lived and worked and loved and sang.

Several times Jakobson came to the ranch to take pictures of the family as it did its thing. The idea was to create a presentation on film, to impress potential backers.

There was conflict about the so-called direction the film would take.

It will be remembered that 1969 was the year of the movie *Easy Rider*—a nomadic flick with themes of violence, dope, communes, bikes, dope-dealing, honkies and hatred.

Manson had in mind a movie that could be given a title like "Easy Snuff." He wanted satanism. He wanted robbery and chase. He wanted the men of the family depicted in dune-buggy brigandry. He wanted good Armageddon footage with helter-skelter carnage. In other words he wanted to create an "honest" movie presenting the state of his current insanity and that of his followers.

Jakobson, Melcher, et al., were more interested in the gentler aspects of the family: the singing, the love, the tribal religiosity, etc. They seem to have wanted a here-come-the-hippies documentary with Lowell Thomas type narration.

On May 18, 1969, National Guard troops ripped up Peoples' Park in Berkeley.

Also on May 18, Terry Melcher was persuaded to come to the Spahn Movie Ranch for an audition of Charlie and his choir in their natural setting. Jakobson and Melcher picked up Bob Beausoleil and his girl friend Kitty Lutesinger where they were staying with her parents at the Lutesinger ranch, and they went to the Spahn Ranch for the "audition." Manson took Melcher on a dune-buggy ride. Melcher observed men putting a generator into the tractor truck. Manson told Melcher that the truck was being put together to transport dune buggies and motorcycles out of the city. Shortly thereafter Manson tried to drive the tractor truck loaded with dune buggies to Goler Wash but the truck broke down, thwarted they thought by the magic of the so-called scientologist gold miners.

The audition was held in a clearing in the woods in back of the ranch. The only way of getting to the audition was to Tarzan down the steep creek bank, holding onto a rope that was tied to a tree.

Everybody went down the stream. The girl choir walked in silence, equidistant apart—or so they seemed to Melcher. Charlie Manson sat on a rock as he sang and the girls gave up background percussion claps with their hands and hummed in harmony behind the singing, uttering "yeas" and "amens" as if aroused by revival fervor.

Melcher gave Manson fifty dollars, the contents of his pocket, as a gift to buy hay for the horses at the ranch. "I hope it wasn't construed as an advance on a recording," Melcher later testified at the Manson trial where he tried to assert he never ran around with the family.

People interviewed in the family claim that Melcher told Manson he'd have to sign some contracts—probably meaning film contracts plus songwriting agreements—with one of Melcher's music publishing companies. But Charlie was very much against signing contracts. Too plastic, man. He just wanted the money.

After the audition by the creek, they went back up to the front ranch and lo and behold, they ran into Randy Starr, who was in his pickup truck painted with the words "Randy Starr, Hollywood Stunt Man." Randy was drunk and belligerent and had a gun strapped to his hip, and it seemed he was going to draw the revolver. Charlie stepped in and slugged Randy in the stomach and took the gun away.

Speaking of guns, no doubt there is heavy interest in knowing a bit about the history of the .22 caliber revolver that Manson et al. used in their murder activities in the summer of 1969. It was sometime in the late spring that it showed up at the ranch.

The family acquired a 1952 Hostess Twinkie bread truck registered to the Continental Bakery Company. It was in this truck that Manson visited the Esalen Institute in Big Sur six days before the murder of Abigail Folger and the others. Danny De Carlo, former president of the Straight Satans, bought the bread truck off of one Dave Lipsett, a friend of Manson.

De Carlo traded some stolen motorcycle parts, including an engine, for the Twinkie truck. There had always been controversy over the ownership of the bread truck. Manson has claimed that the motorcycle engine and parts were actually stolen by his devices, therefore the truck should have been his. But Charlie didn't care; everything was everybody's.

One night Bill Vance was rip-roaring drunk and, in the manner of extra Y-chromosome drunks everywhere, he was belligerent and was going to shoot up the ranch. Perhaps there was a dishonor-among-thieves squabble about rip-off booty. Other accounts say that Vance was having hassles with Randy Starr, the stunt man specializing in the neck drag.

Whatever the case, Manson entered the squabble and traded De Carlo's bread truck for the gun that Vance was waving about. De Carlo seemed to protest—my truck, my truck—but Manson told him that Vance wanted to use it for a couple of months then De Carlo could have it back. Okay.

The revolver that Vance turned over to Manson is a sixty-dollar, three-pound item of Western chauvinism, manufactured by the U.S. Firearms Corporation. The description of the weapon in the company catalogue is, for history, as follows: "This long barrel beauty is reminiscent of the Wyatt Earp days when Ned Buntline presented the Marshall with a similar long barrelled gun. Shoots nine shots faster than 'fanning.' Crisp trigger action and button-swaging precision barrel rifling. Genuine walnut grips. Gold finish trigger guard."

This revolver killed Jay Sebring, shot Wojtek Frykowski, shot a black dope dealer in the stomach, and God knows what else.

After Melcher visited, Manson kept asking Jakobson if Melcher was still interested in the project. Evidently there was a period wherein Melcher was to "make up his mind." Manson wanted Melcher's phone number so Jakobson gave him Melcher's answering service number. Manson was really counting on Melcher to come through for him with the movie and the records.

On May 21, 1969, Manson called his parole officer and asked if he could leave immediately for a tour to Texas with the Beach Boys. He was going to earn $5000, or so he said. The parole officer said that he would have to furnish verification of employment. A couple of days later, Manson called back and said that it was too late, the Beach Boys had already left. He told his parole officer that he had a song on the hit parade and that he had just recorded an album which was going to be released in about a month.

On Tuesday, May 26, 1969, Mayor Yorty, blatantly appealing to the racism in Los Angeles, won re-election as Mayor of Los Angeles over black candidate Tom Bradley. Abigail Folger worked long and hard for the election of Mr. Bradley.

Only occasionally can the focus really be precise on actual details of a particular day in the life of the family, especially when they did not believe in time and months and days. It was all Now. One girl claimed, when arrested in Death Valley later in the year, that she didn't even know Nixon had been elected President.

June 3, 1969, however, can be scanned with some precision.

On June 3, 1969, Charlie tried to put out a contract on somebody's life.

On June 3, 1969, Terry Melcher and Gregg Jakobson again visited the Spahn Ranch. They encountered two policemen who were on the set also, investigating Charlie's rape of the girl from Reseda in March. Melcher brought with him a gentleman named Mike Deasy, who possessed a van in which was a complete recording studio. Mr. Deasy had recorded several Indian tribes and was experienced in recording "tribes" in the field, so to speak. Melcher evidently was going to use Deasy perhaps to record the sound track for the documentary or to record an on-site live recording of Manson and the all-girl creepy-crawl chorus.

With Melcher was the beautiful "star" named Sharon or Shara who used to visit the Spahn Ranch wearing wigs. It was not Sharon Tate as Sunshine Pierce thought when he copped a visual on her. Sharon Tate was in London, six months pregnant and happily preparing to return to Los Angeles for the baby's birth.

Sunshine and Tex were changing the spark plugs in the green and white GMC tractor truck with which Charlie planned to haul the tarp-covered trailer to the desert. This was the tractor truck with the Olds engine. Manson had planned, but never accomplished, a false bottom on the trailer in which runaway girls could be hid on their way to the desert (or to a ritual). Hot and thirsty, Sunshine walked up to the front ranch into the kitchen and filled up a quart jar with water.

As he left the kitchen to return to the truck, he saw Melcher, the starlet, Gregg and Manson standing by the couch on the boardwalk. They were arguing, and Charlie was cursing and yelling at them. Sunshine didn't think much of it, because Charlie was always chewing out somebody or other, threat-tripping the weak links in the family and chasing away undesirables, as is wont of a commander.

That morning, Charlie had gone down to "Hollywood" to discuss the film and record project and had come back with Terry Melcher and "this other guy that had come out there and taken pictures of us this one time"—as Pierce later told police. With dedicated intensity, Jakobson had taken many, many photos of the nude commune of lovers, for the album cover. Now they were arguing.

Sunshine Pierce went back down to the GMC, the "jimmy" as it is known in trucker circles, and finished up the plug change. He then lay down under the trailer on a mattress and amused himself with Charlie's pet crow, Devil. About thirty minutes after Pierce had overheard the argument, Manson himself came to join him at the trailer. Pierce thought that, perhaps, Charlie was about to deliver himself of a lecture—as often he did to instruct his followers.

Charlie asked Sunshine how long he intended to stay at the ranch. Uh oh. Pierce was afraid that Manson was going to brick him off the ranch and not a dime had Pierce. His new silver Plymouth Roadrunner Charlie had long since given to Randy Starr. His I.D. too had disappeared. No car, no money, no I.D.—not a condition in which to be set adrift in America.

Sunshine replied that he planned to stay on two, three, maybe four weeks then hit the wind. Charlie asked him if he was interested in helping him pull off a job. After the caper, Pierce could then split. Charlie, according to Pierce, said he'd give him a three-wheeled motorcycle (with legal pink slip)—probably De Carlo's three-wheeler with the word LOVE written on the back with aluminum tubing—and some cash. No one would know about it but them—for that was a rule; you didn't discuss anything Charlie talked about with you, unless he said it was okay to speak.

Sunshine was interested because he thought, as he claimed, that the project proposed involved some sort of robbery. There had been action aplenty, of course, during the six weeks that Pierce had lived on the ranch: the antiques and paintings, the proposed armored car heist, the offed travelers' checks, the trading in dope. So Pierce thought that Charlie was going to cut him in on some plunder.

It was murder. Charlie revealed that he wanted Sunshine to help him kill someone, saying, in substance, according to Pierce: "Well, you know, if you ever want to get anything and you want it bad enough, you can't let anybody come between you when you are going to do something."

This was something new to the twenty-year-old lad from Midland, Texas, so he told Manson he'd have to think about it and would let him know soon.

"He said that he had one person in particular he wanted me to help him kill and he said that there might have to be some other people killed.

"He said he could probably round up maybe $5000 or more and give it to me if I helped him pull this job."

Later that evening, Pierce learned that the argument on the boardwalk was over the "direction" the film would take—already they'd shot pictures and made tapes for a presentation. The NBC officials, on the one hand, wanted a verité hippie-commune movie with a narrator. But Charlie hated hippies. Charlie wanted to make an honest movie presenting the family in an as-is situation, adding marauder elements, bikers, creepy-crawlie capers—in order to magnet in on potential followers and attract them.

And what about Pierce? Later on, after the arrests, he told the Richardson, Texas police the following: "I thought it over for a while. I figured, well, it's something I couldn't get away with and if I could get away with it, I don't know if I'd like going around knowing that I done it. So I told him no. And so, right after that, well then I called my mother in Midland and told her where I was."

The next day, June 4, the girls patched his pants for him, his mother wired him some money, and Sunshine Pierce flew back to Texas.

On June 4, 1969, Charlie Manson was arrested as a result of a follow-up investigation on the rape in March of that girl from Reseda. But he got out the next day on bail of $125. Nothing ever happened with the charge and once again Charlie Manson got away with encroachment.

On June 6, Mike Deasy, the man with a recording studio in his van, visited the Spahn Ranch where he recorded Manson singing. Family gossip has it that Deasy took an acid trip with Manson, flipped and had a death-trip involving Manson that later required entrance into Jungian analysls.

Manson gave Deasy some four- and eight-track tapes of "the music" for his listening pleasure. Manson called him later and wanted him to bring his kids out to the ranch. No thanks.

In early June and once also in July at the Jack Frost Surplus Store in Santa Monica, Charlie Manson bought several hundred feet of white nylon three-ply rope, forty-three feet eight inches of which only sixty days later would be looped over the ceiling beam of the Polanski residence. The rope was fairly expensive but it was taken care of by running a phony credit card for it. Some of the rope was used around the ranch to tow vehicles. Charlie gave George Spahn part of the rope. The blind George felt the rope and admired it. Around 200 feet of the rope Charlie kept behind the bucket seat of his command dune buggy.

Danny De Carlo recalled one escape scheme Manson dreamed up for the rope: "He had a winch on the front of his dung bug, and the thing, what he wanted to do was, when the police were chasing him, see, he'd like take this winch and he'd throw the line out there and he'd winch himself up in a tree, the police would just drive right on by. You wouldn't see the dune buggy sitting up in the tree up there."

Manson became more and more involved with blending violence into his transactions. He seemed to be eager to see which of his "program people" would kill.

After all, Manson said, "We are all one." Killing someone therefore is just like breaking off a piece of cookie.

And did not the Manson adage say, "If you're willing to be killed you should be willing to kill?"

One of Manson's potential "program people" was the Vietnam veteran, the six-foot five-inch Panamanian ranch hand Juan Flynn. One day sometime in late May of 1969, according to Juan Flynn, Manson and Juan Flynn went to an ice cream parlor in Chatsworth and Manson talked a little about Juan's family, some of whom lived at the Porter Ranch, located in the north part of the valley, not far from the Spahn Ranch. Juan Flynn testified about it at the Manson trial: "So I wanted to see where they lived at, you know, and I was looking into it, you know.

"So I says, 'Why don't we look up this address and go down and see where my family lives.' " Manson agreed to drive him there. After they'd looked for the house and the street and they'd found it and parked, Manson asked if they had a little dog in there, and Flynn replied, "Yes, they have a little dog.

"And then he says, 'Well, why don't we go in there and tie them up and cut them to pieces,' " Flynn told the court in volume 103, page 11903 of the trial transcript.

Juan Flynn has claimed that on several occasions he and Charlie drove around Chatsworth, near the ranch, and Charlie tried to get Flynn to enter the houses, tie up the occupants, force-feed them LSD, kill the children in front of their parents, then kill the parents when they were going berserk.

There was another occasion when Manson wanted Juan to help him kill a black man.

Around June 13, 1969, Manson and Flynn drove in a dune buggy down the paved storm sewer of Brown's Canyon Wash, which twists down through Chatsworth and past the two-block section of Gresham Street, where the Manson family had once lived. Manson pointed to an apartment building near the former family house on Gresham Street, where some black dope dealer lived. And Manson asked Juan to help him kill him because the guy had been giving "his" girls dope and balling them.

Manson has denied, however, that there ever was any trouble with the black guy on Gresham.

Manson's snuff-offers to Sunshine Pierce and Juan Flynn pose a grim question: Was Manson, through his extensive fourteen-year connections with the California underworld, becoming a "hit man" who took murder contracts?

Charlie had trouble with his federal parole officer in June of 1969. He seems to have almost got his parole revoked because of his associations with other federal parolees. Federal parolees are denied close contact with one another to prevent collusive criminal activities.

The three were dope dealers whom Manson gave access to the harem. One of the federal parolees visited the Spahn Ranch then returned to his home in Las Vegas where he mumbled something to his wife about living off the land and getting a dune buggy.

One wife of the parolees was upset because Manson tried to seduce her when he visited them in Las Vegas.

Another worry for Charlie, in this summer of pressures, was that he really hated to lose a follower, once the follower was enmeshed in the nets, so to speak.

Charlie was always talking about scientology in his various raps, and it should have been no surprise when some of his followers decided to investigate it. Around the middle of June, two of the family, a boy and a girl, evidently left to pursue formal training with the Church of Scientology.

Vern Plumlee, who came to the Spahn Ranch in the middle of June, said this about the matter:

"They left right after I got there. They met some guy from scientology and the dude who was interested in scientology—he started talking to these two people and they left and Charlie'd been down on them ever since."

Charlie was miffed. It was not enough that sacred Goler Wash was being held by Crockett and crew but now his followers were defecting to scientology. Pressure, pressure, pressure.

Manson was a knife-freak. Everybody used to throw knives at the haystack. After all, the police could hear gunfire for miles in the desert but blades would be silent. And shrieks melt easily in the distant air.

He gave the girls lessons in knife throwing and later that year he actually got into lessons in throat slitting and skull boiling—evidently having in mind adorning the Barker Ranch with human skulls.

Machete chauvinism was one of Manson's ultimate devices, unless the stories are true that the family was into filming human sacrifices of young female Caucasian victims.

Charlie had an old sixteen-inch army surplus machete and he was the only one who could throw it. Charlie could throw it fifty feet, the family claims, and stick the target. He used to put girls up against the haystack and see how close he could throw the machete to them.

In his universe, women had no soul. They were to be slaves of Man.

The girls were required instantly to submit to the men Manson stated to be on the grope-list. Any time, anywhere. The girls supposedly were not allowed to ask for sex but had to wait, though they could smile alluringly if they wanted. Sounds like the Protestant ethic.

Manson is known to blame women for the institution of capital punishment, for jails and for practically all repression.

"We live in a woman's thought, this world is hers. But men were meant to be above, on top of women."

He hated women.

"I am a mechanical boy,
I am my mother's boy,"

went one of his songs.

Manson decreed that only the men could talk to the babies. The women, though they still cared for them, could only speak gibberish to the children. There was rebellion on this. Mary Brunner told Linda Kasabian that she didn't care what Charlie said, she was going to love and talk to Pooh Bear, her baby.

The women were not allowed to discipline the children in any way. After all, the child was the perfect state.

As noted, the women offered food to the dogs before they themselves ate. The children were often fed sour milk, according to Sunshine Pierce. Infant sexuality was encouraged. Susan Atkins told a cellmate later that she used to perform fellatio on infants.

More incredibly, the women in the family were not allowed to ask questions. The word "why?" was banned. Only a few knew exactly what the men were doing. The men had almost a separate life.

The girls were always saying, "He's not our leader. He

falls down at our feet. But doesn't let us step on him." If they did, he'd punch them in the face.

When Charlie would beat any of the girls, they'd say, well, it was really because they wanted him to do it. Snake Lake, for instance, then fifteen, was to become a kind of punching bag for Charlie during his anger spasms. But she stayed on. The family claimed she wanted "attention," so she deliberately angered the Devil. The girls would fight among each other, but the rule was when a man told them what to do, they had to do it immediately. The girls would say, "I don't care or know about you, I've got my love for me." They talked his raps, spoke his language, but over and over again, he told them that he was not really telling them what to do. As a matter of fact, that was the reason that Manson was amazed that he got indicted for murder. Because he claimed he never told anybody what to do. They'd walk around singing little ditties about themselves as "die, Leslie, do die," for that was the essence of the message, to die in the mind in order to live in The Hole.

But Charlie's greatest hold on the girls was fear. Threatening to cut off their breasts was one of his favorite snarls. He'd always manage to commit a few felonies in front of them and to get them involved in murders and the burial of bloody clothes and the wiping down of houses for criminal fingerprints and the forging of checks and the planning of robberies. They'd think they were equally implicated in events, even though they had merely witnessed them. He'd always blend them into this plexus of gore and grime and crime.

Early in the day Manson would "program" the girls—give them a list of things to do. They sewed a lot. Charlie always wore his corduroy vest—embroidered with those witchy whorls. Each girl wove a part of it, sometimes adding locks of human hair with bright threads depicting snakes, dragons, humans and animals in a mural of religious meaning that the family understood very well—it told stories and illustrated the concepts of Charlieism.

And people ask how on earth it happened.

All anybody has to do is open the nearest anthropology book and check out any number of weird religious cults throughout history that, among them, have believed every conceivable thing. Manson's scam was the old live-forever chosen-people hype.

It was all summed up by Country Sue:

"This group of people has come up from millions of years. It's like every one of them is just so familiar that each person is perfect. It's like, you can remember—after you took acid and stuff—you can sort of remember all the lives you've lived, all the people you've been and all the struggles and all the dying and coming back and over and over and over. But this is the last time. Like, the way I feel is like I've got exactly the body I wanted, you know for the last time. The perfect, the strongest one, the one that's going to make it through. And like, I'm willing to die for anyone, anyone who's me, 'cause it's like one soul. . . ."

Manson used to brag how he was a "man with a thousand faces." In a life-style where everything is a hype and a con, that is an assertion of virtue.

On the crime front in May and June of 1969 Manson was in full frenzy. Naturally there are many gaps in trying to depict criminal activities in the summer of '69.

Like any entrepreneur must, Charlie had to scheme constantly since only a certain percentage of the capers could come to fruition. He talked about a thousand capers. He wanted to rob an armored car. He wanted to break into a military reservation and steal weapons.

They had set up a whole network of crime, enabling them to fence anything or readily to get hold of any psychedelic substance they should require. They had a fence and a dope source in Santa Monica for sale of hot items. Manson had a strict rule that whenever he discussed with any of the family members any proposed illegal venture, the person was not allowed to discuss the criminal activity with any other person in the whole universe. Charlie sat at the top of a pyramidal structure of small criminal bricks.

Tex Watson had acquired extensive contacts in the Hollywood area when he was a co-owner of that wig shop on Santa Monica Boulevard. He was active in handling dope deals for Manson. He was completely under Manson's power.

Once someone with a full beard visited the ranch and Tex admired the beard, saying, "Maybe someday Charlie will let us grow beards." And Tex wasn't just dealing nickel bags for Charlie. They were dealing big in acid, hash, pot and sometimes coke.

One L.A. dope dealer interviewed by this writer requested that if one ever ran into a certain family member, now under indictment for murder, one was to ask him for the $2000 he burnt him for in fake hash-bricks in 1969.

Vern Plumlee has told of the large amounts of cash the family sometimes obtained:

"There have been times when the family had $25,000, $40,000—gee, you know. At one time right before I came they had $30,000 and they went down and bought all kinds of sitars, guitars, drums, all kinds of things.

"Then they went out and they set 'em up in the back ranch house. Everybody dropped some acid, got loaded and started, you know, working out on the drums and everything. And at the end of the acid trip there wasn't an instrument that was playable."

It is known that Charlie was considering feeding four of the girls into a Hollywood prostitution syndicate. Manson probably kept up his ties in the pimp-hype from the 1950s when he claims he operated a whore scene out of the Roosevelt Hotel.

When stolen travelers' checks were brought in, various men would try their hand at forging the name. The one able to copy it was the one honored with cashing them.

In early summer 1969, members of the family stole an NBC-TV station wagon loaded up with film equipment. There was tens of thousands of dollars' worth of cameras, lenses and Nagra recording equipment aboard. The truck was dumped and the film equipment buried. Manson approached Gregg Jakobson to try to locate a purchaser but Jakobson refused to serve as a fence for it.

Most of the film equipment was given away. Manson took an NBC camera with him to Death Valley in September 1969.

With the sound-pack the family recorded their song sessions and other activities including the re-creation, in song form, of one of the murders.

Charlie hungered for male additions to the family and specialized in attracting youths with kleptomaniacal tendencies.

John Phillip Haught aka Christopher Zero aka Zero,

and Scotty Davis were young boys from Ohio who got enmeshed in the webs of creepy-crawlie. Zero would die in the fall under suspicious circumstances. A young man named Lawrence Bailey aka Little Larry arrived from a chicken farm in Oklahoma and he joined up.

Zero, Scotty, Vern and Bill Vance formed a crack squad that plundered San Fernando Valley, stealing cars, robbing service stations and uttering forgeries. They even stole a bunch of checks from the back of George Spahn's checkbook and bounced them around the valley.

A human named Brother Bill was an antique dealer in Santa Monica who had helped the family in the past. The family was hard up for mon but Brother Bill refused to continue to give.

Bob Beausoleil aka Jasper Daniels took Bill out to breakfast one morning while Charlie et al., strangely enough, happened along and looted Brother Bill's store of $70,000 worth of antiques and paintings, which were taken to the Spahn Ranch. Bill came storming out to the ranch later claiming that Beausoleil had set him up. But once again, the family waltzed away free.

They buried items like ritual films or Wojtek Frykowski's credit card. Less sensitive material they could hide by crawling beneath the wooden foundation timbers and sticking it on a rafter.

They were always burying things—food caches, the helter-skelter maps, guns, antiques, film. To this day, Manson's Spanish guitar lies buried in Death Valley, awaiting his escape. Shudder, shudder.

They set up a creepy-crawlie dune-buggy assembly plant in the trash dump behind the corral of the Spahn Ranch. They stole Porsches and Volkswagens and brought them to the Devil's Dune Buggy Shop in back of the corral, and then the man would strip off the body and fenders, and cut everything up, and load the cuts onto a truck and cart it away. Then they'd make some dune buggies out of the skeleton Porsches or Volkswagen frames. They would then sell the fresh fashioned dune buggies somewhere out on the desert, in exchange for dope and money. It was creepy-crawlie capitalism.

They ripped off an electric welding set and tools from a rental agency. They ran up an incredible electricity bill for George Spahn by day-and-night welding and drilling at the trash-dump buggy works.

Sunshine Pierce observed it: "He would go out and trade these dune buggies to these guys in the desert. . . . They were hippies, and he would trade these dune buggies to them for dope and money and things that they would steal from these little towns and stuff out on the desert."

They were forced to learn methods of quick auto theft. The family record for hot-wiring a vehicle was evidently held by Sadie aka Susan Atkins. It was rumored that she could hot-wire a vehicle in thirty seconds flat.

On June 24, 1969, thirteen-year-old Virginia Lynn Smith was found murdered in Cobal Canyon, Claremont, California. A person who spent time living at the Spahn Ranch had been dating her. Somebody from Florida has confessed to the slaying. However, considering that over twenty people have confessed to the evil Black Dahlia murder in L.A., anything is possible.

On June 27, 1969, twice-married twenty-year-old Linda Darleen Kasabian, a blond girl with a sixteen-month-old baby girl, Tanya, flew to Los Angeles from Milford, New Hampshire.

Since April 1969, she had been separated from her husband Bob and had been crashing with her mother in Milford. Prior to separation, she and Bob had been residing in communeland, Taos, New Mexico. In 1968, as was noted, they lived for a while in L.A., where once Linda had peyote fruit punch at the house next door to the residence of Leno LaBianca.

At her husband's invitation, she flew west for reconciliation. Bob Kasabian and a human named Charles Melton aka Crazy Charlie invited Linda on a trip they were planning to South America, where they intended to buy a boat and sail the seas.

It is necesssry to discuss at this point the hostilities Manson, particularly in June '69, had with a black drug dealer named Bernard Crowe. The hate scene culminated in Manson shooting Crowe in the abdomen and leaving him for dead.

Bernard Crowe, twenty-seven years old, five feet nine inches, 290 pounds, was a man bearing the nickname Lotsa Poppa. Numerous times he had run afoul of the laws regarding sale of drugs.

He lived in a house at 7008 Woodrow Wilson in the Hollywood Hills above Sunset Boulevard. The house was a famous crash pad in the area, with numerous complaints by neighbors regarding sun-deck sex and dope trafficking.

Manson seemed to have become entangled in hassles with a so-called black dope syndicate in Hollywood, the true facts of which are only partly known.

At the time there was definitely a group of black dope dealers in Hollywood, some of whom were arrested during the investigation of the murders at the Polanski residence.

There was plenty of gossip among those interviewed who lived in the group of houses near Crowe's place on Woodrow Wilson that Manson and his crew were hanging around Woodrow Wilson and Loyal Trail (a short road running right behind Crowe's place).

It seems clear that Manson and select associates used to hang around the Woodrow Wilson area both at Crowe's house and, according to several sources, at singer Cass Elliott's house.

"I've heard that Charlie went down to Mama Cass's place and like they were all sitting around jamming for hours and she'd bring out the food. Squeaky and Gypsy were down there. Everyone would jam and have fun and eat," related a former family associate named Melton.

Hearsay emanating from a tuba player for the Los Angeles Philharmonic Orchestra (who lived near Crowe) says that Manson spent time on Loyal Trail. A lady living right next door to Crowe claimed that the family bus had been parked there for a while. This would have had to have been late '68 when some sort of blue-covered Manson bus was roaming around the Hollywood and Bel Air hills.

One former family "member" interviewed said that in late 1968 some of the family used to visit "Bernie's house" somewhere in the Laurel Canyon-Woodrow Wilson area.

Snake once referred to Crowe as "the Negro member of the family."

The family also stole a red Toyota Land Cruiser for use in Helter Skelter which was owned by a person named Kemp who lived on Loyal Trail about a hundred feet from Crowe's house at 7008 Woodrow Wilson.

Gregg Jakobson has claimed he heard Manson say he

was going to shoot Crowe days before the act was accomplished. It appears that Manson had actually been trailing Crowe, that he had Crowe staked out under surveillance, so to speak.

Sometime in the evening of June 30, 1969, Manson arranged for Tex Watson to burn Bernard Crowe. Watson never made a move without Manson's "programming." All the dope dealers in the family, except Manson, have stated that it was totally Manson's idea to burn Crowe.

In March of 1969 Tex Watson met a beautiful girl named Rosina who lived at 6933 Franklin Avenue in Hollywood, right next to the Magic Castle. (The Magic Castle is reputed to be the home of the Count Dracula Society, a society of well-known film-men and writers who groove behind old vampire movies.)

Tex spent a lot of time at the house on Franklin and occasionally Manson and some of the girls would also visit. A lovely member of the ill-fated Acapulco, Mexico production of the musical, *Hair,* was a roommate of Rosina.

Crowe's version, uttered under sworn oath, at the Manson trial, is that beautiful Rosina Kroner, Tex Watson and Crowe drove to an address in El Monte, California to cop dope. Crowe forked over $2400, allegedly to purchase marijuana. Tex left the automobile and entered the building, then left by the back entrance to return cackling to the Spahn Ranch.

Crowe and Rosina waited for a while, then returned to her apartment on Franklin Avenue. Crowe was enraged, vowing to maim the burners.

In a subsequent interview in a hospital after Crowe got shot in another altercation, this time in the foot—he keeps getting shot—Crowe claimed that it was actually a $20,000 deal and that the $2400 was merely a portion of it.

11

The Locusts (July 1969)

About 2 A.M. on the morning of July 1, a phone call came in over the pay phone by the corral. T.J. answered the call. It was Rosina Kroner and she was hysterical. Bernard Crowe was at her house. He wanted his money and was threatening to kill her. She was calling from her apartment at 5933 Franklin Avenue in Hollywood. She wanted to talk to Charlie.

Charlie talked to her and then to Crowe. They had a heated conversation during which Crowe threatened to come over and shoot up the ranch. Charlie said, "Don't come over here. I am coming over there."

Tex and Bruce and T.J., Danny and Charlie were alone by the dusty corral. Charlie told them that Crowe threatened to do in everybody and he had to be stopped. He said, "I'm going to go over there. Does anybody want to go?" It is not recorded whether or not any hands were raised.

"Come on, let's go," said Charlie to T.J. the Terrible.

Charlie got into the car and put the revolver on the seat between them, the Buntline Special which later was to kill Jay Sebring. The automobile was wrangler Johnny Swartz's yellow-white '59 Ford—the same car which was to be driven to the murder of Gary Hinman, to the Polanski residence and to the LaBianca house.

It was a thirty-minute freeway ride from the Spahn

Ranch to Miss Kroner's residence. Charlie got out of the car and walked up to the front door. T.J. picked up the gun from the front seat and followed Manson. He handed the revolver to Charlie, who stuck it in his belt.

Bernard Crowe wasn't there when they first arrived. Rosina answered the door. There were two men in the apartment, Dale Fimple and Bryn Lukashevsky, a friend of Dennis Wilson. They told Charlie that Crowe was enraged because of the burn. He wanted his money or else he was going to take vengeance on the girl and raid the ranch.

When he entered, Charlie placed the revolver on the table. In a few minutes Crowe re-entered the apartment, and he and Charlie were talking calmly. Charlie told him to the effect that you can't take my friend's life, you must take my life. When Crowe said that no, he didn't want to harm Charlie, just the people that had burned him, Charlie had him where he wanted him.

According to Dale Fimple, Charlie performed some sort of "ritualistic dance," and then got ready to leave. He picked up the gun. Rosina was sitting on the bed; T.J. and the other two men were at the door. Charlie was standing about eight feet from Bernard Crowe, gun in hand. Crowe stood up and said, "Are you going to shoot me?"—putting his hand to his abdomen, the evident trajectory of any possible bullet.

Charlie pulled the trigger—click. Nothing happened. Charlie, perhaps in an act of instant theater, laughed and said, "How could I kill you with an empty gun?" The trigger clicked again and then there was a shot—and Crowe fell down in the hall, clutching his stomach.

Charlie turned to one of the men and said that he liked his shirt and wanted it. It was a leather shirt; Charlie liked leather shirts. Quickly the guy gave it up, fearing a bullet. Charlie then walked over, kissed Bernard Crowe's feet and told him he loved him. Other versions say he kissed the feet of the guy who gave him the leather shirt. Then he split.

Manson thought Crowe was dead.

When they were driving back to the ranch, T.J. claimed that Manson told him he didn't like the way T.J. was looking at him because it made him question himself and he shouldn't question himself. Not Jesus. It was his first public gunfight, an act that triggered two months of violence, leaving around fifteen people dead.

Tex, Bruce and Danny were sitting on the boardwalk in front of the bunkhouse when they arrived. Charlie told about the shooting and T.J., freaked out by the apparent murder, walked back to the corral where he spent the night meditating with the horses. The next day he left the ranch.

An ambulance picked Crowe up at 4:15 A.M. and took him to the USC General Hospital Medical Center. He sent a telegram announcing impending surgery to his sister in Philadelphia, then was operated on by two surgeons. He evidently stayed in the hospital till July 17, after which he returned to 7008 Woodrow Wilson to recuperate.

The bullet lodged in Bernard Crowe's torso remains there to this day. In the spring of 1970, Bernard Crowe was incarcerated in the L.A. New County Jail, where he ran into Manson again. If it is true that Charlie thought Crowe was dead, it must have been a weird surprise to see him in the jail. When the prosecutor learned that the bullet was still inside Crowe, he was very eager to secure possession of it since it would definitely link Manson with the murder weapon. They offered to send Crowe to the Mayo Clinic for a painless extraction of the lead, but Crowe refused.

The next morning after Crowe was shot, things were panicky at the ranch. There were scared looks in the eyes of Tex, Charlie and Bruce Davis. Tex pulled out a wad of money—saying that it was $2500—and blew air into Danny De Carlo's face by fanning the bills.

T.J. was in grim shape. He announced that he didn't want anything to do with "snuffing people." And Charlie was, in the words of De Carlo, "chewing his ass off" about "getting on his case"—as they say in jails when a person butts into the affairs of another.

After the shooting of Crowe, there occurred a fluke event that had dire consquences. Tex Watson recalls that the next day "a report came in on the news that the body of a Black Panther had been dumped near UCLA the night before. This made us a little uneasy, since we hadn't figured on getting involved with the Panthers." That is, for some reason difficult to analyze, the family thought Lotsapoppa Crowe had been the Panther. Manson's paranoia about blacks grew grotesquely thereafter and vomited itself into modern history.

The story of the shooting of the black man spread throughout the family, but in mutated forms. Always it took the form of a so-called Panther meeting, not in its real context of a dope burn. The Crowe shooting is so garbled in its telling that there is a suspicion that there were several blacks shot and that only Crowe's shooting has surfaced.

One story, for instance, has it that there was a black guy chopped to death at a "meeting" attended by about ten people at a location near a college campus. This story emanated from a girl who supposedly overheard the family talking about it. Dan De Carlo said Manson said that the two witnesses called a couple of days later and told Manson they had dumped the body in a park.

In any case, Manson subsequently was to tell several versions of the shooting of Mr. Crowe, usually placing it in the context of a Black Panther meeting.

Manson seems to have considered any self-assertive black man a Black Panther. He certainly didn't know anything about the Panthers since in a jail interview he didn't know of Huey Newton, for instance. Manson was totally paranoid over reprisals from the "Black Dope Syndicate."

More specifically, the family was afraid that the black friends of Bernard Crowe would storm the ranch and kick faces. Each night armed foot patrols were set up to guard the grounds. Often men with guns would stand on the roof above the boardwalk at night awaiting the supposed Black Panthers. Little Larry slept on top of the haystack as a sentry.

One day, De Carlo discovered the Buntline special used to shoot Crowe sitting in its holster in the "gun room" on top of his radio. They wanted him to clean it, which he was hesitant to do because Dan was afraid it had been used to snuff the black guy.

In the first few days of July, Bob Beausoleil and his pregnant girl friend moved to the Spahn Ranch from their place in Laurel Canyon. Bob and Kitty moved into one of the "outlaw shacks," perhaps the one painted "Alice's Restaurant." Two humans named Little Joe and Fat Frank lived in nearby shacks, according to a dope dealer who dealt in the neighborhood.

At his second murder trial, Beausoleil testified that he returned to the Spahn Ranch because Gregg Jakobson had called him and said that the movie deal was on, that Terry Melcher wanted to do it. Jakobson, according to Beausoleil's testimony, wanted Beausoleil out at the ranch to help with the music for the sound track.

Just before he went back to live at the Spahn Ranch, Beausoleil second-storied the Gerard Agency to snatch up his contract and his demo tapes. He was seen by Gerard Agency employees slithering out of a second-story window. Shortly thereafter a videotape system was stolen from the Gerard Agency building which former Gerard executives suspect may have been ripped off by Beausoleil or Manson.

It is known that Manson approached his old friend and former manager of the Galaxy Club, stage hypnotist William Deanyer, with a videotape system to sell. Manson told him that the video system would help him in his hypnotism act.

On July 2, Tex Watson went to Butler's Buggy Shop on Topanga Canyon Boulevard to get a dune buggy customized for desert specifications. He wanted a forty-gallon gas tank installed so that the machine would have that 1000-mile raid diameter. The frame was to be fixed so that there was a sleeping area within it. He paid for it with $350 cash in advance.

On July 4, Gypsy aka Yippie aka Cathy Share and aka Manon Minette, saw fit to take herself to Topanga Lane near the beach in Topanga Canyon to visit Charlie Melton, a bearded friend who lived in a canvas-covered stake truck notable in that it had an automobile seat perched atop its cab. There Gypsy was to fall into a scheme which would add considerably to that helter-skelter contribution jar in the saloon.

Linda Kasabian, her husband Bob, Blackbeard Charles and Jim and Juli Otterstrom—all were living in the stake truck, preparing for that trip to South America. Charles

Melton had inherited around $23,000 and some of that was going to pay for the trip. The rest he had been giving away, much to the delight of various Topanga residents.

Inside Melton's trailer, Gypsy picked up his guitar and began to sing "Cease to Exist." Gypsy began to tell Linda about the Spahn Ranch and particularly about Charles Manson. She said that children were the most important thing at the ranch, that everything was communally owned, that everybody was going to live in the desert. She told her about The Hole, and the river of Gold which Linda had already heard about from Hopi legends. It sounded out of sight.

According to Linda, Gypsy told Linda that Charlie was above wants and desires—he was dead. That it wasn't Charlie any more. It was the Soul. They were all Charlie and Charlie was they. And the men. There were men there who were great lovers, lots of them, ready for love that was total. The others in the trailer were shining Gypsy on but Gypsy said that their ego wouldn't let them listen to the Truth.

Mrs. Kasabian, though reconciled with her husband for only seven days, was having trouble with him. It seems that already he and Charles Melton had cut her out of the trip to South America. Gypsy invited her to come to the Spahn Ranch.

Linda had been planning that day to go to the July 4 Love-In on Topanga Beach but she went to the Spahn Ranch instead, taking her sixteen-month-old Tanya with her. Everybody hugged her when she and Tanya arrived at the ranch. They took from her her identification and her carried belongings. All was love and peace.

And she was ready for it for she had grown up in the dope-trip love generation, roaming sweet from commune to commune since she was sixteen. Tanya was taken, of course, to join Pooh Bear. Linda was told that Tanya's ego must remain free from the programs of the mother, therefore she was not to speak to her with the English language.

Mrs. Kasabian soon became pregnant after intercourse with Beausoleil, Manson, Tex, Bruce, Danny, Karate Dave, Clem et al. It was Beausoleil, however, who claims to be the father of the child.

It is interesting to note that the family scarfed up all I.D.s and credit cards to be held in one central place, usually with Squeaky, in George Spahn's house. When a new runaway appeared they would gather up the i.d. almost like a ritual. Linda Kasabian was no exception. Thus, when Charlie told her to drive to Sharon Tate's house, she had to obtain her driver's license from the central i.d. cache.

That night Linda Kasabian encountered her first mystic experience at the ranch. She and Tex Watson made love in the dark shed and it was, as she later testified, unlike anything she'd ever experienced. It was total, but eerie, as if she were being possessed by some force from without. Her hands were clenched at her side at the culmination of the sex and her arms were paralyzed.

Later she asked Gypsy about the meaning of such paralysis. Gypsy reportedly told her that such things occurred when you don't give in completely to a man; her ego was dying.

Tex, during the loving, learned about the inheritance money that Charlie Melton had in his truck. He was all ears. He kept up a steady chant of there is no good/there is no evil, and everything belongs to everybody. She accepted it and decided to rip off Charlie Melton.

Linda slept that first night on the mattress on the roof of the Longhorn Saloon. That was the last night that Charlie allowed anyone to sleep on the roof. "The Panthers could easily spot us and kill us," he said.

July 5 was a day of happiness for the family. In the morning Tanya, Linda, Gypsy and Mary Brunner went to Topanga Canyon to go to the beach. They ran into Charles Melton and Bob Kasabian behind the Topanga Shopping Center by the creek. They smoked some hellweed and Bob and Charles went off to downtown L.A. to get their passports for their trip.

Linda and the girls drove to Melton's canvas truckhouse to get her possessions. She dug up a buried Bull Durham pouch full of thirty pink acid tabs she had brought from the East.

She packed up her gear, including household utensils and the tape-handled knife that was later to kill Abigail Folger and the old Buck clasp knife that Sadie would lose in a stuffed chair at the Polanski residence. Then she went into Melton's duffle bag and removed a Velvet tobacco pouch containing fifty $100 bills which she took to Chatsworth to give the Wizard: $5000.

Charlie was working on his dune buggy with Snake and Brenda when Linda was brought to him to be introduced. To Linda, Manson looked magnificent dressed in his buckskins. Charlie asked her why she had come to them. Linda told him that her husband didn't want her any longer and that Gypsy said she'd be welcome here. Charlie received the money. He scanned Linda's legs: "He felt my legs; seemed to think they were okay," as she later testified with a smile. He was pleased.

He was told about the probability that Charles Melton and friends would be coming to the ranch to get back the money. Manson then decided to send Linda to the cave down the creek behind the ranch, to hide from the wrath of her husband.

For her efforts, Linda was rewarded with a grotto grope. When on the night she stole the money, July 5, Manson came to the cave where Linda was staying, Manson and she got after it on the cave floor in the presence of Gypsy, Ouish and Brenda. Up to his old tricks, Manson told Linda that she was hung up on her father. She admitted that she had a stepfather she didn't dig.

All the next day, high up the hill by the cave, the young ladies scanned the dirt driveway of the Spahn Ranch below with binoculars. And, just as predicted, Mr. Melton, Bob Kasabian and Jim Otterstrom pulled into the drive in their stake-bed truck.

Charles Melton asked someone by the boardwalk to locate Gypsy and Linda. The person left and returned with Manson, who rewarded Meiton with kill me/kill you routine.

According to Meiton, Manson said, "Who are Linda and Gypsy? I can't even remember their names."

Melton replied, "They took $5000 from me."

Manson said, "What's money? Nothing is yours." Then Charlie took out his knife and handed it to Melton, urging him to kill Charlie with Charlie's own knife.

Mr. Melton refused the proffered knife. Manson said, "Then maybe I should kill you to show you that there's no such thing as death."

At this point, Melton and company were quick to drive away into the wind.

The person named Bryn Luwashevsky who witnessed the shooting of Bernard Crowe called Dennis Wilson several days later and told him about it. Gregg Jakobson heard the conversation and evidently told Melcher. Melcher was very upset about it and that may have been the cause of the final rupture in any and all plans to record or film Manson. And Manson was really counting on Melcher to come through.

One day Manson asked Jakobson if Terry had a green spyglass set up outside of his beachhouse in Malibu.

"Yes," Jakobson replied.

"Well, he doesn't now," chortled Charlie.

So it was Doris Day's telescope that the family used when scanning for Black Panther raids from the Santa Susanna hilltop.

Slowly, Manson began to become infuriated with Melcher. He was welching on his commitmnents. One day Manson sent Leslie and another girl to Malibu Canyon to see Melcher. Melcher wouldn't see them but talked to them through the intercom at the door. "They used to talk about kidnaping him," Miss Lutesinger remembered.

Kasabian leaped with full force into the ranch lifestyle. Tex Watson and Linda Kasabian became close companions, a fact which may hold the answer to many baffling aspects of the so-called Tate-LaBianca murders.

When Gypsy testified at the trial she spoke of Linda Kasabian's eagerness after stealing the $5000.

"She got a whole lot of attention for that. She just kept on bringing back presents."

Manson quickly accepted Kasabian, she claims, and began, she says, to give her trusted assignments. Manson told Linda about the good old days long gone when he had his bus full of girls traveling freely. Those were the days.

Manson would paraphrase a song by John Lennon:

"Christ you know it ain't easy,
You know how hard it can be,
They're gonna crucify me."

This was absolute proof that Lennon was gonna take

the cross upon himself. "They crucified me last time but now John Lennon is taking my place," Charlie chortled.

Charlie promoted himself as a miracle healer. Once he cut his arm and said to Kasabian something like, "Someday I'll be able to heal myself." Another time supposedly he sat down and talked with a dying horse, Zane Grey, and miraculously the horse recovered. Then there also was the miracle of the club foot. Someone, unknown as of this writing, came to the ranch who had an enlarged foot and limped. Charlie allegedly cured him over the days, gradually, by a series of commands.

Things remained crusted with a sense of normalcy though family life was rapidly becoming berserk. Every evening George, Ruby Pearl and one of the family, usually Squeaky or Ouish, would drive to the International House of Pancakes in Chatsworth to eat. On the way back they stopped to load the truck up with corn for the horses. Then Ruby would drive to her own house and aged George would sack out in his house by the movie set, attended by his teenage geriatrics squad.

The girls spent a lot of time cleaning tools and dune-buggy parts, organizing them and helping to build the buggies. Leslie, Katie, Little Patti and Brenda, for the most part, were occupied with the children.

But Charlie was really jumpy.

Once Snake dared to talk during one of his lectures at dinnertime and Charlie grew furious and told her never to speak when he's talking.

One day in July Charlie was late for chow so the family started to eat without him, a sin. He got really angry when he arrived and stormed out of the house. Tex, Bobby, Clem and Bruce followed him out, begging forgiveness. Soon they all came back and Charlie played the guitar and they held a songfest. All was happy again.

And his raps about imminent death from the blacks caused waves of paranoia—especially on acid trips. Charlie loved the fear emanating from the silent circle of paranoid young men and women in the Longhorn Saloon listening for the oncoming footsteps of the marauder-killers.

On July 10, Charlie Manson took a wad of $100 bills into Butler's Dune Buggy Shop and purchased for $2400 four dune buggies for the battalion. His trusted assistants, Bill Vance, Danny De Carlo, Tex and Bobby, now would possess their own legally purchased iron horses of Helter Skelter—and the work began on them immediately to modify the dune buggies for the north desert campaign.

One day, around the 10th or 11th, a black man with a dog stopped on the road by the Spahn Ranch and checked it out. He then drove down and looked at the trash dump—where the dune-buggy assembly line was located. Tanya and Bear were playing by the "gun room" on the boardwalk. This triggered off the fear that perhaps the Panthers might sometime gun down the children, so it was decreed, and it came to pass, that all the children were to be kept at a new camp by a waterfall in the hills about a mile north of the Spahn Ranch on the other side of Santa Susanna Pass Road. They set up a tent and a campfire to cook. All runaways, all children and some of the older girls were kept there.

It was possible to walk up the Spahn Ranch creek to the new camp. Charlie wanted to be able to drive the dune buggies all the way up to it, which was difficult because of the rocks and boulders in the creek bed. He ordered the girls to remove the boulders. They did.

Linda was proud when she was named by M. to drive the girls back and forth on the creek bed from the waterfall to the ranch.

There was also a visit from two carloads of black men with cameras. Charlie hid in the hollowed-out haystack by the corral; the girls ran to hide in the trash-dump dune-buggy factory. The blacks, eight in number, took pictures and generally checked out the ranch, then split. Family paranoia dictated that this had to be an advance Black Panther snuff unit who were out to wipe the aware white world-savers. They found candy wrappers in the weeds across the road from the ranch—another sign that the Panthers were watching them.

On July 14, Danny De Carlo and Bruce Davis went to a store called Surplus Distributors on Van Nuys Boulevard in Van Nuys. There they purchased several weapons including a .45-caliber pistol and a nine-millimeter Radon pistol, under assumed names, a violation of federal law. Davis used the name Jack McMillan and De Carlo used Richard Allen Smith.

Davis later told the police that Crowe had said he was going to kill them, therefore they bought the weapons.

On July 15, Officer Breckenridge of the Los Angeles sheriff's office was hovering above the Spahn Ranch in a 'copter when he noticed "at least three" Volkswagen floor pans scattered about, indicating to him at least the possibility of car theft and car strip. The sheriff's office was beginning to gather data on the car-theft aspect of the ranch. In a month they would raid.

Late one night during the five days that the family camped at the waterfall, the girls were busy sewing an ocelot skin upon Charlie's dune buggy. Malibu Brenda had liberated various furs from her mother's closet. Her mother was to flip out when she was to see her furs, worth thousands of dollars, garlanded upon his buggy in the *Life* magazine cover story a few months later.

Just before dawn, Charlie sent Brenda from the ranch with scissors bearing a wonderful announcement: it was time for the sacred witchy Tonsure Rite. Charlie said that they were ready to cut their hair—for, at last, their egos were dead. It was special privilege time. Snake announced that she did not want her long red tresses shorn. She was told they'd hold her down and do it anyway so she submitted to it. Katie was spared the hair chop because her full witchy mane was to serve as the magic blanket when they were to find refuge in The Hole.

The next day the tonsured young ladies went to the ranch to reveal themselves to the Wizard. They had left one long lock uncut, each of them, hanging down. The girls, according to legend, each buried one of their cut hairs and each also burned a hair in the fire. They saved their hair, each wrapping and typing their own into a swatch which they gave to the Soul. Charlie was pleased. "It looks good." He then told four or five others to snuff their hair also.

Around July 15, 1969, Charlie decided to move everyone in the family about three miles up Devil Canyon to a secluded spot in the woods, off a fire road. There they remained for about a week until a motorcycle patrol of police rousted them off the set.

From the ranch, from the cave and from the Fern Ann Falls campsite, around twenty of Manson's followers thronged to a new location, a pleasant grassy croft with a birch tree bent over the edge of it, providing a natural tent pole. The girls set up a ten-man tent and placed a parachute over the dune-buggy factory as camouflage.

Unfortunately, fire trucks used a nearby road and there was a riding trail cut just up the hill from the camp, so that quickly the camp was spotted. Almost at once a police helicopter checked out the camp. Manson or somebody in the family seems to have threatened firemen patrolling the dry fire trails with menacing motions of their "Tommy guns"—as the family called their submachine guns.

They camouflaged with brush the short entrance driveway that led from the fire road to the camp. The girls strung a telephone wire a mile or so down the rocky Devil Canyon so that the field phones could be set up for guard outposts.

There was a twenty-four-hour guard set up at the mouth of the canyon on a hill that overlooked the Spahn Ranch itself. The purpose was to watch for the police and the "Panthers." If any should invade, the watch was to phone up to the camp with a warning. The watch was divided into three shifts.

Charlie decided to have the NBC motion-picture camera handy and to string up lights as if a movie were in preparation. That was to be part of the excuse to the police, should they raid and find long-hairs and young girls.

At one point Charlie told Linda and Vance to go hot-wire a large truck with a generator on the back and drive it to the camp. They drove a car to the location of the truck; she was to drive the car back, he the truck. The mission was aborted, however, when Vance couldn't get it started, and Kasabian became afraid. Charlie and Vance went back and started it up. They drove it up the steep canyon to the camp. Tex needed the generator so he could work on his dune buggy and finish it.

They used the generator for three to four days after which Vance then took it back and parked it a block from the owner's house. Linda and an unknown visitor went to pick Bill up and drive him back to the ranch.

When everybody moved to the canyon, they left a skeleton geriatrics force back at the ranch to take care of George and to help cook for the ranch hands. Included in the group left at the ranch were Little Patti, Zero, Squeaky and Ouish.

Charlie told the girls to hang "witchy things," usually made from beads, feathers and leather, from the trees so that, by touch, they might return to the campsite at night. The girls set up a camp kitchen. Staple sustenance was provided by a hundred-pound sack of brown rice. The girls were told to secure additional food from the wild, a difficulty in such dry unfertile country. Linda Kasabian located a hot sulfur spring which soothed with its mud the endemic family skin problems: sores and lesions.

People would swim in a large wooden water tower nearby. At night they would lie about on sheepskins and sleeping bags while Danny played drums and Bobby or Charlie would sing and play the guitar. And the creepy-crawlie chorale would raise itself in unison.

Devil Canyon is rather dry but heavy rains in the winter of 1968–69 had kept the creeks full of water even into the summer so there was water aplenty in which to bathe and to wash the dishes nearby but no one was to go there in the daytime or in large numbers.

On Sunday, July 20, 1969, some of the family listened to the Apollo II moon landing on Danny De Carlo's radio in the bunkhouse and gun room, located at the end of the Western movie set, by the corral.

Around July 20 a sixteen-year-old boy named Mark Walts was found by the roadside in Topanga, gored to death as if struck by an automobile several times. His brother, according to Danny De Carlo, came storming out to the Spahn Ranch to confront Manson about the death since the young boy had been supposedly staying there. Several police officers visited the Spahn Ranch to investigate the death.

Sometime in this era, a young girl, referred to in police records as Jane Doe 44, was murdered and buried in a shallow grave near Castaic a few miles northeast of the Spahn Ranch on Whitaker fire road. The girl, totally unidentifiable by the time she was found months later, wore a short, puffy-sleeved dress which several have identified as a dress they saw at the Spahn Ranch.

Around July 20, the day on which Mark Walts died in Topanga, Charlie went into one of his fits of anger. The only known reason was that Gypsy had sinned by rolling a conga drum down a hill.

Ella, Sadie, Mary and Ouish ran down to the ranch from the Devil Canyon camp upset and sweaty. Charlie was beating Gypsy. In fact, he was going nuts. Kicking her in the ribs, hitting her in the head, until she couldn't move. He had yelled at Mary, in substance: "Why don't you take Bear to your mother? That's what you want to do." Then he smashed his guitar, drums, saying something about how "nobody cares enough for the music." He even smashed the sound-pack for the stolen NBC camera.

The police found the outside container of the sound system by the Devil Canyon camp. After the recorder was smashed, the transistors from it were placed in Baggies and were hung around the canyon and ranch as those witchy nighttime trail markers.

Within two days after Manson went berserk, the police raided the Devil Canyon creep camp and everyone had to move back to the ranch. Fortunately for Manson, the artist John Friedman and his family, who had been living in the back ranch, moved out, hauling with them the out-of-service International Scout given to the family by Juanita, and Helter Skelter was able to move in.

Charlie made arrangements with George to rent the back ranch. He moved the trailer truck back there and for a while everyone, including the children, lived in the ranch building. Nouveau mattress-on-floor was the decor of the barren back ranch.

The police raided again, however, so Charlie had a few girls set up the tent in a thicket of woods down the creek across from the house. This is the residence referred to as "the wickiup" in the testimony of Barbara Hoyt, a family follower who was later fed an LSD-drenched hamburger in Honolulu to keep her from testifying. The children and all runaway girls were enjoined to sleep in the wickiup.

The dune-buggy works was set up again in the dump behind the bunkhouse. Security precautions were established by Manson. No one was to hang out at the front ranch, except those assigned tasks there by Satan.

When they moved into the back ranch, some of them reminisced about the good old days of 1968 when they had first lived there, how groovy it was with all those tapestries and pillows bought with Juanita's money. They also recounted the tale of the fire orgy of October '68 where no one got burnt even though they were hurled into the flames.

But it was tough going. It will be remembered that the Transcontinental Development Corporation was hot in pursuit of the various properties in the Spahn Ranch area for that German-American resort. Unfortunately for Manson, and another pressure upon him, was the fact that George Spahn's property line ran right through the middle of the back ranch building causing some problem regarding who actually owned it. Transcontinental had purchased a chunk of land adjacent to the back ranch and claimed the back ranch belonged to them. The officials of the Transcontinental Development Corporation were naturally eager to wipe the hippies out of the area so they began to pressure the family to leave the back ranch.

In honor of reacquiring the back ranch, Charlie decreed that there be an orgy, an event far-famed in the annals of Manson family lore, for it was to be the Initiation of Simi Valley Sherri. Simi Valley Sherri was a fifteen-year-old local girl who tended horses at the ranch. Her last name is not mentioned here because she has since returned to high school.

The orgy was attended by about twenty people plus four "guests"—whose identity is unknown at this writing.

The event probably took place about July 22, 1969. Some people have claimed that it was filmed. Charlie positioned the fifteen-year-old in the center of the assembly, then stripped her bare except for her bikini underpants. Everyone stared. Cameras whirred. She was less than willing. Charlie pushed her to the floor and began to touch her head to toe. He started to kiss her neck and her breasts. Simi Sherri bit Manson on the shoulder, causing him to punch her in the face.

According to Linda Kasabian, a key participant in the orgy, Manson said, "Sherri, remember the time when I chased you down the creek with a brick in my hand and said if you didn't make love to me I was going to hit you over the head and rape you?"

She lay quiet and Manson ripped off her panties. He

told Beausoleil to make love with her. This Beausoleil did.

Then Charlie flashed the signal to begin indiscriminate apertural-appendage caress and conjugation. "The whole scene was perversion like I've never seen before," declared Linda Kasabian. And was she active.

There was tri-love between Kasabian, Leslie and Tex Watson. Clem then lay with Linda. Snake Lake twined in love with the twenty-year-old Mrs. Kasabian. "Sometimes I looked up," Mrs. Kasabian testified at the trial when asked if she observed what was happening in other parts of the room.

12

Getting the Fear

One of Manson's summer 1969 raps was about how groovy fear was—is. "Getting the Fear," as he called it, was an exquisite physical experience. It's actually an old LSD phenomenon—conquering a period of intense fear. But Manson decided that the entire substance of expanded consciousness was fear—the "infinite plain of fear unto infinity."

He says the girls kept asking him what he meant about getting the fear. Manson would tell them, in substance, "Well, I go into Malibu and pick a rich house. I don't steal, I walk into the house and the fear hits you like waves. It's almost like walking on waves of fear."

He advocated going into wealthy homes where there were lights on. He taught that "the rich piggies" inside would be too scared themselves to do anything. He showed the followers how to shim open those pushover summer climate doors with a thin plastic card. He demonstrated how to cut open a screen with a knife.

"Do the unexpected," he said. "No sense makes sense. You won't get caught if you don't got thought in your head."

Forthwith all the trusted girls of the family began to jump in the waves of fear, crawling into houses and stealing jewelry and furs. They would wear dark clothing and open windows silently and crawl about in that Malibu living-room fear surf. Then they would leave, taking booty.

The actual term "creepy-crawl" began to be used in July of 1969 and was invented by the girls. "I didn't tell them to creepy-crawl. They just did it," Charles Manson said on June 24, 1970.

Sadie, it seems, was a creepy-crawler among creepy-crawlers. Dressed in a black cape and her newly purchased genuine Roebuck jeans, she would go scout for targets, peeking into windows. De Carlo says it like this: "And that's all they did. Spend all their time up in the rich district up there in Beverly Hills, and the Brentwood area. All around there where all the rich people hang out. And their theory was to make such a gruesome thing out of it, like he wanted to go as far as hanging 'em up by their feet and slice 'em."

It seems strange that all of a sudden they got into wearing black capes. The girls made Charlie one that reached to the floor. With a flourish Manson tried it on, remarking how no one for sure now would see him when he creepy-crawled. Mary Brunner had a black cape. Sadie had a cape. Squeaky, according to Danny De Carlo, used to dye clothing black in a pot in the Spahn Ranch kitchen.

There are subjects associated with the Manson case that are so soaked in evil that the mere knowing of them is like a nightmare.

All kinds of people, including Beausoleil, Manson, Vern Plumlee and others, admitted that people sometimes made motion pictures of family activities. The family made films in Topanga Canyon, Malibu Canyon, Death Valley, in Hollywood, at the Spahn Ranch.

Vern Plumlee said this about family filmmaking: "They made home movies; yeah—I watched the family make movies, you know, just crazy movies."

"What about subject matter?" he was asked.

"Well, just anything, you know, just anything that came up, like if a person was having a heck of an acid trip, they filmed that, you know. And like just goofy things."

Plumlee said that they had three super-8 film cameras with which they filmed.

He was asked about violent films. "Like dancing, you

know. Like, they'd be dancing with knives, you know, and they'd pretend they were cutting each other up or something like that. I really didn't think that much of it—just another weird thing that they did." (Laughs.)

Another family associate independently described in an interview what seems to be the same pretend-to-hack type of film. He was more exuberant about it than Plumlee was: "It's really a trippy flick—uh, it's maybe seven minutes long—but it's Charlie and everybody like running round in a circle . . . with knives—you know, the belt with the knife on it—and they're holding the knives, you know flicking around and uh—for about three minutes this goes on and then they just start, you know, starting charging everything and everything with the knives, you know, trees, to the house, and so on."

Plumlee told of several friends of the family who processed films for them. One was a person who lived on a dirt road in Granada Hills, east of the Spahn Ranch, who may have done film developing for the family. For a long time, the family films seemed merely to be sexual—with the added spice of a few famous faces and bodies. Ho hum.

Once this writer was in Los Angeles posing as a New York pornography dealer with Andy Warhol out-takes for sale. There was an opportunity at that time to purchase seven hours of assorted erotic films including Manson porn collected during the pretrial investigations. But the price was $250,000. Then there was a note which was written to a reporter by a person named Chuck, a friend of Gary Hinman, claiming possession of films of "Malibu and San Francisco ax murders."

Finally a person was interviewed who had been hanging around on the edges of the family for about two and a half years. He told a tale which, if true, and it seems to be, ushers in the ugly age of video-vampirism. He told about movies which the family would show at night, evidently in the woods behind or above the Spahn Ranch. It was sort of an outdoor light show with several movies shown at the same time.

"The family had things where they'd show flicks, you know, like light-show type things; they were running four or five different movies at once; you know, playing tapes at the ranch."

He said they played various tapes as a sound track. For movie screens they hung up white sheets. They rented four or five battery-operated eight-millimeter movie projectors down in Los Angeles for these grim events. The batteries supposedly ran the machines for a half hour or so. And the films shown seem to have been reels of family happenings, music, the already noted knife dance, lots of sex—but other films also.

According to a study called "The Blood Sacrifice Complex" by E. M. Loeb (printed in the *Memoirs* of the *American Anthropological Association,* Volume 30) there were human sacrifices performed in much of prehistoric America but somehow the California area was spared—spared, evidently, till recently.

The person who has been interviewed shall remain anonymous for obvious reasons.

After graduation from high school in the Midwest in 1968 this individual came to Haight-Ashbury where he met the family when they were crashing on Clayton Street. He possesses a lot of information about the Haight, the Haight-Ashbury Free Clinic, the Waller Street Devil House, etc. Manson, he says, invited him down to live in Los Angeles. He claims to have scrounged around with the family off and on since then.

During a year of investigation, there were numerous rumors and reports from people interviewed that there had been occult and magic ceremonies on various secluded beaches north and south of Los Angeles.

He alleged that the site of some of the filmed ceremonies was located on the beach by Highway 1 near the restaurant called Pete's Beef across the street from the County Line Mobil station. He also pointed out other locations.

There were three types of films that he seems to have witnessed: (1) family dancing and loving; (2) animal sacrifices; (3) human sacrifices.

The dates he gave for the making of the films varied. He claimed that some were made in 1969 and some, O Lord, in 1970 in the summertime.

In most of the films, he claimed that a lot of the participants were dressed in black and were wearing crosses, though some of them, however, wore white clothing. Some wore black hoods but others had no hoods on.

In the dog-blood flick, the film allegedly began with everybody sitting around singing. Then it was all hideousness.

Here is his description of the dog-sacrifice movie:

"It was like a nighttime thing. It started out with the people, you know, everybody was sitting around—and they just, uh, one of the cats came, and uh, it was about eleven o'clock at night and uh, they started their trip, right—and uh, type thing. Just sitting around and a guy brought out a thing of blood and everybody took a hit. Then the guy was, you know, poured it over everybody. Then, like, this other cat came by and uh, and then this whole funny trip . . .

"They cut up a dog. Then they brought in a girl in there—two girls. They took their clothes off and poured the blood of the dog on top of the girls. They just held the dog. And they took the girls and they put the blood—and the bodies—all over both of them. And everybody balled the two girls . . . it was a couple, two couples—they were being, uh—but I'm not, you know, this was a while ago. But I remember they were all taking hits of blood. It was really weird . . . I recognized maybe eight to ten people in that film. You know, people that I know, people that I've seen come to the ranch, you know, people that have, you know, for the weekend or so . . . They had two or three similar to that that I've seen of theirs."

He further fingered two key Manson female followers as having taken part in the drinking of blood, one of them having sexual intercourse while blood was poured on her. All on film.

"I've only seen a few sacrifices," he said. "I've seen one with the dog. I seen, uh, one with the cat—that cat was the most gruesome."

Here is part of the interview dealing with the cat:

Q. Where was it?
A. It was outside. This was the one I was talking to you about, on the beach.
Q. Where they had the cat?
A. And the dog.
Q. Same place?
A. Yeah. I think they had their monthly things there. The out-of-doors freak-outs.

Q. You know where on the beach that is? Malibu Beach?
A. No. It's a private beach, uh, it's like just on the boundary line of Los Angeles County and Ventura. It's on Highway 1.
Q. What's the name of the house?
A. It's not a house. It's just a beach.
Q. Who owns it?
A. I don't know. Nobody. It's like a private beach I don't even know who owns it.
Q. What day of the month (do they meet)?
A. Wednesdays.
Q. Full moon?
A. Or full moon, whatever.
Q. Every other Wednesday?
A. Something like that, but, you know, I've seen three or four movies like that and the cat movie was the stupidest one I've seen; it was gruesome. They took firecrackers . . . what do you call it, M-80's, and lit it and had the cat sit on it. Blew the cat to smithereens. It was just so gruesome. Sickening.
Q. What'd they do with the blood?
A. They just smeared it all over themselves and poured blood all over themselves, you know, they had maybe a pint of blood, they were, they'd pass around and everyone'd get a hit off of it. Those movies were really gruesome.

He gave considerable information about a short movie depicting a female victim dead on a beach. This film, he contended, was part of a larger movie.

He was asked initially if he was aware of such movies.

A. I, I, I knew, I know, I only know about one snuff movie. I, uh, you know—
Q. Which snuff movie do you know about?
A. I just know like a young chick maybe about twenty-seven, short hair . . . yeah . . . and chopped her head off, that was . . .
Q. Whereabouts was that?
A. Probably uh, from the scenery, somewhere around Highway 1, and the beach.
Q. Who'd they look like? Who was in the film besides the decapitated girl?

A. It didn't show anybody's face. It just had everybody on black creepy-crawlies with the black hood and uh—
Q. What do you mean black? Black hoods with eyeholes you mean?
A. (*Nods*) and uh—
Q. What else?
A. You know, long black type dress(es).
Q. Any crosses on?
A. No, it was all black and with these kind of straight type things to go over their faces with slits and they, uh, people were just dancing around it. Nobody ever said what it was. It was a short thing maybe five minutes.
Q. What'd the girl look like? What was the scenario?
A. What was the what?
Q. What was the scenario? Was she tied up? Did she look willing?
A. She was dead. She was just lying there.
Q. She was already dead?
A. Yeah. Legs spread, uh. She was nude but nobody was fucking her. They said her head was just chopped off and she was just laying there.
Q. That's when the movie started? They didn't show the actual sacrifice?
A. *(Shakes head no)* They showed people throwing blood all over, all around the circle.
Q. Did it look like anybody was the leader?
A. No, maybe it was a short. You know what I mean, don't you? It could have been just something, you know, shot, you know, that they didn't edit in one of the other movies. It was only five minutes long. It was just a small thing.
Q. Five minutes is thousands of frames. It sounds like one I know about. It was inside the footage that was shot this summer?
A. (*No answer)*
Q. What was the rest of the movie like?
A. I didn't see it. I just, you know—
Q. Red-haired?

A. Yeah.
Q. The head was just lying there?
A. Right next to the body.
(Gives a demonstration with his own head)
Q. How many people were in the film with black clothes?
A. Five. They were circling around the body.
Q. Was there a campfire?
A. Campfire was about here *(points)* and you could see a few other people walking around, but you know.
Q. Were they in robes, all the other people too?
A. It could have been a continuation of something else, but I didn't . . . It was kind of an interesting flick. (!!)
Q. Was she lying on a rock?
A. No, she was just, you know, on a beach.
Q. On the sand?
A. Yeah. Just really weird.
Q. Did it look like a protected area?
A. Boy, you can't do stuff like that unless it's really protected.
Q. Do you think it's that area on the beach on Highway 1 where that restaurant is?
A. It doesn't look—I mean—there was so mu—you know—you can usually tell that one place if you've seen it, but you know it wasn't that place—it could have been somewhere else along Highway 1; they could have done that and dug a little hole and dropped in the remains. You can hide shit like that. This was a short one. Only five minutes long. The only difference in the Apogee one and the dog movie was that there was no crosses.
Q. In the dog movie they had the hoods on too?
A. Well, they didn't have them on all the time. Sometimes they had them off.
Q. But sometimes they had the pointed cowls on?
A. But the thing is, you can tell who it was by the faces, you know. It wasn't always the same.
Q. You don't think it was the same people then?

A. It probably—unless they didn't have crosses on. One time they had crosses, another time they didn't.

Q. They wear gloves?

A. No.

Q. What kind of knives did they do their work with?

A. Bowie. Twelve-inch Bowie knives. It's the ones I've seen. I saw Bowie knives and a hatchet. One of the persons had a Bowie knife on this side and a hatchet on this side.*

*[Footnote from 1989: In the eighteen years since this interview, no films depicting actual murders or murder victims have surfaced. See Chapter 25.]

SECTION 2

THE MURDERS

(July 25, 1969–August 15, 1969)

13

The Death of Gary Hinman

Compared to the Spahn Ranch, the house on Cielo Drive was like a citadel of mental health.

Things were pretty casual at 10050 Cielo Drive while the owner, Mr. Altobelli, and the lessees, the Polanskis, were all in Europe during April, May, June and July 1969.

John Phillips, the songwriter, told a reporter that there were weirdos hanging out at 10050 Cielo Drive that summer of the type he had been studiously avoiding for years.

In April and May of 1969, Abigail Folger took an active part in the Tom Bradley mayoralty campaign. According to a co-worker, she worked at the Youth Headquarters on Wilshire Boulevard. She also worked for a few months as a volunteer helping children in Watts. During the mayoralty campaign, Abigail Folger became interested in a black group called the Street Racers who evidently served as security forces for the Bradley rallies and offices.

Sometime in June, after Mr. Bradley's defeat on May 26, Miss Folger and her mother visited New York City for a while. Abigail would travel frequently, almost commuting from Los Angeles to San Francisco.

In the spring and summer of 1969, Mr. Frykowski made lengthy daily entries into notebooks in order to work on his grasp of the English language. He was hoping to become a movie scriptwriter.

In early June, Sharon Tate was seen at a party in London's Mayfair section. After the party she was driven home in her new Rolls-Royce. "It was Roman's birthday present to me," she said. "We're taking it back to Hollywood to be with our seventeen cats, three dogs and the new baby. I can't wait to get back to start on the nursery."

Around July 7 or 8, Frykowski learned that Sharon was coming back around July 20. He and Miss Folger began to move clothing from Cielo Drive to their own home on Woodstock Road.

A Polish artist named Witold Kaczanowski aka Witold K. had been brought to the United States through the kindness ot Roman Polanski. He naturally came to live in Los Angeles where he cultivated the Polanskis' circle of friends. He was staying, during the summer of murder, at the Woodstock Road home of Abigail Folger and Wojtek Frykowski. He was a frequent house guest at 10050 Cielo Drive during the spring and summer of 1969. An actor friend of Voityck by name of Mark Fine also had been staying at the Woodstock address but moved out the second week in July, having stayed one week.

Early in July, several friends of Frykowski from Canada promised him samples of a new drug called Methlenedioxylamphetamine or MDA, a euphoric stimulant with overtones of aphrodisia that was coming into vogue. According to police reports, Frykowski was being set up to serve as a wholesaler of quantities of MDA manufactured in Toronto.

Both Mr. Frykowski and Miss Folger were enjoying MDA on the night they died.

In mid-July Frykowski's friends from Canada went to Ocho Rios, Jamaica allegedly to create some sort of movie about marijuana use there. This Jamaican movie project was a front for a large marijuana import operation involving private planes secretly winging the dope to the United States via Florida and Mexico. Investigation into the operation after the murders resulted in one of the biggest dope busts in Jamaican history.

They were making films on Cielo Drive. One day in July William Garretson, the caretaker, saw Wojtek Frykowski taking pictures of a nude lady in the swimming pool. A cable-TV repairman named Villela came to the

Polanski residence and encountered some sort of a nude love set going on.

Around July 14 Wojtek ran over Sharon's Yorkshire terrier, Saperstein. The dog had been named Saperstein after the doctor in *Rosemary's Baby* who prescribed weird herbal drinks during her satanic pregnancy. Wojtek called London with the news. In London, Roman Polanski then purchased another Yorkshire terrier, which was named Prudence.

Sometime in the middle of July, Brian Morris gave a catered party for 150 at the Polanski residence, seemingly to round up members for Bumbles, a new private club that was to serve the Polanski circle.

After finishing her filming in Rome, Sharon joined Roman in London, where he was finishing the script for the talking-dolphin spy thriller, *Day of the Dolphins,* which he was scheduled to direct for Paramount Pictures. Sharon ran an ad in the *London Times* for an English nannie to come to L.A. and interviewed dozens of candidates, selecting one named Marie Lee.

Sharon was too pregnant to travel by over-ocean air, so she booked a stateroom on the *QE 2.* She had just read Thomas Hardy's *Tess of the d'Urbervilles,* which she left in their bedroom in London and told her husband it would make a wonderful movie. When he kissed her good-bye, as he later wrote in his autobiography, Mr. Polanski had a premonition he'd never see her again. While walking back to his car, he told himself to snap out of it, "forget I'd ever had such a morbid feeling . . . have a ball, see some girls."

Mrs. Polanski asked Abigail Folger and Wojtek Frykowski to stay at 10050 Cielo Drive until her husband was to return from London. On Sunday, July 20, Abigail Wojtek, Jay Sebring and Lieutenant Colonel Paul Tate and Sharon watched the moon landing at Cielo Drive.

In the days before her death, Sharon was seen in local department stores purchasing baby supplies. Her white Rolls-Royce was on the way home from London. The nanny would come as soon as her papers cleared immigration.

She was bubbling with happiness over the impending birth of the baby. She was exercising in preparation for the delivery. She bought books on child care and supplies for the nursery, which was being built in July in the north wing of the house.

Jay Sebring was a frequent house guest at the Polanski residence whenever he wasn't overseeing his far-flung business interests.

Jay Sebring served in the U.S. Navy during the Korean war. He was short, about five feet six, and slender, weighing maybe 125 pounds, and intense. Paul Newman, according to the San Francisco *Chronicle,* said that Sebring's method prevented him from losing his hair. Actor George Peppard allegedly spent $2500 to fly Sebring to a movie location to trim his locks. Frank Sinatra used to fly Sebring to Las Vegas to cut his hair. "He was a legendary name in hair styling," commented his friend Art Blum.

He was born with the surname Kummer, the son of a CPA in Detroit. In Hollywood, he changed his name, incredibly enough, to correspond to that of an automobile racetrack, Sebring.

Actors and singers and businessmen would play chess in Sebring's shop. When a particularly illustrious client would arrive, he would rush to cut his hair himself. By the time of his death, the fee for his personal haircut was fifty dollars. If his assistants performed the cut, the fee was about a third as much. Is it possible to imagine paying fifty dollars for a haircut at the time?

The corporate offices for Sebring International were located above the hair shop at 725 North Fairfax in Hollywood.

In partnership with public relations executive Art Blum, Sebring opened another shop in the summer of 1969 in San Francisco at 629 Commercial Street. Shortly afterwards Sebring rented a houseboat in Sausalito, California, just north of San Francisco. Throughout the summer, he flew frequently north to check on his new enterprises. On several occasions he visited Colonel Tate and family at Fort Barry. Mr. and Mrs. Tate would stay at Sebring's houseboat in Sausalito when they came to San Francisco. One Saturday, either the last Saturday in July or the first Saturday in August, Sebring threw an afternoon publicity party at his hair shop in San Francisco attended by Paul Newman, Miss Folger and a throng of guests. In the days following, Mr. Sebring was in Los Angeles where he spent a great deal of time at the Polanski residence with Abigail Folger, Wojtek Frykowski and Sharon Tate.

There was a so-called darker side to Sebring. The police, after his murder, found films at his house which revealed an interest in hoods, whips, studded cuffs and people chained submissively to fireplaces.

Every day for about a week Charlie instructed Mary, Bruce Davis, Bobby and various others to use a bunch of the ripped-off credit cards to purchase a large supply of helter-skelter equipment. They bought hundreds of dollars' worth of sleeping bags, dune-buggy tools, lots of Buck clasp knives, mess kits, baby clothes.

Each girl wrote down her measurements. Charlie wanted each one to have a straight-looking dress and a dark creepy-crawlie outfit. Included in the clothing were ten or so sets of dark blue T-shirts and genuine Roebuck jeans.

A young man from Simi Valley named Hendrix came across a car wreck in San Bernardino where a man named Dries had died and his credit cards were strewn on the highway. Hendrix grabbed up the credit cards and took them to the Spahn Ranch.

Hendrix, a seventeen-year-old known to the family merely as Larry, was an example of the psychopathic youth attracted to the family. He was another gun freak, operating a gun business "on the street." He was also a teenage demolition expert, claiming that he once blew a hole in the side of a mountain. Once he was arrested and accused of blowing up a house.

Hendrix incurred Charlie's wrath by stealing a huge motorcycle using one of the family automobiles. Someone spotted him. He buried the bike in the sand and later claimed that as soon as he was released from the insane asylum, he was going to dig it up and it would be all his.

Late in July the family bought some bayonets and sharpened them at a shop on Devonshire. These were added to the arsenal in De Carlo's "gun room." The bayonets and swords, etc., were all kept in readiness in a slit between the door and the wall.

There was one caper discussed in July '69 involving the robbery of a gambling casino near Box Canyon. Manson and Linda Kasabian, according to Kasabian, actually drove up a steep dirt road to the casino to plot the caper. The plan was he'd have one of the girls stand at a nearby stop sign and ask for a ride from anyone leaving the casino. Manson would follow behind him and make him pull over then seize the person's wallet. An alternative was to follow someone to his home and then get all his valuables.

A person named by the family "Karate Dave" spent several weeks during July at the Spahn Ranch. He helped the group with karate lessons—which Tex Watson would use when he was kicking bodies at the Polanski residence.

There was a car shortage in the family in late July. The '68 Plymouth Roadrunner had been repossessed. The sleazy dune buggies could not be legally driven on the road. De Carlo's bread truck had not reappeared as yet. About the only good automobile, a yellow and white 1959 Ford with back seat removed to accommodate garbage crates, belonged to a ranch hand named Johnny Swartz, who lived in one of the house trailers. It was the car driven to the Polanski residence and to the LaBianca residence.

Manson seemed to have a number of private interpersonal relationships, outside of his so-called family, where he was the tormentor. There was one girl who worked at the Moonfire Inn in Topanga on whom he pulled a terror scene. He threatened to kidnap her baby and take it to the mountains. When a fireman named Witt came to the ranch and told Manson to cut the weeds for fire safety reasons, Charlie threatened to gouge out the fireman's eyeballs. Manson threatened to kill Dennis Wilson's son, Scotty, when Wilson refused to give him money. And then there was Hinman.

Thirty-two-year-old Gary Hinman was near to getting his Ph.D. in Sociology from UCLA. He had always helped out the Manson family. People in Topanga Canyon would send people to crash for a night at his house. For about a year he had been intensely interested in Nichiren Shoshu Buddhism, a militant sect headquartered in Japan with Los Angeles headquarters located on the Coast Highway at the Santa Monica Beach.

In Hinman's house were found considerable lists of names of potential converts to Nichiren Shoshu Buddhism. Found in the house were an abundance of gohonzas to give to new members. A gohonza is a religious scroll used by the sect.

Hinman had a small setup at his house where he made quantities of synthetic mescaline. A young married couple who lived with Gary right up to several days before his death were partners with him in the manufacture of the mescaline. "We were making mescaline. It was a really long, long process but the advantage was that it was really cheap. You bought things and no one would ever connect the things you bought with what you were going to do. You could order zillions of them from the chemical supply houses and they'd never get hip, not unless somebody really did some thinking. Gary had a degree in chemistry." His partner's wife has indicated that Hinman had developed a method of manufacture whereby two steps in the process were eliminated.

About four days before Gary Hinman was murdered, Eric, the mescaline partner, visited Hinman's house at 964 Old Topanga Canyon Road. When he entered the small hillside house he found Gary Hinman on the phone, arguing with Manson. He says: "When I came into the house they were arguing. Like, Gary was really into Nichiren Shoshu and the concept of leadership and the concept that people needed to be directed, which was something that Charlie was very opposed to, and so they were in a heated discussion about that and then it was like there was a response: it was pretty together and I talked to Gary afterwards to verify what Charlie said—He said, you know, like it's your last chance, Gary. And Gary responded to that: 'I'm sorry, Charlie. I'm not going to sell all my things and come and follow you.' Those were his exact words.

"And so Charlie said, in response to that, that he couldn't be responsible then for the karma that Gary was going to incur. He then reiterated that it was his last chance. And Gary said, 'I'll decide . . . I'll take care of my own karma.' "

Manson has claimed to jail visitors that Hinman had made drugs and that certain individuals had threatened Hinman as a result of the sale of bad dope. Hinman, he said, came to him seeking protection.

On Thursday, July 24, Manson sent Ella Bailey aka Ella Sinder over to Gary Hinman's house to get the money and then to kill him. Miss Sinder had been a close friend of Hinman. Although she was a long-time Manson follower, she was not willing to snuff anybody for him. Bill Vance, who loved Ella, tried to intercede with Charlie, but Charlie was furious. So Ella and Bill Vance left the ranch together and went to Texas. The family was enraged with this, muttering among themselves how they were going to kill Bill and Ella if the two should dare to come back to the Spahn Ranch.

Everything was murder. One day around this time, Cathy Gillies Myers went off by herself without checking out. When she returned Tex threatened her. "Don't you ever leave here without telling someone where you're going, next time I'll kill you, your life means nothing to me," he said, according to Linda Kasabian.

The next day, July 25, 1969, Kitty Lutesinger asked Beausoleil if she could leave. She was getting a little weary of living at the ranch, the constant hassles, the raids and the general atmosphere of impending doom. So Bobby said that he would ask Charlie if she could leave. He asked Charlie and Charlie said that under no circumstances could she leave the ranch.

Charlie and Kitty apparently never got along, for Charlie would say that she looked too much like his mother, also a thin, short redhead. Manson came up to Kitty and accused her of trying to trick Bobby into leaving the family. He threatened to torture and to kill her. That afternoon Manson was seen pacing up and down the Spann Ranch boardwalk, sword in hand, fencing with his shadow, jabbing the sword at bales of hay, angry.

Also that afternoon, Bobby and Charlie went for a ride in his dune buggy up Devil Canyon. They checked out an old abandoned mine whereupon, according to Beausoleil, Manson noted that it would be a good place to hide a body. Manson was armed. Indeed, he was armed: the magic sword was stuck in a metal tube on the steering column of the dune buggy; a pistol was in a holster on the bucket seat between Charlie's legs; and there was a knife strapped to his ankle.

Some say the long hair swatches shorn from the girls were tied together and were affixed to the dune-buggy roll bar. The canopy of ocelot fur decorated the back deck near the machine-gun mounts. Manson shifted in the bucket seat toward Beausoleil and asked if it were true that Bobby was thinking of splitting from the ranch. And when Bob said yes, Charlie, according to Bob, said, "Maybe I ought to slit your motherfuckin' throat." Manson used his old con routine, saying that Bobby knew too much to be allowed to leave.

Abruptly, according to Bobby, Manson changed the subject to Hinman and asked Bobby if he would be willing to go over to Gary's house and try to get some money out of him.

Beausoleil, at his second murder trial, testified that the reasons for getting money from Hinman were to help the family move to the desert. "I was supposed to tell Gary about the idea of making the desert a place for a lot of people. Gary is the type of person who would be interested in something like that, making a place for people where they could express themselves in music."

Linda Kasabian remembered that around dusk she was standing in front of the ranch and Bobby and Charlie were in the bunkhouse talking. Sadie and Mary were outside the bunkhouse standing patiently, waiting for Bobby to come out so that they could go someplace. Sadie told Linda Kasabian that they were going to get some money and that she and Mary had been chosen to go in order to work out a personality conflict.

During his trial for murder, Manson admitted several times the Hinman affair was about some botched dope deal. In his autobiography, sixteen years later, he finally revealed what may be the truth. He reaffirmed that Hinman was making mescaline, slowly, in his home lab. "For several weeks," he states, "Bobby had been moving Gary's stuff off on a group of bikers, without any problems. But one morning three of the bikers came riding into the ranch and wanted to see Bobby. The bikers said the latest batch of stuff he had sold them was bad, laced with poison. Some of their own group had gotten deathly ill and some of the people they sold to were also sick. They wanted their money back."

Manson's version could be true, or it could be meadow muffins.

The amount in question, M alleges, was $2,000. Manson called Mr. Hinman, who wanted to take a look at the putatively poisoned mesc. Hinman then balked at forking over two thousand. Manson says he asked for enough mescaline to turn a profit of $2,000, and they'd pay him later. "Can't do that," he reportedly replied. "I'm getting things together so that I can go overseas for a few weeks. Besides, you guys still owe me some on the last stuff you got."

Beausoleil, Sadie and Mary Brunner were driven to Hinman's house by Bruce Davis in Johnny Swartz's Ford, the same car they would drive to the murder of Sharon Tate and the others.

Sadie describes the grim trio climbing the steps to Hinman's house. Mary Brunner was silent, perhaps recalling how Hinman had once helped her keep her baby when the authorities had sought to take it. "Bobby seemed nervous but his natural arrogance compensated for it, and he was as cocky and confident as ever. I thought of his competitiveness, especially with Charlie. He was gripped with the need to prove that he could do anything Charlie could do. He seemed to need to prove it to himself, to Charlie, and to all of us." The death dozens of Beausoleil and Manson was about to begin.

At the Spahn Ranch, while Beausoleil and Sadie and Mary were working Hinman over, the family ran the walkie-talkie system from the movie set a half mile or so to the back ranch. A girl would stand guard at the front ranch, prepared to call the back ranch in case of any invasion by the police or the blacks.

Hinman had been living with a young, red-haired girl named Diane right up to the end of his life. She and Gary were seen the day before the family began to torture him, smiling and waving as they drove through Topanga Canyon in Hinman's 1958 red and white Microbus with a red thunderbird emblazoned on the side. It is hoped that Diane, believed to have been a runaway from San Diego, was not subsequently killed by the family.

That afternoon Gary Hinman had gone down to Los Angeles to obtain a passport. In two weeks he intended to undertake a religious pilgrimage to Japan. He had taken with him Glen Krell, who owned a music school where Hinman taught piano, bagpipes, trombone and the drums. Hinman called Krell to ask if Krell would sit in as a witness for him in the obtaining of his passport. So about 2 P.M. they drove downtown to Los Angeles from

Hinman's house at 964 Old Topanga Canyon Road, and returned to Krell's house about five o'clock in the afternoon. Hinman stayed there until about 7:10 when he said he was going to go to a meeting somewhere. That was the last time Hinman was seen on his feet.

Krell had wanted to borrow the Volkswagen Microbus for that weekend but Hinman said he couldn't because he was going to haul some rocks in for his driveway. But that Krell could use the Microbus the following weekend.

Hinman was very friendly, and he gave a warm "Hi!" as he welcomed Sadie, Mary and Beausoleil. The welcome did not last. They asked for money and his autos, and he told them to leave.

They talked to Hinman for a couple of hours, but it was no use. Beausoleil had brought with him the nine-millimeter Radon pistol purchased by Bruce Davis in Van Nuys a couple of weeks previous. Beausoleil pulled the gun on Hinman and informed him that they weren't kidding.

Bobby punched Hinman, Atkins recalls, and Gary spit out a piece of tooth. They began to fight. Bobby fired the pistol, then handed it to Sadie, whereupon he and Hinman battled furiously, rolling on the floor. Sadie put the gun on the table, and Gary Hinman lunged for it, picked it up and held it on Mary, Bobby and Sadie.

Then the gentle musician, instead of calling the Malibu sheriff's office, did something that cost him his life. Sadie: "With tears in his eyes, he handed the gun back to Bobby. 'I just don't believe in violence,' he said. 'Here, you take the gun. I don't want it. Why don't you just go? Just leave me alone.' "

Bobby and Hinman went into the living room, where Cupid tried to talk Gary out of the money. Hinman lay on the couch.

They called up the Spahn Ranch and told Charlie it was no use because there'd already been a scuffle and gunfire and Hinman wouldn't do a thing for them. Shortly thereafter, close to midnight, Bruce Davis and Manson, waving his sword, arrived at the Hinman house. Charlie was angry. Right away he barked at Hinman that he wanted "to talk about that money." Hinman began to shout at him, telling him to get out and take his family with him and Manson raised up his sword and hacked

Hinman's ear. It was an ugly five-inch wound, cutting deep into the jawbone area and angling up through the ear.

After this, Manson and Davis split, evidently in Hinman's Fiat. Before leaving, Manson told Hinman he'd better give up the money or else. Those left behind tied Hinman up and placed him on the rug on the living-room floor next to his bookcase, where he lay wounded, cursing Manson and vowing vengeance. They decided they'd stay up all night and keep watch over him so that he should not escape. They pulled up a chair alongside the bleeding body. They gave him a drink of wine or beer, and Sadie went down to the Topanga store to get food, bandages and some white dental floss to sew up his gaping wound. Beausoleil and Mary thoroughly searched Hinman's house, turning it upside down, breaking open a cash box, looking here and there, but they couldn't find the money.

Hinman wouldn't tell them for a couple of days where the pink slips for his autos were. Once Beausoleil fell asleep, and Hinman tried to escape and was beaten badly. Finally Hinman signed over the VW microbus and the souped-up Fiat, dating the slips July 26, 1969. There is one report that they stole Hinman's bagpipes from the house and took it with them to the ranch after they killed him.

On Saturday, July 26, two friends of Hinman, both also associates of the Manson family, tried to contact Gary Hinman while he was held victim by the family prior to his death. One, a boy named Jay, called Hinman's house on Saturday afternoon, July 26. The alleged purpose of his call was to try to get Gary to rent him the lower apartment in Hinman's house at 964 Old Topanga Canyon Road. A girl answered the phone, supposedly Sadie Glutz, talking with an English accent. The English voice told Jay that Gary was in Colorado, where his parents had been involved in an automobile accident. Maybe it was actually an English girl who answered the phone. Another person from Santa Barbara named Dave showed up in Hinman's house in person. A female Caucasian, none of the family acoording to Dave, answered the door and wouldn't let him in.

Sometime late Saturday or early Sunday, they called

the Spahn Ranch and, according to Danny De Carlo, Manson told them to kill Hinman: "He knows too much."

It is known for certain that Hinman was threatening to expose the family and their activities, perhaps to the police, and that the family might have to break up. So it was decided that he would have to die. There is another version that says the death was a result of Hinman suddenly starting to scream.

Manson hints that there was probably enough money around the ranch to pay off the biker creditors. "The bikers had phoned while Bobby and the girls were at Gary's," he alleges, "and my message to them was that we were working on it, but they might have to give us more time. I told them the connection wasn't coming through, and someone might have to go north where we were sure we would come up with enough money to straighten things out.

"Some of what I said were lies, but I was buying time. Truth is, there might have been enough money around the ranch, but if I could come up with some more drugs for them, I wouldn't have to put out the dollars. With the mark-up for the replacement drugs, I could square things up and still be out less than half the money they felt was owed to them. I knew there wasn't much truth to their story of it being bad shit, anyway. But with the situation at the ranch being what it was, I wanted a group of bikers on my side if the blacks did come down on us."

Manson had said that they were all set to take Hinman out to the ranch to let him heal his wounds but that Beausoleil panicked, evidently when Hinman started screaming out the window. Whatever the case, he was stabbed twice in the chest by Beausoleil, one of the wounds cutting the pericardial sac and causing Hinman to bleed to death.

As he died, they put him on the floor of the living room near his bookcase. Above him they fashioned a makeshift Buddhist shrine for the Nichiren Shoshu faith. As Gary Hinman lay dying, they gave him his prayer beads and he chanted "Nam Myo Ho Renge Kyo—Nam Myo Ho Renge Kyo," the chant of his faith, until he lapsed into unconsciousness.

Mary and Sadie removed the bloody bandages from Hinman's thread-sewn face. They gathered all the bloody towels and clothes and took them away to dispose of elsewhere. There was somebody's black cape, bloodied—perhaps Mary's, perhaps Manson's—that was carried out of Hinman's house and thrown away also.

They covered Hinman up with a green bedspread. On the wall in the corner of the room just above Hinman's head, someone scrawled, in Hinman's blood, "POLITICAL PIGGY." To the left someone fingerpainted in blood the paw of a cat, intended to be a panther. With a narrow brush someone painted the claws of the paw. They wanted the police to think that black militants committed the murder.

They wiped the house down for fingerprints and burnt some documents, evidently linking the family with Hinman, in the living-room fireplace. They locked all the doors and crawled out the side window. As they were leaving they began to hear Hinman making a lot of heavy rasping sounds, so Beausoleil climbed in the rear window and went over to Hinman's body and started smothering him, and Sadie came in and grabbed a pillow and put it over his face until he lay still. Mary pulled Hinman's wallet out and removed twenty dollars, then thrust the wallet halfway into his back pocket.

Then they tripped down the steep, wooden staircase to the street, where they hot-wired Hinman's VW van painted with the thunderbird.

According to Mary Brunner, they were hungry after they left the house and drove over to the Topanga Kitchen at the shopping center, where they had some cherry cake and coffee. They then drove back to the Spahn Ranch. When Hinman's Microbus arrived at the ranch, some of the girls saw that there were some paints in the back so they used them to paint some pictures. Then right away Mary Brunner, Linda Kasabian and Kitty took Hinman's Fiat into Simi for a garbage run.

That night, as witnesses later told police, some of the family got together for a songfest and tape-recorded a re-creation of the murder of Gary Hinman in musical form. Each person played a role. Someone played the part of the dying Gary Hinman, who is supposed to have mumbled several times, "I wanted to live, I wanted to live."

One Father Ryan of the Order of St. Augustine claimed

that Charles Manson, or Manson's simulacrum, a short hirsute hippie with a new beard, on Sunday, July 27, 1969, approached the back door of his parish house located about a half-mile from the LaBianca residence. "I'm Jesus Christ," announced the short fierce individual, according to Father Ryan. The Jesus-claimer looked at the father with a cold hard stare beneath heavy eyebrows. He asked the father why he was a priest and evinced an intense dislike toward the priesthood. The father claims he shut the door in Manson's face. The incident has no doubt provided the basis for many a sermon delivered by the good father on Sundays since.

Later that eventful day and night of July 27, around 1 A.M. Charlie was lurking near the Spahn Ranch on Panther patrol. He had concealed himself and his dune buggy in underbrush near the turnoff from Topanga Canyon Boulevard onto Santa Susanna Pass Road, awaiting the invasion of hostile forces.

A group of police cars from the California Highway Patrol and from the Malibu sheriff's station, about five in number, turned onto Santa Susanna Pass Road, preparing another raid on the Spahn Ranch about a mile and a half away. The police gathered together near the turnoff to finalize their raid game-plan because they came across Manson's hidden dune buggy.

Officer Sam Olmstead of the sheriff's department approached Manson and asked him what he was doing. According to Olmstead's testimony at the trial, Manson said that he was watching for Black Panthers who were expected to attack the Spahn Ranch.

According to Sheriff's Deputy George Grap, Manson said, "We got into a hassle with a couple of those black motherfuckers and we put one of them in the hospital," after which Manson told him that the blacks were going to wreak vengeance. He said that the "Panthers" had been out to the ranch several times scouting it out, riding horses.

Manson then pulled a great con routine on the assembled officers. He told them that the people back at the ranch were heavily armed and that, were the officers suddenly to raid, they might think them to be attacking hordes of Black Panthers and open fire. So Charlie obtained permission from the officers to proceed first to the

Spahn Ranch and cool out the gun-toters. The police agreed to this. Charlie then leaped into his dune buggy, peeled out and raced back to the ranch, jumped from the buggy, raced into the Saloon, warned everybody, whereupon the youth pack fled to the four winds, leaving behind only their warm sleeping bags.

The five police cars were right behind Manson when he leaped and ran into the Saloon. The officers checked the buildings but no one was there.

Officers Grap and Olmstead ran what are called DMVs on the automobiles in the ranch driveway to see if any were stolen. One happened to be the red VW bus with the white thunderbird on the side belonging to the recently deceased Gary Hinman. When they called in the license number and it came back as belonging to Hinman, one of the officers said, "Hey, I know Hinman; he must be out here visiting."

Charlie flipped part of his threat trip upon the officers by drawing their attention to the dark steep hills north of the Spahn Ranch. He told the officers that he had people scattered throughout the hills with guns trained upon the officers and that on Manson's command the police could be wiped out. He told police officer Olmstead that only dune buggies could reach his hidden troops, and to forget about reaching them with their patrol cars.

According to Deputy Grap, as he was filling out the standard Field Investigation Report (FIR), Manson approached him about joining up forces to wipe out the "Panthers." "You know, you cops ought to get smart and join up with us; those guys are out to kill you just like they are out to kill us. I know you hate them as much as we do, and if we join together we could solve this problem."

Horse wrangler Johnny Swartz was arrested during this raid for "false evidence of registration" for the '59 Ford.

On Monday afternoon, July 28, Bob Beausoleil went into the bunkhouse-gun room-office-undertaker's parlor where he joined Charlie, Danny and Sadie—who was sewing a knife case for Charlie. Mary Brunner came into the gun room in a huff, angered by rumors that Sadie had told Shorty Shea that "Charlie killed a black man and I don't know who else." According to Beausoleil and Snake

Lake, Mary told Sadie that she was going to kill her unless she kept her mouth shut.

Charlie, taking up the theme, smashed Sadie's head against the wall, muttering something about Shorty "knowing too much." Unfortunately for Manson, there would be no wall in Sybil Brand Jail only three months later upon which he might bash the babbly head of Glutz as she confessed to Virginia Graham.

At 3:07 P.M. on July 30, somebody at the Polanski residence called the Esalen Institute at Big Sur, California. Charles Manson himself visited the Institute only three days later.

On Tuesday, July 30, Bob Beausoleil went back to the Hinman house to wipe down the house more thoroughly for fingerprints. The house was full of flies. Beausoleil neglected to remove a fingerprint from the kitchen door with twenty-six points of identification linking him to the house and to Death Row.

The same day that Bobby went to Gary's house to clean it up, his girl friend, the pregnant, attractive Kitty Lutesinger, ran away from the ranch after Charlie had threatened, according to Miss Kitty, to carve her up, accusing her of trying to lure Bobby away from the family.

Frank Retz, the agent for the Transcontinental Development Corporation, was on the property north and west of the Spahn Ranch at the very moment that Kitty made her move to escape. She went along the underbrush toward the back ranch in order to find a stretch of road away from the main ranch complex whereupon she might hitchhike out of the area safely.

Mr. Retz had driven to the property with the then current owner, a Mrs. Kelly, in order to negotiate purchase of the land. Just minutes previously they had stormed in on the back ranch which, it will be remembered, was on the property line, and demanded that Manson and the others leave the premises. When Mr. Retz and Mrs. Kelly returned to his car they discovered that it had been robbed of Mrs. Kelly's pocketbook. Right at that time, Miss Lutesinger ran through the brush and asked for protection from Manson.

Retz drove Miss Lutesinger to a police station and she was transported by police officers to her parents' horse ranch. This sowed the seeds for the dissolution of Helter Skelter even before the murders were committed. For the police started visiting her home to get information about the Spahn Ranch, which they considered an illegal haven for runaways and an assembly plant for stolen dune buggies.

After returning home Miss Lutesinger was very afraid and kept all doors to her parents' house locked for several days because Charlie, she said, had told her he would kill her mother and sister if she left the ranch. She refused to answer the phone, even when Bobby called to say he was going to San Francisco.

Gary Hinman missed participating in a bagpipe parade in Santa Monica on the 27th and his friends began to worry. On Thursday, July 31, three of his close friends, fellow chanters and Nichiren Shoshu Buddhist adepts, came to his small brown-shingled house and walked up the steep ivy-sided steps to encounter the many flies of death swarming in and out of the open window on the second-floor front of the house. They called the police.

Late in the afternoon, a call came into the L.A. County sheriff's homicide office on the third floor of the Hall of Justice in aromatic downtown L.A. with details of a death in Topanga Canyon, a man badly decomposed, a hippie, so to speak; possibly a suicide. The sheriff's homicide officers handle all murders that occur in unincorporated areas of Los Angeles County and the two officers on duty that afternoon were Sergeant Paul Whiteley and Deputy Charles Guenther, two formiable gentlemen indeed.

They could have left the matter for the evening watch to handle, since their shift was almost over, but they decided to drive out to Topanga Canyon to check out the possible crime. After surveying the scene they felt it was murder, and from the state of the body, the murderer had at least a week's jump on them.

They sent out for a couple of six-packs of beer and some room freshener. The smell in the house was intolerable. For five days Officers Whiteley and Guenther spent almost all their waking hours inside the residence sifting through Hinman's personal effects, trying to locate the culprit. The earliest suspects were the couple who had been making mescaline with Hinman, but they were quickly cleared.

These two sheriff's office homicide detectives, Whiteley and Guenther, were the ones mainly responsible for bringing down the house of Manson, but it would take about ninety days—days replete wlth the screams of uncounted victims.

In fact, the $25,000 reward set up by Peter Sellers, Warren Beatty, Yul Brynner, John Phillips and friends perhaps should have gone to Officers Guenther and Whiteley instead of going, as it seems to have gone, to Virginia Graham, Shelley Nadell and a young man who would find the .22 caliber revolver used at the Polanski-Tate house.

14

The Anvil into Tartaros

On August 1, the pages of the newspapers were crowded with outer space news—the first pictures of the moon, a report from Mariner 6 on climatic conditions on the surface of Mars, astronauts in motor parades across America.

Elvis Presley, with fifty gold records hanging on his wall, opened a four-week engagement at the International in Las Vegas. In San Francisco there were five homicides.

One day in early August, Linda Kasabian and pregnant Sandy Good went to Topanga beach to panhandle and to enjoy the ocean. They were picked up by a movie actor named Saladin Nader in an old white Jaguar. Mr. Nader had starred in a Lebanese movie called *Broken Wings,* about the youth of poet Kahlil Gibran. Sandy and Linda went with Saladin Nader to his apartment at 1101 Ocean Front in Santa Monica. Mr. Nader showed the girls pictures of himself in various movies. There, he and Linda got after it in the bedroom while Sandy took a nap.

Later he drove the girls to a shopping center in the San Fernando Valley. Early in the morning of August 10, Linda and Manson and Sadie and Clem would return to his house on Ocean Front to try to kill him.

Meanwhile, at the ranch, Charlie got rid of the nine-millimeter Radon pistol used at Gary Hinman's murder by trading it to that boy from Simi named Hendrix for a blue '55 Chevy four-door sedan.

Charlie gave one Mark Arneson Hinman's VW Microbus. Arneson also wanted Hinman's souped-up Fiat but Beausoleil needed it. The family wanted Mark for their membership rolls. Leslie Van Houten was working on Mark to join the family and she put him on the no-sex list to put the pressure on him.

On August 1, Charlie was talking about taking a trip up north to gather recruits. Beausoleil testified at his trial that he was called into a trailer where he had a conversation with Bruce Davis and Manson. According to Beausoleil, Charlie told Bruce he should be willing to do what "he" did at Gary's; he told Bruce that Terry Melcher should be ready for death; it was his karma.

Charlie had his ear-hacking sword at hand and told Bruce, according to Beausoleil, that he should be willing to go into the city and cut and slash until he had blood and guts up to here—motioning to his chin.

Around 6 PM. that day, a resident at the Crest Haven Ranch on Fern Ann Falls Road up by the waterfall campsite saw some bikers prowling along the road and he heard automatic weapons' fire coming from the Devil Canyon and Ybermo Canyon area. After George Spahn went to dinner, it was always rifle practice time. The carbine was evidently Charlie's favorite weapon. He'd let all thirty rounds go in a burst of rapid-fire, standing in the surf of Fear.

In the evening, the girls cleaned up the Hostess Twinkies Continental Bakery truck, outfitting the bed in the back for the Wizard's important trip to Big Sur.

Danny De Carlo said that Charlie talked about being gone for about three months. Others say he talked about going north to recruit girls. Beausoleil has claimed that Manson left the Spahn Ranch for the trip about midnight.

The chronology of Manson's whereabouts during the days between August 1 and 8 is filled with gaps.

It is known from interviews that between 7 and 8 A.M. on Sunday, August 3, Manson purchased gasoline in a service station in Canoga Park, near the Spahn Ranch. He must quickly have sped north because his alibi for his whereabouts during a double homicide in San Jose on Sunday afternoon, August 3 was that he was visting the

Esalen Institute in Big Sur, enjoying the hot springs and steam baths.

Manson in his autobiography says he spent the first night, Friday, just outside of Santa Barbara with some old friends. "When I left the next day, it was with a supply and variety of drugs that would take the bikers off our backs and make a lot of the kids at the ranch happy. Following Highway One, my next stop was Big Sur." He spent the next night, Saturday, August 2, he says, in his truck. "And the next day [Sunday], I visited the Esalen Institute to enjoy the mineral baths. It was totally relaxing and I felt refreshed when I left. After leaving the Institute, I parked my truck by the ocean, smoked a joint, played some music and fell asleep. About two in the morning, I woke up and went looking for a coffee shop."

On Sunday the 3rd, Randy Reno, a musician and occasional visitor to the Ranch, visited the family and they told him that Charlie was up in Devil's Hole. Beausoleil later testified at his April 1970 trial that after Charlie cut out, he felt that people were watching him as if to prevent his leaving. Throughout the history of the family whenever Charlie took a bit of time off, that provided the opportunity for people to escape. Tex and Bruce Davis seemed to be keeping their eyes on him. Bobby waited. "I smiled a lot, tried to be myself. It seemed that they were trusting me so I left." He told the girls to clean up Hinman's customized Fiat station wagon which "was full of junk"—as he testified.

Why did Robert Beausoleil leave for San Francisco driving the car of the very man in whose murder he had participated?

So, around Tuesday, August 5, Robert Beausoleil drove Hinman's grill-less Fiat, with Toyota motor and a radiator set at a 45-degree angle, toward San Francisco, unaware that Hinman's body had been discovered.

He passed through Santa Barbara and stopped at a restaurant where he was told by a policeman to take his Mexican sheath knife off. He put it in the car trunk. He continued driving north and sometime in the night the Fiat broke down on Highway 101 near San Luis Obispo.

At 10:50 A.M. a California Highway Patrol car stopped behind the parked car and, as it halted, Beausoleil raised up in the back from a sleeping bag. Beausoleil had no driver's license to show the officer but had identification for Jason Lee Daniels and a credit card plus a business card for the Lutesinger Ranch.

Officer Humphrey of the Highway Patrol called in Hinman's license number to the computer and he learned that the car was reported stolen from Los Angeles. He drew his revolver and arrested Beausoleil. When he arrived at the CHP station, there was a Los Angeles sheriff's office "All Points Bulletin" that the car be impounded and occupants held in regard to Hinman's death.

As part of a prearranged scheme, Beausoleil said that he had bought the car in the week previous from a black man. The Fiat was locked up, to preserve fingerprints, and Jim's Tow Service hauled it into custody in San Luis Obispo.

The same day around 8:30 P.M., homicide officers Paul Whiteley and Charles Guenther and a fingerprint expert named Jake Jordan arrived in San Luis Obispo to interrogate Beausoleil. They brought with them the card bearing Beausoleil's thumbprint lifted from the kitchen door jamb of Hinman's house. They had the man.

Beausoleil remained pretty quiet during interrogation though he finally admitted going to Hinman's house with two female Caucasians. He claimed he did not reveal their names but only that Hinman was injured, when they got there, and that they came to his aid, sewed his face, etc., then left. He said that Hinman rewarded them for suturing his face with dental floss by signing over his automobile to them. Hinman, he said, told them he got involved in some political hassle with blacks and that one of them had knifed his face.

The next day, on August 7, Robert Beausoleil was brought to Los Angeles and booked for homicide. As per California law, he was allowed to call the Spahn Ranch. Linda Kasabian was manning incoming calls that day and Beausoleil gave her the bad news but said that everything was okay and that he was staying quiet.

Beausoleil himself has said that Linda was upset and that she asked what could be done to help him and a discussion was held regarding possible plans of action. According to Beausoleil the discussion involved copycat murders, or murders removing those who might have known about the Hinman matter. Such discussions of possible murder to get Beausoleil out may have served to rev up the family for more snuffs, another example of the self-fulfilling prophecy.

Sadie Glutz testified at the Tate-LaBianca trial that soon after Bobby called, Leslie, Sadie, Linda Kasabian, Katie and others had a homicide-klatch to discuss and to determine how to get Bobby, their brother, out of jail. According to the Glutz-Atkins testimony, one of the girls had seen a movie where copy-cat murders were committed over a period of time, enabling a killer to get out of jail.

They wanted to raise money for him to get a lawyer. The girls decided to hold a night of streetwalking to raise money for Beausoleil. They donned their finery and high heels, and painted their lips and hit the bricks.

Meanwhile where was Manson during all this?

Manson seems to have left the Esalen Institute sometime late Sunday. Manson was then cruising around the Big Sur area in the 1952 Hostess Twinkie bread truck with two unknown male companions.

About 3 or 4 A.M. Monday morning, August 4, Manson met a pregnant seventeen-year-old girl named Stephanie who was entering the ladies' room at a service station. He scarfed her up.

This is her story:

"I was with this guy and we had gone to Nevada, saw his uncle and came back through San Francisco and down through Big Sur. He was weird; he wasn't my boy friend, I just went with him to keep him company. He did everything according to the rules and I was sick of it. So we stopped at this gas station late at night or early in the morning and this guy in a milk truck whistled at me when I went into the bathroom. When I came he went, 'Do you want a sweet roll?' I took one and he started talking to me and showing the flowers to me.

"Then he asked me if I wanted to come with them. He said, 'I'll take you back to San Diego, we will see Big Sur tomorrow as long as you come to my ranch.' I said okay and I was really freaked out and I went. Nobody forced me to, I just went."

During her time with Manson he became attracted to the lovely girl. She made Manson vow that he would not leave her side for two weeks, a vow that has long caused consternation and disbelief among his female followers, who would not have thought such a vow possible. He initiated her into a prolonged session of LSD sex. According to her, Manson took her down into a Big Sur canyon, stuffed a tab of dope into her mouth and ordered her to swallow it. Then he said, according to the girl, "Open your mouth and wiggle your tongue around."

"He wanted to make sure that I took it," she told an interviewer a few months later. "He sure did send me on a trip that one day."

The two male companions who were with Manson when he picked up Miss Stephanie outside the ladies' room, she testified, were hitchhikers who left them shortly thereafter. The two new lovers toured the Big Sur area for a couple of days then headed south for the Spahn Ranch, arriving the afternoon of August 6, 1969.

Manson and Stephanie stayed part of the afternoon and evening at the ranch, then split toward San Diego where Manson, as per the bargain, was to deliver Miss Stephanie back home. They only got a few blocks when they parked and spent the time of night in blissful repose in the back of the Twinkie truck. The next morning they headed south to Jamul, California, where Stephanie lived with her sister and brother-in-law, Mr. and Mrs. Hartman.

At 4:15 P.M. near Oceanside, California, Manson and Stephanie were stopped by the California Highway Patrol.

Manson received a citation for not possessing a driver's license.

They drove on to Stephanie's sister's house. They had dinner with the Hartmans and Charlie talked a lot, as usual. Charlie was attired in gungy blue jeans and his witchy-whorled sequined vest. He rapped for about two hours. It was a general sort of Manson discussion. Slaughter, music, hypnotism and the Beatles.

Manson really weirdized the Hartmans, according to Mrs. Hartman, by saying that soon "people were going to be slaughtered and they would be lying on their lawns dead." Stephanie was afraid her former boy friend was going to show up, so she and Manson had to leave rather than stay for the night. Charlie talked her into returning with him to Spahn land.

They drove in the Hostess Twinkies bread truck to

somebody's lawn, a friend of Stephanie, and the lovers slept on the lawn, the night of August 7.

Miss Stephanie stayed with the family till October 1969 and by 1971 was operating her own dog-grooming shop at the age of nineteen.

In the morning of August 8, Manson and Stephanie drove back north to the ranch, arriving about 1 P.M., with murder eleven hours away.

On Friday, August 1, 1969, a hair stylist named Carol Solomon and a girl named Linda, a Beverly Hills doctor's daughter now deceased through an overdose of doraden, attended a small party thrown by Wojtek Frykowski at 10050 Cielo Drive. Sharon Tate and Abigail Folger were not there. Linda was Wojtek's date and was known to have "hung out" at the home during the summer. Chicken and champagne were served at the pool. It was a quiet scene involving about ten people, some of whom spent time in the bedroom watching TV. The two girls, according to Miss Solomon, were invited over again for the following weekend.

According to the vice-president of Sebring International, Jay Sebring had visited the Polanski residence on Sunday, Tuesday and Thursday, during the week before the murders.

On August 4, 1969, Sharon rented a 1969 Chevrolet Camaro from Airways Rent-a-Car "to be leased from August 4, 1969 till August 8, 1969," as the contract reads. Her red Ferrari was in the garage being repaired, following an accident.

On August 4, Wojtek's actor friend Mark Fine called and reminded him that Frykowski had a meeting with a movie producer on the sixth regarding the sale of a story. Frykowski told Fine that on August 6 he would have to pick up some friends at the airport coming in from Canada.

Sometime during that week, perhaps Tuesday or Wednesday, a dope dealer from Canada, according to an L.A. homicide officer who helped break the Manson case, was whipped and video-buggered at 10050 Cielo Drive. In the days before his death, Sebring had complained to a receptionist at his hair shop that someone had burned him for $2000 worth of cocaine and he wanted vengeance. The dealer from Canada was involved in a large-scale dope-import operation involving private planes from Jamaica. There seem to have been many dope-burns, perhaps like the falling of a line of dominoes, during the days around the Tate-LaBianca murders.

Dennis Hopper, in an interview with the *Los Angeles Free Press*, said, about the video-bugger and the circumstances there:

"They had fallen into sadism and masochism and bestiality—and they recorded it all on videotape too. The L.A. police told me this. I know that three days before they were killed, twenty-five people were invited to that house to a mass whipping of a dealer from Sunset Strip who'd given them bad dope."

On Tuesday or Wednesday, August 5 or 6, there evidently was a party at 10050 Cieio Drive in honor of French director Roger Vadim, in celebration of Vadim's completion of a motion picture and his imminent return to Europe. An area of silence surrounds this event.

Sharon, Wojtek and Abigail on August 6 were at Michael Sarne's house for dinner. Sharon was tired and got up to leave shortly after dessert. Her life revolved around the baby. She floated during the day in a rubber ring in her swimming pool—to take the weight off her stomach.

Mr. Frykowski seems to have acquired a new shipment of MDA two or three days prior to his death. Mrs. Chapman, the housekeeper at Cielo Drive, was off Wednesday and Thursday. Sebring had some films developed at General Film Labs on Wednesday, August 8, so the films may have been taken on Tuesday night.

Another of Wojtek's dope-dealer friends from Canada showed up on August 6 and later claimed to reporters that Frykowski was in the fifth day of a "ten-day mescaline experiment." In fact, the Canadian claimed that both Jay Sebring and Mr. Frykowski were out to lunch on mescaline. The dope-hawker talked to Frykowski about an impending shipment of MDA. The same dealer showed up the next day about 4 P.M. and shared a bottle of wine with Frykowski. He met Sharon Tate that day, indicating that he was a recent friend of Frykowski, or from another circle of acquaintances.

Novelist Jerzy Kosinski and his wife were supposed to come to Los Angeles on August 7 to visit at the Polanski residence and wait for Roman to return for his birthday and for the baby. Kosinski's luggage was lost on the way to New York from Europe so, instead of traveling immediately to Los Angeles, they waited in New York for the luggage. This probably saved his life, because he was not able to arrive in Los Angeles on the 7th or the 8th.

On Friday, August 8, 1969, the housekeeper, Winifred Chapman, arrived at the Polanski residence at 8 A.M.

Around 8:30 A.M. a Mr. Guerrero arrived to paint the nursery. He worked until midafternoon, completing the first coat. He was scheduled to return on Monday to complete the second coat of paint.

Before lunch, Winifred washed down the front Dutch door because the dogs had dirtied it. Pig and a fingerprint would dirty it later.

Mrs. Chapman testified that on Tuesday, August 4, she washed the French doors in Sharon's bedroom, where Friday midnight would find a murderer's fingerprint. Wednesday and Thursday were Mrs. Chapman's days off.

About 11 A.M. Roman Polanski called from London. Mrs. Chapman answered the phone. Then Sharon talked.

Sharon hinted she might throw a birthday party for him on August 18, when he returned. There was a heavy heat wave in L.A., and there was an edge to the conversation. She was anxious for him to arrive soon, so that he might attend a course for expectant fathers. Mrs. Polanski planned to have natural childbirth. She told her husband a little kitten had wandered onto the property, and she was feeding it with an eyedropper.

Polanski was having trouble finishing the script and planning the production of *Day of the Dolphins*. It was difficult figuring out how to make the dolphins talk so that the audience wouldn't think it funny and laugh. He had hired a writer to help him with the final sequences and had postponed returning to L.A. a number of times. "It dawned on me, as we talked," he recalls in his autobiography, "that I was getting nowhere with the ending . . . and that the sequence I'd been working on could probably be cut altogether. 'That's it,' I said, 'I'm coming. I'll finish the script over there. I'll leave tomorrow.'

"I couldn't hop a plane the next day, a Saturday, because I needed a U.S. visa and the consulate was closed, but I made up my mind to do so the following Monday or Tuesday, as soon as the visa was granted."

In the afternoon, the gardeners and groundskeepers of the estate, Joe Vargas and Dave Martinez, arrived.

Joanna Pettit and Barbara Lewis, old friends of Sharon Tate, arrived about 12:30 for lunch. Abigail and Wojtek showed up, after which Mrs. Chapman served a late lunch for Pettit, Lewis, Sharon, Abigail, Wojtek and herself.

Joanna Pettit and Barbara Lewis departed at 3:30 P.M. Around 3:45 Dave Martinez, one of the gardeners, left the property. He asked Bill Garretson to be sure to water the grounds during the weekend.

Jay Sebring called at 3:45. A few minutes later Gibby Folger left in the red Firebird. Wojtek left at 4 P.M. in Sharon's rented yellow Camaro. At 4:30 Miss Folger went to her usual daily appointment with her psychiatrist, Dr. Marvin Flicker.

Frykowski drove to Sebring's house on Easton Drive and picked up a Susan Peterson with whom Sebring had spent the previous night. With her, Frykowski drove to stick-artist Witold K.'s gallery-boutique at the Beverly Wilshire Hotel to get the keys to Wojtek and Abigail's house on Woodstock Road where Witold K. was staying. Mr. K. did not have the keys to the house because they were left over at Mr. K.'s girl friend's house. Mr. Frykowski finally located the keys at the girl friend's house and then went with Miss Peterson to his Woodstock Road house.

There they dallied, listening to records.

At 4:30 Joe Vargas, the gardener, signed for the arrival of Roman Polanski's two steamer trunks because he didn't want to awaken Sharon, who was napping in her room.

As it was extremely hot and dry, Sharon thought it would be uncomfortable in Mrs. Chapman's apartment so she asked Winifred if she wanted to stay over. No, thank you.

Around 4:45 Joe Vargas left the property, giving the housekeeper, Mrs. Chapman, a ride down to the bus stop. When they left, Sharon was alone in the house, asleep.

Sebring was seen on Easton Drive by a neighbor, whizzing past in his black Porsche, followed closely by another sports car, about 5:30 P.M.

Between 6:30 and 7 P.M., one Dennis Hearst delivered a lightweight bicycle to the residence. Abigail Folger had purchased it earlier in the afternoon. Jay Sebring answered the door, wine bottle in hand.

Sharon Tate had invited people over for the evening but later called them and said she was not feeling well.

Evidently Sharon was supposed to stay overnight with an old friend Sheilah Welles at Miss Welles' house. Sharon and Sheilah Welles were roommates for a year in Hollywood. Something caused her to change her mind.

Director Michael Sarne was considering going to Sharon's on Friday night. Also Dino Martin, Jr. and a host of others, including John Phillips. One popular folk singer, according to Leonard Lyons, claimed that he was supposed to go to the murder house that night to get a haircut from Jay Sebring.

If the number of people who claim to have been invited to 10050 Cielo Drive the night of August 8 had shown up, there wouldn't have been room for a murder.

According to a Mrs. McCaffrey, a receptionist at Sebring's hair shop, her boy friend Joel Rostau delivered cocaine and mescaline to the house on Cielo the night of the murders. She said that Frykowski and Sebring wanted more, but Rostau, unable to score, didn't return.

Frykowski called his friend Witold K. in the evening sometime and invited him over but Witold K. was busy laying down a rug in his new art gallery at 9406 Wilshire Boulevard.

The foursome Jay, Wojtek, Abigail and Sharon had a late dinner at a Spanish restaurant, El Coyote, on Beverly Boulevard, about the same time as the coyote-worshiping Charles Manson was plotting his evil.

Miss Folger's mother called from San Francisco. Miss Folger was scheduled to fly the 10 A.M United Airlines shuttle the next morning to Frisco in order to be with her mother for her birthday.

It was about midnight. They were in bed. Wojtek was evidently asleep upon the flag-draped living-room sofa. Abigail was reading a book in the northeast bedroom. Sharon Tate and Jay Sebring were talking in the southwest bedroom when the knife stabbed into the gray screen, scratching and slicing an entrance into the empty nursery at the far north end of the house.

In the early afternoon of August 8, 1969, Charles Manson arrived at the Spahn Ranch, bearing the pregnant runaway seventeen-year-old graduate of Anaheim High School, Stephanie. Charlie called Stephanie the "product of 2000 years of good breeding." He was proud of her. Charlie was quickly apprised of Robert Beausoleil's arrest. The whole trip up north had been a bummer for Charlie, who hated rejection. And now, with Beausoleil's arrest for murder, Manson's whole empire was threatened.

As soon as he got back, driving the 1952 Continental Bakery Hostess Twinkie truck, Charlie sent Mary Brunner and Sandy Good off to run a credit-card caper at the Sears store. Before they left they took Stephanie's credit cards and identification away from her, naturally, and filed them with the master credit-card horde in George Spahn's house.

Around 4 P.M., Mary Brunner and Sandy Pugh—for Sandy was using the name of her former husband at the time—were completing purchases at the Sears store at 1030 Celis Street in San Fernando, California. They bought merchandise with a stolen credit card, recently ripped off from Vern Plumlee's brother-in-law in Bothwell, Washington. Mary Brunner forged the name Mary Vitasek on the credit card. The two young ladies left. If they had split right away, they probably would not have been arrested.

Instead of leaving they decided to make some more purchases at a different checkout counter and again presented the same stolen credit card. The cashier, an alert lady named Mrs. Ramirez, noted that the card was on the "warning sheet." Mrs. Ramirez became suspicious when she noted that the pregnant Sandy kept looking over her shoulder all the time.

The store manager intervened and the girls fled. The Sears's store manager proceeded to follow the girls in his automobile, trying to get them to pull the bakery truck over to the side of the road. Sandy and Mary cut through a service station, trying to ditch the Sears officials. The chase led to the Chatsworth entrance to the San Diego Freeway, where the girls were stopped, evidently having some sort of accident. Sandy had managed to toss the credit cards out the window, but the act was spotted by the pursuers.

Captured with the two young ladies were a creepy-crawl full house of various credit cards from Hancock Gasoline, J. C. Penney, Sears, Gulf, Texaco and Richfield, plus various forms of identification cards. Three of the cards belonged to John Dries, who had been killed in a traffic accident.

The police found the traffic citation given to Manson the day before in Oceanside, California. Mary and Sandy were charged with violations of Section 459 and 484e of the California Penal Code. Mary Brunner admitted that she, in fact, forged the credit card but Sandy Good proclaimed her innocence.

They were booked at the police station just as, thirty miles away, Abigail Folger was ending her appointment with her psychiatrist. Mary and Sandy Good were taken to the police station and then later that evening hauled into downtown Los Angeles where, at 10:21 P.M., they were booked into the Sybil Brand Institute Inmate Reception Center.

Meanwhile, back at the Spahn Ranch, murder was on the minds. Mary Brunner arrested. Sandy Good arrested. Bobby Beausoleil arrested. Charlie Manson rejected in Big Sur. It was a tragic time for California.

In the afternoon, someone went on a garbage run for the evening meal. At the back ranch, they cooked dinner on the Coleman four-burner camping stove. Everybody was excited that Charlie was back. Charlie said that people up north were really not together, they were just off on their own little trips and they were not getting together. "Now is the time for Helter Skelter" is what Charlie Manson said.

At the meal, Charlie issued instructions that all people under eighteen were to sleep in the wickiup by the back ranch. After dinner, the slave girls washed the dishes and Tex Watson and Charlie plotted what to do about Beausoleil's arrest.

When Sandy and Mary were booked into Sybil Brand Jail at 10:21 they probably called up the ranch and told them the grim news. Within an hour, the killers were on their way.

About an hour after dinner Charlie took Stephanie into a trailer and left her there. "He told me he'd be back in a little while," she testified at Manson's murder trial.

Manson didn't return till dawn.

Approximately an hour after the meal, Manson pulled Sadie aside and told her to get a knife and a change of clothes. Sadie immediately called the back ranch over the field telephone and told Barbara Hoyt to gather three sets of dark clothing and bring them to the front ranch.

Linda Kasabian had helped fix dinner, helped to clean up, had walked to the front ranch and was standing by the Rock City Café when Charlie came up and pulled her off to the end of the boardwalk and told her to get a knife, a change of clothing and her driver's license. With Mary Brunner arrested, Kasabian seemed to be the only person at the ranch with a valid driver's license, and one of the few who could be trusted with such a heavy mission as murder. Linda Kasabian walked across the dusty driveway from the Spahn Ranch movie set and went into George Spahn's saddle-lined house to look for her creepy-crawlie accouterments. There she rummaged through a box and found a blue denim mini-skirt made from chopped-off blue jeans and a lavender knitted top. She asked Squeaky, who ofttimes served as the family quartermaster, where her driver's license was.

Squeaky told her to look in some chests of drawers. Not there. In a box on the mantel of the fireplace. Not there. Then she went into the Saloon to look for her knife. Couldn't find one. She was looking for the Buck knife she had brought with her to the ranch. She walked down the boardwalk, east, went into the Rock City Café kitchen, saw little Larry Jones there and got her kitchen knife from him, a knife with a flawed handle that required it to be wrapped with dark electrical tape. Sadie was using Linda's old Buck clasp knife.

Patricia Krenwinkel was already asleep, coming down off an acid trip, when she was awakened and told to get a knife and a change of clothes. She really didn't want to get up but she did, summoned by the Devil.

Someone must have called in advance to the Polanski residence to see who was going to be there or at least that there was no party going on. Vern Plumlee, for instance, has claimed that they thought Sharon Tate was not going to be there.

In the hot August evening, people were sitting and chatting on the boulders and rocks and chairs that were situated in front of the Spahn Ranch, unaware of what was going on. In the presence of Manson, Brenda came up and handed Linda her driver's license. All was prepared.

Manson prepared Watson for the event by blaming him for the "killing" of Bernard Crowe. It was Tex's fault M had to shoot him; therefore Watson owed him plenty. Manson laid out a fairly comprehensive set of instructions, and he wanted severe gore. Watson claims M told him, "Pull out their eyes and hang them on the mirrors."

There may have been a tinge of amphetamine psychosis in the air, because, in violation of family rules, Tex had a secret supply of powdered amphetamine in a Gerber's baby-food jar. He and Sadie had been snorting it constantly for three or four days. When Manson gave the kill instructions, Sadie was already stoned on amphetamine, and Watson went to where the Gerber's jar was hidden on the porch. "I took a couple of deep snorts of speed," he writes, "and went to get the clothes and rope and bolt cutters as Charlie had ordered."

The automobile, an old yellow and white 1959 Ford with another car's license plate on it, was parked and ready in the space between the end of the Rock City Café and George Spahn's house. George Spahn was not at home. It was his custom to dine about this hour at the International House of Pancakes in Chatsworth. Or perhaps he was visiting his relatives, following his meal.

Linda Kasabian got into the car, in the right front passenger seat. Sadie and Katie were in the back of the car. Also in the back of the car were a pair of redhandled bolt cutters and a long, coiled, three-quarter-inch nylon rope. Tex got into the car and the car backed away and then headed out down the dirt driveway toward the exit to the west, by the corral. About halfway down the drive, Manson stopped them. He came over and stuck his head into the window on Linda's side and said, according to Linda, "Leave a sign. You girls know what to do. Something witchy." Then Manson stood alone, watching the car drive off.

Tex Watson's memory was that Manson told him to get money for Mary to get out of jail. "If you don't get enough money at the Melcher house, then go on to the house next door and then the house after that until you get six hundred dollars."

The car belonged to Johnny Swartz, a horse wrangler at the Spahn Ranch. He was sitting in his trailer near George Spahn's house when he recognized the sound of his engine and walked to the window of his trailer just in time to see the taillights of his automobile fade away down the road.

Tex told Linda that the gun was in the glove compartment. Three knives were on the front right floor of the automobile. Tex told her to bundle up the knives and gun and then to throw them out the window if the police attempted to pick them up. This Linda did, bundling them with her very own shirt. Linda Kasabian testified that she believed she was merely going on a second-story caper in Beverly Hills. A second-story caper with forty-three feet of rope and gun, change of clothing and three sharp knives.

After the 1959 Ford, license plate GYY435, had pulled away toward its desolate goal, Barbara Hoyt came trundling to the front ranch from the back ranch, bearing the three sets of dark clothing that Susan Atkins had ordered over the field phone. Charlie was angry at her and snapped, "What are you doing here?" Because it was a rule that all those who didn't have a reason, particularly soul-less females, were to stay in back out of sight and not appear in the public part of the ranch. Miss Hoyt told him what Sadie had asked her to do and Manson said that they had already left.

In the speeding car, the girls seemed to be barefoot. Sadie had on blue denim genuine Roebucks and a baggy blue T-shirt. Linda was barefoot and in her lavender top and dark blue denim skirt. Tex wore moccasins, jeans and a black velour turtleneck sweater. Katie wore a black T-shirt and jeans.

In the car, Tex said that they were going to Terry Melcher's former place, but that Melcher no longer lived there. He described the setup of the house, including the rooms inside, and evidently noted that there was a smaller guest house on the property, and to make sure that the guest house was creepy-crawled also.

According to Sadie, Tex said that they were going to kill whoever was in the house and then get all their money.

They drove there straightaway, leaving around eleven o'clock in the evening. They got lost and ended up going all the way into Hollywood, then back west on Santa Monica Boulevard past the Tropicana Motel and the Troubador Bar, through West Hollywood and the edges of Beverly Hills. Then they cut up past the perfect mansions with their tall elegant palms, to Sunset Boulevard, then to Benedict Canyon, then finally turned left onto Cielo Drive and proceeded to the house on the hill.

15

Death on Cielo Drive

Bill Garretson, the caretaker of the guest cottage at the Polanski residence, got sick Thursday night, August 7, on four cans of beer, a dexedrine and two marijuana cigarettes, so he stayed home all day Friday until the evening.

It was the windup of Mr. Garretson's employment at the Polanski estate. The owner, Rudy Altobelli, who had been in Europe all summer, was due to return. In addition to the thirty-five dollars a week that he was earning, Altobelli promised to buy the young Garretson an airplane ticket back to his home town, Lancaster, Ohio.

It was Garretson's habit to go to bed late and get up early in the afternoon and go check on his mail. By arrangement, Garretson took care of Sharon's Yorkshire terrier and Abigail's Dalmatian. The guest house sat at an angle to the main house, up against a steep hill. Between the two houses lay the swimming pool. Four entrances and numerous windows make the guest house a pushover to creepy-crawl. There is a back door, a door to the dog's room, a door to the back yard and front door.

Unknown people came around 8:30 in the evening who took Garretson down the Canyon to the Sunset Strip. Garretson went to Turner's Drugstore, got a TV dinner and a Coke and a pack of cigarettes, and then walked up, then down, the Strip. Boredom. He then hitchhiked back to Benedict Canyon Drive from Sunset, then hitched up

Benedict to Cielo Drive. He walked up Cielo then up the hill to the back house. It was around ten o'clock. He watched a movie on TV, then he put the TV dinner in the oven. While his dinner cooked, the American boy ate potato chips and drank Coca-Cola. Around 11:45 P.M., Steve Parent arrived unannounced, with an AM/FM clock radio to sell, or one like it. They talked. Parent evidently asked Garretson who the two pretty young ladies were who were inside the main house.

Garretson thought that Wojtek Frykowski was Roman Polanski's younger brother, so Garretson explained that Miss Folger was the "younger Polanski's" girl friend and the other one was Polanski's wife, to which Parent replied, "You mean Polanski has a girl friend and a wife?" And Garretson said, "No, the younger Polanski has a girl friend and the other one was the older Polanski's wife." Finally, Parent got it straight.

Steve Parent placed a phone call around 11:45 or 11:55 or so to a man named Jerrold Friedman on Romaine Street in Hollywood and Parent told him something to the effect that he was at the home of a movie star, "somebody big." Friedman asked him if there was a party going on, and Parent said there was not. Parent was going to help Friedman build a stereo, so they made a date for Parent to come to Friedman's house in about forty minutes, which would have helped put Parent at Friedman's house at 12:30 A.M. Garretson gave Parent a can of Budweiser beer. They listened to the stereo, which was located next to the couch in the living room of the guest house.

As Garretson walked Parent to the door, Christopher, the Weimaraner, began barking and Steve asked, "What's the matter with Christopher?" Garretson said, "Oh, I don't know. He usually barks." According to Altobelli's testimony at the trial, Christopher gave forth two types of barks, a generalized bark and something called a people bark when anyone approached the house. Probably Garretson was not able to distinguish between the two types of barks. The Weimaraner was not known for its gentleness. In fact, at one time, it had even bitten Rudy Altobelli.

Around 12:15 A.M. Garretson said good-bye to the young man from El Monte, Steve Parent. The dog was yipping and barking. Garretson contended that he only walked Parent to the door. He never heard any shots or any shrieks or any screams during the ensuing butchering on the lawn, less than 150 feet from the house. He claimed that he spent the night writing letters to a friend of his named Darryl Kistler and listening to the record player, which was turned up to medium volume. At one point in the middle of the night, the Weimaraner began to bark and Garretson looked up from the couch in the living room and noticed that the bar-shaped door handle had been turned down by something or somebody. He leaped up and walked to the bathroom and looked out the window to see if anybody had tried to force the door. From the bathroom window it was possible to see out onto the screened porch where the front door to the guest house was located. Garretson also noted that something or some force had cut loose the screen to one of the windows in another part of the house near the kitchen.

When the polygraph interrogation officer, Lieutenant Burdick, ran a polygraph examination of Garretson on Sunday, August 10, Garretson admitted that perhaps he may have gone out to the back yard at some point during the night.

Patricia Krenwinkel has contended that they creepy-crawled the back house and found no one there. So perhaps Garretson, hearing the shrieks and the bullets and the screams, ran out back to hide then crept back into the house in the early dawn, fearing either for his own life or that he would be charged for the crimes.

At 12:15, Garretson saw Parent to the door of the cottage. Before he left, Parent reached over and unplugged his unsold Sony AM-FM clock radio, taking it with him. When the police found it the next morning on the front seat of the Ambassador, the clock was frozen at 12:15.

Steve Parent walked off the screened porch, past the redwood picnic table, past the small swimming pool set against the steep hillside; he walked down the east path, on the walkway by the white split rail fence, then down the paved driveway. He got into his car. Sebring's Porsche, Abigail's yellow Firebird and also the Camaro which Sharon had rented while the red Ferrari was being repaired were parked there.

He backed his car out of the driveway so quickly that he broke the split rail fence that borders the parking lot. The paint from the fence was found on the underside of his car the next morning by Officer McGann. He may have seen the killers in the house or coming out the drive or cutting the communication wires. Or he may have heard the splat of the telephone cables as Watson cut them. The parking area narrows at a point a few feet in front of the electric gate. At this narrowing point, on the left side, is the housing box for the electronic button which activates the main gate. Parent never got as far as this button; he never pushed it. Death punched his face.

The white and yellow, back-seatless, 1959 Ford four-door sedan pulled up the paved, winding, cliffside driveway to the top, facing the rattan fence. The car turned around at the gate. The lights were off. Coyotenoia was. They parked the car facing downhill on the right side, away from the main gate, next to the telephone pole that juts up above a cliff-like hill that falls down to the north. Eighteen feet up were the telephone communications lines.

Tex asked for the red-handled bolt cutters from the back seat. They were given to him, and the six-foot two-inch, 190-pound, former All-District halfback for the Farmersville, Texas, high-school football team shimmied up the pole and cut two wires—one a telephone wire which did not fall and one an old communications line from the days when Mark Lindsay and Terry Melcher first rented the property in 1966. Splat. The communications line fell to the ground, but it draped over the right side of the iron-framed, wire electric gate.

Tex Watson slid back down, jumped, hit the road, got into the car on the driver's side and coasted down the hill, lights off. At the bottom of the driveway, he grabbed a right and parked on Cielo Drive, to avoid suspicion. They all got out of the car—Linda Kasabian, Tex Watson, Sadie Glutz and Katie Krenwinkel. All was chop.

The entrance to 10050 Cielo Drive is located at the northwestern edge of the property, consisting of a wrought-iron fence and a gate. The gate is six feet high, twelve feet wide and located in the center portion of the fence. On either side of the iron gate, rattan facing has been placed. On the left of the gate, a cliff falls away. On the right is a steep hillside going up at about a fifty- or sixty-degree angle.

The gate is electronically controlled from both the inside and outside. Affixed to the telephone pole that Tex had just shimmied up was the electronic button. The electronic button was housed in a metal box on a three and a half-foot metal stalk pipe. There was a locking device on the button, to be operated by key, but it was never used. Someone would push the button and the gate would swing inward, allowing them to enter, with the gate automatically closing behind them.

Tex wasn't sure just what sort of line he had cut that had splatted across the electric-eye gate. In any case, it had fallen in a north-south direction, but right over the gate, and they were afraid it was some sort of utility cable, charged with electricity. Fear of electrocution caused the young murderers to hesitate to enter via the front gate. They had nothing to fear, since the wire hadn't been used since the Polanskis moved into the estate. At one time the wire had been connected to two speakers, which were used for communications between the house and the front gate.

So they trudged up the hill, carrying their changes of clothes, their weapons and their rope. They arrived at the gate, where they located an area about ten to fifteen feet up the steep embankment on the right where, by cover of bushes, they were able to climb over the fence. Sadie ripped her shirt on the barbed wire. Tsk, tsk. Then, after they had crossed the fence, as they were creeping down the embankment toward the driveway, lights appeared, a car, moving down the driveway-parking lot. Tex said, "Lie down and be still." All lay down. Tex leaped forward, having evidently deposited the coils of rope from his left shoulder but holding his revolver in his right hand, his knife God knows where—probably in his left hand or in a scabbard.

Evidently Parent spotted them coming in and he said, "Hey, what are you doing here?" Watson seems to have believed, luckily for Garretson, that Parent was the caretaker. Parent must have just been slowing down to touch the exit button when Tex ran up in front of the white, 1966 Nash Ambassador two-door sedan and yelled, "Stop! Halt!" It must have been around 12:30 A.M. Through the open driver's window, Tex jammed his formidable weapon up against Parent's head. It was a weapon right out of the spirit of the American West: a .22-caliber, nine-shot, walnut-handled, blue steel, long-barreled, Ned Buntline to Wyatt Earp, longhorn, fifteen-inch revolver, loaded with .22 long rifle bullets. Parent said, "Please don't hurt me. I won't say anything."

Bang, bang, bang, bang.

Mrs. Seymour Kott, living just over the lip of the hill, on the other side of the driveway, about a football field distance away, heard, just as she was about to go to bed around 12:30, four shots fired in quick succession. Bang. Parent was shot in the upper chest. Bang. Once in the back of the left forearm, exiting on the other side. Shot in the left cheek—exit wound through the mouth. Shot in the lower chest. Somehow, Parent's Lucerne wristwatch got torn off—perhaps Tex was jabbing him with a knife as he was shooting him. It was found in the back seat with a severed watchband. There was a defensive wound in Parent's left arm—a deep wound between his ring and little fingers that severed the tendons.

The young man, Steven Parent of El Monte, California, was attired in a red, white and blue plaid shirt, blue denim pants, black shoes and white socks. His body slumped slightly into the direction of the passenger's seat when he was shot, part of his weight against the armrest that separated the bucket seats, his head leaning back and out to the right, into the separation. Blood was spattered on the dashboard, blood and bone chips, bullet fragments on the rubber floormat and the right front door from Detroit.

Tex reached into the car, shut off the lights and the engine, put the gear selector in neutral, pushed the car back a few feet, turning the automobile a quarter circle to the southeast, out of the way. Then he put the gear in second forward and ran back to the crouching girls by the fence. Tex picked up the rope coils, put them on his shoulder and said, "Come on."

They had stashed their clothing on the estate side of the fence, in the bushes, as per Charlie's Helter Skelter instructions.

On Watson's left shoulder were about seven coils of the white, three-quarter-inch, three-ply nylon line—seven or eight coils, a total of forty-three feet eight inches. And why was this Texan carrying a rope? Part of the game-plan, which later was abandoned in their haste, was to tie the victims up to the beams and draw and quarter them. They walked past the Porsche, the Firebird, beneath the trees that hover over the edge of the front lawn, and up the walkway, where they paused to scout the house. Tex ordered Linda Kasabian to go around the back of the house to check for any open windows or doors. Linda walked around between the north edge of the house and the three-car garage and checked the back porch door, looked into the kitchen windows and the back door into the living room, but there was nothing open. On her way back, evidently she spotted the bouquet of flowers on the table in the dining room, or so she testified a year later. She came around front and found Tex standing at the fresh-painted window of the unfurnished nursery room on the far north end of the house, next to the garage. He was cutting the lower part of the screen, slitting it with his bayonet.

Tex told Linda to go down by the fence and keep a lookout for people coming. She complied, walking down-hill to the gate end of the parking lot, by the fence, and she knelt down on one knee, waiting. She could see Steve Parent, the young boy, slumped over his bucket seat. Sadie and Katie walked up the elliptical sidewalk which curves from a north/south direction to an east/west direction, where it hooks into the covered flagstone front porch. Never say why. Cease to exist. You can't kill kill.

Tex crawled in through the window once he had slashed the screen and pulled it off the frame. There was the smell of fresh paint in the nursery being prepared for the late August arrival of the baby. The first coat of paint had been finished that very afternoon. Tex entered the kitchen walking south, through the dining room, into the entrance hall then opened the front door and let the two girls in. They grabbed a left out of the entrance hall into the large, white-walled, cream-carpeted living room. Bordering the west side of the living room was a loft carpeted and furnished with chairs and a telephone, reached by a redwood ladder, located adjacent to the left side of the large stone fireplace on the west wall of the living room. In the southeast corner of the living room, facing out into the room at a triangular position, was a baby grand piano with a metronome on the left side. On the music holder of the piano stood two compositions. One on the left side: a song called "Straight Shooter" by John Phillips of the Mamas and the Papas, a song off their first album. The song on the other side of the music stand was "Pomp and Circumstance" by Edward Elgar.

The grounds were lit up all around the house. The bug light on the north edge of the two-story garage was on. Several lights out on the front lawn were on. The poolside light was on. The two front porch lights were on.

The stereo inside the front hall closet beneath the shelves of film and videotapes was blaring, which may have prevented the four shots that killed Steven Parent from being heard.

In the center of the east wall was a large desk, jutting out into the living room. On the desk was a candelabra, flowers, various scripts and papers and a white pushbutton phone.

On the high-backed chair next to the desk was Jay Sebring's blue leather jacket, with his wallet, containing four twenty-dollar bills, and a tube of white powder. Nearby was Jay's briefcase, containing hair dryer, mirror, electric clippers and address book, some sort of pilot's map and miscellaneous barbering tools.

Dark wood stereo speaker cabinets were positioned on the east wall. The area of the living room which was to serve as the tableau for the murders was a sort of enclosed section near the large stone fireplace on the west center wall, in front of which was a large zebra-skin rug. Piles of books and movie scripts lined the hearth, as well as several throw pillows. Facing the fireplace, a few feet from the zebra skin, was a large, three-cushioned, beige velvet sofa.

To the immediate left of the couch was an end table, to the east. Two comfortable, cream-colored, stuffed easy chairs were set at angles on each side of the beige divan, forming sort of a closed area, facing the fireplace. Near the chair on the right was a brown, wide-reed, woven basket for holding magazines and a floor lamp.

Above the couch and parallel to it, running the entire length of the living room, east to west, was an apparently solid, four-inch by twelve-inch beam, painted white, over

Charles Manson shaking the hand of a judge at the juvenile center in Indianapolis in 1949. He had been living on his own and had broken into a grocery store to get cash to rent a room. In this photo he was on his way to Father Flanagan's Boys' Town.

Manson on acid, early 1968. (photo credit: Gene Daniels, BLACK STAR)

Sharon Tate. (photo credit: BLACK STAR)

Sharon and Roman toasting the success of *Rosemary's Baby* in London, early 1968. (photo credit: AP/Wide World Photos)

Vojtek Frykowski, author and bon vivant, his lover Abigail Folger, famous hair stylist Jay Sebring, and Steven Parent, all killed at the house on Cielo Drive. (photo credit: AP/Wide World Photos)

Front view of the Benedict Canyon house rented by Roman Polanski and Sharon Tate. The screen at the right was removed by Tex Watson prior to crawling in through the window to open the front door for the killers. (photo credit: Gene Daniels, BLACK STAR)

The home of Leno and Rosemary La Bianca on Waverly Drive in Los Angeles. The couple had just returned from a vacation at Lake Isabella. They were preparing for bed when Charles Manson entered the house holding a short sword and thongs to tie them up. (photo credit: UPI/Bettmann Newsphotos)

Manson's Command Dune Buggy with three murd-molls aboard. The fur cover in back concealed a machine gun mount. 1969. (photo credit: AP/Wide World Photos)

Tex Watson said that Charles Manson and Brenda McCann were dancing naked in front of the Longhorn Saloon at the Spahn Movie Ranch not long after midnight when the killers returned from Sharon Tate's house. Manson and a Family member then drove to the murder house to view the carnage and to wipe away any incriminating fingerprints. (photo credit: AP/Wide World Photos)

Sheriff's deputies reach under the rear porch at the Spahn Movie Ranch to haul out Charles Manson from his hiding spot during a raid a week after the Tate-La Bianca murders. Manson was held for auto theft, but there was a flaw in the search warrant, and he was set free to flee to his final hideout in Death Valley.

A helicopter hovers above the Spahn Movie Ranch during the raid. Sheriff's deputies are examining the yellow and white '59 Ford, which was used to drive the killers to the Tate and to the La Bianca houses. The police thought they were breaking up a stolen car ring, and all suspects were released. August 16, 1969.

Tex Watson and Linda Kasabian. He fought extradition from Texas, and she won freedom by testifying for the prosecution. (photo credit: AP/Wide World Photos)

Susan Atkins, Patricia Krenwinkel, and Leslie Van Houten seem to be singing as they follow Sheriff's deputy Aileen Stagle to a pre-trial hearing in March 1970. (photo credit: AP/Wide World Photos)

During Manson's murder trial, a group of followers continued to live at the Spahn Ranch. Here are five friendly faces from 1970. Left to right: Country Sue, who held Christopher Zero as he lay dying; Sandy Good, whose husband died mysteriously in London; Gypsy Share, later arrested in the Hawthorne shoot-out; Ouish, arrested for spiking a witness's hamburger with LSD, and Squeaky, now serving life for attempting to assassinate Gerald Ford.

View of the Barker Ranch in the Panamint Mountains above Death Valley, forty miles from the nearest phone, where on a cool evening in October 1969, James Pursell of the California Highway Patrol found Manson hiding in a tiny closet beneath a bathroom sink. (photo credit: Charles Moore, BLACK STAR)

Squeaky Fromme being subdued by Secret Sevice Agent Larry Buendorf and others after she aimed a loaded .45 at President Gerald Ford in Sacramento, California. September 1975. (photo credit: AP/ Wide World Photos)

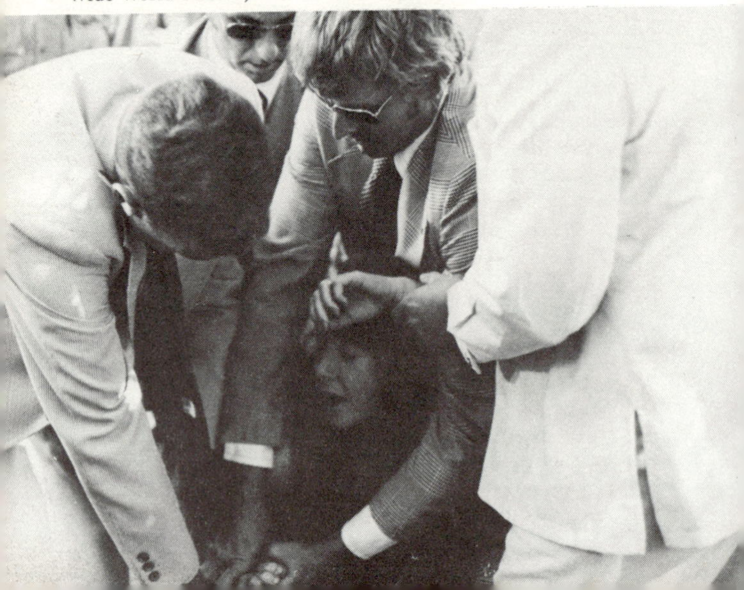

which the satanist Texan was soon to throw the nylon rope.

Draped over the back cushions of the beige divan was a large American flag, turned upside down. This was, in spite of the mutterings of the police officials a few hours later, about the only powerful symbolic element in the decor of the room. The flag, above five by three feet in size, had only been in the house about two weeks, according to the testimony of the maid, Mrs. Chapman.

On the north end of the living room was a bar, serving liquor. Also on the north end of the living room, near the hallway door, were Roman Polanski's two large, shiny blue steamer trunks which had just been delivered that afternoon, while Sharon was taking a nap. They stood stacked one on top of another, just inside the door.

Wojtek Frykowski lay on the couch, in front of the fireplace, dozing off, zonked under the pleasant influence of the moderate psychedelic, MDA. Past the desk and toward the back of the couch crept the death-minded butcher. Evidently Watson walked around, standing on the zebra skin, his back to the fireplace, and leveled the Wyatt Earp revolver at Wojtek's head. He motioned with his knife hand for Katie and Sadie to line up behind the couch, prepared to enact their Helter Skelter exactitude. Wojtek woke up, stretched and asked, "What time it is?"

"Don't move or you're dead."

"Who are you?"

"I'm the Devil. I'm here to do the Devil's business. Give me all your money," said Tex Watson, tall and hairy, knife in one hand, gun in the other. Wojtek must have seen the two girls at this point, standing silently by the flag. The one, Katie, with her long, brown, magic hair that would be the blanket for the chop clan when they went into The Hole. The other, Sadie, with her dark brown hair now shorn closely, except for one long strand which hung over her left shoulder in witchiness. This Southern boy would later, in Death Valley, tell sixteen-year-old Snake Lake "it was fun" to tear down the Polanski residence.

Elegant Abigail Folger was lying alone on the antique bed in her bedroom in the extreme southeast corner of the house, clad in a full-length, white nightgown, reading, wearing her reading glasses, slightly stoned on the euphoric MDA. Most of her and Wojtek's personal belongings had been taken back to their house on Woodstock Road. But she and Wojtek were remaining with Sharon until Roman Polanski should return from London. Her Nikon camera was visible on the chest of drawers. Inside the small bedstand nearby was the box containing capsules of MDA and a Baggie full of cannabis, for spiritual comfort.

In the living room, Wojtek Frykowski kept asking the creepy-crawlers who they were, what they wanted, over and over. "My money is in the wallet, on the desk," he said.

Sadie went over to the desk to look for it and announced that she couldn't find it. Later, Sadie would claim to her jailhouse snitch, Virginia Graham, that she put a palm print on the desk when she was looking for the wallet, but her witchy force field prevented it from being identifiable. She said, "My spirit is so strong that obviously it didn't show up, 'cause if it had, they would have had me by now."

Tex told Sadie to go get a towel in the bathroom with which to tie up Frykowski. Sadie went looking for the bathroom. She took a towel back to the couch by the fireplace and tied Wojtek's hands behind his back with a loose knot. Frykowski was then made to lie back down on his back, trapping his hands behind him. Tex then told her to scout the house for other people. Sadie evidently climbed up the redwood ladder to look in the loft. And then she walked to the south, toward the hallway off which were the two main bedrooms of the house. In the one on the left, Abigail Folger lay reading alone. She looked up, she saw Sadie, and Abigail waved! Waved and smiled and Sadie smiled back and walked away. Hi, death.

Sadie turned, crossed the hallway, walking west and glanced into the bedroom of Sharon Polanski. Sharon, her stomach tanned and full of child, was lying in bed, propped up on pillows, her blonde hair down over her shoulders. She was wearing matching blue-yellow, floral-patterned bra and panties. For jewelry, she had on her wedding ring and gold earpins. The lime green and orange sheets were pulled down. It was about 12:25 A.M. On the edge of the bed where the beautiful Sharon Tate lay sat Jay Sebring, clothed in a blue shirt, black high-top boots and white pants with black vertical stripes. On his wrist was an opulent Cartier watch. They were talking. They did not see Sadie.

On each side of the bed were semicircular, marble-topped tables. The one on the right held a princess phone and an oval-framed wedding portrait of the Polanskis. On the right marble table sat a bottle of Heineken's beer, Jay Sebring's favorite drink.

There was a white, louvered, double French door leading out to the swimming pool on the south wall of Sharon Tate's bedroom. The windows looking out onto the pool area were shuttered also with white, louvered blinds. It was out this door just minutes later that Abigail Folger would run for her life and Katie Krenwinkel would leave her Death Row fingerprint.

There was a large closet in Sharon's bedroom, as well as a bathroom and a dressing room. On the east wall of the bedroom was a tall armoire with drawers near the bottom. One of the drawers was full of photos of Miss Tate. On top of this wardrobe was a new white bassinet for the baby, wrapped in clear plastic; and, to the right, an ornate hookah. To the left of the armoire was a television set and a Sony videotape viewer.

Sadie returned to Watson in the living room and told him that there were people in the bedrooms. Tex was angry. Where was the money? He told Sadie to go into the bedrooms and bring them out into the living room. Sadie unfolded her Buck clasp knife and walked into Abigail Folger's bedroom waving her weapon: "Go out into the living room. Don't ask any questions." She did the same thing on the other side of the hall in Sharon's bedroom.

Sadie waved her knife at Jay and Sharon and they all walked out into the living room, confused and angry. Jay Sebring said, "What's going on?"

"Sit down!" Sebring refused to sit.

A crisis occurred for Katie at this point. She had no knife! So she walked outside and went down past Steve Parent's Ambassador to the gate to get Linda Kasabian's knife with the taped irregular handle. Katie told her, "Listen for sounds," then walked back up the hill to the house.

The tendency of Sebring—cool, experienced businessman—and Frykowski—survivor of Hitler—must have been not to panic or to fight—at first. But when Tex told everybody to lie down on the floor on their stomachs atop some pillows near the fireplace, Sebring would not stand for that and said, "Let her sit down, can't you see she's pregnant?" Then Sebring lunged for the gun and Tex waxed murderous and shot Jay in the armpit. Jay fell, and Tex drop-kicked him in the bridge of the nose. Abigail Folger screamed.

The bullet entered Sebring's left axilla, penetrating downward through the left fifth rib, through the left lung and exited out the left side of his midback. The bullet was found by the coroner several inches from the exit wound, trapped between skin and shirt.

Christopher, the Weimaraner, left the back patio porch of the guest house, barking and excited. The dog evidently trotted into the front door of the main house about this time. Sadie told Virginia Graham that a "hunting dog" came around. Sadie even thought that somehow the dog got hold of her knife: "We looked all over for it. . . . I really think the dog got it."

The sight of Jay Sebring lying on his side gave the former cotton picker, Charles Watson, instant credibility. "All right, where's the money?"

Abigail said that her money was in her purse on the couch in the bedroom. Sadie stuck the knife up to Miss Folger's back and marched her into the bedroom where Abigail opened up her black canvas shoulder bag and took out seventy-two or seventy-three dollars for the satanist. Sadie refused Gibby's offer of her credit cards and they walked back into the living room. Five souls, seventy-two dollars.

Tex then tied them around and around their necks with the nylon rope and threw the end of it over the white ceiling beam and told Sadie to choke the rope so that Abigail and Sharon had to stand up or else strangle. Jay's unconscious body acted as a dead weight on the other end of the rope, which was knotted around his neck. A large hematoma was swelling on his left eye.

Tex was worried lest Wojtek Frykowski should get loose so he told Sadie to retie his hands with a bigger towel. She went into the bedroom and got a larger towel, a beige forty-six-inch Martex bath towel, and tied his hands behind him more securely, then she pushed him back down onto the couch, standing guard over him.

Tex told Katie as he was wrapping the rope around their necks to turn out all the lights in the house. This she did, according to Susan Atkins. The next morning the only lights the police found on in the house were the hall light leading into the back bedrooms and the desk lamp on the east side of the living room.

Katie assumed choke duties on the end of the rope. One of the ladies asked, "What are you going to do to us?"

Charles, the smug muscular boy from Copeville, had them trapped in his own phoneless hamburger universe. "You are all going to die." And again he told them that he was the Devil. Immediately the moans and shrieks and begging rose up from the trussed victims. They struggled to get free.

Tex ordered Sadie to kill Wojtek Frykowski. Wojtek lay quaking up and down, desperately trying to loosen the knot behind his back. Sadie raised her knife and, by her account, hesitated. He wrenched his hands free and reached up from the couch and grabbed hold of her hair and pulled her down, grabbing her knife arm. He hit her on the top of the head and they fell against the end table to the left of the sofa and rolled onto the stuffed chair.

Sadie got her arm free and stabbed blindly, one, two, three, four times, parallel down the front of his left leg. He turned towards the front hall as if to flee. She managed to stab him once in the back but the knife hit bone. Then she stabbed him deeply in the right back lung. The skin surface widths of the wounds were three-quarters of an inch, the same as the width of her Buck knife. In the scuffle she lost her knife somehow, the knife the little terror-addict thought the dog had carried away. The police found the knife lodged blade up between the cushion and the back of the overstuffed chair, seven feet from the north wall and four feet from the west wall. Knifeless, she clung to his back and yelled.

Still, Wojtek staggered onward. Tex ran up, wrestled Frykowski around and shot him below the left axilla, the bullet lodging in his middle back. He shot him also through the front right thigh. Still he walked on. He shot again—

the gun misfiring. (The gun had a history of misfiring, as when Manson shot Bernard Crowe on July 1.) Tex began to club his face and scalp with the gun, holding it by the barrel. Wojtek's blood type was found on the intact left gun grip and on the inside of the cocked hammer of the gun. The right walnut grip broke into three pieces, two pieces falling in the front hall, the remaining tiny piece skittering out onto the front porch.

What was William Garretson doing during the screams and the shots? According to *his* testimony he was sitting in his living room, just fifty yards away, listening to the Doors and a Mama Cass album. And two freeways distant, on the northwest edge of the San Fernando Valley, Charles Manson was waiting by the dusty driveway in front of the Longhorn Saloon for the return of his patrol.

When Tex ran up to the hall door to get Wojtek, Sharon and Jay and Abigail struggled to get free from the knots on their necks. Katie was holding the rope where it trailed down on the other side of the beam. Abigail broke loose and headed for the back bedroom, where the door to the swimming pool led to freedom.

Krenwinkel dropped the rope and gave chase. Abigail, taller and stronger, fought for her life. Meanwhile, Tex spotted the struggling Sebring and ran up. Stab stab stab stab, four times Watson hacked him in the left back, into the lung. The wounds were one and a half inches wide on the surface, penetrating deeply. Tex's knife was sharpened, of course, along its normal cutting edge but the top edge had been sharpened also, for about an inch. The coroner was able to declare this long before the arrests by noting that vital organs were pierced by a double-edged instrument while the skin surface wound indicated that the upper knife edge was thick. Tex kicked his face, then turned, his attention caught by the yells from Katie, his black velour turtleneck beginning to get bloody, his eyes shiny. He ran up to Abigail, who was wounded only defensively at this point, in the hands and arms. Abigail surrendered. "I give up. Take me." He did, slicing her neck and smashing her head with the gun butt. He stabbed her in various parts of her chest and abdomen. She clutched a gaping tear in her lower right stomach. She fell.

Watson glanced up when he heard Wojtek screaming

near the front lawn. He ran to the front porch to see him rise up from the bush into which he had fallen and stagger across the grass toward the southeast, yelling. Sadie Satan told her cellmate, Shelley Nadell, about it. "He got to the lawn and was standing there hollering, 'Help! Help!' and nobody even heard him." An unlikely story. The police undertook noise tests at the Polanski residence and you can hear yells all over Benedict Canyon, not to mention a guest house with open windows. Did you hear those screams? Shut up and go back to sleep.

Deep in flower-power knelt the young mother Linda Kasabian by the dark fence. When she heard the screams, she claims she looked over at the dead Steve Parent and it dawned on her on a sudden that the occupants of the house were being killed. Then, just like a tadpole wriggling toward a light source, she raced toward the shriekers, "to try to stop it," as she later testified. She ran up the walkway, onto the grass. "I ran over to the hedge" —probably the almost s-shaped hedge to the immediate north of the front porch.

"Waited a minute—then I saw Frykowski staggering out the door—drenched in blood—I looked in his eyes—he looked in mine—I saw the image of Christ in him, I cried and I prayed with all my heart."

In her testimony at the trial she mentioned two mental events that occurred as their eyes met: her silent prayer, "Oh, God, I am so sorry. Please make it stop"; and also that in the midst of the terrible glance she began to feel Charles Manson no longer to be Jesus Christ the Son of God. He was a Devil.

Tall Wojtek stood up against the square wooden support post on the northeast corner of the porch and he tried to step from the flagstone onto the sidewalk, holding onto the post. His balance failed; he spun around the post and fell head first into the dirt.

Sadie ran out of the house upset that she had lost her knife. Linda testified that she tried to tell Sadie to make it stop, that she heard voices. Sadie said, "It's too late." They talked and somehow as the witches chatted Wojtek got to his feet and began to scream into the smog, down the Canyon. Someone had to hear.

It must be noted that where Linda claims to have

and the two knives. He pulled off to the right of Benedict Canyon and stopped. Linda threw the bundle down the ravine on the right. It bounced down intact, lodging within eyesight of the road, against a bush.

She was told to throw out the knives. She did—first one, which went down a hillside, then the other, which bounced on the curb as the car moved away. Evidently Tex had turned around before the tossing of the knives because Linda testified that the car was heading downhill. He announced that next they had to find a place to wash up. He pulled off Benedict left onto Portola Drive, just a block north of the street where Jay Sebring lived.

A couple of hundred yards from the turnoff they spotted a garden hose hooked up to the home of Rudy and Myra Weber. They turned the car around and parked the car toward the Canyon road so they could get away easily. They walked to the house. It was twenty feet from the street.

Rudolph Weber was asleep but the sound of running water woke him up. He thought it was a leak in his plumbing so he grabbed a flashlight and walked down to his basement, opened his garage door and went in to check out the pipes. No water was leaking so he figured everything was all right. Then he heard voices, from the street. Goddamn kids. He went over and flashed the light on them. "Just what do you think you're doing?" They looked like teenagers.

Tall Tex dialed his mind to smiling psychopath and said, "Hi—we're just getting a drink of water and we're sorry to have disturbed you." Rudolph walked over and turned off the water. The girls started walking down to the car.

"Is that your car?"

"No, it's not. We're walking."

Weber followed the young folk and by this time Myra was awake and by his side, announcing that her husband was a member of the sheriff's reserve. Tex opened the door for the girls and Weber was offended by the disarray inside. Tex got in and flooded the engine. Weber made as if he were trying to remove the keys from the car, reaching in while Tex was trying to start it. Finally the engine caught and Tex peeled out, wrenching Mr. Weber's clutching hand. As the car sped away, he memorized the number and later wrote it down, GYY 435.

Tex didn't turn on his lights until he reached the San Fernando Valley, where they stopped for two dollars' gas. Tex went to the john to wash, as did Sadie and Katie. Sadie noticed when coming back to the car that there was some blood on it. She hoped the attendant didn't see it. Tex told Linda to drive. On the way Tex evidently threw the Longhorn revolver out the right window down a ravine at a location about one and a half miles from the slaughter zone. It is strange, however, that none of the murderers seems to have mentioned throwing the revolver away. Perhaps Manson threw it away later.

During the remainder of the drive, the foursome seemed to relax, becoming even jovial. The weapons, the blood, the clothes, they were gone, weren't they? They were Helter Skelter's finest butchers. And they began to chit-chat.

To start it off, poor Tex had hurt his foot and it was killing him. Sadie's hair was hurting terribly where Frykowski had pulled it. Katie babbled on about how the knife handle hurt her hand each time she stabbed. All agreed that the knives were inadequate. Next time they would need heavier equipment. Sadie complained about the toughness of Wojtek's legs when she strained to stab them. They had quite a time describing the moans of the murdered, how Sharon kept calling out to God and Abigail kept crying out to her mother.

"How come you're back so early?" Charlie asked when they arrived at the Spahn Ranch. Charlie was waiting in the driveway, sitting by the Saloon. It was 2 A.M.

Sadie told Charlie that she had seen blood on the Ford. He told her to go to the kitchen and get a sponge and water and wash it down. Linda and Katie were to check the interior for spots. They found none, so Manson told them to go into the bunkhouse while Sadie washed the outside of the car. Charlie then took Tex aside to debrief him.

Clem and Brenda were in the bunkhouse when Katie and Linda arrived. They were totally exhausted. Pretty soon Tex and Charlie came into the bunkhouse for a general discussion of the evening. Tex told Charlie that everything had been messy; bodies were lying around, but all were dead. Charlie was happy.

Tex made several laugh when he revealed that he had said to people in the house, "I'm the Devil, I'm here to do the Devil's business, where's your money?" Ha ha. Manson then polled the hackers to see if any felt remorse for what they had done. Katie: "No." Sadie: "No." Linda: "No."

There is some indication that someone removed a credit card belonging to Wojtek Frykowski from the murder site. One witness claims that the credit card was brought out on later occasions as a relic to be passed from hand to hand during family gatherings.

People were sleepy. Kasabian went to the back ranch to sleep. Sadie made love with a man—she thinks it might have been Clem—then sacked out. Katie and Tex slept in the Saloon, according to Kasabian. It was over. But not quite.

There is considerable discrepancy between the scene of the murders, as left by Susan Atkins, Patricia Krenwinkel, Tex Watson and Linda Kasabian, and the one found by the police the next morning. Neither Susan Atkins nor evidently any of the others tucked any face towel over the head of Jay Sebring, yet the police found a towel over his head.

There was not enough slack in part of the rope extended from Sharon Tate to Jay Sebring for her to have been standing and moving around; yet she moved around the room, the killers say. So the rope perhaps was affixed some time after her death. The murderers, including Susan Atkins, do not mention fixing the rope, although the effusive Atkins gave long detailed accounts to anybody who would listen about every aspect of the crimes. Nor did Susan Atkins talk about the brown-framed glasses found by the bloody steamer trunks. These glasses were found face down with the frames open and jutting up perpendicular to the floor. They had belonged to a person with severe eyesight problems.

There were two large pools of blood on the front porch, one to the left of the door mat, type O–M, Sharon Tate's, and the other on the north edge of the porch, type O–Mn, Jay Sebring's. All the females involved, Linda, Katie and Sadie, have claimed that at no time were Sharon Tate or Jay Sebring ever near the front porch. How did the blood get there?

Steve Parent's, Frykowski's and Folger's blood types were all B–Mn, so that none of the blood on the porch could have been theirs. A police report describing the homicide scene said, regarding the blood of Sharon Tate on the front porch, that: "From the amount of blood there it would appear that she remained there for at least minutes prior to movement."

The police also thought that Mrs. Polanski's body may have been moved from one location to another, because of its condition. There were various spatters of Sharon Tate's blood in the front hall and on the door sill, but never, while the killers were at the estate, was she in the hall.

There were two steamer trunks in the living room by the hall door which were knocked away during the night. The killers didn't do it. The right end of the top trunk was resting on the left end of the bottom trunk, and the left side of the top trunk had tipped to the floor. There was a stain of blood, apparently from the same dripping, extending from the left side of the upper trunk to the top of the bottom trunk. It is Sebring's blood, yet the killers claim he was shot and stabbed and killed in one spot and never moved.

The answer is that Manson and a companion returned to the scene of the crime. "I went back to see what my children did," he told a lawyer at his murder trial.

When the killers returned to the Spahn Movie Ranch after the killings, Watson recalls that "Charlie was waiting for us on the boardwalk of the old movie set, dancing around naked with Nancy Pittman in the moonlight. His first words were, 'What're you doing home so early?' "

Tex recounted the killings to Manson, who was upset at the lack of results. Apparently he had wanted some slaughtering in other places along Cielo Drive. "When he asked why we didn't go to any other houses I just shrugged," Watson recalls.

Apparently unknown to the others, Manson then selected a pal to accompany him to Cielo Drive, where they parked, rather boldly, not far from the gate. They crossed the gate at the embankment the way the killers did and paused by the dead Steven Parent's car to wipe it down for prints, then went into the house and viewed the carnage. "I did not feel pity or compassion for the victims. My only concern was whether it resembled the Hinman killing. Would the police now have reason to believe that Bobby was not the slayer of Hinman?" And, of course, did anybody leave prints?

"I'd had thoughts of creating a scene more in keeping with a black-against-white retaliation, but in looking around, I lost the heart to carry out my plans." They took towels and wiped every surface clean, except for Tex's print on the front door and Katie's on the door out to the swimming pool. Manson took a beige towel and hooded it over the head of Jay Sebring, tucking the towel ends under the rope loops.

M's partner had an old pair of eyeglasses used as a magnifying glass to start fires, which they tossed down by Roman Polanski's steamer trucks as a false clue.

Then they were gone.

Danny De Carlo had related to the police about a night around August 8, 9 or 10, 1969, when Tex, Charlie and Clem left one night and returned the next morning. They asked De Carlo if he wanted to go along but he said no thanks. When they returned in the morning, De Carlo spotted Clem meandering in the dirt-way by George Spahn's house. When De Carlo walked up to Clem and asked, "What'd you do last night?" De Carlo looked back over his shoulder and spotted Charlie behind him, smiling. Clem then placed his hand on De Carlo and said, according to De Carlo, "We got five piggies." Then Clem turned heel and walked away grinning.

Stephanie, Manson's new-found love, testified that Manson woke her around dawn the next morning after the murders and took her in to Devil Canyon, probably the waterfall campsite, where she stayed about a week.

It was over. Over for five sparks of the universe, butchered by some new form of programmed zombie-spore.

16

Fear Swept the Poolsides

There were a number of screams and shots reported in Benedict Canyon during the night. Various people in various locations near the Polanski residence heard them between 2 and 4 A.M. Most of the screams were after the murders were committed. Nothing much, just ordinary Friday-night screams.

Between 4:30 and 5 A.M., Steven B. Shannon delivered the morning *Los Angeles Times* to the Polanski front gate and noticed that there was a wire down, draped across the fence. At 7:30 A.M., Mr. Seymour Kott, the temporary resident at 10070 Cielo Drive, walked out of his house to get his paper and noticed the wire down and saw the yellow bug light on the Polanski garage, shining in the distance.

Mrs. Winifred Chapman, the Polanski housekeeper, a well-spoken lady who had been working for them for just over a year, took a city bus to Santa Monica and Canyon Drive at the southern end of Benedict Canyon, arriving about 8 A.M. She was late and was considering calling a cab for the remainder of the trip to the Polanski residence when she saw a friend of hers, a man named Jerry, who took her up Benedict Canyon and Cielo Drive to the front gate of the estate. It was 8:30 A.M.

Mrs. Chapman pushed the button of the electronic gate, noted that the wire was down, picked up the *Los*

Angeles Times and walked up the drive. She reached the garage, snapped off the yellow bug light, then walked past the front of the three-car garage, turned right, out of view of the bodies, walked along the extreme north edge of the house to the back, turned and went into the house through a service entrance door.

She reached up on the rafter above the door and obtained a key from its usual place, unlocked the door, put the key back, walked into the service area, right, into the kitchen where she switched off the back patio light and put her purse down. She picked up the phone. It was dead.

She went into the dining room, walking south, to wake someone up to tell them there was no phone service. She saw the bouquet of flowers that Linda had seen the night before, resting on a small stand in the dining room.

When she reached the front hall, she saw a towel, she saw the steamer trunks, saw blood, saw a door open, saw out over the front porch, over the bloody doormat, saw Frykowski. Panic.

She ran back out of the house as she had come in, picking up her purse on the way. She ran screaming down the hillside parking lot, pushed the bloody exit button at the narrowing of the driveway, the gate opened up and she fled. She rang the doorbell of the house immediately down the driveway from the front gate. No answer. She ran down the hill to the Asim residence, where she encountered fifteen-year-old Jim Asim, a member of Law Enforcement Troop 800 of the Boy Scouts of America.

"There's bodies and blood all over the place! Call the police!" Mrs. Chapman was distraught to the degree that the young Boy Scout called up the police emergency number to seek assistance himself. Three times he called and finally a patrol car arrived, then another and another and another, sirens keening.

At 9:14 A.M., Officer J. J. De Rosa, operating West Los Angeles unit 8L5, and Officer W. T. Whisenhunt, operating West L.A. unit 8L68, were given a call by central dispatch: "Code 2, possible homicide, 10050 Cielo Drive."

Officer De Rosa arrived first, encountering the young man Jim Asim and the hysterical housekeeper, Mrs. Chapman. She told him of the blood and the body and she showed the officer how to operate the electronic gate.

De Rosa, rifle in hand, walked onto the property and encountered Steve Parent slumped in the Ambassador. The motor was off, lights off. As Officer De Rosa was checking out Parent's automobile, Officer Whisenhunt arrived, having "received a call to back up a fellow officer investigating a possible homicide" as he later testified.

They radioed for an ambulance and verified death. Whereupon they walked up into the property again, into the chaos of stilled souls. They noted Parent, then walked toward the garage, rifles ready to fire. They went up into the second story of the garage, where Roman Polanski was to set up his office, by the steps on the side, and checked it out. Nothing.

They walked past Sebring's black Porsche and the Firebird and the Camaro in the garage, and into the front yard, across the lawn where they encountered Wojtek Frykowski, wearing colored bell-bottomed pants and a purple shirt, and buckled, brown, high-top shoes. They saw Miss Folger a few yards to the south, white gown red.

Officer Burbridge of unit 8V5 was the next officer to arrive, joining the two policemen in the investigation. The three policemen could see the great amount of blood on the front porch and, of course, the open front door. They paused. Who could know what sort of maniac might lurk within the house? With De Rosa covering, Whisenhunt and Burbridge went around to the back of the house to check out possible entrances, but the door was locked. Whisenhunt and Burbridge decided to enter the open nursery room window on the far right of the house, the very window that Tex Watson had crawled upon. The window screen, with a slit, was resting against the house.

A few seconds later, Officer De Rosa observed his fellow patrolmen within the house, so he made to join them, walking over the flagstone porch into the hallway, avoiding the blood. He saw the ugly "PIG" scrawled in ugliness. And he walked into the ugly ghostly desolation of Manson's tableau. They noted the bodies and the rope and quickly searched the house, the bedrooms, the loft.

Later, Officer De Rosa was unable to recall seeing the two red barefoot prints on the porch.

Their job was to protect the scene and to make note of the original physical circumstances of the area, leaving it undisturbed.

The officers completed their search of the house and were evidently checking out the rest of the estate, the pool area, and were proceeding toward the guest house when they heard dogs barking. Then they heard a male voice within the guest house yelling at the dogs to quiet down. Five dead bodies and someone yelling at a dog.

Bill Garretson heard the dogs barking as the cops approached and yelled: "Quiet down!" and started to get up from the couch in the living room where he had been sleeping since shortly after dawn, or so he testified. He was a short, tanned boy with slightly long brown hair, age nineteen, barefoot, shirtless, and wearing pinstriped pants. He looked out the window onto the front porch and what he saw was an officer pointing a rifle at him. The officer told him to freeze. Christopher, the Weimaraner, was barking furiously. Garretson saw another officer leveling a rifle at him from the redwood picnic table on the porch. It was time for fear.

The first cop, Officer De Rosa, kicked the front door in and the Weimaraner rushed forward and chomped the officer's leg. They threw Garretson on the porch floor, ripping his pants knee, and handcuffed his hands behind his back. Garretson kept asking them, "What's the matter? What's the matter?"

"You want to know what's the matter? Well, we'll show you what's the matter."

They marched the handcuffed Garretson across the lawn to Abigail Folger, who lay upon her back in her nightgown. He thought the body was that of the maid, so destroyed was it. They marched him over to Wojtek Frykowski. He looked away from the unidentifiable victim. Then they took him to the Ambassador, where he couldn't identify the person inside.

Thinking that the first body was the maid, Garretson was taken aback encountering Mrs. Chapman alive, in the custody of an Officer Gingras, when he reached the front gate. When he asked whose body it had been, he was told in error that it was Mrs. Polanski's.

The police had captured the person who had probably been the last human to have seen the victims alive and the first person to have seen them dead. It was a classic investigation, requiring only that a lot of pressure be forthwith applied until he or she confessed and the case would be solved.

Mrs. Chapman and William Garretson were driven to the police station by Officers De Rosa and Whisenhunt while Officer Burbridge remained behind to protect the location. Mrs. Chapman evinced hysteria and was taken to the UCLA Medical Center for sedation and then was escorted by Officer Richard Gingras to West Los Angeles police headquarters for questioning. Bill Garretson was led daze-eyed into the lockup and sometime later an officer walked up and said, "There's the guy that killed those people."

Fear swept the poolsides of Los Angeles on the hot August morning as the news of the murders seeped through the network of phones.

Media sources, who monitor police radio broadcasts, were quick to note that something had happened on Cielo Drive. Reporters heard something about fires in Benedict Canyon with five people killed and that Sebring was a victim so one of them called Jay Sebring's house and spoke to an employee of Sebring, who had stayed over to paint or to repair the house. After the reporter called, the employee called John Madden, the vice-president of Sebring International, who called Sharon's parents. Mrs. Tate then called Cielo Drive. Even though the phone lines were severed, the telephone appeared to ring, giving the appearance that no one was home. This was not startling. Sharon was supposed to be staying at a girl friend's house.

All at once six squad cars sped up to the gate. Then more arrived.

Sergeant Klorman, the first uniformed supervisor, arrived with Officer Gingras, who took Mrs. Chapman to the station house.

Aerial photos taken a few minutes after the police arrived show the front gate of the estate aswarm with reporters, none of whom was allowed through the electric gate onto the property.

The reporters badgered the policemen as they entered and left the front gate. Security was tight but Sergeant Klorman, the first uniformed supervisor on the set, saw fit to announce to reporters about the condition of the beds: "All of the beds, including those in the guest house, appear to have been used. . . . It looked like a battlefield up there."

And thereafter the police entering and leaving began to give out bits of information on the crimes. One officer said about the murder scene that "It looked ritualistic." Those three words set the tone for early reportage of the events. The *Los Angeles Times* hit the stands that afternoon with a page-one story about "Ritual Murders."

The police gave out so much information that they were depleting the possible supply of "poly keys"—polygraph interrogation keys—which are key bits of information about the murders that only the killers could know, so that on a lie detector test the possible killer could be asked questions about these facts. If the facts were printed or broadcast, they would be spoiled for such a purpose.

One officer told the press that the victims were attired in "hippie type clothes." Another saw fit to announce that one of the victim's pants were down. Another that it looked like a "typical fag murder." There is no knowing what led reporters to print or officers to say that Sebring was wearing a black hood over his head. There is a great difference between a light-colored bloody towel and a black hood.

The police swarmed upon the residence, upon the roof, upon the grounds, scraping, dusting, making notes. It seemed like half the Los Angeles police department showed up at Cielo Drive that day. Over forty officers, including the chief of the Beverly Hills police department, plus ambulance drivers and four members of the coroner's staff, visited the property.

Police photographers took hundreds of photos of everything in the house and grounds. One of the jobs was to find out as much as possible about the victims immediately—with emphasis on enemies and people with motives. There were literally thousands of things to do immediately. First, they looked in purses and wallets to learn the identity of the deceased.

Around 10 A.M. the police called Sharon's mother.

They were terse. They obtained from her the name of William Tennant, her business agent. The police then seem to have located Mr. Tennant at his tennis club. He traveled immediately to 10050 Cielo Drive, arriving about noon, still attired in his tennis clothing.

He identified Mrs. Polanski, Miss Folger, Mr. Sebring and Mr. Frykowski, and left the premises at once, sobbing and holding back his stomach, refusing to talk to the congeries of reporters at the gate. A female TV gossip asked him if it was "really Sharon."

"Oh, don't be an ass," was the anguished reply.

When Mr. Tennant called abroad, it was early evening in London, and Roman Polanski was at the apartment of Victor Lownes, managing director of the London Playboy Club. At first Mr. Polanski thought it was a joke and hung up. The phone rang again and it was true. The rest is grief and tears. "She was such a good person," Mr. Polanski said over and over during the early shock.

Before 10 A.M. a team of West Los Angeles detectives arrived to take charge of the investigation. For the history, they were Lieutenant R. C. Madlock, commander; Lieutenant J. J. Gregorie, Sergeant F. Gravante and Sergeant T. L. Rogers. In addition, there were numerous West L.A. patrol officers on the property.

Officer Rivera covered the bodies with sheets. They went into the guest house to look for weapons, for Garretson at that time was a prime suspect. They checked immediately for signs of robbery and ransacking. There were no drawers open. Sebring still wore his $1500 watch. They went up on the rooftop to trace where the downed telephone and communications wires led. The glasses were found, face down, ear frames open and sticking up, just east of the blood-spotted steamer trunks.

They took for inspection Mr. Polanski's engraved .45-caliber revolver, which had been given to him by the cast of *Rosemary's Baby*. They took into evidence all knives to check for blood.

When Mr. Raymond Kilgrow of the phone company arrived between 10 and 11 A.M., newspaper and media reporters were already flocking at the outside rattan fence. Forthwith, Mr. Kilgrow discovered four lead-in wires fallen down, severed a few inches from the attachment at the top of the pole. He repaired two telephone wires and left two down pending police investigation. The police wanted to know what sort of device had severed the wires, so the phone man examined the wire to see what might have clipped it.

Later, Sergeant Varney found a rivet setter in the driveway and a pair of pliers and shears in the guest house. These were received as possible evidence. The officer cut a piece of the telephone cable to test these instruments on it to see if the cut marks were the same. They weren't. A foot and a half length of wire was cut off containing on one end the actual marks of the instrument used by the killer or killers to sever the wire. This was taken into evidence.

A call went out for the Special Investigation Division (S.I.D.) of the L.A.P.D. to send in blood analysts. Sergeant Granado arrived at 10 A.M. and began to take blood samples from forty-three locations all over the house and grounds. In effect, the officer created a blood-map of the murder house which was useful in determining how the crimes were committed. They removed the flag from the couch since it was spattered. They located three pieces of broken pistol grip from the Wyatt Earp revolver.

Everything was weird. There was that bloody flag. There were those blood barefoot prints on the sidewalk to the driveway. There were bloody pink ribbons hanging on the front door. There was a blood-soaked purple scarf found near Frykowski. These were removed.

Some police officer or other tracked blood on the front porch, leaving three red footprints. This created problems later when the police were trying to recreate the undisturbed scene. They had to find out what sort of soles officers had on their shoes in order to determine that the bloody shoe prints were in fact made by a policeman at the scene.

What seems to remain a part of the mystery is an evident bloody boot-heel print on the flagstone front porch that was not made by the police. Whose is it? Probably not Watson's or Manson's since they seem to have been wearing moccasins.

Sometime around noon the investigation of the murders was reassigned from the West Los Angeles division of L.A.P.D. to the robbery-homicide division of L.A.P.D.

Inspector McCaulay appointed Lieutenant R. J. Helder, supervisor of investigation, robbery-homicide division of L.A.P.D., to take charge. Lieutenant Helder subassigned responsibility for the investigation to Sergeant Michael J. McGann, and Sergeant J. Buckles, Sergeant E. Henderson, Sergeant D. Varney and Sergeant Danny Galindo. These homicide investigators finally arrived between 1:30 and 3:30 P.M.

Officer Jerome Boen and Officer Girt, fingerprint specialists, arrived at the Polanski residence about 12:30 P.M. and immediately began dusting for prints. The ridges of the fingers, palms and soles ooze with oil and fluid, constantly. An impression of the ridge patterns is made wherever surface contact is made. On hard, smooth surfaces the ridge impression or print can be removed.

First the officer powdered the surface with a gray powder. The powder was then brushed away with powder sticking to the ridges of the fingerprint or footprint. The print is then sprayed with iodine and transferred to a card with a special tape. Photographs are made of the precise location of the print.

The fingerprint officers were joined that afternoon at 5:30 P.M. by Officer Dorman and civilian fingerprint expert Wendell Clements. Another method of detection was used on those prints where dusting didn't detect the "moisture ridges" sufficiently because of the faintness of the ridges. They sprayed on an iodine chemical mixture and within twenty-four to forty-eight hours the print appeared.

There were fifty fingerprints found at the Polanski residence. Twenty-two were eliminated, three were "unmakable" and twenty-five remain unidentified. Of this twenty-five, quite a few were located on the freshly painted window sill of the nursery window, indicating that they were left there either the afternoon or the evening of the murders.

The chief medical examiner of Los Angeles County, Dr. Thomas Noguchi, took charge of the bodies. Noguchi ordered the bodies not to be disturbed till he and three assistants should arrive at the scene. The nylon rope connecting Sebring and Tate was ordered severed by Coroner Noguchi. Later the police cut the sections of the rope to trace source, manufacturer and possible purchasers. It was all grim.

A deputy coroner took liver temperatures of the victims as an aid in determining the time of death. Hands were wrapped with bags to save possible hairs and skin from the struggle with the killers. The ambulance crew brought wheeled stretchers and removed the victims, leaving behind pink death slips.

As he ran the query-gauntlet at the front gate of the estate, Dr. Noguchi told reporters he would announce autopsy reports about noon on Sunday, August 10.

Officers quickly went to Sebring's home to look for evidence. Several friends of Sebring rushed over to Sebring's house on Easton Drive to clean it out of contraband, evidently ahead of the police.

Sergeant Varney gathered up all the cutlery in both the caretaker's house and the main house. He also visited the Folger-Frykowski house at 2774 Woodstock and confiscated ten address and notebooks, some or all of which were written in Polish. Also taken into possession were various personal papers of the decedents and a box of "miscellaneous photographs and negatives" as it was listed in item number 65 in the police property report.

Later the police backed a van up to the Polanski house and carted a truckload of stuff down to S.I.D. headquarters for examination. A few days later they evidently brought most of it back and placed it in the same order to try to recreate the original undisturbed crime scene.

Someone picked the glasses up from the floor and put them on the table in the foyer. They were given to Mrs. Polanski's father, who held them for two weeks trying to locate the owner, who would have been a prime suspect.

The caretaker, William Garretson, was "questioned by investigators" at West Los Angeles jail at 4 P.M. He was advised of his rights and agreed to speak without counsel. "He gave stuporous and non-responsive answers to pertinent questions," a police source said. Shortly after the 4 P.M. interview, he retained the services of Los Angeles attorney Barry Tarlow. Garretson was then transported to Parker Center, the downtown L.A. police headquarters, where he was interviewed again, this time in the presence of Mr. Tarlow. It was fruitless. It was agreed that Garretson would submit to a polygraph examination (lie detector test) on Sunday, August 10, with Mr. Tarlow present.

Police instituted a day-and-night guard on the house that lasted almost two weeks. The Animal Regulation Department removed the dogs and the kitten.

The police conducted a dope search. They found a baggie half full of twenty-six grams of marijuana in the living room in a cabinet against the west wall. They found thirty grams of hashish in a box in the nightstand in Frykowski and Folger's room, plus ten MDA capsules. They found cocaine and marijuana in Sebring's Porsche and that vial of coke in his pocket.

Steve Parent's body remained unidentified for quite a while, lost in the rush. A reporter at the electric gate could see the license plate on Parent's Ambassador so he ran a make on it and got Parent's home address. A priest friend of Parent went down to identify the body. Steven Parent's father and mother evidently learned of his death over television. Already the murders were becoming the Tate Murders.

And so it went. Some policemen would not sleep for three or four days, so forceful was the investigation.

There were thousands of things to do. There were grief-whelmed relatives and friends. There was fear as never before. Thousands of rumors poured out of mouths. Acquaintances of the victims, some of them with enemies also, seemed to ask themselves, "Am I next?" What maniac was slouching through the smog with a grudge?

17

The Second Night

Sadie woke up in the morning and went into the trailer to watch the news. Immediately she encountered bulletins of the murders. She was excited. She hurried out to summon Katie, Clem and Tex so that they too might get a few thrillies from the tube. Tex seemed satisfied when the identity of the victims was revealed and commented: "The Soul really picked a good one this time."

Everything was normal at the Spahn Ranch for a Saturday. There were the usual weekenders on the scene to ride the horses. Ouish or one of the girls was in the corral-side office receiving the money from the riders. There was a garbage run down the hill into Simi. Some girls took care of George. Others got a load of corn for the horses. People worked on the dune buggies, preparing for the desert. Groins were clinked. But, in spite of the usual work, things seem to have been pretty tight-lipped. A young runaway named Maureen overheard Charlie chewing out various key people over the sloppiness of the murders.

It was generally known that it had been necessary to discorporate a few bodies into The Hole. Only a few knew who had done it and where. Everyone was acting calmly. Tex was his normal smiling self.

In the late afternoon, Sadie entered Johnny Swartz's trailer and demanded to watch the six o'clock news on

Channel 2. She left immediately after the report on the homicides was over, commenting, "We're going to get all those pigs"—evidently referring to the KNX–TV broadcaster. Juan Flynn, Barbara Hoyt, Katie, Linda and Tex were also in the trailer. The killers laughed during some of the broadcast, seeming to enjoy the report. Miss Hoyt later testified that she received enough information in the trailer to solve the case, had she been a snitch.

There was a garbage gobble about sundown. Everybody sang together and smoked dope, after which there was a cleanup in the kitchen. Kasabian said Gypsy had driven back from the waterfall and was talking about taking more girls there. She gave Linda Kasabian some Zu-Zus—Manson's term for candy—which Linda put in her pocket to eat after the long hard night ahead. Linda was going to go with Gypsy to the fall until Charlie came to the boardwalk and called her and Leslie and Katie outside.

He told Linda to get her license and a change of clothing. Linda has claimed she tried a beg-off with her eyes: "I looked at him—his eyes—my mind told him I didn't want to go—afraid to say it." It didn't work.

Charlie told the girls to meet him in Danny De Carlo's bunkhouse gun room. Stuck in a slit in the wall by the door were four bayonets and the Straight Satans' club sword. De Carlo was not in his room while Charlie briefed his disciples. But later that night when he returned to the room he noticed that the weapons were missing from their slit.

Tex had spent the day tinkering with the dune buggies and snorting speed with Bruce Davis. He had also taken LSD, and he was coming down. To rev himself up for the carnage, Watson went to his amphetamine supply, kept in the Gerber's baby bottle, and took three snorts in each nostril. Sadie too honked up some dope, and the upper-addled acidassins again were lined up on the edge.

There they were: Tex, Sadie, Clem, Katie, Leslie, Linda and the Wizard. Charlie said they were going out again. He seemed upset because of the messy caper of the night before. Tonight he would lead them himself, to show them how it should be done. Vern Plumlee, eager to be cut in on the caper, came up and asked Charlie if they needed any help but the car was too crowded.

Tex complained about the quality of the weapons used the night before. They decided to use sturdy bayonets and the Satans' sword. Once again they would use the yellow and white '59 Ford. Charlie drove with Linda and Clem in the front seat. Leslie sat on Tex's lap in the back with Katie and Sadie.

They started out of the driveway then stopped. Charlie called for Bruce Davis. Several minutes later Bruce came out of the woods where he had been sleeping. Charlie got out of the car and talked for a while with Bruce and Bruce gave him some money for gasoline. Charlie drove away down Santa Susanna Pass Road to Topanga Canyon Boulevard, turned right, drove to Devonshire, turned left on Devonshire. They stopped for gas on Devonshire, after which Linda Kasabian drove. They turned onto the San Diego Freeway and drove to the Ventura Freeway. They drove off the Ventura Freeway at the Fair Oaks turnoff in Pasadena. Throughout the drive Manson kept up a steady reassuring stream of conversation.

The trip to the LaBianca house was hesitant and tortuous. Charlie announced that the mission was to be split into two units of three. Up and down the streets of Pasadena drove the '59 Ford looking for a quiet reserved suitable location. They stopped at a house and Charlie got out. He told Linda to drive around the block and when she returned, Charlie was waiting. He got in and told them to wait and look.

In a driveway a few doors away a rotund gentleman and a lady got out of a parked car. Charlie said, drive on. They were informed that Charlie had seen pictures of children through the windows. Later, perhaps, they might have to harm children, but now they were to be left safe. Still in Pasadena, they cruised into an area of hills and larger houses. Charlie decided to drive. He drove to a hilltop and contemplated the possibility of crawling a two-story house there. He decided against it because of the nearness of neighboring houses. Someone might hear it.

On drove Snuff. Soon they passed a church and Charlie turned off onto the paved parking lot of the fane. God, you could just picture the headlines. But there was no one there. It was locked. Charlie got back into the car.

He drove to the Pasadena Freeway, proceeding westerly; hooked onto another freeway, winding up on Sunset Boulevard whereupon he allowed Linda to drive. She drove west, turning onto a dirt road near Will Rogers Park, not far from Dennis Wilson's house of the good old days. Manson decided to game a bit, directing Linda through a series of turns and maneuvers that left her confused.

She drove up a steep hill to a closed gate in front of an estate of some sort. She went into a series of left and right turns, arriving at a house. Charlie told her to return by the same route she had come. He was pressuring her. Finally he showed her how to get back to Sunset Boulevard.

They traveled east on Sunset Boulevard where it twists through Brentwood Park when lo, Manson spotted a small white sports car driven by a young man, headed the same direction. Manson told Linda, "At the red light pull up beside it." Charlie was going to strike.

Charlie started to get out of the car. Was Satan to write upon the white metal? Luckily for the young man, the light changed and the car got away.

From this point onward the Wizard seemed to know exactly where to go. Straightway he directed Linda to Silverlake. She drove down Sunset Boulevard, past Sunset Strip, past the several miles of garish hoardings advertising the latest rock and roll recordings, through the foothills of hype.

They arrived at the Los Feliz district just south of Griffith Park, pulling up in front of the home of Leno and Rosemary LaBianca on the other side of the street from their driveway. Both Sadie and Linda recognized the house right next door to the LaBiancas' residence. Linda recalled at the trial that she had been served a peyote fruit punch there the summer of the Chicago riots, when Harold True had lived in the house.

Linda said, according to her testimony, "Charlie, I've been here before. You're not going to 'do' that house, are you?'

Manson, according to Linda, then said, "No, the house next door."

Charlie got out of the car, grabbed a weapon and sneaked up the steep driveway, twin thong-nooses slapping his breast. While in the car, Linda lit up a Pall Mall

King Size and passed it around, awaiting the return of the Soul.

On August 5, Mr. and Mrs. Leno LaBianca had gone to the home of Leno's mother, Corina LaBianca, where they picked up their speedboat which they kept stored in her garage. They drove it north to Lake Isabella where their son, Frank Struthers, age sixteen, was visiting family friends. They left the boat there for Frank to use and returned to Los Angeles.

On Saturday, August 9, the LaBiancas returned to Lake Isabella accompanied by Rosemary's attractive twenty-one-year-old daughter, Susan Struthers. Their purpose was to visit the Saffie family where Frank was staying, to pick him up and to haul the boat back to Los Angeles. They spent the day on the lake, had dinner and prepared to leave. Frank Struthers was asked by his young friend, Jim Saffie, to stay on till Sunday. Accordingly, Susan Struthers and the LaBiancas left the Saffie residence at Lake Isabella around 9 P.M., leaving Frank there. They were driving a green 1968 Thunderbird, hauling the ski boat.

They drove immediately to Los Angeles. At 1 A.M. they dropped Susan off at her apartment in the 4600 block of Greenwood Place, not far from their own home. Shortly after 1 A.M., John Fokianos, who operated a newsstand at the corner of Hillhurst and Franklin Avenue, near the LaBianca house, observed their green Thunderbird pulling a boat-trailer, headed east on Franklin. It turned into the Standard station, made a U-turn and pulled up adjacent to Mr. Fokianos' newsstand.

The LaBiancas remained in the car. Leno bought a Sunday *Herald-Examiner* and the Sunday *National Daily Reporter*, a horse-betting publication. Rosemary LaBianca expressed concern about the murder of Sharon Tate and the others so Mr. Fokianos gave her a front-section filler from the Sunday *Los Angeles Times* with its "ritualistic murders" page-one story.

They talked for several minutes about the murders, shocked at the gruesome details. "She seemed quite emotional about it," Fokianos later was to tell reporters. Leaving the newsstand, Mr. and Mrs. LaBianca then drove to their home, parking the car on Waverly Drive just west of the house, with the boat still hitched to the back.

The white one-story house at 3301 Waverly Drive was in a quiet upper middle-class neighborhood near Griffith Park. The house, once owned, according to United Press International, by cartoonist Walt Disney, had been owned for a number of years by Leno's mother. Leno had lived in the house before, for a while, but moved out in 1959 when he married Rosemary. In 1968 Leno and Rosemary purchased the home from his mother, Mrs. Corina LaBianca. They moved to the location in November of that year. Rosemary's son of a previous marriage, Frank Struthers, Jr., also lived in the newly purchased house.

To the west of the LaBianca residence was the former estate of Troy Donahue, movie giant. To the north was an uncccupied hillside. To the east at 3267 Waverly Drive was the large house once rented by acquaintances of Charles Manson during the period September 1967 to September 1968. The three renting the house were Harold True, Ernest Baltzell and Allen Swerdloff. It was at Harold True's house the summer before that some of the family had undertaken a group LSD journey.

Leno LaBianca was the chief stockholder of the State Wholesale Grocery Company which operated the Gateway food market chain, businesses begun by his late father and later managed by Leno prosperously. Mr. LaBianca had extensive property interests in California and Nevada. He owned an enterprise called Arnel Stables and possessed nine thoroughbred race horses, including Kildare Lady, a horse of some prominence. He formerly was a member of the board of directors of the ill-fated Hollywood National Bank. He left $100,000 in various life insurance policies.

He was an avid coin collector, owning at times, $10,000 to $20,000 worth of rare coins. At the time of his death, Mr. LaBianca had $400 worth of uncirculated nickels in the trunk of his Thunderbird. At the time of his death, he was negotiating the purchase of a ranch in Vista, California for $127,000. Whereas his financial affairs were amazingly intricate, one thing remains apparent: he was rich. Leno liked to gamble, visiting the race track often. He did it in style, often betting as much as $500 in a single day. For some reason the LaBianca telephone was tapped. This is known because a telephone repairman was called to the home the day before the murders due to some trouble on the line. The repairman discovered the tap. It is thought that the phone was monitored because Mr. LaBianca may occasionally have used the services of a famous bookmaker known as The Phantom who lived just down the street.

Mr. LaBianca was only forty-four years old.

Rosemary LaBianca was thirty-eight years old. She was co-owner of a successful dress and gift shop, Boutique Carriage, located at 2625 North Figueroa within the Gateway shopping center which her husband owned. She herself was a successful businesswoman, speculating in stocks and commodities. She left her children an estate valued at $2,600,000.

To ward off theft, they removed the water skis from the boat and carried them to the back entrance of the house and set them on the fender of Mrs. LaBianca's '55 Thunderbird, which they had left parked by the garage. When they entered the house Mrs. LaBianca placed her purse on the liquor cabinet in the dining room. She went to the bedroom, turned down the covers and prepared to go to bed. Both put on sleeping attire.

A few minutes later Leno was sitting in his pajamas in the south side of the living room, checking out the *Herald-Examiner* sports section and the racing form, drinking a can of apple beer. The rest of the newspaper and his reading glasses rested on the table in front of the L-shaped sectional sofa on which he was sitting.

He was creepy-crawled. He looked up and saw a short hairy male Caucasian wearing a black turtleneck sweater, levis, moccasins and waving a cutlass. Charlie told Leno, "Be calm, sit down and be quiet." He located Mrs. LaBianca in the bedroom. He told them to stand up and tied them up, back to back, using two forty-two-inch leather thongs from around his neck. The knot was a double square knot. He told them that everything was okay and they weren't going to get hurt. He sat them down on the divan, and then he walked over to the liquor cabinet, removed Mrs. LaBianca's wallet from her purse, and walked out the front door, leaving it unlocked.

Linda Kasabian was just finishing her Pall Mall cigarette when Charlie walked down the driveway to the car and looked in. He'd been inside the house about five minutes.

Sadie claimed later that when Charlie looked at her, she begged off of the mission with her eyes and that Charlie could scan her mind and know that she didn't want to do it. Linda too contended in her various statements that she confronted Charlie with silent vibes so that he would refuse to nod her into the murder crew.

Charlie called Tex, Leslie and Katie out of the car and gave them a few final instructions. They could hear only parts of the briefing in the car. He said there were two people in the house and that he had tied them up. He told them that the people were calm and not to instill fear in them. Then kill them. Then they were to hitchhike back to the ranch. Katie was to go to the waterfall.

Charlie opened the door and Linda slid over into the passenger side and Charlie got in, handing her Rosemary's billfold. He started the engine and drove the Ford away, bearing the second half of the two-part squad.

They walked into the house bearing their changes of clothes. Once inside the foyer and entering the living room, they saw the terrified couple. They went to the kitchen to choose the weapons. From a drawer they obtained a white-handled ten-inch bi-tined carving fork, belonging to a set, and an eight-inch serrated wood-handled knife. They pulled down the kitchen shades to avoid detection. Everything was calm. Nothing was said about the Devil.

The girls, Katie and Leslie, untied Rosemary LaBianca and took her to the bedroom where they placed her face down on the bed. She was attired in a shorty nightgown over which she wore a robe. They removed the pillowcase from one of the pillows and fitted it over her head. Then they pulled out the plug and tied her neck with the cord of a heavy bed lamp which was attached also to another bed lamp, knotting it near the end. Everything was going to be okay, they told her.

Tex pushed Leno back upon the couch and ripped open his pajama tops, exposing the large full stomach of the buinessman. Homicide Sergeant Galindo was to find a ripped-off button lodged in a buttonhole of the pajamas the next night. Tex began stabbing him and Leno struggled and screamed and shrieked, his hands behind him.

He fell against the table, knocking the apple beer and newspaper all over the floor. Blood covered the cushions.

Tex had him down on his back and slashed him four times in the throat leaving the serrated knife buried deep within. He stabbed him four times in the abdomen into the colon, all fatal wounds. He bled to death, helped by the throw pillow with which Tex smothered his face to stop the screams.

When Mr. LaBianca began to shriek, Mrs. LaBianca began to struggle. She fell to the floor pulling the neck-cord taut and the lamp toppled. Over and over again she kept screaming, "What are you doing to my husband!"

Later, when everybody had returned to the Spahn Ranch, Sadie was quick to debrief Katie about what had gone on inside the LaBianca house. Katie told her about the screams: "That's what she'll carry into infinity." Sadie agreed.

Leslie held her, Katie stabbed. She crawled approximately two feet, the lamp cord on her neck, dragging the heavy lamp. Her spine was severed and she was paralyzed, lying on her face, parallel to the bed and the dresser.

Tex left the dying Mr. LaBianca in the living room and raced to the aid of the girls. Forty-one times they wounded her, mostly in the back; three were in the area of her chest. There were three linear abrasions on her back, made with a dull instrument, perhaps the electrical plug. All wounds were made with the same knife.

They pulled her nightgown and her robe over her shoulders and over her head, exposing her back and her buttocks. Leslie was not participating.

Tex wanted Leslie to stab. So did Katie. Leslie was very hesitant but they kept suggesting it. She made a stab to the buttocks. Then she kept stabbing, sixteen times. Later the nineteen-year-old girl from Cedar Falls, Iowa would write poems about it.

They were dead. It was time to leave the world a few signs. Tex took the bayonet or perhaps the metal prongs of the electrical plug and made a series of scratches near the navel proceeding toward the chest of Leno LaBianca which, from a distance, looked like a row of overlapping Xs. Up close the bayonet cuneiform scratching turned into the word "WAR."

Not to be outdone, Katie took the carving fork and stabbed both bodies with it. Seven double punctures she punched here and there into the abdomen of Mr. LaBianca, till she left it embedded in his flesh near the navel to the bifurcation of the tines. Katie said she was fascinated by the fork. She reached over to it as it stood out from his stomach and she gave it a twang and it vibrated.

Knife in the throat, fork in the stomach, acts insanely inspired by the song "Piggies": "You can see them out for dinner with their piggie wives, clutching forks and knives to eat their bacon."

They took the white electrical cord attached to a massive floor lamp near the couch and tied it around his neck, knotting it. They put the small throw pillow over his face. Then they fitted a pillowcase from the main bedroom over both his head and the pillow. They left him on his back, the "WAR" and the fork exposed.

Then they wrote on the walls. They removed a long narrow tapestry on the north wall facing the front door and placed it on the floor. There, in Mr. LaBianca's blood, they scrawled for all to see as they entered: "DEATH TO PIGS." Later, when Sadie debriefed her, Katie told how she had seen pictures of the children in the house. Katie said that she figured that the kids would probably be coming over for dinner Sunday and they'd find the dead bodies.

Six feet eight inches up on the south wall of the living room, directly to the left of the front door, they printed the word "RISE," above a painting. They folded a piece of paper to use as the blood brush. It was found, bloody and frayed on one end, in the dining room.

In the kitchen on the double doors of the refrigerator Katie began to scrawl. She meant to write "HELTER SKELTER" but committed some sort of psychological slip by writing "HEALTER SKELTER" instead.

Leslie wiped the house down for prints, taking her time, wiping all the surfaces they had touched and more, leaving no family prints for the police. Then they took a shower together in the rear bathroom and changed their clothing.

They went to the kitchen. Boy, were they hungry. But first the girls fed the dogs. They patted the three dogs who had watched silently throughout the massacre and who had licked the gory hands of the killers. Then the humans ate, locating some food in the ice box. They left a watermelon rind in the kitchen sink then they found some chocolate milk which they drank and carried with them as they left by the east door, leaving it ajar. Clutching their bloody clothes, down the hill, drinking the milk.

None of the expensive camera equipment, diamond rings, rifles, shotguns, valuable coins were disturbed. Leslie Van Houten seems to have taken a sack containing about twenty-five dollars' worth of rare domestic and foreign coins. These she sorted out at the ranch.

They threw the clothing away into a garbage can a few blocks away. They walked to the Golden State Freeway, found an entrance and began to hitchhike, securing a ride all the way from Griffith Park to Santa Susanna Pass Road, near the ranch. The driver was familiar with the Spahn Ranch, even going so far as to ask them if that was where they were going. Oh no, they said. This person's identity, although known by some, was never determined by the police.

Meanwhile, the second triad of killers had driven away in the yellow and white Ford. After Manson handed her the wallet, Linda Kasabian checked out the credit cards and saw the I.D.—Rosemary with some Italian surname.

They drove quite a distance on the Golden State Freeway out into the valley to Sylmar where they pulled off onto Encinatus Boulevard. They drove into a Standard station where Linda Kasabian walked into the ladies' room to dispose of Mrs. La Bianca's billfold. She placed it inside the water closet above the flushing mechanism where it remained for four months, although it is company policy at all Standard serice stations to change the bluing agent in the restroom water closets once a day.

When Linda returned, Charlie was displeased that she had placed the wallet in so obscure a location as inside the water closet. They drove then to a beach south of Venice, near some oil tanks, where they parked the car on a hilltop. They all got out, Manson with Linda, Sadie with Clem. Then the young mothers walked hand in hand down the beach with Clem and Charlie.

According to Kasabian, Manson asked her on the beach if there wasn't some "pig" nearby that she and Sandy had met. According to Manson, on the other hand, Linda aka Yana the Witch announced that she wanted to waste some "fat pig" in Venice, so he agreed to drive her there but she didn't have a weapon.

The person in question was the actor, Saladin Nader, whom Linda and Sandy Good had met a few days previous on Topanga Beach. It was he who had played a role in a movie about the youth of poet Kahlil Gibran. Nader's apartment was located on the fifth floor of 1101 Ocean Front Street, near the Beach House Market, in Venice.

The four drove there from that beach south of Venice. After they arrived Linda agreed to show Manson Nader's apartment. She said that she took Charlie to the floor below Nader's and pointed to another door, evidently seeking to save Nader. They then walked back downstairs.

Clem, or one of them, went to a biker's house and borrowed a gun.

"If anything goes wrong, just hang it up," Charlie said.

Manson said for Kasabian to knock on the door while Sadie and Clem waited down the hall. When she was able to get into the pad then all should pounce and kill. Charlie gave her a pocket knife and showed her how to slit a throat.

Then Exterminans got into the '59 Ford and evidently drove back to the Spahn Ranch.

Mrs. Kasabian, two months pregnant, having already decided to save Mr. Nader, instead led Clem and Sadie to an apartment on the floor below Nader's apartment. There she seems also to have deliberately spared the occupant. She knocked on the door. Someone opened it a little ways. Mrs. Kasabian then excused herself, saying she had the wrong apartment and the mission was voided.

They walked along the beach. Sadie went into the ladies' room on the beach near a pier. Clem seems to have buried the revolver in a sand pile or by a pier. They hitchhiked north along the Pacific Coast Highway. Someone gave them a ride to the mouth of Topanga Canyon.

Then they stopped to visit a house next to a business known as the Malibu Feed Bin. They went in, sat around in the living room for a while, smoked a joint, then Sadie, Linda and Clem went back to the street to hitch to the ranch. A second ride picked the three up and took them up and over Topanga Canyon and down into the valley.

A third car drove them up Topanga Canyon Boulevard through Chatsworth and let Linda and Clem off at Santa Susanna Pass Road. During the third ride, Sadie and Clem sang snatches of George Harrison's song, "Piggies."

Sadie went further up the highway to the road leading the back way to the waterfall campsite where she and Katie talked about the deaths of the second night of terror.

Section III

MANSON CAPTURED

(August 16—December 1, 1969)

18

The Search

The investigation facing the police was extremely complex and, for the most part, a labyrinth of blind alleys and tedium. Everything at the Polanski residence, even the wastebaskets, had to be sifted for data. Address books, personal papers, house and grounds, everything, sifted for enemies. Police combed the brushy hillsides of Benedict Canyon looking for the murder weapons. Others began to search for the type of revolver to fit the bloody bits of walnut pistol grip found in the residence. 10050 Cielo Drive was kept under continuous police guard for about two weeks.

On Sunday morning, August 10, the Los Angeles County medical examiner, Dr. Thomas Noguchi, supervised the autopsies of the victims, he himself conducting the examination of Sharon Tate. Several homicide investigators were on hand during the autopsies. Included was one of the sheriff's office detectives investigating the Gary Hinman murder. This detective approached the officers handling the Polanski murders and told them about the similarities between the two sets of murders: writing in blood, wounds inflicted by knives, etc. The officers of the Tate investigation considered the similarities insignificant, however, since there was already a suspect arrested for the Hinman murder when the Sebring-Parent-Folger murders were committed.

Press accounts of autopsy findings took care to note that the baby was perfectly formed, evidently to curb possible speculation pertaining to one of Polanski's movies. The wildest assertions appeared in national publications about the physical state of the decedents, based on inaccurate information supposedly leaked from an employee of the coroner's office. All around the world there were articles and broadcasts speculating about the circumstances of the crimes and lives of the deceased. In Los Angeles, reporters thronged at police headquarters for data.

Since everything any officer said was being printed, they had to be careful. On Sunday, Lieutenant Robert Helder, the head of the investigation, told a news conference that efforts to locate the killer or killers were centered on acquaintances of the short, slim caretaker William Garretson. Sergeant Buckles explained later that homicide detectives were "not entirely satisfied" with Garretson's answers to their questions. In the afternoon Garretson was given an hour-long lie detector test, in the presence of his attorney, Barry Tarlow.

Lieutenant A.H. Burdick of the scientific investigation division, L.A.P.D., administered the polygraph examination at 4:25 P.M., August 10, at the Perker Center police headquarters. Investigators had found Garretson "stuporous and vague," as if he were under the influence of some kind of narcotic. During his polygraph interrogation he still seemed confused and unable to remember things.

Garretson was extremely vague about what had gone on at the Polanski residence the evening of the murders. The polygraph examination revealed that someone seems to have arrived at the residence immediately prior to Garretson's trek down to the Sunset Strip where he bought food. Here's what he said: "And so I stayed home all day Friday, August 8, and I cleaned up the house a little bit and did the dishes and everything, and they came around 8:30, 9 o'clock, somewhere around there. And I went to get something to eat, and I went down on the Strip; I had something down there, and I could see her light all the way down from Cielo—not Cielo, but Benedict Canyon, all the way down to the Strip."

Who are the "they" who arrived about 8:30? The

victims returning from dinner at the El Coyote restaurant? Or guests? Garretson was even more vague about what he was doing during the murders. At the trial he testified that he spent the time writing letters to a friend named Darryl and listening to The Doors and a Mama Cass album. During the polygraph examination he admitted he may have gone out in back of his house. The back yard of the guest house is out of view of the main house and grounds so perhaps he hid there. In spite of inconsistencies, his answers regarding his innocence were shown on the polygraph to be truthful, so Garretson was eliminated as a suspect. The matter of William Garretson is far from cleared up however. There remains the possibility that he was hypnotized, drugged and left at the murder site as a fall guy.

Steve Brandt, former press agent for Miss Tate and a gossip columnist for *Photoplay* magazine, arrived on Sunday, August 10, from New York, where he had been working on assignment. He was questioned repeatedly by police investigators and supplied "voluminous information," according to reports at the time, about Sharon Tate and her circle of friends and about dope and Frykowski's ten-day mescaline experiment. Mr. Brandt had been a legal witness when Mr. and Mrs. Polanski were married in London in 1968.

Friends of the deceased began to fly to Los Angeles, and some were interrogated and given polygraph examinations. Rudy Altobelli arrived from Europe Sunday evening. Since the residence was sealed off, he went to a place where he felt he would be safe—to Terry Melcher's Malibu beach house! Only later did he realize the irony. He was interviewed by the police. They asked him about the party in March where Roman Polanski threw a person out. Early speculation held that the "PIG" on the front door was actually "PIC," the nickname of one of the men thrown from the party. They also asked him questions about the relationship between Mr. and Mrs. Polanski. Mr. Altobelli was asked at the trial when he, Altobelli, first thought that Manson might be responsible for the murders. Altobelli replied that he thought of Manson as a suspect on the plane trip back to the United States just after the murders. He did not volunteer the information to the police, he said, because he was not asked about it.

Later on Sunday evening, August 10, Roman Polanski arrived at Los Angeles International Airport and was silent coming through customs when the reporters crowded about with lights and microphones. His friend and associate, Gene Gutowski, read a short statement to the press that spoke against sensationalistic printed rumors of rituals, marital rifts and so on that had filled the front pages and airways of Europe and America. Roman Polanski at once went into seclusion in an apartment located within the Paramount Studios complex.

Late Sunday night police found Polanski's 1967 red Ferrari, license number VAM 559, in a body repair shop where it had been taken for maintenance—thus removing the possibility that it may have been used as a getaway car by a robber-killer. Around this time, artist Witold K., speaking nervously in Polish, called a friend in New York from a phone booth in Los Angeles. He claimed that he knew who the killers were and that he was afraid.

Friends in New York then called a *New York Times* reporter in Los Angeles and related the development. The reporter thereupon called the Los Angeles police.

Since Witold K. expressed fear for his life, the police promised him twenty-four-hour protection if he would talk. Then his friends called Witold K. back at the phone booth where he was waiting and he agreed to the guard. Three police cars picked up Witold K. and took him to the apartment at Paramount Studios where Roman Polanski was in seclusion.

Witold K. told police that Frykowski was offered an exclusive dealership to sell the drug MDA, evidently in the Los Angeles area. Subsequent friction developed, he claimed, and one of the suppliers threatened Frykowski's life. Witold K. claimed not to know the names of the possible killers but to know them by face only. And that they were Canadian. One close friend claims that Witold K. went around, escorted by police, to the many prestigious addresses in Frykowski's notebooks to try to locate the killer—always leaving behind his business card. Witold K. claimed that the identity of the killers was contained perhaps in these notes and diaries but he seems to have said that "it would take two weeks" for him to decipher the killers' identity from Frykowski's notebooks.

Like many new arrivals from a foreign country, Mr.

Frykowski made voluminous notes and took many phone numbers and addresses. He also kept a diary, written in Polish.

Witold K.'s painting career was enhanced by his revelation. One newspaper account showed a picture of Witold K. posing with several of his paintings on the Polanski front lawn. A friend has claimed that Witold K. even sold a couple of his paintings to two policemen investigating the case.

This is typical of the hundreds of leads followed vigorously by the police that led to blind walls of cool, silent traffickers in dope. And nothing is more secret than the big-league dope trade.

Around 8:30 P.M., August 10, the sixteen-year-old son of Rosemary LaBianca by a previous marriage, Frank Struthers, was driven home from his vacation at Lake Isabella and was dropped off in front of 3301 Waverly Drive. He saw the family car, the '68 Thunderbird, parked on the street with boat attached. He walked up the driveway past the kitchen windows, noticed that the window shades were drawn, evidently an unusual condition. He walked up the driveway to the garage to the back door and knocked. No answer. The door was locked. He saw the water skis on the fender of the other car, also a Thunderbird, parked by the garage. He knocked on the den window. No answer. He walked down to a Charburger stand and phoned. No answer. He made another phone call to try to locate his sister, Susan Struthers. In a while, Susan Struthers called back and her brother told her of his apprehension.

About 10:30 P.M. his sister Susan and her fiancé, Joe Dorgan, arrived at 3301 Cielo Drive, where they met sixteen-year-old Frank Struthers, Jr. They obtained the house keys from the ignition switch of Mrs. LaBianca's Thunderbird. The three walked into the house through the back door. Susan stayed in the kitchen while Frank Struthers, Jr., and Joe Dorgan walked through the dining room into the living room and saw Mr. LaBianca "in a crouched position" on the floor. They knew something was wrong. The two about-faced and fled. Dorgan picked up the phone in the kitchen as if to call, then dropped it. They ran into the yard yelling for help, and a neighbor called the police. About 10:45 P.M. police cars began shrieking to the scene.

In short order the property was aswarm with reporters and homicide investigators. The *Los Angeles Times* made it a page-one story with the caption "2 Ritual Slayings Follow Killing of 5," linking it to the murders of Friday night. Police released practically all the major details of the LaBianca murders to the media. The newspapers made mention of the knife and fork in Mr. LaBianca and the word "war." They told of the white "hood"—the pillowcase over his head. What evidently was not released to the media were the bloody words "Healter Skelter" written on the icebox doors. But they did release the fact that there were blood words on the icebox doors. The *Los Angeles Times* story, for instance, mistakenly related that "the words 'Death to Pigs' had been smeared on the doors of the refrigerator, apparently by the heel of a slayer's hand . . ."

Manson's good friend Gregg Jakobson was questioned right after the murders by the police because of his association with Rudy Altobelli. Had the words "Healter Skelter" on the icebox been released to the media by the police, Jakobson, who was one of scores of people who knew what the words meant, certainly would have told the police about the Manson family. Then Manson and crew probably would have been arrested immediately and further murders would have been prevented. It is possible, however, that the police, alarmed by the untoward discussion of the so-called Tate murders by the police at the Polanski residence, may have wanted to make certain that a number of polygraph interrogation keys remained this time. Therefore they may have withheld "Healter Skelter" as well as the bloody word "rise" in the living room.

On August 11, in the afternoon, authorities released the caretaker, William Eston Garretson, having held him for two days. He walked out of custody with his attorney, Barry Tarlow, into a barrage of cameras.

On August 11, police "backed away" from linking the Cielo Drive and Waverly Drive murders. "There is a similarity," remarked Sergeant Bryce Houchin of the L.A.P.D., "but whether it's the same suspect or a copy cat, we just don't know." The difference in life styles, the different circles of friends, the lack of any apparent connection, were important factors in the decision to split up the investigation of the two sets of murders. By Tuesday, August 12, 1969, detectives officially ruled out any link between the Tate and LaBianca crimes.

The LaBianca investigation team was headed by Captain Paul LePage and detectives from robbery-homicide, including Sergeant Phil Sartuche, Sergeant Manuel Gutierrez and Sergeant Frank Patchett, all of whom played considerable parts in bringing down the house of Manson. The LaBianca investigation centered on business dealings and gambling activities of Leno LaBianca. It was discovered that there was about $200,000 missing from Gateway Markets, one of Mr. LaBianca's business enterprises. Mr. LaBianca was a rare coin collector with collections worth thousands of dollars. A rare coin collection, believed to be Mr. LaBianca's, was found in a house on Waverly Drive a couple blocks from the LaBianca residence. This house was owned by a notorious bookmaker known as The Phantom aka Edward Pierce and had been abandoned by him a week after the LaBianca murders.

Close associates of Mr. LaBianca denied the possibility that the Mafia had contracted his death. If it had, they said, they would have heard about it. Police made an activity chart by date divided into half-hour increments showing the activities of Leno and Rosemary LaBianca between August 4 and August 10, 1969. They gave lie detector tests to most major acquaintances of the decedents.

There were twenty-five prints found in the LaBianca house. Nineteen were eliminated, six remain unidentified. 41,634 suspects were checked against the print on the liquor cabinet where Mrs. LaBianca's wallet was stolen by Manson.

The LaBianca investigation team arranged so-called M.O. runs with the CII (State Bureau of Criminal Indentification and Investigation) computer, in Sacramento at the California Department of Justice. The CII crime computer has a huge amount of information stored regarding crime and criminals. An M.O. run collects all crimes with the same methods of perpetration. A police agency can, as in this case, get a list of every murder where the killer tied up the victim, or wrote on the wall, in order to obtain the identities of potential suspects.

One of the problems facing the police in the Polanski residence murders was the overwhelming number of suspects. The decedents' lives were fraught with relationships that could have spawned violent grudges.

The murders provided impetus for a great number of narcotics arrests. Some individuals, however, were promised immunity from dope prosecution if they would provide information about the deceased and possible culprits. Three L.A. homicide detectives went to Vancouver to help the Royal Canadian Mounted police to organize a dragnet for the Canadian dope dealers that Witold K. and others had fingered. The dope dealers were believed headed toward Edmonton, Alberta or already holed up in the western Canadian woods.

U.S. Treasury agents investigated aspects of drug traffic to see if there was a pattern of interstate trafficking. In the days following the murders there were large-scale cocaine arrests around the country which have been linked to the reverberations resulting from the murder investigation. Police traveled around the country administering polygraph examinations. They even went to England to interrogate suspects.

Lieutenant-colonel Paul Tate, Sharon Tate's father, resigned from the service two weeks prior to his scheduled retirement after a twenty-year career. He proceeded to work ceaselessly in pursuit of the killers, concentrating on drug motives. He grew a beard and infiltrated dope lairs. "I guess I've seen just about everything in hippie communes while checking out drug angles," he commented in an interview after Manson's arrest.

Mr. Peter Folger, Abigail Folger's father, according to numerous people interviewed, initiated an intense investigation into the matter, as did Roman Polanski, who was assisted by several famous Los Angeles private investigators. "Polanski worked on it himself. But Polanski didn't realize it was hippies. He was working in his own area," reported one of his investigators. Polanski was protected constantly by two armed bodyguards. In fact, at least ten private investigators in Los Angeles were used extensively throughout the investigation of the case, both by private parties and the district attorney.

In the matter of the movies, police found a bunch of films and videotapes during the follow-up investigations. Some were found in the Polanski residence in the main bedroom closet. One particular videotape was found in a

ıad also had an affair with Beatty in
ıad phoned Warren once and . . . I
drunken, stoned stupor, to lay off other
d get himself seriously injured. Warren
that conversation to Roman, who must
ssed with my anger and potential for

ked into Phillips's Bel Air garage and
ically checked his Jaguar for bloodstains,
, although he found a machete in the
time he was alone in Phillips's Rolls
rifled through Phillips's Gucci diary. "I
the entries, from first page to last, were
k capitals. What chilled me was that the
a distinct resemblance to the word 'PIG'
srawled in blood on the door at Cielo
ly photocopied some sample pages and sent
r with photographs of the 'PIG' inscription,
ng expert in New York." Again no results.
in this mini-investigation, according to John
rred at the Malibu beach house of Michael
was busy directing the movie *Myra Brecken-*
ich Mr. Phillips was composing music. Phil-
there was a full moon, which would have
s the very day that just a few miles away the
were burying the remains of one of their
rty Shea.
e all helping to prepare dinner," Phillips writes.
as chopping vegetables with a cleaver. I was
he couch, still in my bathing trunks. Suddenly
werful hand clutch my hair from behind and
ead back with a violent jerk. I felt the razor-
e of the cleaver pressed against my throat. I
d the shape and strength in the hand from count-
restling bouts. Roman grunted. 'Did you kill
Did you?' "
illips assured him he had not.
ptember 2, 1969, Rona Barrett asserted on KTTV,
media station serving Los Angeles, that Roman
had received $50,000 from *Life* Magazine for
os and story from the murder house. The charge
tly denied by Polanski and his attorneys. Mr.
ltobelli became incensed over the alleged $50,000

room off the living room loft and was booked as item #36 in the police property report. Other films were taken into possession in Jamaica and in Annandale, Virginia. Part of the films involved an elite underground film group in Hollywood that swapped torrid films of each other.

One videotape found at the Polanski residence was of Roman Polanski and Sharon Tate making love. It was not booked into evidence but was returned, after police viewed it, to the spot in the loft above the living room where police had found it.

During Manson's trial, his lawyers were approached by a representative of a rising movie actress who had left a roll of undeveloped 35 mm film containing pictures of herself getting after it at the Polanski residence on the day of the murders. The representative asked Manson if the family had removed the film from the house that night since she had been unable to find out what happened to it, and she felt that if the film were publicized her career would be adios'd.

The police found evidence that some of the residents at 10050 Cielo Drive were into collecting humans from Sunset Strip and from various clubs in the area for casual partying at the estate. It was thought for a while that perhaps the murders were the result of a "freak-out" from one of these pick-ups.

Meanwhile, as the police investigation progressed, all forms of wild speculation were passed from mouth to mouth regarding the crimes. There was speculation from close friends of Frykowski that it had been done by the Polish secret police who took a plane from Los Angeles to Rome right after the crimes, in reprisal for Polanski's defection from Poland. There was every form of speculation regarding mutilation and ritual.

There was a flame of violence in Los Angeles in early August 1969 where from Friday the eighth to Tuesday the twelfth, twenty-nine people were murdered. Ken's Sporting Goods Shop in Beverly Hills sold 200 guns in two days following the murders. The Bel Air Patrol, a private security force serving the exclusive Bel Air area, hired something like thirty extra men. People slept within hands' reach of the electronic panic buttons which could summon the Bel Air patrol. Bodyguards were in great demand. Individuals placed their own homes under 24 hour surveillance by teams of private detectives. People packed guns at the funerals of the deceased.

The spirit of Moloch prevailed. Quickly, the movies in which Sharon Tate had performed were reissued. *Valley of the Dolls* went into twelve theatres in the Los Angeles area, with Mrs. Polanski receiving top billing. Also showing up was *The Fearless Vampire Killers,* starring Sharon and Roman Polanski. Distributors hit the screen again with a movie made in 1966, called *Mondo Hollywood,* a section of which was devoted to Jay Sebring as hair styler of the stars. Also playing a part in *Mondo Hollywood* was Bobby Beausoleil who portrayed Cupid addressing his bow, in a brief section. The role in the flick was the origin of Beausoleil's nickname, Cupid.

Around August 15, 1969, two lawyer friends of Jay Sebring, Harry Weiss and Peter Knecht, hired Dutch psychic Peter Hurkos to scan the murder scene in order to try to pick up vibrations regarding the identity of the killers. On Sunday, August 17, Peter Hurkos, accompanied by an assistant, Roman Polanski, a writer named Tommy Thompson, and a photographer named Julian Wasser went to the death house at 10050 Cielo Drive to enable Hurkos to perform a death-scan. Mr. Hurkos crouched down in the blood-stained living room, picking up the vibes while Roman Polanski gave Mr. Thompson a running narrative about the crime scene. The photographer took Polaroid snapshots and some color photos of the event. The entire event was written up for a photo spread in *Life* magazine several weeks later. Mr. Wasser gave Hurkos some of the Polaroid test snaps which somehow wound up published in the *Hollywood Citizen-News.* It was John Phillips, the songwriter, who talked Roman Polanski into allowing Hurkos into the house.

After his void-scan, Mr. Hurkos announced that "three men killed Sharon Tate and her four friends—and I know who they are. I have identified the killers to the police and told them that these three men must be stopped soon. Otherwise, they will kill again."

It was felt that possibly the Canadian dope dealers involved in that Jamaican grass-trafficking were also involved in a Jamaican voodoo group that was somehow connected with the crimes. According to a reporter named Min Yee, he and John Phillips went to a voodoo astrolo-

ger who informe
fitting time for a
tion that one of th
Frykowski a few
On Tuesday, A
conference at the
He decried the sc
murder house: "A
reason write unbear
wife. All of you kn
often I read and hear
most, if not the most
only a few of you kn
vulnerable." He decrie
and dope, acknowledgi
almost every house in
nied that his wife used d
marital rift, saying: "I c
months as much as the l
were the only time of true
Shortly thereafter, Mr. P
to Jamaica to continue inv
doo, according to Mr. Yee
Los Angeles Police Depart
went to Jamaica where he sp
ing.
Roman Polanski took a li
then began a secret investigati
for a few weeks looking for
quaintances, mingling among
keep them unaware of his sleut
The police gave him the pre
myopic glasses found in the hous
sional lens-measuring device, whic
to check out the lenses of his frien
the mate to the fire-starting glasses
the house the night of the murders.
Polanski was suspicious of John P
of the Mamas and Papas, with w
Phillips, Mr. Polanski had had a one
don while Sharon was filming in Rom
John might have suffered a jealous flip
ography, Mr. Phillips wrote that his w

was separated, "
London, too. I
warned him, in a
guys' wives or he
must have relate
have been impr
violence."
Polanski snea
apparently chem
with no results
trunk. Anothe
convertible an
noted that all
printed in blo
lettering bore
that had bee
Drive. I quick
them, togethe
to a handwrit
The finale
Phillips, occ
Sarne, who
ridge, for w
lips recalls
meant it wa
Mansonites
victims, Sh
"We wer
"Roman w
sitting on
I felt a p
yank my
sharp edg
recognize
less arm
Sharon?
Mr. Pl
On Se
a Metro
Polansk
the pho
was ho
Rudy

and later sued Roman Polanski and the estate of Sharon Tate for around $668,000 dollars, charging "trespassory conduct" regarding Abigail Folger and Wojtek Frykowski in that the house had been rented for one family residency. He also sued for damages, depreciation to property, emotional distress and back rent.

On September 3, 1969, Peter Sellers, Warren Beatty, Yul Brynner and others announced the establishment of a reward of $25,000 for the arrest and conviction of the murderers. "We handed the money over to Roman Polanski and his lawyers in the hope that that would bring the killers to justice," Sellers commented in an interview.

In Los Angeles, after the initial release of information about the crimes, there was a tight lid kept on information about the police investigation. Los Angeles Police Department sent only a three-line homicide report to the State Bureau of Criminal Identification and Investigation (CII)—barely complying with the law that requires information about crimes to be collected with the CII. After a month of investigation the chief causes of the crimes under consideration were a residential robbery, a drug grudge, or a "freak-out" of some sort.

A dope burn, whether large or small, tends to trigger off violence. When a burn involves thousands of dollars, deaths or death-threats often occur. Manson had said several times that, if the true story were known about the Tate-LaBianca murders, there would be a "big stink" of a scandal. He has said that he has chosen silence because of the age-old code of criminal behavior that makes telling the names of people involved in a crime equal to the crime itself. Manson has, naturally, also said that the Polanski murders were the idea of his followers. "I don't care. I have one law I live by and I learned it when I was a kid in reform school, it's don't snitch and I have never snitched, and I told them that anything they do for their brothers and sisters is good, if they do it with a good thought," Manson testified on page 18,123 of his trial. A dope burn, however, remains as the motive.

One former family associate stated that he was told by Gypsy that the burn involved "63 keys [kilos] of grass, something like fifty dollars' worth of smack and some

19

Berserk! The Spahn Ranch (August 10–31, 1969)

Around 7 A.M., Leslie, alone, came to the back ranch. Little Patti, Cathy Meyers, Barbara Hoyt and Snake were there asleep. Into the stone fireplace she dropped a short length of rope, a credit card, a fancy leather purse and a woman's blouse. It burnt with an awful smell. She had a plastic sack of change which she counted out. Then she slept.

Around 7:15 A.M. three or four men came to the back ranch, evidently to rout out the sleepers. Leslie covered herself over with covers and said to Snake, according to Snake, "Don't let that man see me or let him in because he gave me a ride from Griffith Park." One or two of the men entered the sleazy ranch house and one of the men questioned the girls, "Where did you get these field phones?" The man said that the girls had a lousy bunch of men on the ranch. They stayed about three minutes, then split. They cut the clandestine lines tapping the electricity before they left in a pink-colored automobile. Intruders gone, Miss Van Houten came out from under the sheets.

People were completely jittery at the Spahn Ranch in the week between August 10 and August 17 when Charlie began moving stuff to the desert. The removal into the Inyo County area was interrupted by the Great Raid of August 16, but finally, by the first week of September, Manson and his armed chumps were safely in the desert.

On August 10, Sunday, Sergeant William Gleason of the Los Angeles sheriff's office visited Kitty Lutesinger at her parents' ranch where she had fled following Manson's kill-threats. Sergeant Gleason was compiling a file of disturbing information about the Spahn Ranch preparing for a huge police raid to come the following week. He had become aware of Miss Lutesinger when she had run away from the Spahn Ranch on July 30 and Frank Retz had driven her to the police station. During the conversation she asked him if it had been the "Panthers" who had committed the so-called Tate murders. He replied that it didn't appear that any blacks were involved. "I had been programmed to believe it was the Panthers who did it," Kitty recalled.

The same day Tex Watson's mother called a friend of Tex, and the friend contacted Watson at the Spahn Ranch. Manson suggested Watson call his mother; Watson pretended to do so, and then fibbed to the Soul, one of M's nicknames. "I lied to Manson, one of the few times I can remember doing so. I claimed I had called home and that my mother had said that F.B.I. men had come to the house looking for me and had told her I was involved in some killings in Los Angeles. As I made up the story for Charlie, I was hoping he'd decide it was time we headed for the desert and started looking for the entrance to the Bottomless Pit. In a few days he did."

About August 11, Ruby Pearl hired a new ranch hand named David Hannon, a twenty-one-year-old blond boy from Venice, California, who was befriended by Manson. Hannon began to talk with Manson occasionally. Manson told him about the "Black Panther" he had shot. Hannon knew a lot about California desert areas and Charlie was eager to talk about the subject. Manson talked as usual about raiding and plundering small desert towns. Once they walked through the desert together and Hannon killed a rattlesnake. This enraged Manson and he told Hannon he was going to chop his head off.

Hannon, being a newcomer, was actually unaware of the large number of girls living in the area. He only saw two or three, the others of course being hidden in the various hillside camps.

Hannon told Manson about a twenty-six acre ranch owned by his mother in the desert near Olancha, a few miles from Goler Wash. On this property were two ranch houses. The property was located on a remote rural road and Manson was eager to move his family there.

On August 11, Linda Kasabian, on orders of the Wizard, put on her high heels and dress, tease-combed her hair and borrowed David Hannon's '61 Volvo and drove to downtown L.A. to the Hall of Justice court building to see if Mary Brunner had a court hearing. She was supposed to see Bob Beausoleil also but she did not have proper identification. Linda was unable to locate Mary Brunner so the mission was a total failure.

The next day Manson sent her in again to the Hall of Justice. There was a hearing and Sandy Good was set free but Mary was held on a forgery charge under $850 bail. However, Linda never showed up. Having again borrowed the white Volvo and acquiring a credit card from Bruce Davis, the family comptroller, she picked up two hitchhikers she had met the day before and proceeded forthwith to drive to New Mexico. A couple of days later near Albuquerque, she was forced to abandon the automobile when a service station attendant wouldn't honor her credit card for repairs.

David Hannon was sorely unhappy a few days later when Linda sent a letter to the ranch notifying him that she was sorry but his car was parked at a service station outside Albuquerque, should he care to come pick it up.

Mrs. Kasabian's baby, Tanya, was left behind at the waterfall nursery because she felt that those guarding the children might get suspicious if she demanded to take Tanya to the court building with her.

One thing that remains a mystery is why Manson let Mary Brunner remain in jail. Her bail was only around $850, a sum that easily could have been raised by sending a trusted zombie on a bank robbery or perhaps a dope burn or something. Since the credit card that Mary had forged belonged to, or had been stolen from, Vern Plumlee's brother-in-law, the girls were thinking of driving up to see him to try to talk him out of pressing charges, they would pay him back, etc. But Manson, for reasons unknown, let Mary Brunner remain in jail until her release on probation late in September.

Charlie drove around looking for money. On two occasions around the days of the murders he and Stephanie drove to Beverly Glen Drive to try to obtain some money from Dennis Wilson but were unsuccessful. As they were leaving Wilson's house one of the times, Wilson told Manson, according to Stephanie, that the police had questioned him about a guy who was shot in the stomach, evidently referring to Bernard Crowe.

The second time Manson visited Wilson to beg for some money, a human named Richie Martin was there and overheard Manson threaten to kill Wilson's son Scottie, a child by a former marriage. Wilson was visited by his son Scottie on weekends, so this would indicate that it was the weekend of the murders since Manson would be in jail during both of the following two weekends.

Manson visited Gregg Jakobson's house around the time of the murders also, but Jakobson's wife was alone in the house and refused Manson's request to use the shower. Manson looked like a wild man and snarled that if she wasn't Gregg's wife he'd seriously injure her.

Mary Brunner called an old family friend, Melba Kronkite, from jail to ask for bail money but Melba was not able to help her. The following night, probably August 12, Manson appeared at 1 A.M. banging loudly on her door. When she answered, Manson demanded money for Mary's bail. When she refused, Manson left in what the lady later described as a "big black car which he was driving"—and he was angry. The black car that Manson was seen driving belonged, according to a close friend of Manson, to a rich friend of Manson—"a real millionaire" as the friend described him.

Around Tuesday, August 12, Manson threatened to slice up Juan Flynn. Flynn had been working outside, feeding corn to the horses. He then went into the Rock City Café to prepare some food. He then sat down at the table to eat. Several girls were in the café kitchen. Others were sitting and chatting outside on the boulders and chairs on the porch. In the door walked Manson, flashing a signal to the girls in the kitchen to leave, a flicking, brushing motion of his right hand on his left shoulder. They left the room.

Manson, five-foot-six, grabbed the six-foot-five Juan by the hair as he sat in the chair and passed a knife close to his throat. "You son of a bitch, I am going to kill you," he said to Juan. "Don't you know I am the one that is doing all the killings?" Manson said, according to Flynn's testimony.

Manson wanted Flynn to come to the desert to live in The Hole. Charlie proffered his knife to Flynn and bade Flynn to begin killing him but Flynn demurred. According to Flynn, Manson bragged about taking thirty-five lives in two days. Manson evidently offered tall Juan the opportunity to be his actual personal zombie. He wanted Juan to wear a ring in his nose and serve as slave. Manson was always terrorizing Flynn, according to Flynn, and once Manson took a few shots at Juan with a pistol as Juan and a girl friend were walking down the creek.

After knowing Manson only about seventy-two hours, David Hannon, the new ranch hand, offered the family the use of his mother's ranch in the desert near Olancha, California. The ranch was located on the edge of the Panamint Valley, just an hour or so from sacred Goler Wash. It was ideal for the family. The opportunity to move everybody in the family away from the L.A. area couldn't be passed up. Things were simply too hot for the family on the coast of California.

On August 14, Tex and Juan Flynn and Hannon loaded up the bread truck with dune-buggie supplies and, towing a dune buggy affixed to the Twinkie truck with some of the famous white nylon rope, headed for Olancha. They unloaded the skelter gear and drove back to the Spahn Ranch. Tex remained behind at Hannon's ranch in Olancha.

When they arrived back at the ranch in the early morning hours of August 15, Manson asked them to return immediately with more dune-buggy equipment and parts. Hannon and Flynn refused but did help load up the truck. Bruce Davis drove the truck back to Olancha, accompanied by the melancholic sixteen-year-old Snake Lake, who remained in Olancha with Tex.

The architect of the August 16 Spahn Ranch raid, Sergeant Bill Gleason, was an expert on motorcycle gangs for the Malibu station of the L.A. sheriff's office. For a couple of months he had been gathering data about Manson. He knew about Manson's threats to various firemen. He knew about Manson's alleged shooting of that "Black Panther." He knew about the weapons and machine guns at the ranch and about the incident in the spring where

Manson raped that girl from Reseda. He knew about the dune-buggy manufacturing line at the ranch and that the family, so to speak, was girding for a war with the blacks. He had learned from Kitty Lutesinger about the hideous death-threats with which Manson terrorized his followers. From the officers involved, Sergeant Gleason learned about the July 27 mini-raid where Manson announced that he had hidden guns trained on the policemen. A decision was made to mount a large nighttime land-air operation against Manson involving helicopters, horses, patrol cars, submachine guns and 102 law enforcement officers.

On August 12, 1960, Sergeant Gleason, along with "Malibu detective personnel," met at the Van Nuys district attorney's office to discuss the proposed raid with deputy D.A. Robert Schirn. They reviewed the facts, then Mr. Schirn issued search warrant number 2029, dated August 13, 1969, and it was signed by Malibu Justice Court Judge John Merrick. The search warrant was good only for the day indicated upon it but the raid did not take place on the thirteenth. The fearsome Special Enforcement Bureau of the sheriff's office (S.E.B.) whose purpose is "saturation patrol of high crime areas"—in the words of an officer interviewed—was picked to raid the Spahn Movie Ranch.

Several days prior to the August 16 raid a couple of family friends came to the ranch in a blue Camaro to warn Manson about the impending arrest. Among them was the daughter of a law-enforcement officer, and she supposedly had inside information, but Charlie scoffed at the data.

On Friday night, August 15, the Straight Satans came to the ranch in several cars, to get Danny De Carlo back and to collect the club sword and for other reasons unknown. They threatened to kill Manson and burn the ranch. The Satans wanted Danny to leave that night but he talked them out of it. "So they gave me until five o'clock the next day to get my ass back to Venice; they said they would burn the place down"—as he testified at the trial on September 18, 1970, volume 92, page 10,842.

After the sword was taken back to Venice, it was broken up, perhaps deliberately, by the Satans. They may have been fearful that the sword was linked to too many grim deeds. After it became known that Manson's group was responsible for murders, the sword pieces were taken into custody by the police.

There was a great possibility of a gang fight. Clem leaped up on the haystack with a weapon and was going to shoot, but Manson was able to turn the violent affair into a party which lasted far into the night. Charlie decreed an emergency flood of female bodies from the surrounding hills. According to Kitty, Charlie came up to the waterfall and told all the girls to come down to the ranch. David Hannon was amazed at the number of girls that appeared from the hills to make love with the bikers.

Violence was quelled and most of the Satans left. De Carlo got so drunk that a couple of girls had to carry him into his bed in the bunkhouse-gun room. The front driveway was littered with Olympia beer cans, an uncommon scene at the Spahn Ranch, where usually only pot and acid passed the lips.

The night the Straight Satans raided the ranch, Kitty Lutesinger called the Spahn Ranch and asked for someone to pick her up. She had called the ranch several times to talk to Beausoleil. She did not know that he had been arrested for murder. Finally she talked over the phone to Manson, who said that Beausoleil had been arrested but that it was nothing, he would be out soon and why didn't she return to the ranch to wait for him. The seventeen-year-old girl, pregnant by Beausoleil, was having problems with her parents, one of whom wanted her to get an abortion. There was quarreling and she decided to split.

About midnight Sadie, Gypsy, and a male Caucasian named Junior came to Northridge in Swartz's car to pick up Kitty. Right there, in the driveway of her father's horse ranch, Sadie cut Kitty's hair off, leaving the single witchy tail adangle. They told her to burn one hair, bury one hair and turn the rest over to the Soul.

She arrived just in time to party with the Straight Satans, to catch a couple of hours sleep, then to get arrested in the dawn raid of the sheriff.

On August 16, while the family and the bikers were reveling, there was a 2 A.M. briefing at the Malibu sheriff's station given by the nominal head of the operation, one Inspector Graham. Then they darted forth, with a warrant seventy-two hours out of date: 102 policemen in twenty-five squad cars, aided by various support vehicles and aided, according to the family, by a canteen truck supplying coffee. They arrived near the ranch at 4 A.M. in silence.

Large numbers of Special Enforcement Bureau personnel (S.E.B.) started hiking into the ranch from the hills of the south side, some toting their M-15s purchased through the National Rifle Association and some even creeping along with bayonets fixed to their rifles. They surrounded the ranch from the west, east and south, an encircling maneuver, according to Deputy Gillory, that had its origins in techniques used to surround suspected Viet Cong villages.

According to an officer who was in the raid, there were orders not to fire the weapons. Some of the officers had large patches with the word "SHERIFF" sewn on the back of their uniform.

The raid was filmed by the authorities, who wanted to use the raid footage in a training film. Evidently the land-air operation against the Spahn Ranch was the first of its kind and would serve as a model for future encircling raids against alleged hippie communes. Some of the officers appear definitely to be out of uniform in the photos of the raid, wearing an admixture of Marine Corps fatigues and regulation sheriff's-office clothing. During the raid they posed for the cameras in front of their commune arrestees, their automatic rifles held high.

Everything was still when just before dawn the officers kicked down the various doors to the main Ranch Western set, the three trailers, the "lean-to," the parachute room, George Spahn's home. They hauled the suspects out of the buildings and placed them sitting in a circle in the driveway in front of the movie set. Gypsy, Kitty, Barbara Hoyt, Krenwinkel, Little Larry, Sandy Good and Vern Plumlee were arrested in the Saloon.

Manson and Stephanie were asleep in the Rock City Café when the police began kicking. Flash—Charlie was out the back door and under the porch, crawling into the dirt beneath the building.

They arrested Larry Craven and David Hannon sleeping on a mattress at the north end of the green house trailer. They were taken outside to the cong circle. In a ditch, some distance from the ranch, the police found a stripped, stolen and abandoned 1969 Volkswagen providing a legal basis for the arrest of the group.

Out of the back door and off the porch of the Saloon leaped one Herb Townsend, Simi Valley Sherri and beautiful Ouish—they ran down to the creek where they were arrested. John Friedman, the twelve-year-old boy whose parents had moved out of the back ranch, was found sleeping on the roof, was hauled down and herded into the circle. Clem was arrested at the beginning of the raid, trying to glide unnoticed off the front porch.

In the trailer next to an old abandoned 1930 Dodge were the nurses: Leslie Van Houten, Kathy Gillies and Little Patti. They were "sleeping nude" attired in panties upon a mattress, arms and legs dangling upon the floor. With them was the infant, Dennis De Carlo. They were covered with a sleeping bag.

Next to the trailer was a small wooden hut/trailer—the "Gypsy Trailer"—in which were sleeping Sadie, a young runaway named Laura and Malibu Brenda. They were sleeping with Zezo Ze-ce Zadfrak, Pooh Bear aka Valentine Michael Manson and little Tanya Kasabian. The three children, in the language of the raid arrest report, were "detained as non-delinquent, and Mr. Pickens of Probation Intake Control authorized taking them to foster homes."

The ranch was rotten with filth and refuse. The police found a dish of "fecal matter" in one of the iceboxes in the trailer.

At 6:15 A.M., George Spahn sat quietly, his cowboy hat on head, his hands folded in his lap, facing the root beer clock on the opposite wall above a poster for the movie *Roman Scandals*. Near him, two stuffed chairs were pulled together with a blanket and pillow on them as if the slim Squeaky were sleeping there, before the raid. Two officers posed in George's house with a display of booty: a revolver, a rifle and a violin case containing a "tommy" gun. They ripped down the curtains in the front window, evidently to get more light for the photos.

Two bikes were parked outside the bunkhouse, one with a flame job painted on the gas tank, and both with high "sissy bars" on the back end, sticking up. The bikes belonged to Robert Rinehard, a bearded balding Straight Satan, and De Carlo.

In the undertaker/bunkhouse De Carlo lay collapsed upon the floor where two girls had carried him drunk. With him was Rinehard, wearing his thong-laced sleeveless club jacket with the picture of the devil on the back. Deputy Gillory and Deputy Neureither crashed in; De Carlo went for his .45 automatic and Neureither stomped him in the bridge of the nose. The two deputies quickly subdued the suspects, using clear plastic disposable handcuffs. Deputy Neureither guarded while Gillory searched the bunkhouse.

They really cleaned up the bunkhouse, seizing a motorcycle engine, De Carlo's radio, a Polaroid camera, binoculars, the .45, a .30-caliber Winchester carbine, a radio-stereo tape player, a soldering iron, a Spartan bullet crimper, a rifle stock, various ammunition and other important items. Click click went the police cameras. There is a photo, among the file of police shots, of the top of De Carlo's radio, in the room where ten murders were schemed, upon which lay a dusty paperback copy of Hunter Davies's "authorized biography" of the Beatles.

They removed the two bikers from the bunkhouse. They threw De Carlo, nose abraded, down into the dust. Rinehard sat nearby on a truck bed for a while, then they ripped apart his Straight Satan one percent jacket with the devil's head. The two policemen spread it over the hood of a car and posed for photos with their automatic rifles raised erect, one of the deputies bearing a field radio over his shoulder, a monitor in his ear and an antenna on his Marine Corps cap. The police took into custody the Straight Satan cutaway jacket, to hang as a memento upon the wall of the East Los Angeles sheriff's station.

The trailer truck with the electric generator, some dune buggies and Johnny Swartz's '59 Ford with the license plate GYY 435 were found in the alley between the movie set and the barn. In Swartz's car truck the fuzz found an assortment of weaponry: a 30-06 rifle, an Enfield rifle, a .20-gauge shotgun, a pellet gun, a Winchester 67A, a large box of ammunition and powder and a gun cleaning box. Deputy Earl Loobey asked Swartz about the guns in the trunk and Swartz replied: "They brought them up last night and we were supposed to get rid of them today."

All vehicles—the '59 Ford, Randy Starr's '54 Ford truck, the two bikes, the '62 Ford, the four dune buggies—were towed to Howard Sommers Garage in Canoga Park by Howard Sommers Towing Company. The '59 Ford—the Crowe, Hinanan, Tate and LaBianca murder automobile—was to remain in Sommers Garage until 12–2–69 when Officer Granado of S.I.D. checked it for bloodstains.

It seemed surreal. Everybody was arrested and placed in the circle. Two helicopters whirred overhead, creasing the hair below when dipping near. One of the dogs was running around wearing a brassiere placed on it by someone in the family.

But where was Manson?

"Where's Jesus?" The officers began to look about for Satan. At last, they crouched down in the early air and beamed lights into the space beneath the floor of the Saloon among the foundation timbers.

Deputy Dunlop spotted Charlie lying face down thirty or so feet from the back porch. They told Manson he'd better haul himself out. So he did, and when he reached the edge of the porch, Dunlop pulled him the rest of the way out by the hair. As Charlie stood up, a folder of credit cards fell out of his shirt pocket, belonging to a Dr. Weiland of Hayvenhurst Avenue. They dragged him down the alley in front of the barn. They handcuffed his hands behind him and carried him, arms bent up like a plow tiller, to the circle. He was barefoot, wearing buckskin trousers and a light-colored dusty shirt. They dumped him next to De Carlo.

Manson was sure he was going to be arrested for murder. Then they read them their rights and revealed the charge—auto theft! He and Krenwinkel looked at one another with smiles of relief.

Manson was also charged with burglary, probably because of the credit cards that fell out during his arrest. De Carlo was charged with assault with a deadly weapon: Section 245 Penal Code, because he went for his .45 as they kicked in the gun room.

Out of the twenty-five arrested, seventeen used pseudonyms.

Squeaky, as usual, began to cry. She asked if anyone

might stay to cook George Spahn breakfast. Simi Sherri pleaded: who's gonna take care of the horses? The police were concerned about the dirt ratio so they made the group take showers, after which, according to the family, they were sprayed with DDT. That night they slept on blankets at the sheriff's sub-station in Malibu then were transported to the county jail in elegant downtown L.A.

The hippie car theft and runaway ring was smashed. What the sheriff's office unfortunately did not know is that they were arresting murderers, murderers that would be set free again about seventy-two hours after their arrest.

The day after the raid on the Spahn Ranch, either Sergeant Whiteley or Deputy Guenther, the officers in charge of the Hinman investigation, called the number listed on the Lutesinger ranch card found in Beausoleil's jeans when he was arrested. Beausoleil evidently told them that Kitty Lutesinger was his girl friend, so the officers called to find out where she was. They wanted to talk with her about Beausoleil.

The officers at this time knew nothing about the Spahn Ranch or Manson or Beausoleil's connection with the family. Kitty was not home for she had run away the night before. In fact, unknown to the officers, Kitty was sitting at that moment in jail. Mrs. Lutesinger told the officer that she hadn't reported Kitty as a runaway because she'd "been through that before." She was told that her daughter was being sought on a murder investigation warrant.

Mrs. Lutesinger filed runaway papers on her pregnant daughter. Officers Guenther and Whiteley made arrangements with the police station near Kitty's home to be notified should the girl show up. This arrangement sowed the seeds of Manson's downfall.

Bruce Davis returned to the Spahn Ranch from Olancha after he had delivered a load of dune-buggy parts and family equipment and was shocked to find everyone arrested. Tex and Snake Lake stayed behind at David Hannon's ranch in Olancha. On Monday, August 18, Snake was arrested for sunbathing nude in the rocks near Hannon's ranch. While they were at the ranch near Olancha, Tex went into town and returned with a paper that accused "Mau Mau devil worshipers" of the murders. Tex laughed and told Snake, according to Snake, that he killed Sharon Tate: "I killed her. Charlie asked me to. It was fun." Tex told Snake to keep quiet about it and that he didn't want to discuss it further.

Also on Monday, August 18, the evidence for consideration of a complaint against the twenty-five arrested in the Spann raid for violation of sections 487.3, 245 and 12200 of the California Penal Code was rejected as not sufficient. Also, the search warrant under which the arrests were made had not been valid. Manson, Van Houten, Krenwinkel, Clem and the others were set free. All the children, Zezo, Pooh Bear, Dennis De Carlo and Tanya Kasabian, were sent to foster homes. A few days later Sadie kidnapped Zezo back from the foster home.

Johnny Swartz called Shorty Shea from the Los Angeles County jail and asked him to come and help pick them up. Vern Plumlee came instead, driving Shorty's car. Shorty was murdered a few days later.

When they got out of jail, the ranch was in a shambles: doors kicked in; dune buggies, tools and credit cards removed by the Law. The police wiped out the gun room armaments. All De Carlo had remaining, for instance, were his boots.

Manson was only out of jail for three days before he was arrested again.

On Friday afternoon, August 22, Charlie and Stephanie were alone together in an outlaw shack near the back ranch, getting after it. During the love, Sadie quietly entered the shack and placed a wrapped crimp-ended reefer in Charlie's blue denim shirt, then crept away from the Devil and his partner. Afterwards, Manson was sitting, shirt off, and the abundant Stephanie sat also, shirt off, and two sheriff's deputies raided the outlaw shack and arrested them.

Miss Stephanie was asked a year after the incident why they were arrested. Her answer:

"Because we didn't have any clothes on and because we were trespassing and because they found some dope. I don't know who brought the dope in there. I think Sadie may have done it. She may have thought it would be groovy to give it to us. I remember seeing her out of the corner of my eye and I thought she just walked in and out then all of a sudden they saw it there and I didn't even know it was there."

The police loaded the couple into the back of the patrol car and drove along the dirt path that led to the front ranch. Passing the Western set, Manson yelled out the window, "Call the station house." Manson called the Spahn Ranch from jail and issued a command that whoever put the "j" in his shirt pocket should haul themselves down to the Malibu sheriff's station and cop out to the deed. According to Manson, the deputies were disgusted that he should make some follower take the guilt upon herself. Gypsy was going to volunteer to go to the station house and say it was her grass but it was unnecessary.

The police sent the joint to the laboratory for chemical analysis and, truth stranger than fiction, the results came back that it was not dope. Manson says that the girls were growing what they believed to be grass but evidently it was some sort of fool's dope or perhaps male plants, or maybe a few leaves from De Carlo's weak pot plant, Elmer. Anyway, it was not cannabis. And there apparently was no law preventing Stephanie from resting bare-breasted in the privacy of an outlaw shack, and since she denied any fornication, the sheriff could not charge Manson with anything. Once again, Manson was set free.

As for seventeen-year-old, pregnant Stephanie, she was sent by the court to her parents' house in Anaheim and placed on probation. She spent about two weeks at home then she dialed DI 1-9026 and asked to be taken back within the family. Clem and Gypsy drove to pick her up on September 5. "In spite of Charlie, I loved everyone so much," Stephanie deposed, when asked why she decided to return to the ranch.

Manson approached the Butler Dune Buggy Shop to get duplicate sales slips for the four buggies purchased there and seized by the sheriff's office during the raid a week previous. Mr. Butler refused so they couldn't get them back from the police. The buggies removed from the ranch were later sold to the LeMans Salvage Yard for junk. Manson's fur-covered command dune buggy later wound up as a special attraction at a car show in Pomona, California. It really didn't matter because the family quickly stole replacements. They also stole a red '69 Ford that was used a lot in transporting people to the mouth of Goler Wash.

Vance, Vern and Zero used the red '69 Ford to rob a few gas stations in the San Fernando Valley. Vance would conceal a revolver in a briefcase, engage the station attendant in chitchat, draw the weapon and rob the till.

Sometime during this era they robbed the Deer Vale Road home of singer Jack Jones, the husband of Jill St. John. Armed with a sawed-off shotgun, they entered boldly at 2 A.M., even though the lights were on in the house. No sense makes sense, Manson decreed. They stacked everything they wanted from the house by a window. They went down to get the car but by the time they got back the police were there so they kept right on going.

Vance managed to steal one thing, however—Jack Jones' own white Stetson cowboy hat which Vance wore to the Barker Ranch in Death Valley.

In late August, Bill Vance and Vern took a trip up north to Portland, Oregon. They brought back a young girl named Diane Von Ahn and one Ed Bailey to add to the family. After a couple of days spent at the Spahn Ranch, Vern, Ed Bailey, Diane Von A. and Bill Vance moved into a rented house off Victory Boulevard in Burbank. There Vance and Vern continued their rip-off forays until they joined Manson in Death Valley.

Manson was released from his marijuana charge around August 26, 1969. That night the family killed the rotund stunt-man, forty-year-old Donald Jerome "Shorty" Shea. "While he was in jail, Shorty was doing a lot of nasty talking about Charlie," recalled Kitty Lutesinger a year later. Charlie believed that it was Shorty who set up the raid on the outlaw shack where he and Stephanie were arrested.

Shorty and Johnny Swartz were working together to try to get the family thrown off the ranch. Manson threatened Johnny Swartz around this time, saying, according to Swartz, "I could kill you any time. I can come into your sleeping quarters any time." Swartz left the ranch thereafter in fear. De Carlo claimed that Shorty was going to work for the German-American resort builders as watchguard of the back ranch property. Manson had said that he got down on his knees and begged Shorty to stop stirring up dissension against the presence of the family, but that Shorty was relentless, so he had to be killed.

Some family members liked the outgoing Shorty Shea. Shorty wanted to become a movie star so he had at least three friends who allowed him to use their phones as answering services in the event a producer or director should want to call Shea about a movie job. Every day the stunt man would call these friends to inquire if any filmmaker had called. These daily phone calls ceased to exist August 27, 1969.

Another "sin" of Shea in the crazed eyes of the family was that he had married a black dancer whom evidently Shorty had met in Las Vegas. The family was upset because his wife's black friends started coming around. He was working with John Swartz to get the family run off the ranch. But the murder was really triggered because Shorty knew something about the Tate-LaBianca killings.

The murder of Donald Jerome "Shorty" Shea is probably the most sickening of their crimes, if the stories circulated by disaffected members are to be believed. They tortured him and, during the torture, tampered with his mental state, as if they were conducting experiments. The entire family was involved in the offing of Mr. Shea. Some killed, some buried, some burned, some packed his gear. "By that time, we all had our job to do," Leslie Van Houten remarked, discussing her assigned task of burning Shorty's clothes. As she began to burn them, a ranch hand wandered nearby, so she had to abort the mission, cover them up with brush and burn them later.

They buried him during the night down the creek by the railroad tunnel back of the ranch, in a crude, temporary, brush-topped grave.

Full moon for August 1969 occurred at 10 A.M. on the 27th, which is just about the time several girls reburied Shorty in broad daylight. His body was placed somewhere down the road toward Simi, and although they occasionally bulldozed the area, it was not found for several years.

They packed up the belongings of Mr. Shea and loaded

them into the trunk of his automobile, which had been parked at the Spahn Ranch. Bruce Davis left a fingerprint on one of Shorty's trunks, a grievous mistake for Mr. Davis. Gypsy aka Cathy Share later admitted to the police that she helped drive Shorty's automobile to be abandoned in Canoga Park. A bloody shoe belonging to Mr. Shea was taken into custody of the Los Angeles County sheriff but his body, or head, was never recovered.

Three people—Steve Grogan aka Clem, Bruce Davis and Manson—were later convicted of the murder, though Manson noted in his autobiography that the D.A. had overlooked many participants and that "someplace out there . . . he has left several killers to prowl the streets."

Bruce Davis owed De Carlo money, so he gave De Carlo the pawn tickets on Shorty Shea's matched brass-handled pistols. De Carlo evidently bought the weapons out of hock. They were seen around the Spahn Ranch for a while. Later he sold the pistols to a Culver City gun shop for $75, using the alias Richard Smith.

Whereas there was almost a complete silence about the Hinman-Tate-LaBianca murders within the family, the Shea murder was discussed from zombie to zombie. Charlie used to joke about it at campfires. When asked by Ruby Pearl and wrangler Johnny Swartz about the whereabouts of Shorty, Manson told them: "He's gone to San Francisco. I told him about a job there."

At the end of August, Charlie sent Sadie, Katie and Leslie to the Fountain of the World in Box Canyon to seek permission to live there. Charlie had a scheme to slowly encroach upon the Fountain and ultimately take it over. "Sadie blew it," remembered Kate, "by calling a lady at the Fountain a pig." The sister in charge ordered them off the property and as the cropped-headed killers split, they were reported by the sister to have sung a song by George Harrison called "Piggies."

On September 1, an eleven-year-old boy, Steven Weiss of Long View Valley Road, located in Sherman Oaks, was out in his hillside back yard repairing a lawn sprinkler when he located the .22-caliber Longhorn murder weapon in the brush.

About fifty feet up above Long View Valley Road and running parallel to it is Beverly Glen Boulevard, off the side of which the grimy revolver was flung, down into the brush in back of the Weiss residence.

The young boy, Steve Weiss, forthwith turned the pistol over to an officer of the Van Nuys division of the Los Angeles police department. The boy was careful not to touch the revolver to protect fingerprints. The police smudged it up and filed it away, the chambers of the weapon containing seven spent shells and two live bullets. Not till December would the police, after young Weiss reminded them, remember about the revolver found on Labor Day.

20

Rommel: The Barker Ranch (September 1969)

In early September, Manson moved his troops to Death Valley. Over a period of several weeks they stole a bunch of dune buggies, about seven in number. They tried to steal a red Toyota from Dennis Kemp on Loyal Trail just a few feet down the road from where Bernard Crowe was living at 7008 Woodrow Wilson Drive. Kemp was able to drive the robbers away. A few days later, however, on September 1 they followed Kemp's Toyota to Ventura Boulevard and while Kemp was in a house in a card game, the coyotes stole the red, four-wheel-drive Toyota and drove it to the desert.

The same batch of happy people—Barbara, Ouish, Kitty, Sherri, Snake and Charlie—drove to the mouth of the Wash, then charged up the dynamited waterfalls seven miles to the Barker Ranch. Charlie drove back and forth in the various rented and stolen cars, personally escorting his family to the desert paradise. There ultimately were thirty or forty humans living there. Charlie left Squeaky and Katie Krenwinkel behind at the Spahn Ranch to take care of George.

Manson and Tex Watson drove in early September to see Ballarat Bob in Trona, a small town adorned with a plant owned by American Chemical and Potash Corporation. The town is encrusted with a mist of potash and a sulfurous smell hangs in the air. Ballarat Bob told them it was okay with him to stay at the Barker Ranch. He asked Manson to round up his burros for him and take care of them for him because he wanted to go prospecting later.

Sometime in September Manson also visited Mrs. Arlene Barker, the owner of the Barker Ranch, at her home in Sunland. Mrs. Barker flew up on weekends in her own plane to a ranch called the Indian Reservation located just north of Ballarat. Manson asked Mrs. Barker if he could stay a few days and she gave her permission.

In Los Angeles, on September to 4, Linda Kasabian hit town from New Mexico to try to get her kid back from the foster home where it had been placed following the August 16 raid at the Spahn Ranch. She came on timid and anxious when talking to Mr. Kroeger, the officer conducting a dependency investigation for the Department of Public Social Services for the county of Los Angeles. Linda said she had no idea how terrible the living conditions were at the Spahn Ranch and that she had left her daughter Tanya with Mary Brunner and had gone to Arizona to meet her husband.

She said to Mr. Kroeger, "I planned to return in about a week to pick up Tanya to return to New Mexico, and when I called the Spahn Ranch, they told me that Tanya had been placed in custody. I called Sergeant Jones at the Malibu sheriff's station and he advised me to see you." Linda told the officer that she planned to establish a permanent home for Tanya at the Church of Macrobiotics located at a ranch near Taos, New Mexico. She was given custody of Tanya after the interrogation. The young mother took her daughter to New Mexico, then to Miami and finally back home to her own mother's place in Milford, New Hampshire where she remained till she was arrested for murder on December 1, 1969.

On September 4, Robert Beausoleil had a hearing in Malibu justice court where it was decided that he stand trial for murder on November 12, 1969.

And on September 4, Stephanie called from her parents' place and asked the family to help her run away. Clem and Squeaky drove to pick up Stephanie in Anaheim and brought her to the ranch. It had been two weeks since she had been arrested with Charlie at the back ranch and placed on probation. They stayed four or five hours at the ranch and near dawn they took off for the desert in a green 1969 Ford, just rented by Brenda with a stolen credit card.

When Stephanie arrived at the Barker-Meyers Ranch area, Charlie gave her a knife. Charlie gave everyone instructions in throat-slitting. There was talk of decorating the Barker Ranch with skulls. Manson talked about boiling the skulls in large kettles to de-meat them. "We were all sitting around and he asked if we could do it. He asked if it came down to it could we do it and everyone said, 'Oh yeah' and I said, 'Oh yeah,' " Miss Stephanie remembered ten months later when she was interviewed just prior to a class at her dog grooming school. She said, "When I said, 'How? I don't really know how,' he used me as a live demonstration—how you cut from here to there" indicating throat gash—"Then he said, 'You have to know how to hide everything so no one will find it.' We were down in some canyon somewhere."

A few days later Stephanie had a conversation with Manson about going back to her sister's house in San Diego. The *farouche* young lady was standing holding a rifle in her arms. "I guess I looked homesick so Charlie asked me if I wanted to go home." She said that it was true that she was homesick. Manson then told her, according to her testimony at the trial, that he'd give her one more chance to go home.

Then he had one of his anger spasms. "Then he took the rifle and hit me in the head a couple of times and told me to forget about going home."

Months later she was asked by interviewers why she tolerated a person punching her in the face with a rifle butt. She replied, "I never wanted him to hit me but I wanted to be made to see in a different way. And the only way Charlie knew how to make me see in a different way was to do that."

One of the barriers preventing total takeover of Goler Wash was the so-called scientologist gold-miner Paul Crockett, who had snared away two of the family—Brooks Posten and Paul Watkins. Mr. Crockett and his new-found disciples were living in a tarpaper-roofed cabin located at the Barker Ranch itself.

Manson told Brooks Posten that he still belonged to Manson and that he was released from none of his agreements. Manson tried the time-worn "Kill you—kill me" routine with Brooks, handing him his knife saying, "Brooks, kill me." And when Brooks refused, Charlie seized the knife and said, "Then I can kill you."

Manson had a remaining grudge against the sheriff's deputy from Shoshone, who had led the raid against the Barker Ranch in February 1969 after several of the family had given his stepdaughter some marijuana. Posten claimed that Charlie said that if Posten loved Charlie then Posten would walk to Shoshone and kill the deputy. "That was if I loved him," Posten said.

Then Juan Flynn began to consort with the so-called scientologist gold-miner Paul Crockett and the two ex-family members, Posten and Watkins, to the point where he began living with them in their tarpaper shack surrounded by bins of gold ore samples. Another follower was snared away by Crockett. Crockett even began to bad-mouth Manson to some of the girls, an ineffable sin in the eyes of Manson.

One night at midnight, Crockett, Posten, Watkins, Juan and a German shepherd were asleep in the cabin. The dog began to bark so that Paul, Little Paul and Brooks went outside to check it out. They didn't find anything unusual, so they went back to sleep. Later on, the dog began to growl so Juan stood up and looked out the window. In the moonlight he saw Clem and Manson creep-walking toward the cabin. Flynn claimed that Manson had a knife and that the fringes on Manson's buckskins were going swish, swish. Naked, armed with a shotgun, Flynn left the cabin to confront Satan and Satan's latah. But nothing came of it. Charlie and he just had a conversation and walked away.

Many times Charlie put his knife up to the throat of the six-foot five-inch Juan Flynn demanding that he give in and accept the will of the so-called Wizard.

Charlie and the gang, using a stolen Master Charge card, began to buy all sorts of supplies for the end of the world—tools, toolboxes, cases of oil, twenty sleeping bags, lots of knives, food, camouflage parachutes. Over and over he claimed to Crockett and the other miners that all the items brought to the desert were legally acquired. Such a claim was credible because of the several times Charlie had been able to get large sums of money from rich young ladies in search of truth.

He had two large spools of telephone wire which he had brought in to set up desert communication. They stayed away from the Barker Ranch mainly because of the presence of Watkins, Posten and Crockett in the little cabin. But they would visit all the time, roaring in and roaring by. On a couple of nights, the family did build a bonfire and smoke dope. Charlie lifted up his guitar to lead the singing outside the Barker Ranch. In the middle of the night, Charlie would roar into the ranch bragging about all the people he had killed, according to Paul Watkins, and "sending out pictures" of slaughter. According to Watkins and Posten, Manson laughed about how he had made some girls bury Shorty Shea and how he had shot a "Panther." But there was no mention of Tate-LaBianca-Hinman.

Manson talked about General Rommel and desert campaigning. He was going to be the Desert Fox of Devil Hole at the head of a flying V of dune buggies, racing across the desert for plunder. Manson spray-painted his stolen dune buggy and then, while the paint was wet, threw dirt on the paint to create a brown camouflage effect.

They talked a lot about taking over the Death Valley town of Shoshone and also Trona. Manson felt a bit of hostility toward all the desert people, wanting to ping them one by one. Manson talked about terrorizing the police. He talked about killing approaching policemen, removing their bodies from their clothes, then leaving the uniforms and shoes and hats neatly arranged on the desert ground, as if the bodies had somehow just disappeared from their uniforms.

Everybody, even when nude, wore a hunting knife strapped to the leg or waist. The family was so completely into gore that everybody was armed, not so much in fear of the police perhaps, but in apprehension of possible spontaneous slashing from fellow family members. Charlie liked to comment on those whom he considered the weak links in the family. The girls must have been desperate not to be thought of as a weak link. For weak links could find themselves on the receiving end of a satanic ritual. Accordingly, the behavior in the desert was brutal and freakish. For instance, one witness reports Gypsy as being absolutely fearless with regard to handling live rattlesnakes: "She'd just pick it up and hold it and stare at it. . . . It was really far out." No, thank you.

And there were deaths, according to Sadie, Vern Plumlee and others. There are supposed to be two boys and a girl buried about eight feet deep behind the Barker Ranch. They filmed some of their despicable activities also. Several witnesses have described what might be termed the Barker Ranch chop-stab dance, where they danced in a circle, then pretended to go into slash-frenzies—attacking trees, rocks and one another with their knives. God knows what else they shot with their stolen NBC camera.

Torture seemed to comprise the substance of most of the conversation about Manson in the final few days before his capture. He became feral beyond description, mean beyond description. In the wilderness the man of a thousand masks could slip them all off and could assume his cherished role of exterminator. "He got wild when he was out there. I don't know, he was just beating on Snake all the time—or everybody," Kitty Lutesinger remembered a year later. She was asked about the threats and she replied, "Oh, the usual stuff, like 'We'll hang you from the trees and cut out your tongue,' or 'We'll tie you up to a tree and put honey on you and let the ants crawl all over you.' "

At first the family set up camp at the Myers Ranch, a lush, foliage-covered forty acres of patented land, purchased by Kathy Myers's grandparents from a legendary local miner named Seldom Seen Slim for a side of bacon. They also occupied several cabins at the Lotus Mine—owned by Warner Brothers, according to Ballarat Bob—located about a mile down from Sourdough Springs in Goler Wash. They moved from cabin to cabin on orders of the Wizard, spending some time at the Newman cabin, another small dwelling a couple of miles further down Goler Wash toward the dry waterfalls.

At the Myers Ranch, they filled up the swimming pool and fixed some of the watering devices for the wild fruit trees and foliage which made it like an oasis in the high desert.

Once Snake got caught wearing a murdered man's work shirt: "One time I was up at the foot of the Lotus Mine. I was wearing a man's blue shirt and Charlie said,

'Where'd you get that shirt? You've got Shorty's shirt on.'

"I was on acid when he said it."

It was all pain. One night, Kitty committed the pardonless transgression of falling asleep during a fireside rap of Charlie's and he punched her in the face, knocking her into the ashes.

One day Kitty and Sadie were sitting by the Meyers Ranch swimming pool. Kitty was already five months pregnant and unhappy. Nobody talked about Bobby Beausoleil. Kitty tried to strike up a conversation with Sadie about Bobby but Sadie wouldn't look her in the eye. Charlie had told Kitty several times that Bobby was in jail but that it was a minor charge and he implied that Bobby would be back soon.

Kitty was determined to find out about it.

"What's he in for?" asked Kitty.

"Oh, nothing, just some little thing," replied Sadie. But Sadie looked sneaky about it, Kitty thought.

"He's in for murder, isn't he?"

"Yes."

"Is it serious?" asked Kitty.

"Whatever serious is," Sadie replied. Sadie then burst into laughter.

There is a story from Death Valley '69, passed from mouth to mouth, which, if true, relates the first known belladonna truck hijacking. Several people have told how the girls sometimes wore pouches of crushed telache leaves or belladonna with which they could disable people by slipping it into food or water. Leslie, Sadie and perhaps Little Patti were hitchhiking somewhere between Shoshone and Las Vegas when along came a refrigerator truck bound for Vegas bearing a load of fruits and vegetables. Naturally, the driver picked up the pretty young hippies.

Sadie supposedly began a pattern of very positive hints that she was willing to ball the driver. The driver was ready right then and there. But Sadie said something like, "Come on, come on. I know a place."

So she directed him on Route 178 into Death Valley. They turned left just past Ashford Mills on Furnace Creek Road and drove into the desolation. The trucker was anxious to stop immediately and create conjoinment but Sadie said, "No, no, we have to drive further." They passed the road sign that read, "Warning: Road not patrolled daily," and Sadie said, "No, no, drive on." So they drove forward up into the foothills of the Panamint Mountains. Finally they stopped. Sadie said something like, "Before we make love, I have to make you some coffee." Instead of coffee, she made the muddy, brown, bitter telache tea from her little Baggie of flip-out. Allegedly the truck driver passed out from the telache.

Meanwhile, one of the other girls ran to get a brush-covered dune buggy and while the driver was out cold, they broke open the truck hatch, loaded up the produce onto the buggy, took the dune buggy away to the ranch and then drove the driver to an obscure location and abandoned him there.

And so it went with The Hole in the Universe Gang. For about two and a half weeks the family swarmed all over Goler Wash and the southwest part of the Death Valley National Monument. Then Manson flipped out and attracted the attention of the Park Rangers and the California Highway Patrol so the family had to go into hiding. But that's why they went to the desert, to hide. Now it was like hiding within the hideaway.

21

The Burning of the Michigan Loader

On Sunday, September 14, a computer engineer named Gary Tufts, who was a temporary family associate, plus Gypsy, Bruce Davis and Tex Watson drove the red '69 Ford, stolen by Vern and Vance, to the Death Valley area from the Spahn Ranch. They parked the Ford at the slim mouth to the Goler Wash waterfalls and Tex walked up the Wash and returned with the red four-wheel drive Toyota stolen from Van Nuys, California on September 1, 1969, police DR #69-068 #306.

Following Tex back down Goler Wash was Manson driving his mud-painted camouflaged command dune buggy. Fair-voiced Gypsy jumped in with Charlie and the computer engineer Tufts rode with Bruce and Tex in the Toyota back to the Myers Ranch where they spent that night and much of the next day, Monday, September 15.

Around this time Manson humiliated Barbara Hoyt and Simi Valley Sherri. Simi Valley Sherri was commanded to perform an act of fellatio with Juan Flynn. She refused, and for this defiance, Manson beat her up. Next, he ordered Sherri's close friend, Barbara Hoyt, the girl who later was fed the LSD hamburger in Honolulu, to perform the act and, in fear, she complied.

The two girls decided to sneak out after this grim scene and some of the others, like Gypsy and Ouish, expressed desire among themselves to split also, but only the two actually dared to leave, walking down the entire length of Goler Wash to the Wingate Road along the salt lake to the Ballarat General Store, barefoot: twenty-eight miles of sharp rocks. The sneak-trudge occupied the greater part of the dark night and near dawn they crawled exhausted into a car near the store and slept.

Manson was furious when he found out they had cut out. He roared down the gulch the next morning, prepared to kill them. He found them eating breakfast in Mrs. Manwell's Ballarat General Store. He stood outside the door and flashed the girls inside one of his silent signals, evidently, according to Mrs. Manwell, some sort of rolling eye-whirl as indication that he wanted them to come outside for a chitchat or chit-chop.

The girls told Manson that they were leaving, and just like a wind that changes its direction and therefore changes its name, Manson calmed down, commenting that, well, they couldn't leave without money, so he gave them twenty dollars. And away he roared in his iron horse of the hairy locusts. Mrs. Manwell took the two young ladies across the salt lake and down south into Trona where they bought some tennis shoes and caught a bus toward Los Angeles. Later Manson sent Clem down to Los Angeles to find them.

A few days previous, Manson had met on a road somewhere a friendly resident who possessed detailed knowledge of caves, camps, shacks and hot mineral springs in the vast Death Valley-Panamint area. This was a twenty-four-year-old bearded gentleman named Larry Gill, who was evidently living in a cabin off Furnace Creek Wash Road near Ryan, an old borax ghost town, on the Death Valley side of the Panamints. At least this was where he was living a few months later, according to an Inyo County sheriff's deputy.

Mr. Gill, trusting the hirsute group because they were driving a new Ford, agreed to show Manson the hard-to-find springs and camps. So, on Monday afternoon, September 15, Manson led a group of vehicles out of Goler Wash onto the Panamint Valley floor where they set up temporary camp for the night. Perhaps he feared that the cut-out of Simi Valley Sherri and Miss Hoyt would prove that it was easy for any of the girls to leave the area, so he wanted to find a more remote locale for the family.

Or perhaps it was dune-buggy imperialism. In his raps, Charlie talked about stashing dune buggies every ten or fifteen miles all over the desert, with hordes of food, ammunition and gasoline buried near them. Because he had in mind raiding little towns like Shoshone and Trona in some dune-buggy Rommel scene, he naturally wanted to be aware of any potential hideouts and raid outposts.

It is known that he hid some 300 gallons of gasoline near Greater View Spring in the Striped Butte Valley, in an old airplane wing tank. Also there were several other tanks of gasoline that were buried in the desert, not to mention the barrels that the owner of the Ballarat Store saw the miner Mr. Paul Crockett haul down Goler Wash as his own following the October arrests of the family.

Manson, Gypsy, Ouish and an unknown female Caucasian drove away in the red Ford on Monday night, while the others remained at the camp at the mouth of Goler Wash. They went up north through Emigrant Pass up around Devil's Cornfield and down into Death Valley south to Ryan to Larry Gill's cabin to see him about the promised scouting maneuvers.

The next morning, Manson and the girls brought Mr. Gill back to the Panamint camp. And then from the camp a caravan of vehicles headed north to the Hunter Mountain-Race Track area of the Death Valley Monument and on into the Saline Valley to check out certain mineral springs. The red Toyota, the green '69 Ford, hyped from Hertz, the red '69 Ford and a dusty-blue flecked dune buggy stolen from the La Paz Buggy Builders on September 11 formed the caravan.

Gill showed them some camping spots and cabins near Jackass Springs southwest of Hunter Mountain. The red and green Fords were not able to drive into the Saline Valley because of the nearly impassable condition of the road so they were stashed on Hunter Mountain in the forest. There are two roads leading into Saline Valley from the Southern end and the M. brigade drove in via the southernmost route over the high twisting pass and down into the desolate salty valley to the northwest.

The Saline Valley is where two travelers had burnt up in the friable air of around 140 degrees Fahrenheit in July of 1969. But the hot baths known as Palm Hot Springs were especially interesting to Manson in his continuing search for the entrance to chocolate-land.

Late that night, the group ran into a high government official named Boyd Taylor who was evidently camping out with his wife in the Saline Valley. The U.S. Commissioner for the Eastern District of California, Mr. Taylor was later to testify on December 3, in Inyo County court auto theft proceedings against Manson, that he saw Manson "in the middle of September" driving the stolen blue flecked dune duggy at 2 A.M. Also he would bring charges, in his official capacity as U.S. Commissioner, against Bruce Davis because of the gun used to pistol-whip Gary Hinman that was bought by Davis under an assumed name, in violation of U.S. law.

After encountering the campers, the family drove back over the pass to Hunter Mountain and spent the night. Larry Gill evidently drove or was driven back to his cabin because there was never any testimony linking him to the burning of the Michigan skip-loader.

The next morning, Wednesday, September 17, the red Toyota and one or two dune buggies, evidently including the camouflaged command dune buggy, bore the family back into the Saline Valley to the hot springs where once more they encountered the campers. According to Kitty, Charlie talked to them and shortly thereafter they pulled away in their camper.

Kitty Lutesinger and Diane Lake say that the following citizens spent two days exploring and having fun in the Saline Valley: Kitty, Diane, Scotty Davis, Tex, Clem, Ouish, Manson and Gypsy. One incident was related by Miss Lutesinger. When they encountered one of the hot springs, Manson commanded Clem and Ouish Morehouse to jump in and see if they could swim to the bottom, but the water was too hot. Nevertheless, Clem jumped in feet first but was unsuccessful. They then tried to tie a string on a rock and sink it down but the spring-cleft went off at an angle. Charlie mentioned something about getting skin-diving equipment and going down to see if the springs led to The Hole.

Late Thursday night or early Friday morning, September 18–19, Manson led his troop out of the Saline Valley over the bumpy wilderness trail up the mountain pass, the single headlight on his dune buggy his only guide. At the very top of the pass which would have led him down to the Hunter Mountain campsite, he stopped. Right in front of him were two large wide holes in the dirt-way, evidently scooped out by some nearby earth-moving equipment.

According to Kitty, Manson thought the authorities had deliberately dug the holes in his path so that he would crash his dune buggy into them! Manson commanded her and Gypsy to fill up the large shallow gouge-outs with rocks and dirt. As they did this, according to Snake Lake, Scotty, Tex, Manson and Clem removed some gasoline tanks and a grease gun from the $30,000 Clark Michigan skip-loader, the evil machine of the Beast that tried to wipe out Jesus' dune buggy. Then they let out the fuel oil, poured some gasoline on the wires and the engine, then poofed it.

Then the family raced away and the rest of the night was spent in a roaring dune-buggy frenzy. They arrived at the cabin in the forest area near Hunter Mountain and proceeded to get the '69 green Ford stuck in the wilderness. Finally they rammed it into a tree. They stripped what they could off it and then abandoned it, speeding away in the red Toyota, leaving telltale Toyota tracks in the dusty trails for many miles. "It was a wild night," as Miss Lutesinger remembered eight months later.

The burning of the Michigan loader enraged the rangers at the Death Valley National Monument, which owned it. Relentlessly the Park Rangers, the California Highway Patrol and, to a lesser degree, agents of the Fish and Game Commission would begin to track down this uncool group of murderers.

If they hadn't roamed the Death Valley area as marauders, the Mansonists could have lived in that wilderness for years without any trouble. As one of the policemen said after the raid, "You could hide the Empire State Building out there and no one could find it."

It would take three weeks for the Rangers and the Highway Patrol to catch Manson.

22

The Capture of Manson (September 20–October 12, 1969)

Death Valley law officers began to enter the Manson nightmare. The Toyota tracks from the burnt Michigan loader led south, so Park Rangers and the Highway Patrol officers responsible for the area began to work south down into the Panamint Valley, asking questions to try to locate suspects owning a four-wheel-drive Toyota.

On September 20 Officer Manning of the C.H.P. found the smashed green '69 Ford that had been abandoned near Hunter Mountain. Miners in the area advised the officer that they had observed a group of "hippie-type people." Near the wrecked Ford they found Toyota tire tracks which were the same as those found near the burnt-out Michigan loader.

On September 22, some of the girls took the stolen red Toyota into Hall Canyon, which is a beautiful canyon about fifteen miles north of Ballarat, climbing over 10,000 feet into the Panamint Mountains. The girls were exploring waterfalls and old mineworks, wandering from rock to rock, when Park Ranger Powell and California Highway Patrol Officer Pursell drove into Hall Canyon and encountered the group of "four female and one male suspects"—as the police report read. The license plate on the red Toyota did not belong to it but belonged to Bob Beausoleil's old '42 Dodge power wagon which was registered in the name of Beausoleil's wife, Gail. The officers did not have radio equipment to run the plate through the computer. When they reached the Highway Patrol station and learned that the plate was illegal, they then had suspects.

California Highway Patrol owns an IBM system called the Automatic Statewide Auto Theft Inquiry System, which in great part was responsible for bringing down the house of Manson. This auto theft system feeds out data regarding stolen vehicles to 200 police agencies including eight California Highway Patrol offices. It was data from this system that revealed stolen dune buggies.

On September 24, Park Ranger Powell and an Inyo County sheriff's officer named Dennis Cox returned to Hall Canyon to seek out the suspect hippies they had encountered two days previous. They were informed by miners there in the canyon that the red Toyota and suspects had split about four hours after the cops had left.

Park Rangers and other officers began to visit the Ballarat General Store, the only store for about forty miles. Various family members had made purchases there both in 1968 and in late summer '69 so the officers started obtaining data about the Mansonoids. They learned from the owner of the store about the two barefoot girls who had walked twenty-four miles to escape Goler Wash. More importantly, from the view of spotter planes, they learned that a large light green bus belonging to the group was parked at the Barker Ranch where they lived.

Sometime around mid-September Sandy Good-Pugh gave birth to a baby boy named Ivan aka Elf at a hospital in Los Angeles. Why the Wizard allowed Sandy to deliver her baby in an institution is not known. Quickly thereafter, Sandy took Ivan to Death Valley. Danny De Carlo also went to the desert but has claimed that he only spent about three days there before returning to Los Angeles.

On September 23, 1969, Mary Brunner was set free from jail on probation for that Sears credit card forgery. Her child, Valentine Michael Manson, had been taken by its grandmother to Wisconsin. Mary herself evidently did not journey to Death Valley but visited for a few days at the Spahn Ranch after which she went home to Wisconsin.

In the days following the burning of the loader, Manson continued his terror operations against the gold miner Paul Crockett and the trio of former family members that were living with him. Charlie sent girls in once to try to steal their shotguns. Other times he waved his hunting knife at their throats.

During their final days, the family spent a great deal of time in the area of Willow Springs and Mengel Pass and Anvil Springs which is on the Death Valley side of Mengel Pass in the Striped Butte Valley. About a half mile from Willow Springs is a valley where there's a cabin also owned by Arlene Barker. Charlie set up his dune-buggy repair shop at Willow Springs. It was far easier to truck automotive parts to Willow Springs from Shoshone than it was trying to negotiate the waterfalls of Goler Wash from the Panamint Valley.

There was once a road over Mengel Pass from the Striped Butte Valley down to Goler Wash during the gold rush in the early part of the twentieth century but it had long ago washed away. Mengel Pass was named after a prospector named Carl Mengel who lived from 1868 to 1944. He was a famous local prospector and operated a mine near his cabin. He filed for water rights on Anvil Springs oozing out of an abutment below his cabin on the west ridge of the Butte Valley. When he died, his ashes were buried on the pass top beneath a steel-banded conical pile of rocks, with a large cherry-shaped rock on top. Inside this rock pile with his ashes was buried Mr. Mengel's wooden leg. Near Carl Mengel's old cabin, Manson and crew hid 300 gallons of helter-skelter gasoline in an old airplane wing tank.

It's always a mistake when a guru makes a claim or a prediction that can never happen. Manson made a big one that fall. He couldn't come up with The Hole. His followers were counting on it. It was one thing to rap about it around bonfires to one's bedoped disciples; it was another to produce it, especially a Hole with such astounding attributes. According to Tex Watson, this underground paradise zone came outfitted with twelve magical trees bearing wondrous fruit and an underground lake which gave everlasting life. There was a different tree for every month of the year.

Nevertheless, they went Hole-batty. It wasn't just magical trees; they needed The Hole to hide from the police. There were a few clues, such as great beflittings of black bats that swarmed into Goler Wash at dusk, which the M group was certain had flitted up from the Abyss. They searched everywhere, crawling into old mine shafts, looking for the vein to paradise. But no Hole, no molten Hersey bar factory beneath the Armagosa River.

"It began to look," Tex Watson later commented, "as if the Abyss would be harder to find than we'd first thought."

On September 29, 1969, Park Ranger Richard Powell and Highway Patrol Officer James Pursell paid a visit to the Barker Ranch. The officers approached the ranch from the northeast over Mengel Pass. They checked out the two dwellings at the Barker Ranch where they encountered what they termed "two females uncommunicative"—evidently two family members who were rifling through Crockett's cabin. The girls said that the person who lived at the ranch had gone to Ballarat and would be coming up Goler Wash.

That morning Juan Flynn and Paul Watkins had gone away to get supplies and make arrangements to go to another place to live until the Manson problem was solved.

Charlie had hauled to the mouth of Goler Wash a batch of tires, tubes, batteries and equipment for servicing his dune-buggy assault squad. Crockett agreed to haul the supplies to the ranch and drove down the waterfalls in Beausoleil's old orange truck to pick them up. As he was driving back up the sheer creek bed, he ran into California Patrol Officer Pursell and Park Ranger Powell. And as Crockett later recounted it, "They wanted to know what it was that I was doing and what I had in the truck and what was going on."

Also in the back of the truck, Officer Pursell noted, was a big movie camera with a power pack. He asked about it and was told that someone was making a movie.

The police officers asked Crockett and Posten to tell them about the family. Crockett agreed to talk but the battery in the truck was low so he couldn't kill the engine. Therefore, the officers followed Crockett back to the Barker Ranch for a discussion. Crockett filled them in on Manson's schemes of becoming a Devil Hole Rommel and so forth.

Crockett did not reveal much to the cops because of fear that Manson was perhaps listening. "He can sneak into Shoshone and sit six feet from you in back of a window and hear everything that is going on and the next time he sees you he tells you the whole conversation and he starts laughing at you and tells you how stupid you are. . . . I didn't know whether he was ten miles away, a hundred miles away, or six feet."

Posten, who was riding with Crockett in the orange pile wagon, told them that the entire family had been arrested on August 16 in Chatsworth for grand theft auto. This information enabled the Inyo County authorities to coordinate their investigation with the Los Angeles sheriff's office.

After the officers left Crockett's cabin, they were scouting around the area in their four-wheel-drive vehicle when they encountered a nude group of hippies, seven in all—scampering away in a draw near the Meyers Ranch. They also found a red Toyota, which did not have a license plate on it but they noted down the vehicle inspection number and were able to run it through the computer when they got back to discover that it was Dennis Kemp's Toyota stolen during that card game on September 1. They also found a dune buggy which they later learned was stolen in Santa Ana. Both of them were concealed by tarps and sleeping bags and clothing.

While the police were chasing the suspects, Manson came running up the canyon, ran into Crockett's cabin and grabbed Crockett's double-barreled shotgun and sped up over the hill, evidently taking a position on the ridge between the Meyers and the Barker Ranches. Brooks Posten said that he heard Manson fire the shotgun three times. Manson claimed later that he dodged around behind the rocks, shouting, trying to unnerve the police.

That night into the Barker Ranch compound roared Rommel and his teenage vampires in their attack vehicles. They had an engineless dune buggy set up in the front yard. Tex and some female Caucasian called Linda, probably Little Patti, and Manson asked Crockett to help them haul in a motor for the buggy which they had stashed in the canyon behind the ranch. Crockett helped them lift the motor onto a wheelbarrow and they carted it down to the dune-buggy frame. They put the motor into the dune buggy by lantern light and then drove away, giving forth the family coyote yips and shooting off pistols.

Around 10 P.M. on September 29, after the officers returned from Goler Wash, the policemen had a strategy meeting. Homer Leach, Chief Ranger for Death Valley National Monument, contacted Sergeant Hailey of the Lone Pine Resident Post of the California Highway Patrol and informed him about the situation in Goler Wash. Accordingly, four representatives of the Inyo County sheriff's office, four National Park Rangers and six California Highway cops drove back in to the Barker Ranch area in four-wheel vehicles to snare the hippie car thieves.

At dawn, Ranger Powell and Officer Pursell came to Paul Crockett's cabin and asked Crockett and Posten if anyone had come into the campsite during the night. Crockett told the officers about the dune-buggy motor-mounting and that the family had ridden away into the night, possibly proceeding over Mengel Pass.

Then many of the officers converged on Crockett's cabin for a chitchat. Crockett gave them some more information but they were suspicious of him. They suggested to Crockett that he haul himself out of the area there but Crockett claimed that he felt that he was still of use to Charlie so that Charlie wouldn't kill him yet. Therefore he thought he'd stay on at the ranch. The cops told him to drive out in the old orange pile wagon if Charlie came back but Crockett felt that Charlie's forces would be guarding both exits on the Barker Ranch, the exit west through the mouth of Goler Wash and the exit northeast over Mengel Pass. Therefore he and Brooks would have to walk out by night.

On September 30, spotter planes buzzed overhead to locate the hippie deployments. But the family covered themselves with tarps or froze in their tracks and evidently were not seen.

That day the police raiding party drove over Mengel Pass where they located two vehicles near Willow Springs: a gold-flaked 1962 Volkswagen dune buggy stolen in the San Fernando Valley and a yellow 1967 Volkswagen dune buggy stolen in Culver City. They also located all the automotive supplies that were being hauled in the day before by Posten and Crockett. They removed the wiring and the distributor caps and rotors from the dune buggies to prevent their use.

That night, Crockett and his helpers were sitting on the front porch of the Barker Ranch when they heard a noise. They went to get their two shotguns out of the cabin. That night someone creepy-crawled the cabin, the dog growled, the door was open and Crockett claimed that Charlie had a half dozen girls chasing around to grab the guns.

It was right about that time, after it became really obvious that the police were after him, that Manson banned all daytime activity. By day everybody was to remain hidden in the wilderness. They were to freeze if there were any spotter planes or cover themselves with camouflage parachutes and remain completely out of the way. Food became scarce. No one was allowed to use the Myers Ranch swimming pool for baths.

After splitting from Death Valley, Simi Valley Sherri spent time with Danny De Carlo in Venice prior to his arrest. De Carlo got the bread truck out of the impound garage around October 1. It had been there since Sandy and Mary had been arrested the day of the Polanski residence murders.

Bruce Davis and Clem were dispatched to Los Angeles to look for Sherri and Barbara—perhaps to kill them. De Carlo caught Clem going through the glove compartment of the bread truck somewhere in Venice. Clem brought back to Death Valley a sixteen-year-old boy named Rocky whose mother was an official at the Fountain of the World sect near the Spahn Ranch. Rocky was infatuated with Katie aka Patricia Krenwinkel, talking with her for hours about motorcycles and horses.

Around October 1, Vance, Vern, Zero and Diane came to the Goler Wash camp, bringing with them an advance copy of the new Beatles album, *Abbey Road*, which was played on a battery-operated machine. Late on Wednesday night, October 1, Crockett and Posten were asleep hugging their shotguns. Around 2 A.M. Charlie and Tex drove up and gave them some tobacco.

Earlier that night, at the other end of the Panamint Valley, one Fillipo Tenerelli, a biker from Culver City, California, was shot near Bishop, California. It was first listed as a suicide. However, three days later his car, a

Volkswagen, blood smeared on the inside and on the outside, was found 400 feet down a cliff near Crowley Peak which is on the road between Ballarat General Store and Olancha. It is quite a distance between Bishop where the body was discovered and Crowley Peak, where his car was found.

Manson handed Tex Watson a shotgun on October 1 and told him to hide out in a little crawlspace above the slatted porchway at the side door of the Barker Ranch and wait for Officer Pursell and Ranger Powell to return, then blast them to death. Watson waited up there until the morning of October 2, at which time he decided no longer to kill for M.

"Even though I was willing to die for Charlie," he has written, "I was getting tired of breaking my back for him. It seemed as if every day there was less chance of finding the Pit, no matter how much we drove around over the desert, no matter how many abandoned mine shafts we crawled through. We were short of food, we were allowed only one cup of water per day and, worst of all, the drugs were running out."

Tex rummaged through the common clothes pile to find the outfit most suitable for splitting, then fired up the '42 Dodge power wagon, drove down Goler Wash to the mouth of the Wash and, running low of gas, tried a shortcut across the large semidry salt lake toward the Trona Road, where he mired down in the salty mush and also ran out of gas.

He spent the night sleeping by the side of the road. The next morning, a man named Mr. Holliday, a pipefitter, from Rialto, California, picked up Watson. Watson told him that the Forestry Department was after the commune he was living in so Holliday drove Watson to the heliport in San Bernardino and then to the San Bernardino railroad station where he dropped Watson off. Watson said he was going back to Texas where his parents owned a chain of supermarkets. When he returned to the commune he was going to bring a truckload of groceries because that was what the commune needed most.

Watson's parents wired him money, and he returned to Texas. He was there for a while, then fled to Hawaii, then back to California, first in L.A., then back to Death Valley, where a prospector told him in the middle of the night the entire family, including Manson, had been arrested. Watson's parents again wired him money, whereupon he returned to Copeville, Texas, where he seems to have maintained a routine existence, dating a doctor's daughter, till the end of November, when he was picked up by his cousin, the sheriff of Collins County, Texas, for murder.

On Thursday, October 2, there was a hostile confrontation between Manson and Paul Crockett. Manson went into a snuff-spasm when Crockett told him that the police had accused him of abetting and aiding a fugitive from the law, namely Manson. "He told me just before I parted and walked out that I should be more afraid of him than the law," Crockett said. Crockett and Posten, in order to save their lives, packed up a few cans of food and walked out over Mengel Pass, down the Striped Butte Valley to the trailer camp near the Warm Springs talc mines, where they found safety.

The next morning, October 3, early in the morning, Crockett and Posten had a nice long discussion with the police, which was taped. Crockett offered the suggestion that the best way to get Manson was either to pick the family off one by one or to mount a large raid against them. They also told the police that Manson had seized Crockett's shotguns and that all the girls were armed with knives and that the girls were all like zombies trained for instant obedience.

With Crockett and crew ousted from the set, Manson began to use the Barker Ranch as headquarters but only at night. Everybody, by this time, was on hand, including Sadie and Katie. By night and by day the police tried to catch them.

Once a day, after dark, the girls would prepare a large meal for everybody in the Barker Ranch kitchen and everybody would skulk in and get a little chow. Sometimes in the middle of the night they'd have to walk for supplies from the Barker Ranch eighteen miles over Mengel Pass to Willow Springs and back.

"We walked to Willow Springs and back in one night. We had to because of the police. Of course, we were helped by some good sunshine," said one of the girls a year later. "We were carrying dune buggies down the hills when the police were chasing us," she said.

They began to leave false campfires to lead the police away from their real campsites.

Some of the girls spent the light of day at a campsite about a mile and a half east-northeast from the Meyers Ranch where they carried sleeping bags and bottles of water. Other girls were required by day to hang out in the hot rocks near Mengel Pass. They "hid out all over the hills, hiding in parachutes," according to Kitty. By night, after supper, they were honored with the task of building the so-called bunkers.

Manson issued an order that all of the girls were to stop smoking cigarettes. Subsequently, he asked for a show of hands as to who exactly had obeyed his order, and was chargrined to find that there were some who had ceased to obey. So he commanded that those who refused to stop smoking cigarettes dig several bunkers by night which were to serve as hidden shelters. Evidently, against the police and against the winter air.

They built a bunker on a hill south of the Barker Ranch which they roofed over with metal and on top of the metal they placed sand and stones. Inside the bunker was a huge Playboy mattress on which bounced the bodies of Helter Skelter. They had a telephone set up. They ran field wires leading from this bunker up to a rectangular rock command post about 300 feet up the hillside so that from this bunker by telescope a spotter could look about a mile and a half down Goler Wash.

There was a set of bunkers to the north in a draw between the Myers and Barker Ranch, one a rock-lined hillside bunker, and down in the gulch near a spring was another bunker built with debris and old window frames.

According to Dianne Lake, just before the police finally netted the family, Charlie sent Cathy and Zero down to Los Angeles in order to kill her grandmother, enabling Cathy to inherit the Meyers Ranch. This would have legitimatized Manson's position in the area. This grim caper was aborted evidently when the automobile they were driving broke down.

On October 8, Manson and Bill Vance left the Barker Ranch area and traveled to Los Angeles together. There's not much known about the reasons for this little trip but it had to be important because Manson had been sticking close by his followers.

As usual the golden opportunity to escape the family occurred whenever Charlie took a trip away. This was no exception.

Life was grim for the pregnant girls, Kitty and Stephanie: little food, no showers, living by night, hiding by day, fearful, threatened by a maniac, confused. Kitty recalled it: "Now when I start thinking about it I remember how bad it really was. How he just talked about it so much that you just . . . you know . . . about snuffing people and torturing them, and all kinds of different orgies. You get so you just can't listen to it any more. It really was pretty bad."

So, on Thursday night, October 9, Kitty and Stephanie sneaked away a couple of hours after sunset. Clem had been assigned bed-check duty and discovered the girls missing. He yelled immediately for everybody to roust out and capture the runaways. Manson had issued proclamations that if they found anybody escaping, they were to beat them up, or worse.

Night held the young girls in safety as they wandered up the Wash to Mengel Pass and on to the Willow Springs area. They had gone in the opposite direction that Barbara Hoyt and Simi Sherri had taken when they escaped in September. Clem and Rocky went to sleep down the Wash in the middle of the creek bed armed with a sawed-off shotgun, prepared the next morning to go out looking for the young ladies.

On October 9, 1969, the same night that Stephanie and Kitty skulked away from the camp, the police set up their final net to catch the car thieves. There had evidently been careful surveillance of the area by the police who determined that the ranch was being used until daylight. Patricia Krenwinkel had been assigned the job of seeing that everybody got out of the Barker Ranch and out of sight before dawn. It was getting cold in the high desert with winter approaching, and on this morning it was very cold and the family hung around the Barker Ranch area too long and were caught.

By cover of darkness the police approached the Barker Ranch from two directions: from the mouth of Goler Wash and from the Striped Butte Valley over Mengel Pass and down the long seven and a half miles to the ranch. The California Highway Patrol supplied radio equipment for these two advancing parties so that when they got close enough they could communicate with each other and exchange information.

Up Goler Wash came the following officers: Brad Hailey, E. B. Anderson, A. B. George, J. B. Journigan of the California Highway Patrol. Also in this crew was Ranger Powell. The party was directed by Lieutenant Hurlbut of the California Highway Patrol.

The other party parked their four-wheel drive vehicles at the summit of Mengel Pass and walked down through the wilderness on foot. The Mengel Pass party was comprised of James Pursell and Officer O'Neill of the California Highway Patrol and others, including a warden of the Federal Fish and Game Commission by the name of Vern Burandt. There were numerous Inyo County officials, including the Inyo County D.A. and assistant D.A., on this important mission. The idea was to converge on the Barker Ranch at dawn.

Just before dawn the two advancing teams of police officers achieved contact via walky-talky. The team of officers coming in from the west, from the Panamint Valley up Goler Wash, encountered, sleeping in suspicious tandem on the creek bed between blankets, Clem and Rocky. Near Clem's head was Clem's sixteen-inch sawed-off shotgun and twenty-four rounds of ammunition.

Officers Journigan et al. awakened them and put them under arrest for having a sawed-off shotgun and for arson and for grand theft auto. The officers parked their four-wheel-drive vehicles evidently in a small draw to the west of the Barker Ranch. Officer O'Neill took a position high on the south slope across from the Barker Ranch up above the bunker. It is not known if the police were really aware of this disguised bunker. However shortly after dawn, Sadie, wearing a red hat, emerged from the hidden bunker to relieve herself. She was evidently spotted by the cops. The cops, according to the girls, let loose a friendly shotgun blast on top of the metal hidden bunker roof causing the girls to come out.

Arrested at the south hill dugout were Leslie Van Houten using the name Louvella Alexandria, Sadie, using the name Donna Kay Powell, Gypsy, using the name Manon Minette, and Brenda, using the name Cydette Perell. Inside the ranch house, the cops arrested Marnie

K. Reeves aka Patricia Krenwinkel. They arrested Robert Ivan Lane aka Soup Spoon. They arrested Linda Baldwin aka Little Patti. Some of the girls were nude. Official note was made of it on the arrest report:

"When the initial group of female prisoners were arrested, several of the females disrobed. Several of them urinated on the ground in the presence of the officers. They also undressed and changed clothes in the presence of the officers."

Proceeding north in the small draw between the Myers and Barker Ranches, the police raided the "spike camp," as they called it, where they arrested Sandy Good, who was carrying Sadie's baby Zezo, Ouish, using the name Rachel S. Morse and carrying Sandy Good's one-month-old baby Ivan, and Mary Ann Schwarm aka Diane Von Ahn. The babies were burnt raw from the sun and one of them had a large cut on his face.

The three girls had in their possession a Miramar mail bag which contained the magic swatches of hair which had been cut off during the tonsure rites of the preceding July. Also in the mail bag was a stolen .22-caliber single-shot Ruger pistol and a ring of keys, one of which fitted the stolen red Toyota.

All day long the police stayed in the area checking it out. Finally, around dusk, a group of ten women, three men and two babies were chained together and transported down Goler Wash. Followed by police vehicles, they walked down the steep waterfall area to the mouth, the chains clanging in the night.

They were all transported to Independence, California by Sergeant Hailey and Warden Burandt, to be booked for arson and theft and receiving stolen property.

As officers searched the area they found the stolen Toyota at the dry wash camp a mile and a half northeast of the Myers Ranch. The Toyota was out of gas and covered over with sage brush. The same Toyota was used to escort Clem and Rocky and Soup Spoon down Goler Wash on the way to jail.

Officers continued to search the area, and in addition to the dune buggy at the bottom of the canyon and the stolen Toyota, they rediscovered the two vehicles that were dewired on September 30. They called the Don Lutz Tow Service of Olancha, California, 130 miles away, and requested the company to haul the stolen vehicles out. What a towing charge.

Then they proceeded to search north along Mengel Pass and found the mud-painted command dune buggy down a cliff with punctured tires and seemingly abandoned although it was covered and camouflaged with brush. The police took color photographs of the vehicles and the arrests.

It was nighttime before the rest of the officers drove over Mengel Pass, their mission accomplished. As they drove toward Death Valley, through the Striped Butte Valley near Anvil Springs, Kitty Lutesinger and Stephanie Schram stepped out of the brush and flagged down the officers. They told the officers they had run away from the family and were afraid for their lives.

Clem Grogan called up the Spahn Ranch from the Inyo County jail in Independence, California and asked to "speak to the Devil." Clem told Charlie about the arrests. Manson for reasons unknown seems to have left for Death Valley about a day later.

Early in the morning of October 11, Stephanie and Kitty were allowed to call their parents, collect. When Kitty called her mother at the Lutesinger Ranch, her mother asked her if she knew that Officers Guenther and Whiteley were looking for her in regard to the murder of Gary Hinman. She did not know. Kitty wanted her parents to come and pick her up but her mother said that she would just have to turn her over to homicide officers anyway, so they couldn't pick her up.

Kitty's mother spoke to Officer Dave Steuber, an energetic auto theft officer for the California Highway Patrol, and told Officer Steuber the details concerning her daughter's connection with Robert Beausoleil. Afterward, Officer Steuber contacted the L.A. County sheriff's office, homicide division, and evidently spoke to Deputy Guenther. Officer Steuber supplied Deputy Guenther with considerable data regarding Charles Manson's activities on Death Valley and the August raid on the Spahn Ranch. This is evidently the first time that Deputy Guenther had learned of the connection between Beausoleil and the Spahn Ranch.

Officers Whiteley and Guenther spent a day researching the Spahn Ranch, Manson, the August 16 raid and various other activities involving the family there. They obtained pictures of the people arrested at the August 16 raid from the Los Angeles County sheriff's office, auto theft division, and on October 12 they proceeded to drive up to Inyo County to secure possession of Kitty Lutesinger. It was the beginning of the solution of the Tate-LaBianca homicides.

The same day, perhaps on the same road, that Guenther and Whiteley were driving to Death Valley, Charles Manson also was on the way there. October 12, 1969, was Aleister Crowley's birthday, a fit day for the arrest of killers.

Why was Manson returning to Death Valley?

He probably realized the amount of fear he could generate to keep everybody in line was greater if he were near his followers. Also, Manson knew that Bruce Davis and others were in Las Vegas getting supplies so he wanted to avert their arrest when they returned.

What did he have to fear? Manson had been arrested that year alone on March 30, June 3, August 16, August 23, for a variety of charges and had walked away free. He had shot, killed, plundered according to his own schedule and gotten away with it. Why not now?

There are indications that Manson was about to undertake his wildest scheme of all, a series of assassinations of prominent Los Angeles citizens against whom he held grudges. The dune-buggy locusts would raid from The Hole, destroy, then return. Perhaps he liked the media attention given to the Tate murders. After all, he had been trying for fame as a recording artist for several years. Now he could be Charlie the Knife.

Central to a discussion of plans to kill famous people is the "list," about which a heavy area of silence has been created. The "list" was found in Death Valley and it marked out those to die.

In one report it contained thirty-four names of stars and businessmen to be killed. This "list" of family enemies included supposedly those who had helped out in the past but had ceased to aid. It is a common phenomenon for cults to have a hate list or enemy list. At least two groups operating in lower California, besides the Mansonoids, have, or had, enemy lists.

High Inyo County officials visited Miss Lutesinger down

in L.A. following the Barker Ranch raids and told her they had in their possession a written list of people to be killed, and she was on the end of the list.

Taken into evidence by the Los Angeles police department from the family material seized by the police in Inyo County was a mysterious pack, perhaps Manson's, which may have confirmed visual aids for the preparation of the "list."

The "army type pack," as the police report read, contained, among other things, sixty-four movie and TV star magazines, one canvas money bag marked "Federal Reserve Bank of Dallas" and one paperback book *Stranger in a Strange Land* by Robert A. Heinlein.

Manson may have returned to his original game borrowed from *Stranger in a Strange Land,* where the novel's Vallentine Michael Smith took to murdering or "discorporating" his enemies. There was one occult shopkeeper on Santa Monica Boulevard who reported selling Manson a copy of *Stranger in a Strange Land* around this time. The movie magazine may have been brought in to help stir up hatred.

Quite a few of the family members escaped arrest on the October 10 raid. Among them were Dianne Lake and Claudia Smith aka Sherry Andrews. Both of these girls hid under a canvas not far from the front ranch gate of the Barker Ranch when the raid occurred. So they were around when Charlie got back. Others had fled and were lurking in various parts of Goler Wash, never to be caught. The police seized the last of the stolen NBC film equipment, a camera loaded with unexposed film. Bill Vance is supposed to have disappeared later with some of the Death Valley footage.

Late in the afternoon of October 12, Charlie walked up to the Goler Wash, stashed his pack near the Lotus Mine, then proceeded to the Barker Ranch, guitar in hand, ready for chow. He was in the company of three other male Caucasians. Bruce Davis, in a stake truck that Clem had rented, came back from Las Vegas and got the stake truck stuck in the sandy wash between Mengel Pass and the Barker Ranch and abandoned it.

California Highway Patrol Officer Pursell and Park Ranger Powell and another Ranger went back in to the Barker Ranch area on Sunday, October 12, to look for more dune buggies and check out the various family campsites for contraband. A passing motorist told them that a stake truck was abandoned in the Wash so the officers checked it out. Pursell and the two Park Rangers located the Chevrolet truck still loaded down with drums of gasoline and supplies. They decided that uncaught hippies, perhaps even Manson himself, had reentered the Barker Ranch area.

So Pursell reached out on the C.H.P. radio equipment and talked to other officers. It was decided that then was the time to noose Satan. About five o'clock in the afternoon police entered the area and took up clandestine positions near the Barker Ranch. They waited. Meanwhile other officers were summoned who were on the way up to Goler Wash from Ballarat.

From a position on a ridge up above the Barker swimming pool north of the ranch Officer Pursell and Ranger Powell observed Manson and a couple of other people walk up the gulch and into the house. Manson was carrying a guitar case. Ranger Curran worked his way around to the front of the ranch so that he could meet the officers who were coming up the Goler Wash from Ballarat. They began to hear giggling and laughter and conversation from the house so they knew there were quite a number of people in there.

The chief Ranger for the Death Valley National Park, Homer Leach, Deputy Don Ward of the Inyo County sheriff's office, and Al Schneider of the sheriff's office arrived just after dark. Then they radioed Officer Pursell, who walked down the hill in the back, slinked along the back side of the cabin just to the left of the Barker Ranch and walked in under the ivy-trellised side porch, kicked open the side door and said, "Stick 'em up." He slid along the wall to the left using it as a cover in case any of them should care to attack him and he told them to put their hands on top of their heads. In slow-motion defiance, the killers complied.

"I ordered the subjects out backwards one at a time where Deputy Ward took charge of them," Pursell recounted later. Once again, as in the Spahn Ranch raid of August 16, the question had to be asked: "Where was Jesus?"

It was about six-thirty in the evening. Seven dirty hippies had been hauled out and handcuffed. The quick desert darkness was imminent. Officer Pursell carried the single candle which had lit the supper around the four-room cabin. He paused at the small blue bathroom with a poured concrete bathtub and a small blue lavatory. Beneath the lavatory was a little cabinet out of which, as the officer placed the candle's flame near, protruded hair. Then he saw wiggling fingers and he said, "All right, come on out, but slowly." And before he could ask, the small human uncoiling from the tiny cabinet said, "Hi. I'm Charlie Manson."

After the police arrested Manson, Pursell went back into the house and ran into Bill Vance standing in the bedroom. After being handcuffed Vance had somehow gotten away and was hiding in the house.

The girls arrested were Beth Tracy aka Collie Sinclair, Dianne Bluestein aka Snake Lake, Sherry Andrews aka Claudia Leigh Smith. All suspects were marched down to the draw and when they got to police vehicles they were escorted in the vans to the head of the waterfalls whereupon they walked down to the Panamint Valley.

They put them in units of three and began to march them down to the draw toward the vehicles which were parked in the Barker Ranch dump area. Men arrested were Manson, John Philip Haught aka Christopher Jesus aka Zero, Kenneth R. Brown aka Scott Bell Davis who was a partner of Zero from Ohio, and David Lee Hamic aka William Rex Cole aka Bill Vance, Vern Edward Thompson aka Vern Plumlee, Lawrence L. Bailey aka Little Larry, and Bruce Davis.

As the chop-fallen killers were walking down the wash from the Barker Ranch, Manson tried an escape caper. He told the officers that he had left his pack very near there and he requested the officers to help him find it. The officers looked and they couldn't find it so Manson asked them to open his handcuffs and let him look around in the darkness for his pack. Then he might have escaped. The pack, probably the one containing those movie mgaazines, subsequently was found by one of the officers and "booked with the rest of the property."

The officers noted that several times during the walk Manson said something and his followers replied with "Amen, Amen"—as if in gospel response. Also, a mere hostile glance from Manson was enough to cause the giggling of the suspects to lapse into silence. Manson told the officers that the blacks were going to take over the country and that the blacks would wipe out the police.

Just as the car thieves arrived at the mouth of the wash, followed by the bouncing headlights of the four-wheel-drive police vehicles, Country Sue and Cathy Myers were arriving at the Goler Wash in a black Oldsmobile full of $500 worth of groceries. The two girls also were arrested. The food was taken in custody also to save Inyo taxpayers money by supplementing the jail diet of the prisoners.

23

The Breaking of the Case (October–November 1969)

Mark Arneson, the person to whom Manson had sold Gary Hinman's Microbus, sold it in turn for $350 to someone named Louis Puhek. In Puhek's possession, the bus still looked the same with the thunderbird printed on the side. It even had the same license plate PGE 388. Someone, however, had put a new engine in the vehicle. There was an all-points bulletin out for the stolen Microbus. Sometime around October 5 or 6 police in Venice, California stopped Puhek and ran the license number, discovering that the vehicle was to be impounded regarding the murder of its owner. Police in Venice questioned Puhek and it was learned that one of the possible owners of the vehicle had been Danny De Carlo of the Straight Satans, who then became a possible suspect in the murder.

Around October 7, Sergeant Whiteley asked Sergeants Gleason, Elliott and Sims of the sheriff's office about Danny De Carlo and if they had a present address on him. They also wanted general information on the Straight Satans regarding possible connections with Hinman. The officers promised to check out De Carlo and get back to Sergeant Whiteley with the data later.

When Sergeant Whiteley and Deputy Guenther learned about Kitty Lutesinger they temporarily forgot about Danny De Carlo, however. October 12 they drove to Inyo County and brought the girl back to the San Dimas sheriff's station, where she was interrogated.

The words "gas chamber," when uttered by police officers, had a magical way of causing some family members to wax loquacious. At first the officers suggested to Kitty that she was one of the girls that had accompanied Beausoleil to Gary Hinman's house. She replied that the girls were "Sadie and Mary" but certainly not she, and that they had "screwed up" at the Hinman's residence, having been sent there by Manson merely to acquire money.

Another factor that caused mouths to open was that Manson evidently uttered a few threats over the phone directed against weak links, either when Clem called him down at the ranch or when Manson called out after he was arrested. She was worried about her life and that of her parents.

The next morning at 9 A.M., October 13, the officers flew from the Ontario, California airport to Independence to talk to Susan Atkins aka Sadie Glutz. They arrived about noon. They brought with them photos of the family. The Inyo County jail was so crowded with car thieves that interrogation was difficult, so Officers Whiteley and Guenther took Sadie to Lone Pine substation of the Inyo County sheriff's department for a chat.

During the officers' skillful interrogation, Atkins admitted participation in the Hinman murder and shortly thereafter even did some talking about Shorty Shea. But she refused to tape-record it. They talked for about twenty-five minutes. Then the officers flew with Miss Atkins back to Ontario. They drove her to the San Dimas sheriff's station and booked her for suspicion of murder. The next day they drove back to Inyo County.

On October 13, Kitty was interviewed by the Los Angeles sheriff's office regarding auto thefts. Sergeants Gleason and Sims interrogated her for four hours. She told about the Michigan loader arson, about various dune-buggy thefts, about stolen credit cards, about the crashing of the '69 Ford from Hertz and about the Hinman case. Kitty was held for several days in Juvenile Hall then released in the custody of her parents.

Sadie Glutz was arrested under the name Donna Powell but the police had been able quickly to determine who she was. The identity of the "Mary" who had been at Gary Hinman's house remained a problem. Patricia

Krenwinkel had been arrested as Marnie Kay Reeves, and had a prior arrest under the name of Mary Scott. Therefore she was taken down to Los Angeles on October 14 as a possible murder suspect.

Kitty had revealed that "Mary" was a slim redhead, because Officers Whiteley and Guenther also took red-haired Squeaky Fromme aka Lynette Alice Fromme aka Elizabeth Elaine Williamson with them. On the ride down to Los Angeles, Squeaky, according to legend, told the officers that Charlie had the girls perform fellatio with dogs as part of his mental-death program.

Krenwinkel quickly told the police that it was Mary Brunner, not she, who had gone to Hinman's house. Krenwinkel, Sadie and Squeaky were held in the Los Angeles sheriff's facility in Lancaster.

The team of investigators working on the LaBianca murders had requested from the Los Angeles sheriff's office information regarding any murders carried out in styles similar to the Waverly Drive homicides. The LaBianca team had rigorously pursued its investigation.

They had connected the bloody "Helter Skelter" and "Rise" with the Beatles album, catalogue number SWBO 101. Also they had correctly interpreted the knife and fork in Mr. LaBianca: "The words in the song 'Piggies' make reference to a knife and fork in the bacon"—as a police report read.

By the time of the LaBianca team's second homicide investigation progress report, dated October 15, 1969, Manson and crew were prime suspects in the LaBianca murders although Manson had not yet been interrogated. Manson's association with the Satan Slaves was noted. Several Satan Slaves had been suspects previously in the LaBianca matter.

The murders were similar, the police noted. Blood writing on the wall, knives as the weapons, both crimes involved the placing of a pillow over the victim's face. And one suspect in the Hinman murder, Susan Atkins, had been free the night of the LaBianca crimes, unlike Beausoleil, who was in jail. Because of all this information about Manson supplied by Officers Whiteley and Guenther, the LaBianca team began to concentrate on the family.

Plans were made by the LaBianca investigators, as of October 15, to compile a list of everybody who had lived at the Spahn Ranch and to obtain a handwriting sample and fingerprints of each. Sometime evidently in mid-October Manson submitted to a polygraph examination but terminated it in the middle. He must have known that the noose was set around his operations and several deaths may have resulted to create silence and fear.

Sadie and Katie were asked to write Helter Skelter to see if either had written it on the LaBianca refrigerator.

On October 15, fourteen of the Mansonoids were arraigned in Inyo County Superior Court on twenty felony charges. The bail totaled out at $263,500. Ten were set free with charges dropped.

Kitty Lutesinger testified that she had been at the Lotus Mine, located high on the steep side of Goler Wash near the turnoff to the Barker Ranch, and had seen Manson down below, roaring past in one of the stolen dune buggies. She recognized the unique air scoop on it. Her testimony enabled Inyo County to link Manson with a specific crime and thus hold him. Otherwise he too might have been set free.

On October 15, Danny De Carlo, a Straight Satan named Al Springer and six others were arrested in Venice for receiving stolen property and possession of marijuana. De Carlo's charge stemmed from a hot engine he traded to acquire his bread truck. De Carlo was released on bail. His troubles were mounting. De Carlo had a child custody hearing on September 12 to try to gain possession of his son Dennis, seized during the August 16 raid at the Spahn Ranch and placed in a foster home. At the hearing De Carlo was arrested on a federal charge of purchasing a pistol under a fictitious name. De Carlo also had a five-year conviction for smuggling marijuana in from Mexico which he was then appealing. Danny's many troubles with the law forced him a few days later to finger out the family as the killers of Sharon Tate and others.

Meanwhile, up in Independence, California, where the so-called family was being held, the brave girls would raise their dresses in the exercise yard. Manson would utter coyote yips and his disciples would yip in return. Once during their stay in jail there they asked for peanut butter and honey for a purification rite, whatever that meant. It was all happiness.

On October 16, Inyo County sheriff's deputies plus Los Angeles sheriff homicide and auto theft teams, and CHP officers scoured the Barker Ranch area for incriminating data. There they located some more dune buggies and, according to the police report, numerous food and equipment caches and, perhaps most important, a grease gun and cartridge that witness Lutesinger had earlier described to the investigating officer in San Dimas as being stolen from the National Park Service loader prior to its being found by the hippie group. The cached vehicles were covered with sage brush, willow branches and camouflaged parachutes.

On Thursday, October 16, Susan Atkins aka Sadie was arraigned in Malibu Justice Court for murder. A preliminary hearing was set then for November 12.

In the afternoon of October 17 the sheriff's office in Lancaster called Patricia Krenwinkel's father. Mr. Krenwinkel drove to pick her up. Katie stayed with her father for five days and then on October 23, 1969, she flew to her mother in Mobile, Alabama via National Airlines.

Also on October 17, assistant Los Angeles Police Chief Robert Houghton told a press conference that the initial part of the Tate investigation was over and that now the police would backtrack over the entire case and compare notes. More than 400 police interviews had been conducted to that date.

At the end of forty days of intensive investigation, the chief possible motives for the Cielo Drive homicides were considered to be a drug burn or a drug freak-out.

October 20.

Officers Whiteley and Guenther were impressed that Miss Lutesinger told them that she had overheard Susan Atkins talking about stabbing a man in the legs as the man was pulling Susan's hair. The man was someone other than Gary Hinman, and since Susan Atkins had been free the night of the so-called Tate murders, they felt that she might have something to do with it.

Whiteley and Guenther informed the Tate team about Manson. The Tate detectives waited until October 31, eleven days after they were informed, to interview the young lady.

October 21.

At the Inyo County Courthouse in Independence, California preliminary trials were held for Leslie Sankston aka Leslie Van Houten, Nancy Pitman aka Brenda McCann, Manon Minette aka Gypsy and Robert Ivan Lane aka Scotty. The theft charges were dismissed but all four defendants were held to answer to charges of violating section 182 of the California Penal Code.

October 22.

Charles Manson "aka Jesus Christ"—as noted on the arrest report—Manon Minette (Gypsy), Dianne Bluestein aka Snake Lake and Rachel S. Morse aka Ouish were held to answer for violations of Section 449a of the California Penal Code, referring to the burn-job on that Michigan loader.

October 23.

Sandy Collins Pugh-Good and Mary Schwarm aka Diane Von Ahn and Ouish were held to answer in the Inyo County Court at a preliminary trial on the charge of receiving stolen property (the Ruger pistol that was inside the Miramar mail bag with the witch-swatches of hair, when the three young ladies were arrested in the gulch back of the Myers Ranch).

Zero, Bill Vance, Little Larry, Vern Plumlee, Sherry Andrews aka Claudia Smith, Beth Tracy aka Diane Von Ahn, Sue Bartell and Cathy Gillies were all released with charges dropped.

Quite a few of the freed family then went to Los Angeles, where they stayed in Venice at the residence of one Mark Ross, located at 28 Club House Drive, just off the ocean. It was there that Zero would die.

Manson realized that if he couldn't control what family members said to the authorities it was all over. "Some heavy scheming and a lot of communication had to be done," he later wrote. "The police made both avenues possible when charges on several of the kids were dropped. With their release, I had the means to spread the word, 'Clam up, no talking! Find out where the cops are getting their information.' "

Two of his most dedicated gore-spores, Squeaky Fromme and Sandy Good, came to Independence, California, where M was being held, and stayed in a motel. They were Manson's eyes and ears, and they pretended great benevolence. No one could run the We-are-sweet-innocent-flowerwaifs scam as well as they, and they ran it for years, all the way to 1975, when Squeaky would aim a .45 at President Ford.

"They were my link to everything that was going on," recounts Manson. "Though in jail some six or seven hours' drive from L.A., I had Lyn and Sandy burning up the highways and telephone lines with daily reports on who was saying what, and to whom."

The threat of death went forth.

October 25.

At the Sybil Brand Jail for women, in Los Angeles, news broadcasts were available to the inmates, and Sadie was stimulated to babble more than once by news bulletins about the investigation into the Tate murders. Around October 24 and 25, the airways were filled with announcements of a hot new clue in the homicides—the possibility that the murders were commited by a nearsighted bullet-headed freak with deformed ears. A newspaper had printed the story of the pair of glasses found near Mr. Polanski's blue steamer trunks, lying open with the ear bars sticking straight up, as if the murderer had been wearing them and they had fallen off. Local radio stations flashed broadcasts derived from newspaper accounts of the glasses. The police had taken the glasses to a Hollywood optometrist who opined that the glasses, because of certain bendings in them, belonged to someone one of whose ears was lower than the other, and who was very very myopic and who had a rounder head than most humans. So, when the broadcasts occurred about the glasses, Sadie talked about it with a fellow inmate nicknamed Casper aka Roseanne Walker, a young chunky brown-haired lady in jail for various offenses.

Casper was that sort that you find in many jails, a businesswoman selling cigarettes and candy to fellow inmates on the sly. She would have people hold her merchandise and her excess profits for her, since it was against prison regulations to have more than a certain fixed amount of money or cigarettes. According to Casper, Sadie became friendly with her because of her pleasant open disposition and because literally Sadie had not a dime, and Casper had lots of candy and cigarettes she was willing to share.

before Sadie visited with Sue. When Sue told her about the roulette, Sadie, enthusiastic as ever about gore and death, rushed out to tell Ronni about it, in gruesome detail.

November 6.

At 1:30 P.M. Lieutenant A. H. Burdick of the scientific investigation division of the Los Angeles police department, the gentleman who ninety days previous had administered a lie detector test to William Garretson, was in Independence, California, interviewing Leslie Van Houten. He claimed, in a report to Sergeant Patchett of the Los Angeles police department robbery-homicide division, that Miss Van Houten indicated to him that there were "some 'things' that caused her to believe that someone from her group was involved in the Tate homicide but denied knowledge of the LaBianca homicide. At this time she declined to indicate what she meant and stated that she wanted to think about it overnight, and that she was perplexed and didn't know what to do." The next day, Miss Van Houten had gained her composure and refused to speak any more about the matter.

The friendly runners, Sadie and Virginia Graham, ran messages all day till 3:30 P.M., then they went to dinner, returning to the 8000 dormitory about 4:35 P.M. Virginia was all set to go take a shower when Sadie came over to Virginia's bed and asked if she could sit and talk for a minute. Virginia said okay. They talked. Somehow the subject centered at first on LSD, which the thirty-nine-year-old Virginia had taken for the first time on October 1, a few days before her arrest. Sadie had taken hundreds of trips, so it was something in common to talk about.

Then Sadie began to talk about the Hinman matter, confessing freely to participating in it. Miss Graham reproached Sadie for her loose talk.

"I told her that I didn't care particularly what she had done, but I didn't think it was advisable for her to talk so much," Virginia remembered later. Graham told Sadie she had heard of cases where people in jail were victims of entrapment after confessing to crimes to cellmates who later snitched.

Sadie replied that she wasn't worried because looking in Virginia's eyes, she just knew she could trust Virginia. April Fool.

Sadie then began to talk about Death Valley and the people arrested up there and the Underground City for the chosen. And she began to talk about Manson. Then Sadie became visibly excited and began to talk quickly. What triggered it off? Evidently a general discussion of crime and murder.

"We were talking about crime and, you know, various murders, and all that," remembered Miss Graham.

And Sadie said, in the course of the conversation, according to Graham, "Well, you know, there's a case right now. They are so far off the track they don't even know what's happening."

There was a pause.

"What are you talking about?"

"That one on Benedict Canyon."

"Benedict Canyon?"

"Benedict Canyon, yes."

"You don't mean Sharon Tate?"

"Yeah," Sadie said. Then she grew excited even more and the baleful words of chop-mania were spewn out. "You're looking at the one that did it."

Several times Sadie raised her voice and Graham had to tell her to lower it. Out came the horror, the deathly details, the scenarios. And Miss Graham began to ask questions to determine if Sadie was really telling the truth, querying Sadie about the rope, what the victims were wearing, etc., in order to trip her up. But the story seemed to hold, except that Sadie claimed to have left a palm print on the living room desk and to have lost her knife in the fray, events unmentioned in the media. (And any palm print would already certainly have led to Sadie's arrest.)

For just over an hour they talked. At 6 P.M there was a jail prisoner count so it had to stop, but not before Miss Graham's mind was filled with an unforgettable mixture of shocking data. Right away, Miss Graham rushed over to her ten-year friend Ronni Howard and told her what Sadie had related. They weren't totally convinced but they planned to try to find out more from Sadie.

"We'll ask her certain questions that only a person would know who had been in on it," Miss Howard said to Miss Young. "Try and ask her what color the bedroom was, or what the people had on or anything."

Because Sadie had moved into the bed right next to Ronni, Ronni was able to begin to talk to Sadie, by night, in privacy. Since the prison matrons counted the sleeping inmates each half hour, it was possible by means of a system of lookouts to visit each other intimately for half-hour periods in between head counts.

November 8.

Virginia Graham didn't want to rouse Sadie's suspicions, so she waited to bring up the subject of murder. One day, she told Sadie approximately two or three days after the bedside conversation, this: "Hey, you know . . ." revealing to Sadie that she and her former husband years before, around 1962, had been to the residence at 10050 Cielo Drive to see about renting it. "Is it still done in gold and white?" Taking a shot in the dark, because she had never actually seen the interior.

"Uh huh," Sadie replied.

On November 8 or 9, Sadie came to Virginia's bed with a movie fan magazine in her hand. The magazine was opened to a picture of Elizabeth Taylor and Richard Burton. Sadie seemed jolly as she disclosed to Virginia a list of future victims, including Richard Burton, whose groin was to be trimmed of appendage, Elizabeth Taylor, Frank Sinatra, Tom Jones, who was singing over the jail radio at that moment and Steve McQueen—although Sadie said that she hated to have to do in Tom Jones because he turned her on. She also expressed enmity for Frank Sinatra, Jr. The most hideous of deaths Sadie plotted for those on her list.

November 12.

Both Susan Atkins and Bob Beausoleil had hearings at the Santa Monica Superior Court, on the Hinman matter, but before different judges. Sadie appeared before Judge John Merrick, in a hearing to determine if she should be held for a trial. Her lawyer was court appointed, a Mr. Gerald M. Condon.

Deputy Guenther, of the Los Angeles sheriff's office homicide division, testified about information obtained from her on October 13 at the Lone Pine sheriff's station house. Officer Guenther also testified that Sadie told him that she held Mr. Hinman while Beausoleil stabbed him. Deputy Guenther told of interviewing Kitty Lutesinger, who evidently had overheard a phone conversation wherein

Susan Atkins had talked about killing Hinman, "indicating that Bobby and Susie had screwed up, that they had to kill Hinman." Sadie was angry, to be sure, at Kitty when she heard this.

Judge Merrick found that there was sufficient cause that Miss Atkins be brought to trial and, accordingly, he set a trial date of November 26, 1969.

Sadie came back to Sybil Brand Institute an upset woman. Evidently, she had made notes which she showed to Ronni Howard. Gosh, how could Deputy Guenther testify that she held a 200-pound man's arms, little old she, while Beausoleil stabbed him? What she told Graham and Nadell was that she stabbed Hinman, not Bobby.

It so happened that on November 12, Virginia Graham had a parole hearing and it was decided to send her back to Corona State Prison for Women. Just before she left (after Sadie had returned from her own court appearance) Ronni and Virginia had a short conference about what to do about Sadie's confession.

Ronni said that she had been talking every night to Sadie, commenting, "Boy is she weird."

Ronni aka Shelly aka Veronica felt that she could ask Sadie the question that would determine if Sadie was telling the truth. Ronni knew what it was like to stab someone, since she had once stabbed her former husband. So Ronni decided to ask Sadie what it was like, physically, to stab someone.

Ronni evidently agreed with Virginia that the key might be to start out by talking about LSD trips, since that seemed to get Sadie going. As Virginia Graham left to go to Corona, she told Ronni that if she found out more, she could then go to her parole agent.

Ronni replied that, since she worked down in receiving, there were always lots of homicide detectives coming to the jail, and she'd just tell one of them. Whereupon Virginia said that, if Ronni decided to tell anybody in authority about the matter, Virginia could be reached at Corona State Prison.

The hour for lights-out in dorm 8000 at Sybil Brand Institute is 9:30 P.M., and that very night, after taps, Sadie and Ronni Howard were talking face to face. "Oh, how I got her to tell me about it; I told you we were talking about an acid trip. You know, because not too many of the girls take acid in there and I guess I was one that she could talk to," is how Miss Howard described her method of getting Sadie to talk.

Ronni had taken twelve acid trips. Sadie told her that there was nothing that could shock her, nothing that she hadn't done. Then upon the subtle prodding of Miss Howard, the subject somehow shifted to butchery and Miss Atkins began to tell all. Ronni scoffed enough and asked enough questions to force Sadie to reveal all the details, whispering in the dark dormitory.

Each night from November 12 through November 15 or 16, Shelley Nadell aka Ronni Howard would lie down with Sadie Glutz in the darkness, collecting data. Sadie really upset Ronni, however, when she told Ronni that the deaths were going to continue and that they were going to occur at random!

Venice detectives interviewed biker Al Springer in the L.A. County jail. Springer had not been able to raise bail. The police were interviewing anybody who had any connection with the family in the hope of finding someone with information who would talk. They hit pay dirt this time, a rare occurrence because of the veil of fear that kept the family quiet. Springer told them about a conversation that Danny De Carlo had allegedly heard from somebody after the Tate murders, something like "we got five piggies."

The Venice detectives located De Carlo living with his mother, who was caring for Dan's two-year-old son Dennis. Hesitant to talk, De Carlo had so many charges against him that pressure forced him to loosen his tongue.

Then the LaBianca detectives interviewed both Springer and De Carlo on November 12, and the road to victory was entered at last.

November 14.

Testimony was heard against Robert Beausoleil, following jury selection which took most of the preceding day. Because the case had not yet become such a media trip for the district attorney, it was agreed, with trial Judge John Shea concurring, that the death penalty was not being sought. Testimony was heard from twelve prosecution witnesses and one defense witness so that the trial was scheduled to conclude after two days of testimony, with the closing arguments of defense attorney Leon

Salter and prosecuting attorney Ross to be had on Tuesday morning, November 18.

The case against Beausoleil, at that time, was circumstantial and fairly weak, until the very day that the trial would probably have ended, when the prosecution learned about De Carlo and the confession that Beausoleil allegedly had made to him.

Around November 14, Virginia Graham claims to have decided to talk about Susan Atkins's confession. She filled out a "blue slip" or request to speak with a staff member and sent it to the psychologist at Corona State Prison, Dr. Vera Dreiser, with the note: "Dr. Dreiser, it is very important that I speak with you."

Dr. Dreiser sent a "blue slip" back indicating that Miss Graham was to talk with Dr. Owens, Dreiser's administrator. Finally about twelve days later she told her counselor, Miss Mary Ann Domn, about the Manson family.

November 16.

Police called Gregg Jakobson to make an appointment to see them about Manson. The next day, several officers including Lieutenant Helder, the head of the Tate investigation, and Sergeants Patchett and Gutierrez of the LaBianca investigation came to Jakobson's house on Beverly Glen for a long interview. A key incentive for Jakobson to talk, as in the case of De Carlo and Lutesinger, was that Manson was in jail and off the streets, therefore seemingly unable to harm. They asked Jakobson to relate everything he knew about Manson's group.

At 3:30 P.M. on November 16, an unidentified body of a girl was found in the Hollywood hills off Mulholland Drive near Skyline Drive. The girl, referred to by the police as Jane Doe number 59, had been dead for about a day. Again the crime had been committed with savagery.

November 17.

Ronni Howard aka Shelley Joyce Nadell aka Veronica Hughes aka Veronica Williams aka Connie Johnson aka Connie Schampeau aka Sharon Warren aka Marjie Carter aka Jean Marie Conley had an appearance in Santa Monica Superior Court before Judge Brandt regarding her false prescription charge.

California law allows a defendant a phone call for each separate court appearance, so Ronni called the Hollywood division of the Los Angeles police department, because she believed that the Hollywood division was handling the Tate investigation. She told them about Sadie's confession.

After Miss Howard returned to Sybil Brand Jail from court, L.A.P.D. Special Investigators Brown and Mossman came to Sybil Brand and talked to Ronni in a private room for about an hour and a half. She supplied them with most of the information that Sadie had given her, except she left out some of the names involved.

What made it totally believable to the police was that Sadie had told Ronni of things only the killer could have known, such as the Buck knife that Sadie said she lost in the house.

There are some interesting aspects to Ronni Howard aka Shelley Nadell snitching to the police. Nadell testified at the trial that she told certain details to Officers Brown and Mossman but that she never repeated these details later.

On Monday, November 17, the same day Ronni Howard aka Shelley Nadell was telling the police about Susan Atkins, other officers at L.A. police headquarters were taping a long interview with Danny De Carlo of the Straight Satans. De Carlo came in voluntarily.

The interview ranged over every aspect of the family and De Carlo's memory was very exact. He told them about the white nylon rope found at the Polanski residence. He talked about the Hinman murder, the Shea murder, the death of the sixteen-year-old boy in Topanga and numerous other crimes.

When interrogating officers suggested that De Carlo, since he was seen sporting one of Shorty Shea's matched .45's after his death, may have been involved in the murder, De Carlo replied, "I got no balls to put anyone's lights out."

De Carlo was uptight about reprisals from Manson and Bruce Davis. The family girls now set up headquarters in Venice where they had been spotted by the Straight Satans. The police assured him that Manson was going to remain in jail. But Davis was a free man.

De Carlo was interested in obtaining some part of the $25,000 reward in order to put his boy Dennis through military school. The police agreed not to turn De Carlo over to federal authorities on the gun violation nor to turn him in on a charge filed in Van Nuys.

Late in the afternoon Sergeant Manuel Gutierrez called Deputy Guenther of the Hinman investigation and told him of De Carlo's statements bragging about Hinman's death. He gave Guenther De Carlo's home address.

November 18.

In the afternoon Dan De Carlo had a hearing in Santa Monica Superior Court regarding his theft bust in Venice on October 15. He agreed to testify against Robert Beausoleil in exchange for the Venice charges being dropped. Accordingly, De Carlo waited by the phone all morning for a phone call summoning him down to court to testify.

Both prosecution and defense now rested in Robert Beausoleil's trial and both sides were set to discuss jury instructions with the judge, when the prosecution became aware of De Carlo. Around 10:30 A.M., the deputy district attorney, Mr. Ross, requested a continuance till 2 P.M. He told the court that there was an "individual" with information relative to the case.

That morning Sergeant Whiteley and Deputy Guenther were handling a kidnapping case on trial at the Hall of Justice in downtown L.A. At the noon break the officers sped out to Santa Monica Superior Court where they apprised the prosecution of De Carlo's evidence against Beausoleil. Thereafter the policemen returned to downtown L.A. to continue their testimony in the kidnapping case.

At 2 P.M. the D.A. requested a week's continuance till Monday, November 24. The motion was granted over the strenuous objections of Beausoleil's attorney, Mr. Leon Salter. After all, both sides had rested and now there was to be more evidence given against Beausoleil.

Evidently only one lieutenant and five detectives were still assigned to the Polanski residence case. Right away, after Ronni Howard aka Shelley Nadell snitched, the full investigation involving two lieutenants and sixteen men was reactivated. With the evidence supplied by Nadell, De Carlo, Kitty, Jakobson and others, it was all over.

On November 18, 1969, at 2 P.M., District Attorney Evelle Younger assigned Deputy D.A. Vincent T. Bugliosi and Deputy D.A. Aaron Stovitz to handle the case.

These two energetic gentlemen proceeded to coordinate the gathering of conclusive evidence against the murderers.

November 19.

Deputy D.A. Vincent Bugliosi, Sergeant Calkins, Deputy Guenther, Sergeant Whiteley and other officers went to the Spahn Ranch to gather data. They were looking for .22-caliber shell casings and also for knives. They had not located yet the Buntline Special turned over by Steve Weiss on Labor Day and stored by the police. The officers obtained George Spahn's consent to search the ranch. Sergeant Lee, of the special investigation division of the L.A. police department, found twenty-two .22-caliber shell casings around 100 yards south of the Western set and also a quarter of a mile up the canyon toward Hialeah Springs. White panels were placed on the gulley where the .22-caliber casings were found so that a plane overhead could take aerial photos.

Deputy D.A. Aaron Stovitz, possessing a search warrant for the green and white bus, traveled to the Barker Ranch to acquire data, leading a team of L.A. police officers.

Various law enforcement officials in the Inyo County area, notably Sergeant Dave Steuber of the California Highway Patrol, prepared detailed reports regarding the Mansonoids. Officer Steuber produced, on November 20, a skillful document titled: SUMMARY OF THE ARRESTS AND THE CRIMES COMMITTED IN THE DEATH VALLEY AREA OF INYO COUNTY BY A GROUP OF HIPPIES KNOWN AS "THE FAMILY" UNDER THE LEADERSHIP OF CHARLES MILES MANSON.

November 21.

Sergeant Phil Sartuche of L.A.P.D., robbery-homicide, who had been a part of the resourceful LaBianca team of detectives, collected from Inyo County courthouse a large quantity of boots, moccasins, shoes and clothing seized at the Barker Ranch. Officials had not yet located the bloody attire used by the murderers and possibly wanted to match the boots and shoes with the new heel print on the Polanski sidewalk. All items were turned over to Sergeant Granado for analysis at the L.A.P.D. crime lab.

Also taken into custody by Sergeant Sartuche was that "army style pack" containing the sixty-four movie star magazines, the copy of *Stranger in a Strange Land,* the Federal Reserve money bag, etc.

On the evening of November 21, 1969, two scientology students, one of them a girl friend of Bruce Davis, were murdered near a scientology commune called Thetan Manor located at 1032 South Bonnie Brae. The victims, particularly the girl, were unspeakably slashed.

Doreen Gaul, twenty-one—a scientology "clear"—from Albany, New York, and James Sharp, fifteen, of Crystal City, Missouri, were living in the Westlake area near L.A. scientology headquarters in separate residences. Miss Gaul lived at Thetan Manor, an old three-story Victorian house then filled mainly with students of scientology. Several humans connected with a voodoo group lived there also, according to an official of the Church of Scientology who investigated the murders.

They were last seen alive at 7:30 P.M. hitchhiking in front of Vons Market. Their desecrated bodies were found four hours later at 11:30 P.M. dumped in a nearby alleyway lined with pastel-color garages lettered with strange and ornate teen-gang spraypaint writing called placa.

November 23.

Around this time Bruce Davis went back to England, where, according to a homicide detective with the L.A. sheriff's department, he attended a scientology school. The reader will recall that in late '68 and early '69, Davis had also resided in England and then had been employed at a scientology facility.

Sergeants Patchett and McGann of the L.A.P.D. in the evening interviewed Shelley Nadell at the Sybil Brand Institute. The next day, Nadell was removed from the dormitory where she slept alongside Susan Atkins. Nadell could not continue to stay in the same dormitory lest it appear to the court that she had attempted to entrap Miss Atkins into a confession.

November 24.

The trial of Robert Beausoleil for the murder of Gary Hinman ended with Danny De Carlo being allowed to testify. With De Carlo's added testimony, the Beausoleil jury went into deliberation and after considerable debate was unable to come to a decision. The jury remained locked 8 to 4 for conviction so a mistrial was declared. This was unfortunate for Beausoleil, for in the retrial of

April 1970, the district attorney decided to seek the death penalty and ultimately secured it.

The night of November 24, a newscaster for Channel 11 in Los Angeles announced, after a tip to one of his sound men from a detective, that a "Break was coming soon in the Sharon Tate murder case." The press entered the investigation of Manson several weeks before the December 1 arrests. Reporters checked facts with the police and the police, in turn, learned details from the newsmen. An official of Los Angeles radio station KFWB reported that his staff uncovered a link between the Hinman case and the Tate case in the middle of October 1969.

One radio station picked up on the family after it noticed that an unusual number of L.A. sheriff's deputies were filling out travel sheets for Independence, California where the killers were incarcerated.

By November 19, the *Los Angeles Times* had a general knowledge of the Manson family and had a page-one story already written a week before Police Chief Davis announced the breaking of the case to a press conference.

TV camera and light crews who roam L.A. tragedy sites began to get informed, "in strictest confidence," that the case had been solved. Helicopters bearing TV camera crews showed up in Goler Wash. CBS considered venturing to the Barker Ranch via dune buggy but heard that the family was armed and that they employed walky-talky warning devices. A helicopter was used instead.

Pressure mounted for the solution to be publicly aired. On the other hand, the press refrained from announcing details because of the possibility of further murders or suicides or that crucial evidence would be destroyed.

Some police officers have expressed privately that, had the arrests been held off for a while, "we could have got them all." One key homicide investigator stated that the murder of Jane Doe 59 probably would have been solved had the arrests been delayed. But the police knew about Zero's death, and about possible connections with murders in Bishop, Ukiah, Topanga, etc., so there was great concern to get such maniacs immediately off the streets.

November 25.

Sergeant Gutierrez of L.A.P.D. robbery-homicide visited the Spahn Ranch. There he talked to Juan Flynn, who showed Gutierrez a cabinet door in his trailer bearing "various writings." Flynn allowed the door itself to be removed from the cabinet and brought into custody. The writing on the door was as follows: "1, 2, 3, 4, 5, 6, 7—all good children go to heaven—Helter Skelter." At the bottom of the writing was the inverted Yoni-sign or peace symbol.

Police reinterviewed Mrs. Nadell-Young-Howard-Conley-Hughes-William-Lopez at Sybil Brand jail and taped it. Police informed Mrs. Nadell that there were perhaps two or three others with whom it would be necessary to share the reward. Ronni asked the cops, or suggested to the cops, that they send her back in to get more information from Sadie, for if Ronni had returned to Sadie's bedside, it would have meant more data.

"You mean to say that you couldn't forget your code of ethics or something like this because this is something out of the ordinary, really."

To which Sergeant Patchett told her, "We have to take this thing to court to prosecute these people and to do so we can't put you back in there; because you will be our agent then."

On November 25 the Los Angeles police department took a half dozen prisoners (Clem, Gypsy, Ouish, Brenda, Snake and Leslie) from Independence, California to Los Angeles, on subpoenas from the grand jury. The end was near. Manson was left behind in Independence.

All prisoners were intensively interviewed to attempt to get information incriminating Manson, but not even the words "gas chamber" seemed to loosen their tongues. Susan Atkins's confession to her cellmates could only be used to convict Miss Atkins. It could not be used against Watson, Manson, Krenwinkel, Kasabian and the others, because of strict rules pertaining to admissibility of so-called cellmate confessions.

November 26.

Sadie/Susan had a court hearing in Santa Monica on the Hinman matter.

Richard Condon was relieved of his job as court-appointed attorney and Richard Caballero, a former assistant district attorney, was appointed to represent Miss Atkins, at county expense. Mr. Caballero had a long, lengthy discussion with Atkins. She was evidently confronted with the considerable evidence against her from her cellmates. She was made to believe that the evidence was overwhelming against her, Manson and the others. Somehow she was convinced by her attorney that only if she made a full confession to all the murders and cooperated with the police could she hope to avoid the gas chamber. Now the case was truly broken.

In the morning of the same day that Susan Atkins agreed to confess, her former cellmate Virginia Graham related to Miss Mary Ann Domn, Graham's counselor at the Corona State Prison for Women, what Miss Atkins had told her about the homicide.

The same day, at 3:15 P.M. Sergeant Mike Nielsen of the Los Angeles police department taped an interview with Miss Graham at the Corona State Prison.

November 28.

Sergeant Mike Nielsen, of L.A.P.D. robbery-homicide division, called Joseph Krenwinkel and asked where his daughter Patricia was. He told them that Miss Krenwinkel was to be found in Mobile, Alabama. She would be arrested several days later in Mobile, where she was staying with her aunt.

On November 30, Charles Denton Watson was picked up in Copeville, Texas for murder.

At 2 P.M. on December 1, Los Angeles Police Chief Edward Davis held a press conference in an auditorium at Parker Center, the L.A. police headquarters, where he announced the solution of the Tate-LaBianca-Sebring-Folger-Frykowski-Parent homicides.

Facing about fifteen microphones and a knot of jousting cameramen, Chief Edward Davis announced that 8,750 hours of police work had brought down the house of Manson.

On one level it was over. On another level, it was just beginning.

SECTION 4

THE FAMILY:

The Trials and Aftermath (1970–1989)

24

Flower-Waifs with Knives (December 1969–June 15, 1970)

Manson's P.R. apparatus reached out to the media tirelessly. Family members wrote letters, approached editors, visited newspapers. For a while they attracted interest in the underground press, which printed sympathetic articles, interviews and letters from Manson and the family.

Stripping away all the reporting about communes, drugs, and free love, the evidence was not overwhelming. There was a chance—if only a slight one—that some or all of the defendants were innocent, or they were being framed.

All through the months preceding the trial, the world media flared up with a revulsion of fascination. Coverage had an anticounterculture and antihippie flavor, as if the Mansonites, by their single set of transgressions—including their orgies, their wandering busses, their life-style in the age of the abused credit card—had been the real funeral of Hippie. It was as if the funeral of Hippie conducted on the Haight in the fall of 1967 was really held two years later, in the transgressions of Goler Wash and Cielo Drive, as amplified by the media to the world.

While to the press the family presented a flower-waif image, they gave out another image to potential witnesses as they tried to squash any cooperation with the prosecutors.

Early in the year, the family came into the very secure offices of the *Los Angeles Free Press*, whose front entrance was bomb-proofed because of the threats of right wing anti-Castro partisans. They brought with them a swirl of confusion and imprecation. The mix of P.R., sweetness, polite manners, satiny end-of-the-hippie-era attire, nipples and innocence had a certain power to it: Gypsy leaning over the desk of a reporter as one breast dropped out of its loose wrapping, while out in the hallway Clem Grogan was standing with his arms around the ten- or eleven-year-old daughter of a Freep staffer (unbeknownst to her mother), chanting "There is no good, there is no evil."

Meanwhile, the strange deaths continued.

Sandy Good's husband, and former family associate Joel Pugh, age twenty-nine, was found at six o'clock in the evening of December 2 in Targarth Hotel, on Targarth Road in London. He was lying on his back, unclothed except for a sheet over his lower body, his throat slit twice, slash marks on both wrists, and two bloody razor blades nearby.There was no note, but there were "writings" in blood in reverse on the mirror, along with some "comicbook-type drawings." The hotel's manager recalled only the words "Jack and Jill."

Mr. Pugh had checked into the room on October 27, accompanied by a unknown young woman who had left after three weeks. His room was on the ground floor and could be entered and exited through a window. No fingerprints were taken, and the case was listed as a suicide and closed. Although Sandy Good was always hesitant to talk about him, she did say he was a zoologist and had gone to South America. She had apparently met Mr. Pugh while she was a student at San Francisco State, and he had joined several other of her acquaintances who were lured ınto the world of Charlie.

The L.A. sheriff's department homicide team later received a report from the State Department indicating that Bruce Davis had been in England at the time of Mr. Pugh's demise.

As retired Los Angeles sheriff's department detective-sergeant Paul Whiteley said, "That thing just stunk to high heaven." There was no Scotland Yard investigation, he recalls. "It was handled just by a routine patrolman and they kissed it off as a suicide."

When Sandy Good and Squeaky Fromme left the motel on the outskirts of Independence, in Inyo County, where they were staying and keeping track of things for M, they abandoned papers in the room. Among them was a letter from an unknown person that said, "I would not want what happened to Joel to happen to me."

On December 3, Susan Atkins rapped out a two-hour version of the murders to her attorney Richard Caballero, who later played the tape for the deputy district attorneys, Mr. Stovitz and Mr. Bugliosi, and a group of L.A.P.D. detectives. Now at least they had a correct list of those to indict.

On December 4, the district attorney's office made a written deal that if Atkins testified truthfully before the upcoming grand jury, they would not seek the death penalty, nor would they use her grand jury testimony against herself or any codefendant. It was not a very good deal for Atkins, but at least it avoided the peachlike fumes of cyanide. A better deal would have allowed at least for a lesser sentence or probation. A few days later she wrote to a friend: "My fate so to speak is in the hands of the beast."

On December 5, a grand jury of seven men and fourteen women began to take testimony. On December 8, they indicted Manson, Watson, Krenwinkel, Atkins, Van Houten and Kasabian on seven counts of murder and one count of conspiracy to commit murder.

Meanwhile, sheriff's deputies were digging at the Spahn Ranch, looking for Shorty Shea, a process that at times involved bulldozers and which would not bear results for another eight years. Early in December Mary Brunner had told them where to find Shea's '62 Merc, which had been left for months near the Yellow Submarine house on Gresham. Inside the car were blood-caked boots belonging to Mr. Shea and his foot locker smirched with Bruce Davis's palm prints, a miscalculation that would lead ultimately to Davis's conviction for murder.

On December 9, Sergeants Phil Sartuchi and Manuel Gutierrez of the L.A.P.D. brought Manson from Inyo County to L.A. Squeaky and Sandy closed down operations in Independence, leaving behind the letter mentioning Joel Pugh in their motel. They shifted their efforts to L.A., where they lived at various locations, but always visiting M for instructions. The Manson family may have been history's first nongovernmental murder team with its own P.R. apparatus.

Officers Guenther and Gleason of the L.A.S.O.'s robbery-homicide unit went to Inyo County, and Officer Pursell of the C.H.P. took them up Goler Wash to the Barker Ranch to look for clues to the Hinman or Shea murders. Stuck on a fence post by the Ballarat General Store, in the fashion of Western cemeteries, were a pair of Shorty Shea's cowboy boots. Deputy Guenther did not have the rugged foot apparel required for a trip up the bumpy wash, so he borrowed Mr. Shea's for the day.

In Los Angeles, Judge William Keene issued a gag order on December 10, which forbade anyone connected with the case—defense attorneys, the L.A.P.D., the sheriff's office, the deputy district attorneys—from discussing the evidence with anyone in the media. This gag order was, with one or two exceptions, weakly enforced. There was always a glut of data available, even to reporters from the underground press.

The gag order was too tardily imposed to prevent her attorneys from selling the publication rights to Susan Atkins's confession. A man named Lawrence Schiller had approached Richard Caballero and his law partner Paul Caruso to set up the deal. Using the Susan Atkins tapes, *L.A. Times* reporter Jerry Cohen wrote the text. Serial rights for the story were sold all over the world, with couriers picking up text hot from the printers. Forty thousand dollars were picked up for English rights alone. Also in this quickie packet was a mass-market paperback titled *The Killing of Sharon Tate*.

During the next few months around $100,000 in royalties was obtained from the confession, none of which reached the pockets of Susan Atkins or the other defendants.

Rosemary LaBianca's wallet was found in the bathroom of the Standard service station in Sylmar in early December, left there the previous August by Linda Kasabian, who'd been instructed by Manson to deposit it in a Black neighborhood. The neighborhood did have a percentage of Blacks, but it was not Watts.

On December 11, Manson was brought in his buckskins before Judge William Keene. Attorney Paul Fitzgerald of the L.A. public defender's office was appointed to represent him. Fitzgerald was in charge of the special trials section of the public defender's office and the previous year had briefly represented Sirhan Sirhan. "The rule in those days, and today, is that if an indigent can't afford counsel, the county of Los Angeles will provide it," says Fitzgerald. "So I was appointed initially to determine, number one, whether or not these people had the financial resources to hire private counsel. And number two, if there was a conflict of interest that existed between or among them that required the appointment of independent counsel."

The *Los Angeles Times* had somehow obtained the transcript of Atkins's confession and printed it on December 11. It was the first time the public had been exposed to the full story of the murders on Cielo Drive, and it triggered some detective work by the public, which proved very useful to the prosecution. For example, on December 15, a KABC-TV crew, following the getaway path related by Atkins in the *Times,* found the clothing thrown away by the murderers. They did this by driving down from Cielo Drive and clocking how long it took for them actually to change their clothes, after which they pulled off at a wide shoulder at 2901 Benedict Canyon Road and searched the hillside.

On December 16, a young man named Steven Weiss, later to win $1,000 of the $25,000 reward put up by Roman Polanski's film friends, had also read about the pistol toss in Atkins's account, and he called police to remind them that on September 1 he had found a .22 caliber revolver by a sprinkler on the hill in back of his house and had turned it over to police. At the top of his backyard hillside was Beverly Glen Drive, down the side of which the killers had tossed the Buntline Special. Mr. Weiss had taken care at the time to preserve any prints, though the officer receiving it had smudged the surface with his own hand. The pistol was retrieved from the police station where it had been stored.

On December 17, Manson appeared in court and asked to fire the public defender, Mr. Fitzgerald, and to become his own attorney. Even to this day, Manson smolders for not having been allowed to represent himself in his murder trials.

Manson wanted the control befitting his cosmic station

—to choose the girls' attorneys, for instance. To plot the strategy. To keep up the squeeze on weak links. As an *in propria persona,* or pro per defendant, he would have access to the phone and to the law library in jail. He was used to being in the command dune buggy. And the command dune buggy wanted to drive out of this case, its driver chortling with freedom.

Judge Keene arranged for famed attorney Joseph Ball, a former counsel to the Warren Commission, to meet with Manson. Ball reported back that Manson "has a very fine brain" and was able to defend himself. On Christmas Eve, Judge Keene allowed M to be his own attorney.

It began to look like Tex Watson was not going to be on hand for the trial. A judge in Texas granted a number of delays, and authorities were loath to send the former Texas high hurdles champ back to babylonic L.A. and the certainty of cyanide.

Up in Inyo County, Deputy D.A. Buck Gibbens and the D.A.'s investigator Jack Gardiner began to pick up information from Snake Lake. Slowly she began to talk, and her testimony would take its place in the quilt of remembrances the prosecution stitched together.

On January 2, Vincent Bugliosi ordered Spahn Ranch toll-call lists, which the telephone company would have destroyed after six months. Although some of the Spahn records had already been lost (for April and July 1969), the prosecution claimed that for May, June and August there was no phone contact between or among the Spahn Ranch, LaBianca, or Polanski phones. It's not clear whether Jay Sebring's phone records were checked.

Meanwhile, the family put together an album of Manson's tunes. Not long after the case had broken in December, Dennis Wilson was paid a visit by Squeaky Fromme, who told him that if he didn't give up the tapes Manson had made at Brian Wilson's house she was going to kill him. Wilson told her he had already turned them over to the D.A., a slight fib, since the Beach Boys' manager, when the case first broke, had placed them in a vault, where they may reside even to this day.

From another source the family obtained some tapes of Manson singing, which needed some "sweetening," as they say in the biz, so the extant family went into a studio and laid down harmonies and instrumental overdubs. The man in charge of preparing the album was none other than Phil Kaufman, the gentleman who had helped Manson with his first demo tape of Universal in late 1967, when the black bus first hit Topanga Canyon.

Even though he was known to a few hundred million people around the globe, there was not exactly a bidding war among record labels for the M croon. Mr. Kaufman wound up financing the album himself. It was an unspectacular release. While Manson's words held a certain fascination for some, he was not very adroit in the fashioning of melody lines, and he never learned how to record. The tapes could have used an echo track from the Hole in Death Valley. But if the family was holding faith in the formula that said having a record out equals lots of money, they were going to be very disappointed.

On January 17, Manson represented himself pro per before Judge George Dell to present some unusual motions. "Charles Manson, also known as Jesus Christ, Prisoner," assisted by some other pro per prisoners operating under the name of "The Family of Infinite Soul, Inc.," filed a habeas corpus, charging that the L.A. County sheriff, who was in charge of the running of the jail, was depriving him of spiritual, mental and physical liberty, in an unconstitutional manner not in harmony with the laws of man or God, and asking to be freed at once.

Dell denied the request. Manson's unusual pro per papers ultimately gave the court an excuse take that status away. Dell assigned the murder case to the courtroom of Judge William Keene, who would soon also conduct the second murder trial of Robert Beausoleil.

On February 11, Kitty Lutesinger gave birth to her child with Robert Beausoleil. Although she had supplied some of the good early evidence against the murderers after she had run away from Death Valley the previous fall, Lutesinger pingponged back and forth between her parents' ranch in the Valley and the lairs of the family. She loved it, she loathed it, and she recounted at the time how the Spahn family threatened to kill her genetic family at the Lutesinger Ranch in Northridge, not far from Spahn.

On the legal front, the prosecution's case was still fairly weak, especially against Manson. Their main witness, Susan Atkins, to whom they had promised not to seek the death penalty, could flake off at any point—especially after a threat or cajoling from Charlie. The family began a blizzardly attempt to reach her, a strategy that ultimately worked, since a lonely lawyer being beseeched by knife-edged murd molls as he tries to visit his client is likely to cave.

The overall M strategy was to use a blizzard of letters, telegrams and the like to get Beausoleil, Atkins, Kasabian, et al., to dump their attorneys, repudiate any incriminating statements they had made and engage in a united defense.

Perhaps sensing that the prosecution's case was weak against a united defense, Manson asked the court for an early trial, and Judge Keene set a trial date of March 30. On February 16, M asked for a change of venue on the grounds of adverse publicity, and Keene denied it.

After one of those family mail blizzards, Patricia Krenwinkel asked to be brought to California from Mobile. Once in L.A., she requested Paul Fitzgerald of the public defender's office as her attorney.

On February 24, Fitzgerald became Krenwinkel's attorney, agreeing to stick with her to the end.

In March, Fitzgerald resigned from the public defender's office and went into private practice. It had been decided that since the public defender was handling Beausoleil's second murder trial, it would have been a conflict of interest also to conduct Krenwinkel's defense.

One bit of good news appeared among the headlines of war and death: On March 1, DDT as a pesticide for grapes was banned in the state of California.

In late February, the prosecutors Stovitz and Bugliosi made a deal with Linda Kasabian's attorney, Ronald Goldman, that should she testify fully and truthfully at the trial, after her testimony had concluded, the prosecution would apply to drop all charges against her.

Meanwhile, the family kept up their attempts to sway Susan Atkins. Atkins demanded to confer with Manson, and there were, apparently, also personal visits from the family. Finally, on March 5, 1970, she was taken to L.A. County jail to see Manson, with her attorney present in the room.

"Sadie, are you afraid of the gas chamber?" Manson

asked. "No, I'm not afraid of it now," she recalls replying. "In that instant," she later wrote, "I was back under his control. I knew it and he knew it. But I was still afraid."

During the visit Manson undertook an amazing spew of gibberish, which made investigators think the family had some sort of secret language. It was, as Atkins recalled, "a sort of doubletalk, with real words dropped in every now and then. The others had practically no idea what he was talking about, but I grasped most of his meaning, I believe. The essence of his remarks, which were tantamount to directives, was that I should fire Caballero, drop my moves toward an insanity plea, and refuse further discussion with Bugliosi."

The gibberish-spew worked, and the next day she sent word to the judge that she wanted a new attorney. Soon she repudiated her grand jury testimony and blew her deal with the district attorney for no death penalty.

With Atkins back under the spell, the strategy became to prevent Linda Kasabian from making a deal with the prosecution. I overheard one conversation between an attorney for one of the women defendants and Linda Kasabian's attorney, in which it was suggested that if Kasabian refused to testify, "then everybody could walk." Several family members, including a barefoot Clem with a snake around his neck, visited Kasabian's attorneys to make their point. The snake in question had been caught at the Spahn Ranch. Somehow Clem had managed to bring it with him in a basket when visiting Manson. Manson, always a snake lover, waxed miffed and told him to free it at once.

On March 6, a press conference was called at the Spahn Ranch to announce the release of LIE, Manson's one and only album. Producer Phil Kaufman bit the buck and pressed 2,000 copies with his own money. The album jacket was based on the December 1969 *Life* magazine cover story, with its horrifying shiny-eyed shot of M on acid, glowering beneath the headline "The Love and Terror Cult." The *F* had been removed from *LIFE*, for the album.

The same day as the LIE press conference, Manson appeared in court to ply a number of novel motions, including one that asked the court to incarcerate the deputy district attorneys, Mr. Stovitz and Mr. Bugliosi, for a length of time under the same circumstances as were facing Manson. Manson also requested that he be free to travel to places he deemed proper in preparing his case.

Judge Keene recounted from the bench some of Manson's various motions as a pro per and then removed his pro per status. This outraged the handful of his supporters in the courtroom. Gypsy, Sandy Good and Mark Ross, at whose pad Zero had died from pistol fire the previous fall, were arrested for protesting the decision. Keene appointed Charles Holopeter as Manson's attorney.

Not being allowed to be his own attorney joined the list of primal resentments in Manson's psyche. His treatment as a child by his mother, being gang-raped by creeps in a reform school, his low-light-level education in juvenile homes and jails, his rejection as a pop singer, and later, when President Nixon would declare him guilty during the trial—all were issues that smoldered and burned.

On the other hand, a prisoner is not often denied the right to defend himself in California, and the trial might not have gone on as long as it did had Manson been allowed to direct his own defense. It would have revealed the true strength of our legal system, and it wouldn't have mattered anyway, for the ghosts of Cicero, Daniel Webster, Clarence Darrow and all the legal sages of eternity could not have won for M.

On March 7, Angel, child of Linda Kasabian, was born in jail, after which Linda's mother took the baby back east to New Hampshire. In their interviews with Ms. Kasabian, the prosecutors were impressed that they actually had a person who was showing signs of remorse. She could actually weep for the victims.

On March 11, Atkins requested Daye Shinn as her attorney, and Richard Caballero was relieved as her attorney of record. Mr. Shinn was the attorney for one of Manson's friends at McNeil Island, William Ross Phillips, who brought him to Manson's attention. Initially, Shinn had helped Manson set up a music company for the LIE album.

Manson soon fired Charles Holopeter after the latter made a motion to sever his case from the other defendants and to have a psychiatric examination of Mr. M.

Nobody shrinks the Big J, so Manson substituted Mr. Ron Hughes, who made a motion for M to revert to pro per, which was denied. Hughes, a witty, tall and slightly portly attorney with a beard and a compendium knowledge of the counterculture, would stay with the defense till he drowned later on in the year during a flash flood.

In March, the prosecution located Bernard Crowe and asked if he would allow an extractive operation to remove the bullet in his abdomen. If acids had not yet erased the ballistic markings on the slug, it might have been evidence to match the bullets used to kill Wojtek Frykowski and Jay Sebring. Mr. Crowe turned them down. Why undergo a major operation? And besides, he joked, it was a conversation piece.

On March 24, Judge Malcolm Lucas heard arguments for another motion, prepared by the attorneys for Manson and Krenwinkel, for a change of venue. There was a catalogue submitted of 183 newspaper articles from August 1969 through January 1970 that revealed the journalistic hippie-sexmaniac-knifer-doper pancultural image of the family. Also admitted was a feature article in *Los Angeles Magazine* for February 1970 titled "Could Your Daughter Kill," which was filled with facts of the case. Judge Lucas denied the motion.

Malcolm Lucas later became chief justice of the California supreme court. Fitzgerald recounts Lucas's decision, issued that day: "He agreed with us that we had received more publicity than any other case. The judge agreed that this case was horribly prejudicial. However, the judge said that the publicity was universally pervasive throughout the state of California and that it wouldn't make any difference if the case was transferred."

The defense disputed that contention, but not forcefully. "We would have loved to go to the San Francisco Bay area," Fitzgerald added, "because it would have been much more receptive to the sort of hippie kind of attitude."

On a theoretical level, the case was still fairly weak. But on a practical level, it was grim. "It was a slam-down case," Mr. Fitzgerald said later. "No matter what these people would have done, they were going to be convicted. The climate was such in Los Angeles that they lost this case when they lost the change of venue. And that irrevocably set the tone for the trial."

Manson and his followers at that point decided to defy everybody. Fitzgerald puts it this way: "Once the defendants saw that they were all joined together, that they weren't going to get any change of venue—it was at that point Manson said, 'I am going to be a court jester, I am going to provoke this society into showing its own hand.' "

In March, Sandy and Squeaky flew to Wisconsin to try to convince Mary Brunner not to testify at the second trial of Robert Beausoleil for the Hinman murder. Where they picked up the cash for such peregrinations was never clear. Brunner had made a deal with the sheriff's office that if she testified, charges against her in the same case would be dropped.

On April 13, Manson filed an affidavit to remove Judge Keene from trying the case. Keene was reportedly eager to have such a prestigious assignment, but on April 17, the motion was granted. Judge Charles Older, fifty-two, appointed by Governor Ronald Reagan in 1967, was given the case. Older was to remain the judge throughout the Tate-LaBianca trial.

Robert Beausoleil went on trial for the murder of Gary Hinman and on April 21 was convicted. Beausoleil, at whose first trial the prosecution had only sought life imprisonment, was caught up in the glare of the love and terror cult, and the second trial, orchestrated by deputy district attorney Burton Katz, sent him to Death Row.

In May, Susan Atkins formally repudiated her grand jury testimony, and deputy district attorneys Stovitz and Bugliosi interpreted that as a repudiation of her signed agreement and put her on the Death Row list with the others.

In early June of 1970, Manson substituted Irving Kanarek for Ron Hughes. Kanarek, a former rocket engineer with several classified inventions to his credit, had the reputation of being able to extend a legal proceeding indefinitely through motions, arguments and the application of legal minutiae. There was the chance the trial might now last a couple of years. The prosecution was very upset.

Stovitz and Bugliosi were so anxious about Mr. Kanarek that they suggested to Judge Older that M be allowed to represent himself, an argument the prosecution would lose. Mr. Kanarek remained Manson's attorney for the trial's duration.

In the famous Onion Field murder case, made into a book by Joseph Wambaugh, Mr. Kanarek had been the attorney for one of the defendants, and his courtroom tactics helped cause a district attorney to quit the case. The prosecutors in the Manson case were afraid of his courtroom strategy of multiple objections on all grounds and the creation of such a cloud of confusion that the facts of the case might become obscured.

During the spring and summer of 1970, the remnants of the family, never more than eight or ten in their public array, lived in a trailer in front of the Western town movie set at the Spahn Ranch. George Spahn had a soft spot for them, and perhaps they were good for the horse rental business. Squeaky Fromme began again her loose-limbed intimate care of the eighty-three-year-old Mr. Spahn.

In February, Bruce Davis was indicted for the Hinman murder, although I met him at the Spahn Ranch shortly thereafter. Later he would vanish to live in the Los Angeles sewers. Sheriff's officers were very eager to arrest Davis because the Hinman and Shorty Shea murder cases were in their jurisdiction. They visited the ranch regularly, looking for him. Homicide investigators felt he was a weak link and that they could break him. In conducting these visits, the detectives never bashed heads but were fairly respectful of civil liberties.

I asked Sandy Good during a visit why they stuck it out at the Spahn Ranch. She said, "We're all gonna die in the gas chamber. The only way we can survive is if we stay together."

On one evening in late April, Clem led the singing after a garbage run. Gypsy played the violin, and the others clapped, hummed and sang the songs together. They sat in a circle around candles in the movie-set jailhouse. By the doorway nearest the creekbed (for quick escape), sat several runaways around ten to twelve years of age. The singing was actually very accomplished and the harmonies pretty good, although the structure of the songs themselves was not that far advanced. And throughout it all it was obvious that there was a spirit of love among these remnants of the family.

In the front driveway out of which the forays of slaughter had occurred just a few months previous, there was now a floodlight. Family members joked that whenever they shot it out, sheriff's deputies would raid. They speculated that there was a officer stationed in the hills across the street to monitor them, a charge the sheriff's department has always denied.

A young filmmaker named Robert Hendrickson began working on a documentary movie about the family in the early part of 1970. They filmed at the Spahn Ranch and went a couple of times back to Death Valley and to family haunts in the Striped Butte Valley and Goler Wash. I went to Goler Wash with the film crew and some of the family. The very individualistic residents of the desert haunts of the M group were not very happy to have them roaming around again. On one trip, the police intercepted the group near the Barker Ranch and asked for identifications.

Once we stopped at the pouring pipe of a spring to get water. The nearest phone was twenty-five miles away. A motorcyclist was filling his canteens in the spring as we arrived. Clem leaped out of the van we were driving in and proceeded to advance upon the spring in a sort of gallop. The guy filling his water vessels looked up, abandoned his canteens, leaped on his bike, and split off down the valley, with the water pouring upon the green coverings of the canteens. You could see his dust for half an hour.

On May 8, Paul Fitzgerald filed a sixty-one-page petition to the court of appeal for a hearing to overturn Judge Malcolm Lucas's decision not to grant a change of venue on grounds of adverse publicity. The arguments were persuasive. Manson, Goebbels, and Attila the Hun were getting basically the same ink in Los Angeles. Except for Manson, Krenwinkel, Atkins and Van Houten were still innocent before the law. The petition, needless to say, was not granted.

On May 30, the famous Jerry Rubin, then a revolutionary, one of the Chicago 7 and a partisan of violent overthrow, visited Manson. A few days later, Squeaky and Sandy called him at his apartment for advice on how to get a book published.

Yes, a book. On June 3, I went to an apartment near Big Al's on Valley Street, one block up the hill off Alvarado Street, a decaying stucco building of kitchenette-type apartments. It was not far from the jail where Manson was being held. On hand were Gypsy, Sandy, Squeaky and Clem.

Squeaky was typing the text for a book of short stories, drawings and photos of the family. They let me read through it. Visions of moolah and acceptance were dancing through their heads. It was a project on which they would work for the next five years.

In the same room, Sandy Good was completing a cinch-neck camouflage canvas raincape. She gave a demonstration of how she would crouch when hiding in the desert with it pulled over her head. She then began talking about all of them fleeing to the wilderness. From what they said, it was obvious the plan included an escape attempt for Manson. I told them I didn't want to hear about it.

I had already heard too much about their escape plans. Clem had asked a member of the film crew, "What would you say would happen if one night seventy-five heads were cut off?" They talked of blowing up oil towers near Manson's jail, at 441 Bauchet Street, to create a diversion.

Manson, the story went, had maps of the Los Angeles sewer system, and they had determined you could escape through tunnels all the way from downtown L.A. out through the San Fernando Valley to the edge of the desert.

At the time, filmmaker Bob Hendrickson told me Manson had sent some of the girls down into the sewer tunnels to see what it would be like to live there. For his documentary, Mr. Hendrickson wanted to take a shot of them running into the storm sewers. Later, Bruce Davis and Nancy Pittman AKA Brenda McCann actually lived in the tunnels, until Manson ordered them to surrender late in the year. Hendrickson told me the family wanted him to use his uncle's airplane to parachute food to Davis, but he refused.

Clem and the girls had observed Manson being taken

from court back to the county jail late each afternoon. They said he sometimes briefly stood alone, without handcuffs, by the police vehicle. Then he would get into the back seat guarded by two sheriff's deputies. There was a manhole cover near where Manson stood, which would lead to freedom.

The escape attempt was to occur the first day of the trial. They would shoot the deputies, and then M would leap down into the manhole, meet his disciples, and head for the Hole.

They talked of chopping off heads as a distraction during the escape, and there was to be a limousine bearing a Manson lookalike that would deliberately get chased and caught in rush-hour traffic further to divert the attention of police.

I wasn't sure whether or not these casual remarks, which I had pieced together from several sources, were just meadow muffins, but nevertheless I decided to go to the authorities. I met with Carl George, a fine reporter who was covering the trial for CBS, and told him what I knew. Together we made arrangements to tip off the police.

Whenever my rock band, The Fugs, played Los Angeles in the 1960s we always stayed at the Tropicana Motel, located on Santa Monica Boulevard near La Cienega. There was a banana tree by the pool and beautiful hibiscus bushes with large red flowers, and there was always a party. During the summer of 1970 while I attended the Tate-LaBianca trial, I stayed with my wife, Miriam, and six-year-old daughter at the Tropicana. Others in the music business, including Kris Kristofferson, the Fifth Dimension and Janis Joplin, who was cutting her beautiful final album, were also staying there that summer. In the afternoons, the tables by the pool would fill up with visiting friends, including Phil Ochs, the writer John Carpenter, and the singer Rita Coolidge. The musicians were anxious—very anxious—that I not bring any of the Manson family to the Tropicana. A few vowed to move out if I did, and I promised I wouldn't.

One afternoon two hirsute young men, unknown to anyone, came to visit me at the Tropicana. Their names were Glenn Frey and J.D. Souther, and you could hear the shudders rippling on the tanned stomachs around the pool, where everyone was certain I had violated the ban against Mansonites.

Frey, one of the finer rock stars of the '70s, whose band The Eagles would sell 44 million records, in 1970 was nevertheless in the spaghetti-and-catsup portion of his career and not at all attired in the threads of a star. His partner, J.D. Souther, author of many hit songs during the ensuing decade, was similarly bedecked. Later I assured my pals around the pool that they had not been visited by banned knifers.

One Saturday I went with some of the family to the Spahn Ranch. During the trip I was reading the Book of Jeremiah. I was searching for a tone to take in setting to text the accumulated gnarls of data that were swirling in my travel cases and filing cabinets. I liked those throbbing, tightly constructed Old Testament lamentations as we drove through the San Fernando Valley past Universal Studios.

After arriving at the ranch, one of the first orders of business was a garbage run. I went with a carload of family members. We were heading down Devonshire Boulevard when I heard Cathy Gillies say, "I have a picture of lots of good stuff at the Market Basket." This was so, because when we pulled around back to the Market Basket loading dock, the throwaway bins were packed.

There were two salmon-hued lidded bins about four by five by six feet in size. The left bin teemed with a fluff of corn husks, oodles of loose celery stalks, halves of watermelons, tomatoes mottled green and pink, floppy pieces of lettuce and a glut of bell peppers whose sin had apparently been their slightly mutant, distended shapes. Several cardboard boxes of these free items were seized by the young women. It was extraordinary to see them bent over inside the sweet-sour confinements of the bins, where the only test for fruit-rot was the sniff test.

It was good the remmants of the M group were vegetarians, because within the second trash bin at the Market Basket were piles of the fatty tissue of dead bovinity draped upon some stained peach boxes. The odorous, pinkish-brown, wavy blobs of suet one saw when raising the lid were nearly enough to bring on the dry heaves.

Dinner was served in the Long Horn Saloon, where Manson had attempted in the spring of 1969 to open the

Helter Skelter rock club. We sat on the floor and passed dishes around. The meal consisted of raspberries in Russian dressing, fresh corn ears, dates stuffed with peanut butter, a cheese-celery-nuts-tomatoes-and-lettuce salad, orange juice, mushroom soup, and puffs of marijuana.

On hand were Clem Grogan, Sandy, Squeaky, Gypsy, Kevin, Bo, and Cathy, plus several runaways, girls about twelve or thirteen years old who were, as usual, stationed so that they could flee out the back and up or down the creek if the police should raid.

After dinner Clem played the guitar and the family sang a round of Charlie's songs. My album *Sander's Truckstop* had just been released by Reprise Records. One of the stunt men living at the Spahn Ranch, Larry Cravens, came up to me that afternoon when I arrived to say how much he had enjoyed listening to it. He was wearing cowboy chaps and a wide-brimmed cowpoker hat. His face had been bruised considerably, apparently from taking a fall from a balcony during a film stunt.

As we sat in the lanternlight of the Longhorn Saloon, they asked me to sing for them. I could not bring myself to do it—I just couldn't mix my music with theirs. And then there was the eeriness of the dialogue. Clem Grogan had a particularly scary way of speaking in praise of what he perceived an important aspect of the "Muslims": "They aren't afraid to splurk," he told me. The word "splurk" was accompanied by his hand hitting his chest in a pretend act of stabbing.

That night after singing, someone brought up the current issue of the *National Enquirer*, whose cover bore the headline "Yippie Leader Jerry Rubin Urges Students: 'KILL YOUR PARENTS.' " Rubin was quoted from a speech given in Cinncinati: "We've got to tear down institutions. You've got to stand up for yourselves. Kill your parents! Yeah, go home and kill them tonight!"

Clem Grogan, who was later convicted for the Shorty Shea murder, happened to be on probation at the time, and one of the conditions of probation was that he had to live with his parents. Clem sat there for a while in silence, smiling and stroking his chin. "Um," he said finally, pausing slightly, "kill your parents."

Everybody burst into laughter.

It seemed absurd to have to urge a teenage Manson

follower not to kill his parents. But I did. I mentioned how the words "kill your parents" were not meant to be taken seriously, but, uh—how could one put it—perhaps "symbolically."

After the singing, a couple of the women took me to a very enticing lace-draped cabin and invited me to stay. Squeaky had asked me not long before, "When can we have your babies?"

From the pay phone beneath the glaring searchlight by the corral, I called my wife at the Tropicana to lay out the plan to stay overnight at Spahn. Wives don't dig their husbands shacking with caressing murd molls, so I asked Clem to take me to L.A.

There were four of us in the car as it departed about midnight. On the freeway Clem smiled and said, "I haven't done this in a long time." Then I realized in a jolt it was almost a year since Clem had driven with Manson, Watson and the others to the LaBianca house. The young woman known as Bo asked, in a nervous voice, "Where are we going?" In a great lapse of taste I said, "Creepy-crawling." "I'm afraid!" she cried. "Relax, relax," I assured her. "We're not going creepy-crawling. He's dropping me off at my place."

I didn't want the Manson group to know where I was staying. There was another motel near the Tropicana at which I considered having Clem drop me off, but I recalled the rumor I'd heard that Jim Morrison was holed up there with my friend the poet Michael McClure (an unfounded rumor, it turned out), working on a movie script, so I couldn't be left there either. I settled on the nondescript Hollywood DMZ at the intersection of Santa Monica Boulevard and La Cienega, waited for Clem to streak away, and trotted to the Trop.

By early June it was obvious the trial was about to begin. On June 10 a hearing to bar Kanarek as Manson's lawyer resulted in victory for Kanarek, who commented, "One man's obstructionist may be another man's lawyer."

On June 12, the Friday before the Tate-LaBianca trial actually began, Robert Beausoleil had a hearing before Judge William Keene on a motion for retrial. Mary Brunner had flown back from Wisconsin to try to recant her testimony against Beausoleil. Ms. Brunner had made a deal to finger Beausoleil as the killer in exchange for charges in the same case being dropped against her. Brunner took the stand, but Judge Keene threatened her with indictment for murder and she balked. On June 15, prosecutor Burton Katz read from T. S. Eliot's *Wasteland* in arguing against commuting Beausoleil's sentence to life, and Judge Keene sentenced the young musician known as Cupid to the gas chamber.

The same day as Robert Beausoleil's motion for a retrial, Manson made one more demonstration to complain about not being allowed to be his own attorney. On Friday, June 12, with jury selection to commence the following Monday, he came into the chambers before Judge Older and sat down near his counsel, Irving Kanarek. The three women walked into the courtroom and were seated in their usual position to the right of the bailiff's desk, to the left of the swinging gate separating the judicial area from the spectators, against the railing. After a minute, Manson stood up slowly, attired in his dark blue jail-issue denim pants with white ass patches and his chambray work shirt. He bowed his head and his chin touched his chest. Rather slowly he outstretched his arms and then let his body sag slightly, as if his arms were bearing the weight of it. It was obvious to the assembled body of reporters that Charles Milles Manson was depicting his crucifixion. Or was it a reminder to those few who actually BELIEVED he was J? The three women defendants also stood and stretched out their arms in similar fashion, bowing their heads.

The judge, Mr. Older, waxed wroth: "I order you, Mr. Manson, to sit down. I order you to sit down, sir!" He motioned to the three bailiffs standing behind M to push him back down in the chair. One of them grabbed his outstretched arms and made to twist them behind his back. Manson, still rigid, lost his balance backward but did not fold into the chair as they wanted. They stood above him, dividing the chores: one twisting his arms in order to handcuff him to the chair, another choking his neck, the last trying to pick up his feet. There was an indescribable noise—mix of body thuds, chairs scraping, and scuffling shoes coming from the fray. Finally, one of the bailiffs grabbed Manson's long hair and forced his head back and proceeded to drag him out of the court into the tank, tugging him by the mane. The other two grabbed his torso and legs.

The girls voiced protest over the rough-up of M but did not join in physically. They remained in their seats, attempting to stand up and assume the cross stance whenever the female bailiffs guarding them took their hands from them. Older ordered them marched out of the courtroom to their tank.

Susan Atkins yelled, "Why don't you kill us now? We can't have a fair trial!"

Krenwinkel shouted something puzzling: "Don't you know who we are? Don't you know who we are?" Perhaps she was referring to a belief that they were messengers, seraphim or angels existing within the substance of the Second Coming.

After the tussle, Manson was placed in the so-called Sirhan Sirhan cell, located on a floor above the courtroom in the Hall of Justice, built for the man who shot Robert Kennedy, a cell in which M was kept under twenty-four-hour surveillance.

25

A Trial in the Hall of Justice (June 15, 1970–March 31, 1971)

During the final legal motions before jury selection, TV crews began having jousting matches with their cameras as they attempted safety blitzes and red-dogging techniques borrowed from football to get close to lawyers, prosecutors, family members and the defendants.

Reporters flew in from all over the world. Out of ninety-two seats in courtroom 104 on the eighth floor of the Hall of Justice, fifty-five were reserved for the media. Seventeen were for the general public, and the rest for security, the district attorney, the judge and four seats for the defense.

In the hallway outside the courtroom was a long, light bluegreen table on which resided ten telephones—direct hookups for the *L.A. Times*, the *Chicago Tribune*, and others. There was also a wire-service teletype machine and an operator on hand to type text. One of the few actual pleasures of this trial was to stand by the long table and watch some of the first-rank reporters phone in their stories in a style that was half spontaneous and half delivered from notes.

Some of the better reporters were Mary Neiswender of the *Long Beach Independent Press-Telegram*, Theo Wilson and Michael McGovern of the *Daily News*, Stan Atkinson of the NBC affiliate in L.A., Carl George of the CBS affiliate, Sy Gorman of the *Chicago Tribune*, and Linda Deutsch of the Associated Press, joining those from *La Stampa, Il Messaggereo, Deutsche Presse-Agentur, France Soir, Washington Post, New York Post, Toronto Star, London Daily Express, Axel Springer, US News and World Report, Newsweek, Time,* et alia multa. Seats were secured from court officer Harold Frediani, a burly gentleman with dark-rimmed glasses and modified flat-top crewcut, who was in the zenith of glory as reporters treated him extremely deferentially. He had a folder of beseechings from *Harpers,* the *Village Voice, Der Spiegel,* among others, that he could not satisfy. It was SRO.

Judge Charles Older sat at his wooden elevation in front of a columned wooden tablature with pale yellow pleated curtains; to his left was the flag of the state of California, to the right that of the United States. Fitted upon the tablature above and in back of the judge was a sloped wooden cornice somewhat like a roof. To the left was a door with a small screened window to the lockup, and to the right was another door.

News accounts sometimes inserted "no nonsense," "strict," and "stern," in association with Older's name. He'd been a fighter pilot in World War II and Korea. He'd flown with the Flying Tigers, then the U.S. Army Air Corps in the China-Burma-India Theater. Later he was an attorney in private practice for fifteen years, till appointed by Governor Reagan to the bench on December 19, 1967. He oversaw this freakathon with a ruddy-faced stoic calm. He rarely rose to anger, and he ran a tight flight.

The defense attorneys were led by **Paul Fitzgerald**, then thirty-three, a graduate of St. Thomas Military Acadamy in St. Paul and a philosophy major at the University of Minnesota. After law school, he moved to California in 1964. He'd been in charge of the special trials section of the office of the Los Angeles County public defender; at time of trial he was in private practice. He tried to understand and become sympathetic with the positive sides of his client and associates.

Ronald William Hughes, who'd replaced Ira Reiner after jury selection, was born in Los Angeles, a 1967 graduate of UCLA law school. Then thirty-five, he was witty and living in postbeatnik splendor in a house with holes in the roof through which the sun shone. This was his first case, but he took the job of protecting his client from the gas chamber very seriously.

Irving Kanarek, fifty-one, was born in Seattle, a chemical engineering graduate from the University of Washington who'd worked for eight years in chemical propulsion research. At the time of the trial Mr. Kanarek held two unclassified patents regarding the manufacture of rocket propellants, as well as two or three more he thought classified and wouldn't speak about. One was a computerized method for selecting the right combinations of oxygen, nitrogen, hydrogen and flourine molecules for the maximum pounds of thrust per cubic inch of flow of the propellant. Another, he said, involved a method of using HFI combined with nitric acid in a propellant system for stabilization at high temperatures. He studied law while an engineer and had been in private practice since 1957.

Daye Shinn, fifty-two, born in Sacramento, was a graduate of San Francisco State University and Southwestern Law School in 1961. This was his first murder case.

Ira Reiner, later district attorney for L.A., was for a while the attorney for Leslie Van Houten, until she fired him after jury selection. Then thirty-four, Reiner was a graduate of USC and had been with the legal department of ABC-TV and later with the criminal division of the city attorney's office.

Vincent Bugliosi led the prosecution. Then thirty-five, he was born in Hibbing, Minnesota, and had been a 1964 UCLA law school graduate. He had a way with words, was sharp at the bench, and relentless in his investigation.

Aaron Stovitz, forty-four, headed the district attorney's trials division, supervising seventy-five deputy district attorneys. He was a graduate of Brooklyn College, with a law degree in 1950 from Southwestern University in Los Angeles. He had a reputation for combining toughness with a gruff, zero-bullshit affability.

The district attorney was **Evelle Younger**. Associated with the prosecution was deputy district attorney **Miller Leavy**, who had prosecuted and attended the execution of Caryl Chessman. Mr. Leavy was known as a fanatical supporter of the death penalty.

The first order of business was jury selection.

The jury in L.A. was culled from the ranks of registered voters, who were paid only six dollars per day plus parking. Because of the financial hardship in serving on a lengthy trial, only those with money or who work for a company that pays employees during jury duty could serve. Thus the jurors tended to come from large companies such as Hughes Tool or the phone company, or they worked for state or local government.

The jury was to be sequestered at the Ambassador Hotel during the nine months of the trial. They could have conjugal visits on the weekends, but the husband or wife had to pay for the extra hotel expense.

Manson instructed Mr. Kanarek to accept the first twelve jurors selected, the theory being that he was already convicted and on Death Row. Kanarek attacked the method of jury selection, and among his points was that there were no nomads on the initial panel of possible jurors; and since Manson himself was a nomad, the jury did not represent a group of peers. The American judicial system, on the other hand, defines "peers" as a bunch of people who don't know anything about the defendants, and Kanarek lost.

There was a brief storm in the defense camp when Manson tried to get Atkins, Krenwinkel and Van Houten to fire their attorneys when they asked questions of potential jurors.

Even during jury selection, the district attorney continued to try to flick Irving Kanarek off the case. On July 2, Evelle Younger held a midmorning press conference at room 600 of the Hall of Justice, where he accused Kanarek of being both a professional obstructionist and incompetent. Younger was going to go into state supreme court to try to force Judge Older into requiring an evidentiary hearing on Mr. Kanarek's qualifications. It didn't work.

Short and bulldoggy, even burly, with eyes that looked full and sad, Kanarek was there to stay, lugging to the defense table his bulging briefcase and mountains of law books and papers and raising blizzards of points and objections.

A month-long jury-selection, even in a hot case like this, made reporters worry about their stories being buried in the used-car sections of their newspapers. Reporters could be heard talking to defense attorneys: "Pull us out of the back page! Do something!"

Defense lawyers, of course, noted the tendency of the women defendants to wear micro-minis and further noticed their casual unconcern whether or not spectators gazed at their legs and crotches. The jury box was right on the beaver-shot eyeball flight path, so Squeaky spent weeks preparing creative pants suits for the courtroom. She fashioned for Patricia Krenwinkel a green velveteen pants suit with matching brown hand-embroidered cape. Ms. Atkins's outfit was remarkable in that her left pants leg was very light green and the right was a dark green. When she wore it to court, however, there was a problem. The smooth green cloth around the breasts was clingingly diaphanous, so that the full shape of them and her nipples were very visible. She had to have a brassiere brought to the lockup.

On July 14, a jury was at last selected. The foreman was a middle-aged mortician who said he had learned of Manson while listening to the casual chatting of pall bearers before funeral services. There was a wine-faced seventy-four-year-old ex-employee of the Los Angeles County sheriff's office, a retired lady drama critic, a lady in her forties who wore various puffy, shiny wigs to match the day, a sixty-seven-year-old retired security guard for Goodyear Rubber, and a mod-dressed reactor operator for Ashland Chemical Co in his midtwenties, who read books in the courtroom during recesses. The last mentioned was the token peer, his Breck-ad sandy roan hair long enough for the establishment press to depict him as a "long hair." Two employees of the school system, three employees of the state of California and a lady in her forties who tended to wear white gloves each day rounded out the jury. Ahead of them was nine months of what could only be called a hideo-video.

On July 18, Leslie Van Houten dismissed her attorney, Mr. Ira Reiner, the future district attorney of Los Angeles. Three times during jury selection she had arisen to request that Judge Older fire him. Reiner kept asking questions of prospective jurors, violating the M-ban. Ms. Van Houten hired Ron Hughes, who had already briefly served as Manson's attorney.

Susan Atkins's attorney, Mr. Shinn, recalled the firing of Mr. Reiner as Manson's doing. "He told me to go find Ron Hughes." But Hughes was afraid. "I found Ron

Hughes. I said, 'Come on back, Ron.' He said, 'No, no, they threatened me.' I said, 'Don't worry about the threats. Charlie wants you to come back in on the case,' and so we brought him back in."

Mr. Shinn viewed the climate of threats from the family as woof-woof. "Their bark was worse than their bite," he recalled years later. "You know the girls threatened everybody, but they didn't mean it."

A few days before testimony began, the issue of films surfaced on two fronts—as possible secret film evidence and the possibility of weird films (and photographs) having been seized in a case involving some of the most popular stars in Hollywood.

On July 15, a defense attorney called me at the Tropicana Motel, after a reporter for a television network had asked if the defendants had removed any undeveloped 35-mm film from the house on Cielo Drive. The film purportedly showed a rising young starlet in very compromising positions. He wanted to know if the defendants could be asked if perhaps they took the film and threw it over the hill with the clothes bundle. The police claimed not to know anything about it. The starlet was worried it might destroy her film career.

As the jury was being selected, there was a cover story in *Rolling Stone* by Dave Felton and Dave Dalton on the upcoming trial. In a taped interview given to Dave Felton, deputy district attorney Aaron Stovitz had described the state of the evidence against Manson, Atkins, Van Houten and Krenwinkel. I acquired the taped interview and listened to it carefully. In a part not used in the article, Mr. Stovitz said the following: "On LaBianca, I'll rap with you on the level. Our case is not that strong. There are no fingerprints, no one saw them, there are no motion pictures."

In July of 1970 I met a young man who worked for a private investigator and who claimed that an L.A.P.D. officer who worked on the Manson case was a secret partner in the private-investigation firm. The young man had been told there was secret evidence, a film with the defendants in it, which might be introduced into evidence. The young man said that authorities were afraid Manson would talk, and if it came down to Manson escaping justice, then they would bring out this evidence.

Manson later made the following assertion in a letter to a Hollywood gossip sheet: "Dennis Wilson gave me a $5,000 videotape, TV thing for tapes that fit only to an elite bunch (porno ring) that was worldwide." Videotape equipment in the late 1960s was still expensive and fairly unavailable.

Two other reporters approached the defense attorneys about reverberations in Hollywood. Some in the movie industry were worried that the implications of this case might finish Hollywood. They said that lots of porn, including that of the homemade, handheld variety, had been found as part of the investigation. The reporters said that influential movie people had put a plea to the district attorney to lower the charges against Manson to manslaughter, evidently to keep him quiet.

There were some amazing names supposedly involved. Rumors of porn-films, of course, had surfaced right after the case had broken. It was one of the first things reporters talked about.

One private investigator (not Larry Larsen) connected with the case told me that his associates had acquired a porno ski epic starring a famous film comedian shot in Squaw Valley in the fall of 1968 with a "cast of thousands," though it was "hard to tell who was in it." One reporter for an L.A. television station told about erotic footage of a well-known actress and one of Howard Hughes's attorneys.

In the authorized biography *Doris Day: Her Own Story*, by A. E. Hotchner, her son Terry Melcher was asked about the murders. Melcher said, "For the past two months that's all anyone talked about. I hadn't been in the house since I moved out, but I had presumed that the murders had something to do with the weird film Polanski had made, and the equally weird people who were hanging around that house. I knew they had been making a lot of homemade sadomasochistic-porno movies there with quite a few recognizable Hollywood faces in them. The reason I knew was that I had gone out with a girl named Michelle Phillips, one of the Mamas and the Papas, whose exhusband, John Phillips, was the leader of the group. Michelle told me she and John had had dinner one night, to discuss maybe getting back together, and afterward he had taken her up to visit the Polanskis in my old house.

Michelle said that when they arrived there, everyone in the house was busy filming an orgy and that Sharon Tate was part of it. That was just one of the stories I had heard about what went on in my former house."

The defense team was given as part of its discovery information a set of interviews with a young woman named Charlene Cafritz, who claimed to have made motion pictures of Manson and the family.

The police had learned about Cafritz from Gregg Jacobson. Cafritz, a friend of both Sharon Tate and Manson, had taken numerous motion pictures and photos of the family in Reno and at Dennis Wilson's house, as described in Chapter 23. There had been a misspelling in her name and police didn't locate her until April 6, 1970. They located her in St. Elizabeth's hospital in D.C.

While Charlene was in St. Elizabeth's her mother told authorities that motion pictures were in the basement of her home. Charlene Cafritz called the Spahn Ranch on August 11 from St. Elizabeth's. She said she had tapes and photos that the police didn't know about. A lawyer friend of Bruce Davis was going to send the tapes to Gypsy. She also wanted to donate some money.

The only footage listed on the official L.A.P.D. evidence reports was the video Lieutenant Deemer brought back from Virginia, which, according to prosecutor Bugliosi, showed nothing more than Abigail Folger, Wojtek Frykowski and two friends, eating dinner in front of a videocamera; one other was apparently the videotape of Roman Polanski and Sharon Tate making love, which Sergeant Calkins of the L.A.P.D. robbery-homicide unit told Paul Fitzgerald had been returned to Mr. Polanski on August 10, right after the murders.

No motion pictures ever surfaced, but talk of them added to the spice and fervor of the early portions of the trial.

Friday, July 24, was "X-day." As I walked into court just before ten o'clock, I saw Paul Fitzgerald talking through the small screened window on the door to the lockup tank to Mr. Manson or to Mr. Manson's attorney, Mr. Kanarek. We had heard rumors during the weekend that Manson would mark his forehead with an X by incising it with a razorblade, a symbol that he had X-ed himself out of this civilization. The X, to Manson, would also serve to ward off God's wrath when the march of the locusts, as spelled out in Revelation 9, devours the world. When Manson was brought into the room, there it was, located above and slightly to the left of the nose axis.

My investigative associate, ace private eye Larry Larson, later talked with an intelligence officer for the Los Angeles sheriff's office, who supplied the following analysis for the Manson forehead X. Manson was being held at the Hall of Justice. He'd been put into a cell with two blacks, one of them a Black Muslim. Manson was scared. One of them apparently suggested that M slash an X, and therefore, when the holocaust came and Muslims took over the world, the Muslims would spare the marked people. Manson hastened to comply.

Wise in ink-dinking, Manson had his followers put out an actual press release on the forehead cross. It began: "I am not allowed to be a man in your society. I am considered inadequate and incompetent to speak or defend myself in your court. . . . I have x-ed myself from your world."

Van Houten, Atkins and Krenwinkel also burned X's in their foreheads with hot bobby pins, so that by Monday, when the testimony began, they too were marked. X-mania ultimately spread among other members of the family—to Sandy Good, Squeaky, Gypsy, Ouish, Bruce Davis, Kitty Lutesinger, Cathy Gillies, Sue Bartell, and the rest.

It was obvious that the prosecution's main witness was going to be Linda Kasabian. Defense attorneys had heard that the prosecutors wanted Kasabian to remain in jail until all appeals were over. No dice, said her attorneys, Gary Fleischman and Ronald Goldman. On July 17, the attorneys sent a letter to codify the substance of her deal with them from the previous March. That is, if she testified truthfully, the prosecutors would go into court and urge all charges against her be dropped, and she'd walk immediately.

Before the trial began, I acquired copies of Linda Kasabian's handwritten account of her association with the family. She had a clear mind and, more important, a very exact and exhaustive memory.

On July 27, the day of Kasabian's opening testimony, I went with Ron Hughes and Gypsy during the lunch hour out to the Topanga Restaurant in Topanga Canyon, looking for people who might have seen Ms. Kasabian take LSD. The only hope for the defense was either to cause her to have some sort of breakdown on the stand or to show that her mind had been shredded from too much dope.

I mentioned to Gypsy how Manson's X had already seemed to heal. Gypsy agreed. She exclaimed while snapping her fingers, "Spskew! Charlie can heal himself just like that!" A few days before, three people had been horribly hacked on the beach near Santa Barbara, one surviving and two dying on the spot. A sergeant in the Santa Barbara sheriff's department recalled that one of the victims, who was in very bad shape, mumbled about chanting assailants wearing robes. Gypsy spoke excitedly about the beach blood, calling it "Maxwell's Silver Hammer."

I grew to like Ron Hughes. A few days later we went to a sale of movie props at MGM, where I purchased a white naval officer's jacket reputedly worn in a flick by Gregory Peck. Hughes bought a sports jacket once used by Chill Wills and an elegantly tailored brown jacket formerly belonging to Spencer Tracy. These he wore to court. He passed up the togas used in *Ben Hur*, a surprise, since at one point he had considered appearing before Judge Older in Roman garb like a modern-day Cicero delivering the Verrine orations.

And so the Tate-LaBianca murder trial at last began. The principle of "murder will out" was much in evidence throughout its nine-month course. Or rather it was the principle of "murder will mozaic out." For, with the exception of the testimony of Linda Kasabian, much of the oral evidence was like a mozaic of what could be called "confessionlets," little pieces of confession blurted out by the killers and remembered by a procession of witnesses, which, when coupled with physical evidence—the gun, a couple of fingerprints, the rope and the knives—comprised a quilt of guilt.

Vincent Bugliosi outlined the case. He noted that the prosecution did not have to supply a motive to get a first-degree murder conviction, but he had one. The motive, as he saw it, was the triggering off of a strange race-war armageddon inspired by a British rock tune known as "Helter Skelter."

In order to nail Manson, the prosecution needed a lot

of *folie à famille* evidence that pointed to his domination of the killers. Thus there was evidence, too much evidence, of a sexual and drug-taking nature, which helped give to the trial its unfortunate Death of the 'Sixties ambience.

The defense reserved its opening arguments until after the prosecution had presented its witnesses, which, it turned out, would take till November.

The first testimony on Friday, July 24, was given by Colonel Paul Tate, Sharon's father, who was wearing a double-breasted dark blue blazer with gold buttons, dark blue trousers, and a neatly trimmed moustache and beard. Colonel Tate testified as to the last time he had seen his daughter and identified a photograph of her. He was followed by Steven Parent's father, who wept when shown a photo of his son. Then there was Winifred Chapman, the housekeeper at Cielo Drive; then William Garretson, who was stoned and listening to records in the guest cottage during the murders; and then Frank Guerrero, who was painting the baby's room the afternoon of the murders; then Tom Vargas, the gardener; then Dennis Hurst, who had delivered a bicycle at around eight o'clock on the final night and was met by Jay Sebring at the front door. Testimony concluded at the end of that first day, with everybody waiting with a kind of shuddering anticipation for the next witness.

Then, on the following Monday, July 27, Linda Kasabian's devastating testimony began. There were about forty people waiting outside for the public seats. The line had formed at 5:30 A.M.

Her initial appearance levelled the courtroom with its keening incantations of murder and desolation. She began with details of her life with the Manson group from early July till around midnight on August 8. At first the prosecution elicited as much information as possible on drugs and fucking, so that the early editions of the newspapers had headlines such as "Linda Tells Manson 'Cave Love' "; then the story shifted to blood, and the headlines screamed "Night of Terror" in the L.A. *Times* and "Linda Tells Horror at Tate's" in the *Examiner*.

Kasabian's first full day of testimony, delivered in a way that was eternally believable, ended with Wojtek Frykowski just recently dead upon the lawn in front of the house on Cielo Drive, bloody face, screams silent, leg muscles hack-shredded, head clubbed by gun butt, shot, liver temperature dropping, heart erratic, alpha rhythms lapsing into silence, pulse dead, brain dead, gone.

The prosecutor had large color blow-ups of the victims, and when Kasabian was shown one of them she cried, "I don't have to look at the pictures. It's in my head!" and began sobbing into a squared handkerchief.

The jury was frozen. Fifty reporters scribbled chaotically while straining to see and hear. Reporters began to dart out and stand next to their phones, filing their stories from the chaos. "It was just horrible. Even my emotions can't tell you how horrible it was!" Linda Kasabian groaned. Uncontrollable sobs. A blonde bailiff brought her a glass of water. Kasabian was wearing her hair in pigtails with a perfect center part, a red and blue dress—red bottom, blue top with red wavy bunting and long sleeves. At all times she was attended closely by her attorneys, Mr. Goldman and Mr. Fleischman.

Colonel Tate watched the testimony. A former officer in Army Intelligence who was reportedly involved in the protection of nuclear missiles and who therefore must have had a fairly exalted security clearance, he had nevertheless been searched and patted down prior to entering the courtroom. He sat quietly, with arms folded, as Kasabian described loud human screams, people pleading for their lives, and Tex riding one of the victim's backs into the yard. There was a woman crying in the back of the courtroom, consoled by a lady deputy.

Kasabian had to walk the eye-gauntlet past Sadie, Katie and Leslie and Charlie to the chart depicting the layout of the house and grounds. There was more and more and more, until one reporter, as the hearing ended, exclaimed, "Oh, God!" checking his notes, white faced. Knots of reporters stood comparing pads for accuracy, for the correct stabbing chronology. They filed out, looking in one another's eyes in stunned shared knowledge of bloodbath.

It was difficult to breathe. Death and violation floated among us. So filled was the room with the vibrations of disturbed psyches, one almost became unconscious with the weight of it, so touchable were the pitiful wails of grief floating up from the Hollywood smog.

Although the trial would heave onward for another eight months, it was obvious that it was over. All pretense that this was somehow connected with flower power was forever gone. Kasabian's testimony made it obvious that the trial was going to go against the defendants, and though she testified for over eighteen days, no one could break her.

Not long thereafter I had one further overwhelming experience, one that made me vow to finish this book whatever it took. I was out for lunch with someone close to the case, and we were chatting over our finished plates. He brought his hand forward, its clean white fingers holding a photo, which he tossed across the table so that it landed in front of me—a small snapshot of Sharon Tate lying dead upon the carpet with the noose around her neck. It was the most horrifying thing I had witnessed in my life since the moment, at age seventeen, when I first saw my mother in her coffin.

I couldn't look at it. I covered it with a couple of 3×5 index cards and moved them slightly, revealing only segments of the photo and never its entirety—her left hand clutching her halter as if to try one last time to breathe, her gravid stomach shifted over to touch the floor, her long and elegant legs crooked up beneath her, an American flag draped upside down on the sofa in back of her, her long blonde hair somehow neat and orderly, her right arm thrust up to cover her eyes, and blood, a life's worth, covering the floor, with various matchbooks tossed about amidst small candle-pots near the body. To this day I am horrified when I recall that image. It was then I realized I had to reveal the Manson family as it really was and to describe the murders in a way that would tell for all time what these people were about.

The prosecutors prevented M family members from being in the actual courtroom by subpoenaing all of them as prosecution witnesses, thus excluding them. That did not stop them from hanging out in the hall. Thus we were treated to the bad taste on July 31 of Sandy Good following Colonel Paul Tate down the corridor, saying, "I don't know how to tell you this. We're sorry, but we're not guilty." Mr. Tate escaped by entering a telephone booth and said nothing.

Nor could the authorities apparently stop them from

carrying knives into the courthouse. On the afternoon of August 13, I encountered one of the prime murd molls sitting in the corridor outside Older's court, with a bone-handled sheathed hunting knife in her lap. Squeaky was there with her. She said, "I hear Nadell got killed in Detroit." This referred to Shelley Nadell, to whom Atkins had originally confessed.

"No," I replied. "She got stabbed in Minneapolis a long time ago. Do you think her life's in danger?" Squeaky replied simply, "Yeah."

On another occasion, I observed a group of knife-bearing family members snake-dancing through the Hall of Justice corridors as if it were the homecoming game at the School of Murder. They were followed closely by camera crews. One reporter yelled out to Mary Brunner, "Turn around—let's see your Bowie knife!"

Prosecutor Vince Bugliosi was spotted going up in disbelief to Sergeant Manuel Gutierrez of the L.A.P.D. homicide division and asking, "Is it legal? Is it legal?" Apparently it was, for there are liberal weapons regulations in the state of California.

Twenty years of searching have not yielded the single word to describe the creepy-eery-surreal-ghastly-moany-groany ambience of this trial. People involved in the case would periodically get together and have a fear klatch—that is, trade fear stories. "Everybody in this case thinks they're going to get killed," one of the attorneys said at the time. Poor Terry Melcher required psychotherapy for a number of months because of not "knowing the new facts early." He had mistakenly thought, because of something the police had told him early in the case, that the murderers had been looking for *him* when they went to Cielo Drive. Only at the end of the trial did he find out he wasn't a target and that, in fact, Manson harbored no grudge against him.

Some well-known actors attended the early portions of the trial—Peter Falk, for instance, and Sal Mineo, among others. Manson sometimes got into staring contests with spectators. He must have been able to paralyze his eyelids, for there was no way to beat him. And then there was the way he sometimes ran sharp pencils across his throat as he stared. It was eery, or downright oo-ee-ooey.

Against this background of fear and freakiness, a legendary trio of Los Angeles County sheriff's homicide detectives was quietly and methodically monitoring and reeling in the remnants of the Manson family. These officers, of course, were Sergeant Paul Whiteley, Deputy Charles Guenther and Deputy Bill Gleason. They were everybody's dream team of detectives.

Whiteley had entered the sheriff's office in 1957 after leaving the Air Force. "I worked fugitive detail and station detectives, and then I was brought up to homicide in 1966" is his one-sentence history of his career in the Homicide division. The sheriff's department is different from the L.A.P.D. Robbery and homicide, are two separate entities in the sheriff's department, whereas in the L.A.P.D. robbery-homicide is one unit.

Sergeant Whiteley's partner was Deputy Charles Guenther, and the two received praise all during their service together and for decades afterwards. Defense attorney Paul Fitzgerald once described them with affectionate humor: "One [Whiteley] was a very suave, handsome, charming, smiling, almost Don Juan type. The other [Guenther] was this exuberant, effervescent, hard-charging adolescent—totally fixated at adolescence. Broad-faced and broad-shouldered and pudgy. They were a famous team. And they fit together perfectly. They could play good guy, bad guy. But Guenther had a sort of incorrigible, hard-charging unconventional way of investigating cases. He was outrageous and ridiculous and Paul Whiteley was the model of decorum. And they were a marvelous team. Guenther in his own way was a genius. As unconventional and as boyish, in terms of the results he achieved—confessions he was able to obtain from people; the way he put together certain items, the physical evidence. His ability, his theoretical mind, he really had a keen analysis of the murderer. He was a fantastic homicide investigator. And he had a sort of keen sense of decency too that was very refreshing and everybody sort of picked up on it."

The third member of the team, Deputy (later Sergeant) Bill Gleason, was also known as a formidable and relentless investigator. He was the archivist: "Whiteley and Guenther were working Hinman mainly, and I was working Shea. And Whiteley, being a sergeant, was the team leader, so to speak, of the three of us. But my main assignment was to kind of keep track of these people and identify the new people that were coming around and I maintained a card file on all the players."

William Gleason had been born in the San Fernando Valley and went into the sheriff's office in 1959. He first worked in a unit that maintained information on motorcycle gangs, and then he was transferred into the detective division and assigned to the motorcycle-gang unit in the Hall of Justice. "And it was because of Manson's involvement with the Straight Satans that I became involved. Because the Straight Satans were going to the Spahn Ranch and partying. And one of their members, Danny DeCarlo, had a machine gun that they kept test firing up in the hills." A fully automatic machine gun was illegal.

Officer Gleason would stay with the Shea case for years, right up to the day in late 1977, eight years after the murder, that he wielded the shovel that would finally locate the body of Mr. Shea near the Spahn Ranch.

During the trial the detectives conducted a massive search for Bruce Davis, who lived for a time down in the Canoga Park storm sewers with Brenda McCann. Davis was the second in command in Manson's power structure, so to speak, and it was felt that if he could be made to talk, then a number of other crimes—not only the Shea and Hinman cases, but perhaps also Joel Pugh, Jane Doe 59, and the Gaul-Sharp slayings—might be solved.

There were some irritated feelings between the sheriff's office on the one hand and the D.A.'s office and the L.A.P.D. on the other. It had been the relentless legwork of the sheriff's homicide unit that had broken the case, but the homicide unit seemed not to share in the triumph. The prosecutors resisted having the Hinman-Shea case attached to the Tate-LaBianca case. As one homicide officer told me later, "There was a big delay, you know, in the filings on the Hinman and Shorty Shea case, and that was because Bugliosi didn't want the case filed at the same time. He wanted [Tate-LaBianca] to be the big case. He was worried it was going to be all put together." At issue was the possible draining away of media attention from the Tate-LaBianca spectacle.

An assortment of other law-enforcement agencies looked

into the Manson group during the early 1970s. These included the intelligence division of the Los Angeles County sheriff's department, which had at least three officers collecting information on the family. An agent for the California State attorney general's office looked into the November 1969 murders of Doreen Gaul and James Sharp, who had been living at a scientology commune in L.A. An officer for the Immigration and Naturalization Service did a study of possible connections between the Manson group and an English satanic society. The California Department of State, according to an officer from the sheriff's homicide unit, developed a list of thirty-five murders from around California they were examining for possible connection to the M group. Even the Internal Revenue Service (the Intelligence Division) looked into Mansonland.

Inyo County district attorney Frank Fowles helped set up an informal network of district attorneys from other counties, which, in loose conjunction with other law-enforcement agencies, looked into various homicides that might possibly be related to the Manson group. There was an investigation of possible connections among and between a trio of groups—the Manson squad, an English satanist society, and an international religious organization. In addition, they also looked into the question of a connection between Manson and the Zodiac killer. "Zodiac" was a truly creepy serial killer who operated in northern and southern California during the 1960s, taunting the police with messages containing his telltale sign, a circle with cross hairs imposed upon it. "Zodiac" is thought to have perhaps later died in Vietnam.

There were a number of big-time private investigators who worked on the Manson case, some of whom had been hired by the district attorney's office. During the trial, there was a fiscal investigation in several cities, including Kansas City, Kansas, and a coastal city in Texas, to check on assets in banks for various members of the family, including Manson, Atkins and W. R. Vance. This was apparently part of an investigation into the possibility that the Tate-LaBianca murders were conducted under contract.

Meanwhile, the trial continued.

I had just had lunch with actor Sal Mineo in the cafeteria in the Hall of Justice on August 3. Paul Fitzgerald had finished his cross-examination of Linda Kasabian, and then it was to be Irving Kanarek's turn, when word came in over the teletype in the hall about something rather dumb uttered by then-president Richard Nixon.

In early August, Nixon had come out to San Clemente for the weekend. Being a media freak himself, the story went that Nixon was miffed that the Manson case was grabbing all the headlines and that newspapers were not bestowing enough ink on his historic visit to his Casa Pacifica pad.

On Monday, August 3, Nixon flew to a conference of law-enforcement officials in Denver and fingered M. "I noted, for example, the coverage of the Charles Manson case when I was in Los Angeles, front page every day in the papers. Here is a man who was guilty, directly or indirectly, of eight murders without reason. Here is a man, yet, who, as far as the coverage was concerned, appeared to be rather a glamorous figure, a glamorous figure to the young people whom he had brought into his operations, and, also, another thing that was noted was the fact that two lawyers in the case—two lawyers who were, as anyone who could read any of the stories could tell—who were guilty of the most outrageous, comtemptuous action in the courtroom—and who were ordered to jail overnight by the judge, seem to be more the oppressed, and the judge seemed to be the villain."

It should be noted that Ron Hughes had been put in jail overnight for using the word "shit" in front of Judge Older. And Irving Kanarek the same day had been imprisoned overnight for repeatedly interrupting Linda Kasabian's testimony with objections.

The Chicago Seven trial had gone on in Chicago, and contempt for judicial proceedings was part of the era.

Manson was upset. One of the the attorneys quoted him as saying, "Here's a man, Mr. Nixon, who has murdered hundreds of thousands of Vietnamese who has the temerity to accuse me of murdering eight people." In later years, Manson came to believe that it was Nixon who had in great part caused the jury to find him guilty. His letters would indicate a sore hunger for vengeance. "I want to go to the desert but I would like to go take

Nixon's head, give him this shit of his I been carrying and show him some Manson justice," railed one of his letters.

The bus taking the jurors to their sequestering at the Ambassador Hotel after court on the afternoon of the Nixon statement had its windows soaped to prevent jurors from viewing newsstands.

The next day, while prosecutors and attorneys were in conference at the bench, Manson flashed the headline "Manson Guilty, Nixon Declares" for about five seconds to the jury. Aaron Stovitz happened to be looking in the direction of the spectator section and he alerted the bailiff, who grabbed the newspaper and turned it over to Stovitz, who turned it over to Bugliosi, who took it to Judge Older. It turned out that Mr. Shinn had found the newspaper on a nearby filing cabinet; he had been reading the golf section, he testified, then set the paper aside, whereupon M had beamed it at the jury.

Shinn was held in contempt of court and sentenced to three nights in county jail. His wife, who did not speak English, was reportedly afraid he was cheating and, who knows, perhaps spending the nights in the orgy cabin at the Spahn Ranch.

On August 6, Spahn Ranch stunt man Randy Starr died. Starr was the gentleman Terry Melcher had watched Manson beat up that spring night of 1969. I recalled with a shudder how one afternoon at the Ranch I had seen him yelling louding at Squeaky, Sandy, Gypsy and Clem: "This is a horse ranch, not a place for hippies!" He had been scheduled to identify the Tate-Sebring rope as the same as Manson's, and he would have sworn he'd given M the .22 caliber Buntline Special. An autopsy found that he had died of an infection, but his death was scarey news.

In August of 1970, Snake Lake was released from Patton State Hospital and given to the custody of Inyo County district attorney's investigator Jack Gardiner, who became her guardian. She went to school in Inyo County and later to college, and she finally became a bank executive.

In late July, a young man named Rabbit called the *Los Angeles Free Press* from Berkeley and said that he was organizing a benefit for the family for early August. He was trying to interest big-name rock groups to participate, but he was not having much success. He said that the family was allowing him to show some films of them at the benefit, which included footage shot previous to the arrests. Gypsy and Squeaky, he said, had given him a short segment of a film with Manson in it, a frame of which he was supposed to use for a poster. He also said he was going to make family T-shirts to sell.

Rabbit had first met the family in San Francisco in 1968 and had a loose association since then. That summer he lived with the M group at the Spahn Ranch. Rabbit was one of a group of young humans who were both attracted and repelled by the family. They came, they went, they came, they went, like a cloud of gnats that drifts back and forth across a creek.

Later I interviewed Rabbit in Berkeley, and he told me that just before the trial began they had asked him to come down from Berkeley to the Ranch, where they tried to convince him to commit some murders in order to free M. "I came down for three days. They called me down, four o'clock in the morning, up in Berkeley. I got up and split, hitched and I got there." He hitched holding a sign that read "SPAHN RANCH." "I got there," he said, 'and, uh, Gypsy, said like, uh, the only way to save Charlie was to go back to San Francisco and duplicate it. You know, exactly as it was, and then if I get busted to say I did the other ones too and that way it would save Charlie. And her and Clem and Squeaky spent three hours trying to tell me that it's the only thing that would help Charlie, you got to do it, and I kept saying okay.

"They had me hid; they didn't want anybody else to know I was there. . . . Only Gypsy, Squeaky and Clem knew I was there. That's when they convinced me to go out, to come back to San Francisco."

Thankfully, Mr. Rabbit did not follow through after his assurances. "It'd be interesting to go down to L.A. again," he said. "I don't know how much they want to see me, since I didn't do what they wanted me to do." Although he was hesitant to murder for M, he said he was thinking of breaking into a house in Berkeley and spray-painting letters on the walls.

"There's one thing I plan on doing—Gypsy wanted me to do. But, well, I've been scouting this one house for the last six months. It's in the Berkeley Hills. I have two people who want to go with me. . . . I'll steal stuff, and we're going to have black and red spray paint, and we're going to write 'Helter Skelter' and we're going to leave some of the stuff in the house when we steal it. We won't have to do anything else."

I pointed out he was such a media freak that he most certainly would be nabbed.

Rabbit claimed to have seen a number of hemic films shown by several members of the family and to have stolen a short film showing members of the family sacrificing a dog. We strove mightily to acquire this film but failed. An editor for a national magazine later viewed the film and commented as follows: "There's very little question in my mind but that the film's authentic. Nobody trying to manufacture a rip-off would produce a loop of such incredibly poor quality. I've been assured that if I know the Manson group's faces well, I'd be able to identify them in the film; but, thanks to my ignorance, I can only tell you that, while the camera does some gratuitously pyrotechnic pan-in/pan-outs, a group of people, sitting around a fire, *apparently* slaughter a dog (or a cat, or a goat—or maybe just a teddy bear), then *apparently* anoint themselves with blood, then *apparently* take some of their clothes off, then do a weird—but not *too* weird—little dance.

It was during the interview in Berkeley that Rabbit made the startling claims outlined in Chapter 12 of this book, about having been shown a short film of hooded people on a beach next to a decapitated human. (In 1971, just after the trial had concluded, this strange young man ran for mayor of Berkeley on the Manson ticket, announcing, "I am running to vindicate Charlie Manson." He picked up 122 votes—the winner had 22,000.)

The benefit that Rabbit was trying to organize in Berkeley for early August of 1970 fell through. The defense could have used the money. Daye Shinn had obtained $22,000 from the sale of the rights for Susan Atkins's book, *The Killing of Sharon Tate*, but the rest of the lawyers—Fitzgerald, Hughes and Kanarek—were hurting for cash. Television reporter Carl George told me that he had learned of an assets check that had been run on Kanarek because of the ill-founded rumor that a secret Hollywood source, perhaps to keep Manson silent, was paying for his defense. George told me there was no money coming into Mr. Kanarek's coffers.

On August 12, Mary Brunner and Squeaky went to Phil Kaufman's house to get some money. A small East Coast jazz label, ESP, had purchased distribution rights to the LIE album. The family wanted some of the front money, and Kaufman called the cops on them. ESP had the reputation of paying royalties less than swiftly, if at all, so perhaps Manson, with his ability to apply rather relentless pressure, may have accomplished what a number of acts could not do—i.e., actually get paid some royalties.

On August 13, all charges were dropped against Linda Kasabian, and she was set free. For a while thereafter she was a minor media celebrity. The writer Joan Didion was at that time proposing to write a book about her. A few weeks after Kasabian had returned to the East Coast, Didion wanted to visit her and work on the book, but Kasabian couldn't oblige because she was going to be spending the weekend at Yale, watching the football game.

On or around August 31, Charlie told Sadie to act sick—a strategy to get Atkins severed from the case; thus it might be easier for the others to walk. It was difficult for the prosecution to believe that Sadie would want to sever, because the case against her would then be so formidable. Four court days were lost while Atkins complained of stomach pains. Finally, she was brought to court to testify about her ailment, and although she was quite dramatic in her lamentations, Judge Older became convinced she was faking, and ordered the trial resumed. After the hearing, Aaron Stovitz told reporters, "It was the best act since Sarah Bernhardt."

For that remark, District Attorney Evelle Younger removed him from the case. Stovitz had been instructed after the *Rolling Stone* interview to refrain from talking with the press. Two young deputy D.A.s, Donald Musich and Steven Kay, were assigned to replace him.

Stovitz feels to this day that Evelle Younger was politically motivated. He points out that Younger was running for state attorney general and was putting out a news brief every day and no one was paying any attention, whereas the attention of the world press was focused day and night on Stovitz and Bugliosi.

On September 4, Charlene Cafritz died of an accidental overdose of nembutol and was buried at Mt. Olivet Cemetery in D.C. The films of the Manson group she had made never came to public light.

The next day began the famous LSD hamburger caper in Honolulu. There was a witness named Barbara Hoyt who had lived at the Spahn Ranch from around April until after the murders in August, during which time she oberved some things that bolstered the prosecution's case. Hoyt was prepared to testify she had heard Susan Atkins talk about the killings to Ouish. Barbara's mother said Barbara had received a threat that if she testified she and her family would be killed. On September 5, the family contacted Barbara and offered her a free trip to Honolulu in lieu of testifying. She went. Hoyt spent the night at the Spahn Ranch, then another at a family hideout in North Hollywood.

One Dennis Rice, a recent addition to the family, took Ms. Hoyt and Ruth Ann Morehouse to the airport, gave them some cash and credit cards, and they flew to Hawaii, where they booked the penthouse suite at a Hilton hotel. They goofed around for a couple of days, then Ouish called L.A., received instructions from Squeaky, and told Hoyt that she, Ouish, was returning to L.A. but that Hoyt had to remain in Honolulu. During the course of a meal at the airport while waiting for Ouish's flight, Hoyt's ground beef was sprinkled with a multidose LSD mickey. Ouish boarded the plane, whereafter Hoyt went lycergically bonkers *pro tempore* and was later found collapsed on a sidewalk and taken to a hospital. Her parents flew to Hawaii to get her; she recovered from the dopeburger fairly easily and subsequently testified.

Denied the right to attend the trial, Squeaky and Sandy and several other women and men began to camp out at the corner of Temple and Broadway in front of the Hall of Justice. At night they slept in a white van, which, according to a law-enforcement source, had been given to the family by a publisher of occult books.

About this time, the family members also cut X's into their foreheads. "It's a falling cross," Squeaky Fromme called her mark when she later testified in the penalty phase of the Tate-LaBianca trial. At first, she said, they cut the X's with knives. Later, when the scar tissue began to fade, they burned them into the tissue above their eyes, apparently using a heated screwdriver edge. Squeaky vowed to kneel in front of the courthouse unto the end of time, or until Charlie were released.

Squeaky Fromme promised Manson she would remain on the sidewalk for as long as it took to free him—a promise she violated and which Manson never let her forget, a fact that may have contributed to her decision five years later to point a loaded .45 caliber pistol at President Ford.

After two months of prosecution witnesses, the defense began trying to come up with a unified strategy that was fair to all defendants. The problem with unity was that it was skewed to the benefit of Manson. On September 14, one of the defense attorneys told me that the women were thinking of taking the stand and blaming the drug STP, how it was all foggy, there was blood, but they didn't really remember. They didn't want dragged into the murd mud the holy substance known as LSD. They didn't want to blame it on Tex, either. They liked Tex. Nor did they want retaliation against Beausoleil. And most assuredly they didn't want to take the stand and LIE about Charlie! "What if they ask me who was driving the car the second night?" one of the defendants had asked.

On September 18, Tex Watson made an appearance in the spectator section of the Tate-LaBianca courtroom, after the U.S. Supreme Court had refused to grant further stays of extradition, and he at last was brought up from Texas, gaunt and subdued after losing about thirty pounds. He looked a bit like Spock of *Star Trek*. The three women defendants blew kisses at him.

On September 26, 1970, the Spahn Movie Ranch burned to the ground, caught in a rage of a fire fluffed up by eighty-mile-an-hour winds that charred over 100,000 acres.

On October 5, Juan Flynn had just offered some damaging testimony, and Sergeant Paul Whiteley was just about to step from the witness stand after his own testimony, when Manson announced he wanted to ask questions of Whiteley. Older refused. Manson insisted, saying, "I am going to fight for my life one way or another. You should let me do it with words."

"If you don't stop I will have to have you removed," replied the judge.

"I will have YOU removed if you don't stop. I have a little system of my own." Manson leaped over the counsel table brandishing one of his hyper-sharpened pencils, landing on one knee and obviously headed toward Older. Bailiff Bill Murray landed on Manson's back, and two other deputies joined in, scooped up M, and scurried him to the lockup. M shouted, "In the name of Christian justice, someone should cut your head off!" Manson had leapt about ten feet, according to a measurement by the bailiff.

During the fray the women chanted "Nam Myo Ho Renge Kyo," the chant of the Nichiren Shoshu sect to which Gary Hinman had belonged and which Mr. Hinman himself reportedly sang as he lay dying.

October 5 was a particularly busy day, for in addition to the above freakout, at one-thirty in the afternoon prosecutor Stephen Kay conducted an interview with Virginia Graham, who, it will be recalled, had brought to the police the jailhouse confession of Susan Atkins the previous fall. Graham ultimately received $12,000 of the $25,000 reward offered by Yul Brynner, Warren Beatty, Peter Sellers and other friends of Sharon and Roman.

Ms. Graham had some astounding new revelations, which she said she'd held back originally because she feared no one would believe her. On page 16 of the 25-page statement came the stuff of headlines. She said Atkins had spoken of the family's plan to take a bus across country and commit random murders. She said Atkins was keen to kill movie stars also, although it was not certain whether it was just Atkins's effusion upon reading a movie magazine, which she was holding in her hand, or whether it was the plan of the family. She was going to kill Elizabeth Taylor, Steve McQueen and others; she was going to adze Richard Burton's groin and make Frank Sinatra into little pouches she would peddle at hippie shops so that everybody could have a "little piece of Frank."

Graham said Atkins talked about animal sacrifices: "She described to me that on various occasions Charlie would put himself on a cross. And that a girl would kneel at the foot of the cross and that he would moan, cry out as though he was being crucified, and that they also would sacrifice animals and drink their blood as a fertility rite, because Charlie wanted the girls to produce children."

This interview leaked out in garish headlines, another serious violation of the selectively enforced gag order.

On October 8, Judge Older called Bill Farr of the Los Angeles *Herald-Examiner* into his chambers, and the latter conceded he had obtained copies of the Graham statement. The judge reiterated the concept of the gag order and, while noting Farr had immunity under California law, asked him to disclose his source. Farr declined. The next day an article was published in the *Herald-Examiner* under the headline "Liz, Sinatra on Slay List." Judge Older ordered the windows of the jurors' bus again soaped so they would not see any newsstands on the way to their hotel. After the trial was over, Farr would serve over fifty days in jail for refusing to reveal to Older those who had given him the Graham document.

In early October, the defense subpoenaed Mama Cass Elliott as a witness. She was due to host the "Tonight Show" on NBC the next day and was afraid her distress over the subpoena might impinge on the show. On October 15, the defense also subpoenaed John Phillips, serving the papers at the Troubadour nightclub in Los Angeles, where he was performing to a half-empty house.

There was talk of calling the Beatles to the stand. Later that month, the Beatles issued a statement in London saying that Manson's interpretation of their lyrics was ridiculous. John Lennon was back in England after a few months of primordial screaming with a Los Angeles shrink.

On October 19, the day Gregg Jakobson testified, author Truman Capote visited the court. Ostensibly he was there to cover the trial for the *New York Times* Sunday magazine. I was very anxious to learn if he were going to write a book about the family, so I introduced myself. He assured me he was not. "Where's Chaaaarleeh?" he asked, in his trademark drawl, walking back toward the jurors, two of whom were wide eyed in recognition. One even put her knitting away.

Mr. Capote was wearing a fashionably baggy set of gray European trousers, light green sunglasses, tasseled shoes, and he carried a pocket book. The sheriff's office, of course, searched everybody coming into the courtroom, and when they opened Mr. Capote's bag they discovered that it was packed with bundles of money. He needed it for bail money, because he was liable for arrest in California for refusing to testify at the retrial of a murderer whom he had interviewed for an abandoned ABC-TV documentary called "Death Row, U.S.A."

The prosecution had made a large-scale drawing, six feet by forty inches in size, of the Tate-Polanski house and grounds, which included every single blood stain, and the type of blood. I had obtained a copy and studied it diligently. Based on the way Krenwinkel and Atkins had said the murders occurred, and on the details of the large map, it seemed obvious the crime scene had been disturbed *after* the killers had left. On a hunch, I sent a question on October 19 to Manson through one of the attorneys: Did he go to the Tate house after the murders? He replied, "I went back to see what my children did." He also admitted he had put the googoo-eyed glasses there as a false clue.

There was a hearing on the sanity of Tex Watson. He was being nose fed, had to be shaved and washed by others, and was "rapidly reverting to a fetal state." The former all-district halfback for Farmersville, Texas, High was down from 165 to 110 pounds. On October 29, Judge George Dell ruled that Watson was at present incompetent to stand trial and ordered him to Atascadero State Hospital.

Manson, in front of witnesses, offered to bring Tex out of it. "Just give me twenty minutes with him alone and I'll bring him back," he said.

Around Halloween, the reporters held a Helter Skelter party at a nearby hotel. They came in various costumes appropriate to the case. One newsman, for instance, made himself up into a very eery semblance of the gaunt and starving Tex Watson. Deputy district attorney Burton Katz felt that Watson was malingering, and he commented at the Helter Skelter party that Watson had been spotted beating off under a blanket in his cell.

In the USA they call it "crunch time." Around the end of October 1970, as the prosecution was coming to the end of its presentation, there was a series of hostile meetings between Atkins, Manson, Krenwinkel and Van Houten and their attorneys, Fitzgerald, Hughes, Shinn and Kanarek. Vincent Bugliosi had stated he was going to rest the prosecution's case shortly after the testimony of Snake Lake.

On October 29, there was an important meeting. Manson again spoke of having the women testify in order to absolve him. Another option was not to have a defense. Or to get some Black Muslims to testify that Manson was a "Prophet." Or Manson thought he might call Tex to the stand and let him take the blame. Or Manson thought he himself might take the stand and tell "why" it all had happened. All during those days there was a hiss and closed-room thunder of death threats—against Judge Older, against the attorneys.

Late in October, the sheriff's homicide unit had scuba divers search a water tower near the ranch looking for Shorty Shea's head, on a tip from Vern Plumlee, who had been with the family the summer of murder and part of the creepy-crawl robbery teams. CBS reporter Carl George and I visited L.A. coroner Thomas Noguchi, whose office was located in the basement of the Hall of Justice. We had heard that maybe Shea's head had been found. There was no head, Dr. Noguchi assured us, although he said they'd found some Indian skulls earlier in the year, apparently in Devil's Canyon. He chuckled, noting that they were "seventy or eighty years old. We don't care about any murders that far back."

On Monday, November 9, Manson again talked about Judge Older allowing him to represent himself for the defense part of the trial. It was obvious Older was not going to do it. If Older refused, M threatened to cut off the heads of the judge's family, including his two daughters. "I have twelve people out there who will do whatever I ask," M bragged. He said he could order deaths from the pen also, by taking the brain of a con, making the person a zombi, and sending him out.

Atkins felt guilty about her original snitching and testimony before the grand jury. Krenwinkel felt guilty about the arrests at the Barker Ranch, for she had been responsible for awakening everybody and getting them away from the ranch every morning after the family slept there. Yes, they had plenty of guilt, from Mr. Manson's point of view, so they owed it to him to get him off. It would have been one of the greater injustices in the history of jurisprudence, had they gone along with it.

Van Houten, Krenwinkel and Atkins decided to testify and spring M. They prepared question lists they wanted their attorneys to ask.

On Monday, November 16, the prosecution introduced their 320 items of evidence, including those grim full-color death photos. Late in the afternoon, Bugliosi rested the prosecution's case.

Thursday, November 19, the defense was to begin. Paul Fitzgerald was told by the court, "You may call your first witness, Mr. Fitzgerald."

Fitgerald replied, "Thank you, Your Honor. The defendants rest."

The three women shouted they wanted to testify. They tried to approach the judge but were blocked by guards. Daye Shinn refused to ask the list of questions Atkins had prepared.

Judge Older ruled the women defendants could testify, but the defense attorneys said they would not ask the questions because it would lead to conviction.

Paul Fitzgerald: "I told the judge I am not going to ask these people any questions—you're going to have to ask them the questions. It's not going to be me, because I cannot ethically as a lawyer, whether it means going to jail or not."

On Friday, November 20, 1970, with the jury absent, Older ruled the women could make statements in narrative form, rather than q & a from attorneys. Bugliosi objected, suggesting they make their statements with the jurors removed from the room. The women refused, wanting the jury present. In the midst of the fray arose Charles Manson, who wanted to testify, and he was willing to do it away from the jury.

Older allowed Mr. M to go ahead, as a sort of preview of what a narrative presentation would be like.

Manson took the stand and filled up about sixty-one pages of trial transcript. It was a good performance. It gave a hint of his power around the campfire, structuring his acidassins. Unfortunately for him, there was no campfire, no cult klatch, no acid—just a murder trial, and the peach-scented fumes of the gas chamber the likely reward.

Manson began in the mode of a hillbilly lounge lizard, with a kind of "aw, shucks! me, a killer?" attitude. He said things like "I never went to school, so I never growed up in the respect to read and write too good, so I have stayed in jail and I have stayed stupid, and I have stayed a child. . . ."

Then he ran his standard rap that he was just a reflection of his associates' emotions and prejudices. In fact, the mirror job was on everyone: "I am just a reflection of every one of you." Manson said, "I have killed no one and I have ordered no one to be killed." As to being the Big J, he said, "I may have implied on several occasions to several different people that I may have been Jesus Christ, but I haven't decided yet what I am or who I am.

"My father is the jailhouse. My father is your system, and each one of you, each one of you are just a reflection of each one of you." He forgot himself for a moment and waxed murder-batty: "If I could I would jerk this microphone off and beat your brains out with it because that is what you deserve, that is what you deserve."

Unfortunately for him, M seemed to forget his purpose, or he confused his testimony with a rap around a campfire or a nightclub performance. When Manson left the stand and passed the table where Atkins, Krenwinkel and Van Houten sat, he said, "You don't have to testify now."

A dumb move on M's part. He was probably so pleased with his rap or performance he hadn't the drive to continue trying to force the other defendants' testimony. The spasm was over, but so was his scheme for freedom. Manson didn't want to testify before the jury, either—he told the judge on page 18,192 of the trial transcript—because "I have already relieved all the pressure I had."

After Manson's monologue, Judge Older decided the narrative form of testimony, without the questions of defense and prosecution attorneys, was unmanageable. He then recessed court for ten days for attorneys to prepare their final arguments.

Thanksgiving night, November 26, Ron Hughes left a message for me with my pal Phil Ochs at the Bitter End bar. But he'd gone up to a place called Sespe Hot Springs to prepare his closing arguments by the time I tried to call.

Sespe Hot Springs is in the Ojai Mountains, 130 miles northwest of L.A., in Ventura County, within the Los Padres National Forest. It is one of the wildest and most uncertain places in the California wilderness system. Hughes loved hanging out in the hot water. Sespe is subject to very dangerous flash flooding. Two years before, eight or nine Boy Scouts had been swept down Sespe gorge, two of them washing all the way to Oxnard on the coast.

Ron had a team of volunteer investigators helping him, two of whom, James Forsher and Lauren Elder, both seventeen, drove him to Sespe Hot Springs in their 1966 Volkswagen. Then arrived about four o'clock on Friday afternoon. It started to rain, and it poured all night. At seven the following morning, all three got into the car, went a mile, got mired, then walked back to the camp at the base of the hot springs. Hughes was tired and wanted to rest.

After a while the two youngsters went back to the VW, apparently planning to hike to a nearby Naval Seabee base, but they were picked up by campers and driven to L.A.

In addition to Hughes, four people were marooned at the hot springs until Monday, when they were coptered out. Saturday around noon Hughes told them he was going to the car to get trial transcripts, either to read them in the VW or to bring them back. The rain was heaviest that afternoon—a boulder-dislodging and tree-ripping shriek from the sky that poured twelve inches in eighteen hours.

The quickly rising stream crossed in front of Hughes twice between the hot springs and the VW. A tent was later found to be missing from the car. There was speculation he used it as a raincoat on the way back, to protect his transcripts. Ron Hughes, the girth of his body perhaps affecting his balance in the torrent, his mind distracted by the terror of the trial, and trying to keep his court documents dry, must have slipped crossing the floodway. It swept him down for several miles to a spot where he was lodged beneath a boulder, not to be found for four months.

One reporter covering the trial for a newspaper consulted a Chicago psychic about Hughes's disappearance.

People went to his house. Among his papers was a written threat from Manson: "If you obey the judge, you're going to go with the judge."

I went up to Sespe Hot Springs shortly after he disappeared and saw how the flood had left a desolation. I went to his house also, but there was no evidence of malefaction. Others found the threatening note.

He was a friend of mine, and I wept for him. I am convinced his death was through drowning, but at the time it was scary because of the climate of threats.

Meanwhile the trial continued, although the disappearance of Hughes caused a delay.

On November 30, Paul Fitzgerald told me that outside the court building, Gypsy, Bo, Squeaky, Cathy, Sandy, Ouish and a couple of unknowns had threatened to cut off his head. They had said he should grow his hair longer so that prior to the chopping, they could seize it by the hair. They were mad apparently because they wanted to testify at the trial.

On December 2, Nancy Pittman aka Brenda McCann and Bruce Davis surrendered. Davis was charged in the Hinman and Shea murders, and Brenda was wanted on a forgery charge. She was represented by Paul Fitzgerald. Both had lived for months down in some huge drainpipes of the L.A. flood-control system in Canoga Park. Officer Charles Guenther had at one point almost caught them, apparently positioning his men down in the pipes. Another time Guenther had run into Brenda but didn't recognize her immediately, and she had time to dump down through a sewer hatch and disappear. They had also lived in a sympathizer's garage.

Finally, Manson had ordered them to surrender. Paul Fitzgerald: "He just put out the order for it to happen. Because I represented Brenda. We took a recess from the trial—we went out and surrendered them." There was a deal made to drop charges—credit-card-type things—against Brenda. But as for Davis, "they wanted him for murder, and he surrendered—can you imagine?"

On December 3, attorney Maxwell Keith was appointed to replace the missing Ron Hughes as attorney for Leslie Van Houten. Judge Older suspended the trial till December 16, to give Mr. Keith an opportunity to bone up on the 18,000-plus pages of testimony, 1,200 discovery documents and 320 exhibits. There were motions to separate Van Houten's trial from the others on the grounds that Mr. Keith would have to learn so much in just a few days. Older denied the separation motion, a decision that six years later would result in Ms. Van Houten being granted a new trial.

The death threats against the attorneys continued. On December 7, with music in the background Country Sue Bartell, who had once held the shuddering Zero as he lay dying, called with a message to Paul Fitzgerald, saying that Patricia Krenwinkel was going to invade his neck with a pencil. Fitzgerald immediately went to Katie and Leslie in Sybil Brand and said he'd give them the pencil. That was family protocol: If you rushed up and said, "Hey, kill me," then they wouldn't.

Also on December 7, I began my association with ace private investigator Larry Larsen, who worked efficiently, relentlessly and nonstop for months in helping compile the information for this book.

On Wednesday, December 9, the Ventura County sheriffs office informed a defense attorney that a seven-year-old boy had found a postcard addressed to Sharon Tate, dated 11-14-68 and signed Bam and Papa. The card had an Indian on its face. It was discovered about two miles down the canyon from Sespe Hot Springs and in a place, I was told, where there is no direct floodway through which Hughes might have been swept. It was another strange frazzled string joining the hundreds of other threads that dangle from this case.

On December 18, Squeaky, Ouish, Gypsy, Clem and Dennis Rice were indicted for attempted murder in the Honolulu LSD hamburger caper. Murder by acid seemed a bit ridiculous, and the charges were later reduced, so that Squeaky, for example, served only several months in jail for the caper.

And what of Roman Polanski? He came out of the crush of his wife's murder and tried to put together a movie deal for the book *Papillon*, with Warren Beatty agreeing to star, but he couldn't raise enough money.

The Manson slaughters had caused a grim increase, even for Polanski, of ghoulish script proposals. He decided to do a movie of *Macbeth*. He approached Kenneth Tynan, the literary director of Britain's National Theater, about writing the screenplay together. Tynan accepted. Playboy Productions advanced $1.5 million and Columbia, the picture's distributor, another $1 million. Filming began in the fall of 1970 in Wales and northern England of a "terrifyingly grisly" version, to use the words of CBS television's Mike Wallace, of Shakespeare's play.

In January of 1971, Mark, Manson's teenage son by his wife Rosalie pulled a knife on another boy and was cut in half with a .12 gauge shotgun. Manson's former wife was then married to a coal miner and living in eastern Ohio in strip-mine country. She wanted to forget the whole thing with M. The shooting was called justifiable homicide and no arrest was made.

On January 15, exactly seven months after jury selection had begun, the jury began its deliberations. On January 25, Van Houten, Krenwinkel, Atkins and Manson were found guilty on all twenty-seven counts of murder.

The defense lawyers, who had stoutly resisted the girls testifying during the innocent-guilty phase, strangely had no objections to their testimony now during the so-called penalty phase, when the question was whether or not they'd get assigned to the octagonal gas chamber. Paul Fitzgerald told Associated Press reporter Linda Deutsch at the time, "The defendants can take the stand if they want to. It's their lives, and if they want to testify, how can we in good conscience stop them."

Fitzgerald guessed the odds against getting a life sentence were about fifty to one.

Atkins and the others tried in the penalty phase what they had wanted to do the previous November—i.e., absolve Manson. But it didn't work. Various members of the family also testified, including Cathy Gillies and Gypsy, who absolved Manson of everything and instead blamed the planning on Linda Kasabian. Squeaky Fromme swore that it had all been love and friendship and mutual respect in the face of an impending social cataclysm. There was not a shard of remorse among them.

On Friday, January 29, the prosecution called Bernard Crowe before the jury. Mr. Crowe was sporting rectangular Bo Diddley eyeglasses, and he still carried Manson's bullet in his body.

On March 4, Manson trimmed his beard and completely shaved his head. He attempted to cut a swastika upon his forehead, reworking his previous X, but it was executed in reverse.

On Friday, March 26, the jury began its deliberations. It had been sequestered 225 days, and it now had 31,716 pages of transcript upon which to meditate.

It only took two days. Late in the afternoon on Monday, March 29, word came they were ready. For the jury's verdict, all four defendants were X-headed and shaved. It was a hideous sight.

The court clerk spoke *death, death, death* twenty-seven times as he read off the votes of the jurors. During this death chant, Manson tried to get the judge's attention by shouting, "Hey, boy!" and was removed from the room. Outside the Hall of Justice, the vigil looked like a Martian landing zone. Sympathizers had likewise shaved their heads, and there was baleful talk of self-immolation while reporters and spectators crowded about, but, praise be, no one lit a torch.

Susan Atkins shouted, "Better lock your doors and watch your own kids!" at the verdict.

That weekend, fishermen found the body of Ron Hughes lodged beneath a boulder in Sespe Creek, where the flood had tumbled him. Paul Fitzgerald had the grim duty of identifying the body in the Ventura County morgue, which was only possible because of the domelike remarkability of Ron's head. Some of Mr. Hughes's memorable beard, similar to those sported in Sergei Eisenstein movies, was still identifiable.

On April 19, 1971, Manson was ordered by Judge Older to Death Row at San Quentin Prison, north of San Francisco, for execution; Atkins, Van Houten and Krenwinkel were sent to the California Institute for Women at Frontera, about forty miles east of L.A. Manson would stall his transfer till October, but the three women went right away to a Death Row at Frontera that was being specially constructed for them.

26

From Death Row to President Ford (1971–1975)

1971

Atkins, Krenwinkel and Van Houten were taken to Death Row with their shaved heads and oozing X's. A psychological evaluation conducted on Krenwinkel and Van Houten on May 24, 1971, stated that "they acknowledge that 'according to the other truth, which is not the truth, they are guilty of murder,' but claimed that 'according to their truth which is the truth, they are innocent.' " There was no sign of grief. Grief would come, but it was years ahead, years that marked the dissolution of what we have called the family.

There was a schism between Susan Atkins and her mates on Death Row at Frontera. Sadie was the snitch who had gotten them there.

Manson was able to delay his removal to Death Row at San Quentin because of the upcoming Shorty Shea and Gary Hinman murder trials.

Back in December, deputy district attorney Burton Katz had called forty-two witnesses to testify before a grand jury on the Shea case. On December 17, the jury had voted to indict Manson, Bruce Davis and Steve Grogan aka Clem. Grogan was in jail at the time in Inyo County for a sawed-off shotgun-possession charge.

On December 30, there had been a hearing to consolidate the two murder trials—Shea's and Hinman's—for Manson, Davis and Grogan. The Shea case was one of the few in U.S. history in which first-degree murder convictions would be obtained without the body of the victim being recovered. There was always the concern that Mr. Shea would turn up sometime, to the embarrassment of the police, so officers kept up a relentless search for the body.

On May 10, Tex Watson pled not guilty, by reason of insanity, to the murder of Sebring, Frykowski, Tate, Folger, Parent and the LaBiancas before Superior Court Judge Adolph Alexander.

On July 19, writer Bill Farr refused to answer a series of thirteen questions about his sources for his article on the Virginia Graham "celebrity killings" interview. Although the court recognized that reporters are protected under California law from revealing their sources, since the trial Mr. Farr had left the *Herald-Examiner* and was working as press secretary for the new district attorney of Los Angeles, Joseph Busch. (Mr. Younger had moved on, winning the race for state attorney general.) Farr, argued Older, was no longer protected. It was talk or jail.

Shinn, Kanarek, Fitzgerald, Kay, Musich and Bugliosi all denied under oath leaking the story to him. Older found Mr. Farr in contempt of court and ordered him to jail but stayed the sentence, pending appeal.

In July, sheriff's homicide detectives Guenther and Whiteley were successful in helping Kitty Lutesinger finally escape the clutches of the family. She had tipped them off on the location of Dennis Rice's kids, who were living in a cave beneath a chicken coop in Lancaster.

There were separate trials for Manson, Davis and Clem on the combined Hinman-Shea charges. On July 14, Manson announced in open court that he had cut off the Spahn Ranch stunt man Donald Shea's head in late August of 1969. This was not exactly true, since when the skeleton was discovered six years later the head was intact. The prosecutor in Manson's Hinman-Shea trial was Anthony Manzella, and Manson was given a life sentence.

On July 30, Bartyk Frykowski, young son of Wojtek Frykowski, won a judgment of $500,000 from Manson, Atkins, Krenwinkel, Watson and Kasabian.

In August and September of 1971, Tex Watson went

on trial. It was another sordid affair, but Watson confessed freely his participation in the killings. He sported a tie and coat and still looked a bit like a sunken-cheeked, down-and-out Spock.

It was basically a repeat of the trial of his cohorts, with Linda Kasabian the star witness. Deana Martin, daughter of singer Dean Martin, could not recognize him as the one she had met in 1968 at Dennis Wilson's house Watson's attorney was Sam Bubrick; Vince Bugliosi and Steven Kay were the prosecutors. On October 21, Watson was sentenced to death by Judge Alexander.

Steve Grogan aka Clem aka Scramblehead went on trial for the Shea killing. The jury voted the death penalty, but when Clem was sentenced on December 23, 1971, Judge James Kolts decided that "Grogan was too stupid and too hopped up on drugs to decide anything on his own," and he reduced the sentence to life imprisonment. Clem's prosecutor was Burton Katz, who was instrumental in helping a rehabilitated Mr. Grogan get released on parole, fourteen years later.

Meanwhile, the Manson family became intertwined with a neo-Nazi white supremacist group called the Aryan Brotherhood, a number of whose members resided inside the prison system.

After the guilty verdict, word circulated that Manson was worried about his impending transfer to Death Row. He was supposedly worried about his potential Black cellmates. There was the "pig" written in Sharon Tate's blood to cause suspicion that the murders had been committed by Black Panthers, his dislike of Blacks, and the race war he had bumblingly wanted to trigger. Killing a pregnant woman is not a popular offense among criminals. One report from a deputy sheriff assigned to courtroom duty was that Manson had been spotted, as the trial had drawn to a close, practicing karate in the holding tank, preparing for the event that "Black Muslims," who seemed to comprise the prime family fear object, attacked on the Row.

According to a source in a Southern California law-enforcement agency, the Aryan Brotherhood was formed sometime around the mid-1960s and at one point had as an initiation regulation the killing of a Black, but that requirement was dropped around 1967. The A.B. reportedly had connections with the so-called Mexican Mafia, an organization also situated within and without the California prison system, dealing in drugs, weapons and killings. Its murder contracts were given to the Aryan Brotherhood to fulfill, according to prison officials.

The initial A.B. member in the M sphere seems to have been a charismatic guy named Kenneth Como, whom Manson had brought down from Folsom Prison as a witness at the Hinman-Shea trial. Como had managed to escape from the L.A. jail in July of 1971.

On August 21, there was a ten-minute shoot-out between X-heads and police during an attempted robbery of Western Surplus Store, a gun shop at 13355 South Hawthorne Boulevard in L.A. Three family members were wounded in the exchange. Among those involved in the robbery were the most violence-prone family members, including Mary Brunner, Gypsy Share, Chuckleberry, Little Larry and the man named Fatherman (aka Dennis Rice). The leader of the caper was Kenneth Como. They entered the Western Surplus Store and ordered the clerks and customers to lie on the floor, whereupon they set aside 143 rifles to carry out to their white van. A clerk managed to trip a silent alarm that summoned the police.

According to an L.A. homicide officer, the group began a rather too lengthy debate over whether or not to murder the clerks and customers on the floor, who reportedly were so terrified they could not speak for half an hour after it was over. If this laborious debate had not occurred, police speculate that the gun theft might have been successful.

A squad car arrived, and Gypsy opened fire. The policeman was able to get out of the vehicle just as one of the front windows was blast-shattered. The white van was blocked by other police cars and riddled with fifty bullet holes. The family fired about twenty rounds before being taken into custody. Gypsy, Mary Brunner and Little Larry Bailey were wounded.

One report at the time held that the Hawthorne gun store shoot-out was part of a plot that included the hijacking of a 747 to free the Death Row four.

On October 20, Kenneth Como escaped again, this time in a daring five-story dangle on a bedsheet rope from his cell window on the thirteenth floor of the Hall of Justice. From his dangling position he kicked in the window of the actual courtroom where the Tate-LaBianca trial had been held and made his way to a van driven by Sandy Good, who crashed, and Como was recaptured.

Family members on the outside began to associate with A.B. members. There is at least one case of an Aryan Brotherhood member, Billie Gaucher, being met by a family associate as he left prison. They lived together until he was picked up later on for murder.

Manson probably thought it would be brilliant tactics to join forces with the A.B., because in addition to his personal safety, he could also keep track of wobbling spores on the outside. It turned out to be a blunder, because A.B. man Kenneth Como, the leader of the Hawthorne shoot-out, was subsequently able to split the remnants of the family into two bitter factions, the Comoites and the Mansonites.

On October 12, two years to the day that Manson had been arrested at the Barker Ranch, the jury found Tex Watson guilty.

On October 19, after less than three hours of deliberation, the jury found Watson sane. And on October 21, after six hours, they sent him to die in the gas chamber.

In November, Watson was shipped to Death Row at San Quentin. On December 14, Manson was whisked to Q in a bus guarded by three vehicles and a helicopter to join ninety-six others on the Row.

Bruce Davis's trial for the murders of Shorty Shea and Gary Hinman began in December. Steven Kay was the prosecutor.

1972

Toward the end of the Davis trial, Bill Vance was located in northern Missouri pretending to be a Christian minister named William Cole. He was in a house with exfamily person Claudia Smith. The legendary Little Patty, who had been in the sack with Christopher Zero when the gun went off, had also been living with Vance, but he told authorities she had been institutionalized by her parents in Pittsburgh.

Vance had supposedly run off with some of the better

family music tapes. Sheriff's homicide officers also were told he had the tapes on which the family had recreated the murder of Gary Hinman. Sergeant Whiteley: "I went back to see him in Missouri and listened to a couple of the tapes but they were just singing. I didn't hear anything that would relate to murder." It was then that Whiteley began to get letters from Sandra Good and also from Manson. They wanted the Vance music tapes.

On February 18, 1972, the California supreme court voted 6–1 to abolish the death penalty. At the California Institute for Women in Frontera, Susan Atkins was listening in her cell, as was Leslie Van Houten in hers. "That's us!" shouted Leslie. "No gas chamber."

In Los Angeles, where he was a defense witness in the Bruce Davis trial, Manson flashed a wide smile at the news cameras. Davis was found guilty and sentenced to life imprisonment.

On March 29, 1972, Sergeants Bill Gleason and Paul Whiteley went to the Spahn Ranch with Bill Vance to look for Shorty's body, but it was not found.

In June, the U.S. Supreme Court voted 5–4 that the death penalty was to be abolished in cases where the jury in the penalty phase was given absolute discretion and no guidelines.

Death Row was temporarily abolished. On September 9, Tex Watson was sent to the California Men's Colony at San Luis Obispo. Manson was transferred from San Quentin in October to Folsom Prison.

In 1972 the A.B.-family alliance bore its first evil. A young married couple with a small child, Lauren and James Willett, were drawn to their deaths. They were like luna moths who, when flitting around the high hard lights of a shopping-mall parking lot, are devoured by bats.

The Willetts apparently met some of the courthouse vigilers in L.A. Later they moved to a cabin near Guerneville, California, north of San Francisco and not far from the coast, where they shared a house with a couple of Aryan Brotherhood people. There was a string of petty holdups by the A.B.ers, and in early October 1972 several of them were arrested. One A.B. member used Willett's identification papers. Around October 10, James Willett was beheaded and buried on a hikers' trail near

Guerneville, on the coast above San Francisco. Police later speculated Willett was killed because it was feared he might snitch to police.

His wife, Lauren, was apparently somehow kept in the dark about James's demise. She began to stay with several family women and A.B. men in a house in Stockton, California. In a scene right out of a *Tales from the Crypt* horror story, James Willett's hand became exposed at the hiker trail burial site, and someone discovered it on November 8 jutting above the dirt.

Shortly thereafter, police in Stockton noted that James Willett's station wagon was parked outside the A.B.-family house. The police had a warrant out for bail-jumping against the A.B. member who had used Willett's ID. When they visited the house, the cops noticed electrical cords leading from outlets across the floor and down through a trap door. They obtained a search warrant and raided the building, discovering the body of Lauren Willett, dead just twenty-four hours, beneath fresh dirt in the cellar.

To add to the horror, the Willetts' infant daughter, Heidi, was found upstairs, alive and in the care of the family. Arrested for murder and possession of a sawed-off shotgun and marijuana were three Aryan Brotherhood men and three women associated with the family.

And where was Squeaky Fromme during all this? Sometime around the fall of 1972, she abandoned her two-year vigil at the L.A. Hall of Justice, an act for which Manson made her feel guilty right up to the day she lunged at President Ford. Squeaky moved to San Francisco, where she reportedly was living with a "straight woman." She obviously kept in touch with the house in Stockton, because just as the police were raiding, Squeaky called from the local bus station and asked for someone to pick her up. The police obliged, and she was arrested for murder. She had an alibi for the husband's murder and a probable alibi for the wife's, so her charges were ultimately dropped.

Manson, the documentary film that had been in production during the spring of 1970, was finally released, coproduced by its originator, Robert Hendrickson, in association with a gentleman named Laurence Merrick. Sharon Tate had apparently once been a pupil at Merrick's film-production and acting school, the Merrick Studo Academy of Dramatic Arts, in Los Angeles. *Manson* was nominated for an Academy Award in the documentary category in 1972; it did not win.

On November 27, reporter Bill Farr was put in jail by Judge Charles Older for civil contempt after refusing to say who had given him the famous Virginia Graham "celebrity killings" interview during the 1970 trial. He admitted that he had received it from two sources, both lawyers, but refused to name them because of their possible disbarment. Mr. Farr could have been jailed until the mandatory retirement of Judge Older at age seventy, which meant that Farr could have languished in the slams for over a decade.

Finally, after forty-eight days, Farr was released by the great and heroic associate justice of the U.S. Supreme Court, William O. Douglas. Mr. Farr in his later career wrote for the *Los Angeles Times*. He was a gentle and very humane guy, who was caught up through no fault of his own in the Manson milieu madness, for there were numerous violations of the gag order much more injurious to the concept of a fair trial than the forkover by some unknown lawyers of that sleazy little murd-moll pagination.

Later, a special prosecutor for the case, Mr. Theodore Shield, was appointed in Los Angeles at the request of the L.A. Board of Supervisors. There was an investigation by the state attorney general's office and a grand jury look-see, which resulted in the indictments of Vincent Bugliosi and Daye Shinn. Coprosecutor Steven Kay testified that he had witnessed Mr. Farr in Mr. Bugliosi's office when Kay delivered copies of the Graham transcript to Bugliosi and that a few days later Farr asked Kay outside of court to hand a manila envelope to Bugliosi. The indictments were later thrown out by a judge, who ruled the case against the attorneys was legally insufficient.

At one point, investigators wanted to fly to New York to question me, but I vowed not to cooperate. I had also obtained a copy of the Virginia Graham interview but not from anybody associated with the case.

1973: P Street

Atkins, Krenwinkel and Van Houten began gradually to act as individuals, not as "cult drones." Atkins seems to have been helped by taking a class on the women's movement, something she could have used in late 1967 just before she jumped into the black bus.

Sandy Good and Squeaky were separated in late 1972 and early 1973, when Sandy traveled to Oregon and said she spent some time in jail. The duo was reunited around the spring of 1973 when they obtained a dilapidated attic apartment at 1725 P Street in downtown Sacramento, near the State capitol. They wanted to be near Manson, who, after the abolition of capital punishment, had been moved from San Quentin to Folsom Prison, not too far a drive from P Street.

In February and March there was the trial of Kenneth Como, Mary Brunner, Gypsy and the others for the Hawthorne shoot-out, which, it will be recalled, had occurred almost two years previous. How justice doth ooze. The defendants pled innocent by reason of insanity but were given long prison sentences on March 21 by Judge Arthur Alarcon, including Mary Brunner, who received two consecutive ten-years-to-life sentences. The jury was sequestered after reportedly receiving two death threats.

Manson was brought to testify from Folsom Prison, barefoot and shackled, arm and foot. He claimed that "sex paranoia" was the reason the police had applied pressure on the Spahn Ranch in 1968 and 1969.

This trial, plus the arrests for the murders in Stockton and Guerneville, reduced the M Family back to its original 1967 size—i.e., to a carload.

Squeaky of P Street was kept busy during this period completing the book about the family that various members had been writing and rewriting for about three years. Many pages were festooned with intricate drawings, and there were numerous photos. Squeaky wanted it printed in four colors. At one point it weighed in at about 600 pages. According to one of the family's lawyers, Squeaky sent the family book to just about every publisher in America. Clem sent word "to make it more clear." Squeaky knew well the danger of clarity and remarked in a letter: "To make things clear is to lay them out for the Attorney General and his buddies." She was astute, knowing that the California state attorney general had conducted a serious, high-level investigation of the connections between the family and other bloody cults. And so another manuscript hit the closet.

Meanwhile, Manson's problems with the Aryan Brotherhood began to move towards violence. Oddly enough, it appears that part of his hassle with the A.B. was due to M not taking a hard-line position within the anti-Black Aryan movement. Manson was on the left wing of the Nazi movement—that is, he was not violent enough. Kenneth Como was thus able to woo key women in the group, including Mary Brunner, Gypsy and Brenda. As Squeaky wrote in a letter of June 1973: "A.B. moves much on pure hate, as they want him [Manson] to kill black because black is black. He will not do this and they are against him."

Around the summer of 1973, someone slipped Manson some rat poison in a glass of Tang. Manson chugged it down but was able later to note humorously in a letter that rat poison does not really affect him very much, although it did give a "new experience." There was another report that Manson had beaten up Kenneth Como in the yard at Folsom. The A.B.ers had laughed at him, and Como vowed to off M.

In the fall of 1973 and early 1974 there were reports from several law-enforcement sources that Manson was regressing. He was apparently loath to leave his cell at Folsom. His fingernails grew long, and he was hesitant to bathe.

Prison officials, the report indicated, had to cut his hair by force. Rules for long hair had not yet changed, though they would. They felt he was not communicating, that he was regressing, a common enough phenomenon in prisons, which, if advanced enough, could turn a person into a staring vegetable. He was sent to a psychiatric prison facility at Vacaville, California.

1974: The Order of Rainbow

In Sacramento, Squeaky and Sandy Good lived almost anonymously in their dilapidated apartment on P Street.

One might not have noted the healed scar-tissue on their foreheads. They attracted very few recruits. There was one, a woman named Susan Murphy, who joined sometime around early 1973, and she remained with the P Street attic-dwellers all the way until the attempted assassination of President Ford in 1975.

There is a *cursus honorum* in California whereby a public servant can march from district attorney of Los Angeles to the post of state attorney general to the governorship and even higher than that. So it had been with Earl Warren and Edmund Brown. So it could have been for Evelle Younger or Vincent Bugliosi. Mr. Younger won his battle to become state attorney general but lost in his bid for the governorship in a race against Democrat Jerry Brown.

Vincent Bugliosi left the L.A. district attorney's office and ran for the Democratic nomination first for Los Angeles district attorney and then for state attorney general. He lost both bids. His book about the Manson case, *Helter Skelter*, cowritten with Curt Gentry and published in 1974, was a macro-moolah success.

In August of 1973, Richard Nixon stepped down as president. Wesley Hiler, Manson's therapist at the California medical facility at Vacaville, reported that Manson believed his own personal hex on Nixon had caused him to fall. Manson wreaked vengeance on Nixon because of the remarks Nixon had made during the trial.

The landlord and landlady at P Street didn't know for quite some time who their tenants were. In November of 1974, a newsman approached Sandy and Squeaky, their first media attention in quite a while, to ask about an article that had been published alleging a possible breakout attempt. Prison officials monitoring the arcane rhetoric of Manson's letters had apparently located some suspicious Squeaky-Sandy letters along with plans for escape.

There was an article about the incident in the local Sacramento newspaper and, as Squeaky wrote, "We had to steal the newspaper off the porch to keep our mom-like landlady from reading our names. She would either go into shock or ask us to move."

Meanwhile, Manson had formulated a new religion

called nuness, or the order of rainbow. He assigned colors to present and former family people, "like the spectrums of light in thought," as he wrote in a letter. Thus Squeaky became red, Sandy blue, Susan Atkins violet, Leslie Van Houten green, Patricia Krenwinkle yellow, Brenda gold, and so forth. Additionally, Krenwinkle, Van Houten and Atkins were assigned the appellations queen of yellow, queen of green and queen of violet.

Van Houten, Krenwinkel and Atkins had not been communicating with Manson for several years and had, in fact, broken with him, so they sent back word to Squeaky they did not want to be queens of anything. Squeaky replied, in a sample of her humor, that if they did not want to be the queens of various colors, then why not adopt the names Squash, Corn and Bean; thus they could become the "Suckatash Sisters."

There were supposedly seven degrees, or stages of initiation in this new religion—the degrees of witch, queen, goddess, alikeen, and three others for which M had not yet supplied the names. He ordered a new chronological system: "Make a new clock divided into four or six parts. Morning is red, noon is gold, afternoon is green, and the evening is blue, and night is sleep time."

The structure of order of rainbow, or nuness, was speckled with strange terms like *alikens, alikems, pice,* et cetera. As Squeaky stated in a letter of May 1974, "One degree in nuness can be gotten by sleeping in an open grave at the graveyard. No violence. Only completion of old Christian fears."

There apparently were attempts in San Francisco and Sacramento to recruit fresh talent to the order of rainbow. Times, however, had changed, and the years since 1969 had seen a Tower of Babel beseechment of new and old religions on the American landscape. Religious leaders by the dime a dozen were out there hungry as deer flies for converts, so a couple of Manson followers whom the world was quickly forgetting had about zero chance of success.

In fact, the family had all but dissolved, and religion of a more traditional type was helping that dissolution.

Sometime in late 1973 Bruce Davis became a born-again Christian. Susan Atkins began corresponding with Davis in early 1974. His letters, however armageddon-addled with talk about the Four Horsemen of the Book of Revelation, seemed nevertheless to urge her to become a Christian again. Other Christian groups visited her in jail and told her they were praying for her. Someone sent her a Bible. On September 27, 1974, Ms. Atkins had a religious vision of Jesus in her cell, and she too was born again.

1975

Sergeant Whiteley of the Los Angeles County sheriff's office transferred out of homicide and onto the vice detail. The hours weren't as long and weary. Plain old American vice is always easier than murder. His partner, Deputy Charles Guenther, transferred into a different section of the homicide division. Thus ended one of the most legendary teams of recent law-enforcement history. "Everything got put onto Gleason's head," recalls Whiteley. "And Gleason kept track of what was going on after that."

On March 3, 1975, Gypsy Share was released on parole, having been in custody since the Hawthorne gun store shoot-out of August 1971. She promised to disassociate herself from the M group, changed her name to Jessica, and wanted to begin a singing career. Mary Brunner, on the other hand, convicted of the same charge, was still serving hard time as a recalcitrant A.B. hardliner, although she too would reform, earn parole and leave the madness behind.

Manson was upset that his group was tumbling away from him like oat husks in the morning breeze. He issued a bunch of useless threats, against Cathy "Cappy" Gillies, Ruth Ann Morehouse and Mary Brunner for daring to go their own way. A Manson letter from around this time succinctly depicts his disintegrating circle of disciples: "Also tell Cappy she knows what she's got coming. She got no place to hide. . . . Yes Cappy I'm gonna git you, if you don't clean up. . . . I gave you my Good and you played me fool and if you can write Ruth, tell her faces in the night and her sister is first for helping her. . . . Mary's cut her own head off when I see her. . . ." Ruth

Ann Morehouse had moved to Nevada, helped by her sister, and had finally left the world of the X-heads.

Leslie Van Houten had begun her reformation. She had written some short stories, one of which, "Ima Fibbin," had been printed in an anthology of prison fiction. A later psychiatric evaluation noted that during a year that lasted into 1975, Van Houten "began to re-enter the 'normal world of house and car payments, raising children, that sort of thing.' People once again became people in her clearing vision and were no longer 'shells with egos' as Charlie had taught." She began to feel great guilt, she told her counselor, over what she had helped do to Rosemary LaBianca. She felt Mrs. LaBianca's "presence," and it "wiped her out," to use the vernacular of the 1960s. She wept and felt the terror of coming to terms with what she had done and what she had to do to restructure her whole being.

Tex Watson began working at the medical and drug dispensary at Folsom Prison. He had a German girl friend who visited him regularly. Early in the year he'd heard from a chaplain that both Susan Atkins and Bruce Davis had converted to Christianity. Watson recalled those days in 1971 when he lay in the hospital wasting away, a feeding tube greased into his nose, and he'd silently recited in his brain the 23rd Psalm.

By June 15, Watson himself was born again and was baptized by a student chaplain in a large plastic laundry cart outside the prison chapel. He went all the way under the water, as he put it, to "die there with Christ." Later Mr. Watson, as well as Bruce Davis, would become a preacher in the prison chapel.

Brenda McCann had been released after serving time for being an accessory to the murder of the Willetts in 1972, and reportedly she had left off direct connection with the family.

It looked like the so-called family was in permanent and bitter little shreds. Then came the summer of 1975. The summer of Ecokill.

Ecokill was a ghastly twisting of the message of the environmental movement, in the service of which Sandy Good and Squeaky Fromme reunited for their final P.R. work together. The girls who had been Manson's antennae six years before when first arrested, and whom M had used to find out who was saying what to the police, were now performing their final chores as the go-fers of gore.

There had been a change in the attire of Sandra Good and Squeaky Fromme. They traipsed around Sacramento wearing long red gowns with red hoods. The image rip-off continued. In 1969 it had been music, sexual freedom, communal life and roaming, in 1975 it was ecology and save the redwoods, messages delivered with a special Manson family twist. Sandy and Squeaky formed a corporation called Good/Fromme, Inc., whose purpose was "to clean up the earth." Throughout the summer they visited various industrial plants in California announcing "some serious problems" relative to gore if the companies did not reduce factory smog emissions. They fired off letters to industrial polluters with similar warnings.

Meanwhile, as he worked out the format for the order of rainbow, Manson developed a tough antipornography stance. Women were to hide their bodies. They were to carry prayer beads and were instructed to conduct morning prayer-chants. Only television was to be allowed, and newspapers and magazines were to be abolished. Violence on film was to be banned, since M was now rather belatedly concerned that it could wire people up for gore. "We're nuns now . . . we're waiting for our Lord," Sandy Good said.

Manson's writings for the 1974–75 time period indicate he was expanding his thinking to include geoplanning. That had always been one of the Helter Skelter's structural flaws. What were NATO, the Eastern Bloc, and the rest of the world going to be doing when the communications in the Hole beneath Death Valley crackled with static about a new U.S. government headed by someone who picked up his world view from the White Double Album?

He advocated things like putting "the money on a computer—a credit card like" and the reestablishment of "CCC camps—for young people to reseed the earth," and he would also "put the blame on Nixson [sic] and the Pope."

As for the language, he was in favor of paring it down

to 300 essential words, "and we'll sing them." He would "clean up movies and morals, have new marriage laws in threes, fives, tens, twenties, and forties and eighties till everyone is married," and he favored the seat of world government in China.

There was not, however, with this change in philosophy a drift towards nonviolence. In early July of 1975, Squeaky and Sandy appeared in their hooded red robes at Sacramento news offices to deliver a press release titled "Manson Is Mad at Nixson." The text was compiled from Manson's writings. The only obvious threat against President Ford were the words: "If Nixson's reality wearing a new face [i.e., Ford] continues to run this country against the law, your homes will be bloodier than the Tate-LaBianca houses and Mi Lai [sic] put together. The truth of your fear's ignorance and unconcern for your children will come running through your bedrooms with butcher knives."

As violent as that was, it was received in the media with such inattentiveness and ho hum that it may have spurred Squeaky into grim escalation. Paul Fitzgerald spoke to the Sandy-Squeaky duo during that summer, and they warned him something "drastic" was going to happen to put people on notice. Fitzgerald noted that "of late, the media considered them trivial and laughable, and they had become more and more outrageous in their statements in order to attract attention." They had become pathetic but classic late 1960s-early 1970s media freaks hooked on ink and tube.

It was a double-headed sort of attention—for themselves, and for the cause of getting Manson a new trial. Manson wanted to be tried along with Nixon in the same courtroom. He wanted at last to be allowed to be his own counsel, which had been denied at the Tate-LaBianca trial. He wanted to show prosecutor Vince Bugliosi a thing or two. And, most of all, he wanted to be free, to head back out to the fray in order "to pick up the Fear."

And then came the cow tongue.

I received a phone call from my agent in New York City on June 18, 1975. Someone had sent E.P. Dutton, the publisher of the first edition of this book, a package dripping with odoriferous ooze. The package was opened, and—ugh!—there in a shoe box was a cow's tongue, resplendent with tastebuds! On the wrapper were twelve Christmas stamps with winged and red-robed angels. The package was addressed with large red letters to "Ed Sanders, Author of *The Family*." It joined the other weird letters I had received, one with a bloody fingerprint, as a result of Manson interest. The tongue had been postmarked from Sacramento, California. I made arrangements with an attorney to ask red-robed Squeaky if she had sent it, but by the time that was set up, she had already lunged at Ford.

In August of 1975, Stan Atkinson, who had covered the Tate-LaBianca trial for the NBC affiliate in Los Angeles and was now with KTVV in Oakland, scored the first exclusive television interview with Manson. It was broadcast in five segments the week of August 15.

In the interview Atkinson referred to M as a mass murderer, after which he received a phone call from Squeaky, to let him know that she and Sandy were "deeply concerned."

A few days later, Atkinson filmed Susan Atkins, who broke down and wept during the interview. Only in the past year during her Christian conversion had she felt full compassion and grief for her victims. She now believed that she had been brainwashed through drugs into believing that death was an illusion.

Squeaky Fromme belonged to the "ice cream" branch of the family. A Los Angeles homicide officer once described going out to the Spahn Ranch to pick up a couple of the M women for some offense or other, and they projected such an innocent image that he did not handcuff them. When they passed an ice cream stand they asked him to get them a cone, and he did, apparently leaving the "suspects" unattended in the police car. Squeaky had a bit of the ice cream cone in her personality, and she seemed very skillful at triggering off in older men a confusion of fatherliness and sexuality.

She was not nearly as violent mouthed as her partner, Sandy Good. Reading through about a hundred pages of Squeaky's correspondence for 1973–75, one does not find one sentence of violence or anger, other than she was miffed at Vincent Bugliosi's description of her in *Helter Skelter*. So it's not really hard to understand why the police might have considered her more a red-haired groupie of gore, than a threat to President Ford.

The Hendrickson-Merrick documentary of the family has one memorable sequence in which Squeaky caresses a rifle, saying, "You have to make love with it. You have to know every part of it so that you could pick it up any second and shoot." This philosophy of gun-fondle broke down, thankfully, when Squeaky went for Ford, because she forgot to pull back the slide chamber on her .45 caliber automatic pistol and thus, probably deliberately, was not able to fire.

Ford's visit to the state capitol in September of 1975 was not a secret. Ten days earlier, on August 26, Santa Barbara police had arrested a couple of guys at a motel who admitted to a plan to shoot the president during the Sacramento visit. The two suspects, Gary DeSur and Preston Mayo, were arrested after a multistate spree of bad checks and robbed motels. DeSur had escaped from Warm Springs State Hospital in Montana, where he had been placed after an earlier threat against the President. Under questioning by Detective Robert Zapata of the Santa Barbara P.D., DeSur stated that they planned to break into an armory in the San Francisco area, steal rifles, dynamite and a sniper scope, and then go get Ford. The two had left an automobile at the Hollywood-Burbank airport containing written plans for the operation, and the Secret Service was alerted.

The night of September 4, Ford slept on the sixth floor of the Senator Hotel, just a half mile from the frustrated Good-Fromme, Inc., attic on P Street. The next morning Ford spoke at a packed breakfast, returned to the hotel, then left at 9:55 A.M. for the one-block stroll to the capitol grounds and a meeting with Governor Brown in the governor's office.

Squeaky also took a stroll. She posted a letter to Sergeant Paul Whiteley of the L.A. County sheriff's office the same day—a final one, since he has never heard from her since.

She donned a bright red gown with a mammiferous neckline and upon her head what appeared to be a red peaked elf cap. Squeaky placed the .45 into a holster, hidden by the floor-length dress. It was only about eight blocks from 17255 P to the capitol, where she asked a policeman if this was where Ford was to take his walk.

Then the president appeared, surrounded by those wary Secret Service agents. The crowd lined up for possible presidential flesh-press and began to applaud. Ford paused to greet the crowd.

It was then that freaky Squeaky raised up her arm, gun jutting forward, and pushed through the small crowd at the president's side. The gun was just about two feet away from him. There is some indication that Ford may have made a preliminary move to shake the gun hand, when he froze. At the same moment a former Naval Intelligence, now crack Secret Service, agent named Larry Buendorf batted the gun away with a quick, sure hand, as valuable to an agent of the presidential protection service as it is to a guard in the NBA. Agent Buendorf grabbed at the hammer of the weapon and shoved Fromme to the ground.

Sergeant Bill Gleason had been driving on the Long Beach Freeway, listening to an all-news station, KFWB, in Los Angeles. "I was listening to it, driving on the freeway, and they said that somebody pulled a gun on President Ford. Then a couple of minutes later, it was a red-haired girl. And I'm thinking, 'Jeez, there's only one red-haired girl I know that'd do something like that. That was Squeaky.' Then a few minutes later, they said it was somebody in the Manson family."

Later President Ford spoke in Malibu, at Pepperdine University, and Sergeant Gleason and another officer from the sheriff's department went to work with the Secret Service, furnishing mug shots of the family. And then they went out and mingled with the crowd of 10,000 and looked for the faces of M, not too easy a task.

Gleason felt Squeaky "had no intention of hurting Ford. She knew how to operate that gun. We have pictures of her and Mary Brunner firing weapons that we'd picked up over the years. So they were both very familiar with weapons. Squeaky just wanted to get Manson's name in the paper, I feel."

Whether or not she intended to kill President Ford, it is clear that, by her act, Squeaky Fromme had ended her eight-year career as a Manson family drudge. In doing so, she managed to upstage them all—Manson, Sandy Good, and the International Council of Gore, or whatever it was called.

And she picked up oodles of ink! She was on the cover of *Time* for September 15, 1975, and *Newsweek* the same week. *Newsweek* ran a telling photo of her with an agony-filled face being subdued by four Secret Service agents, reaching down to hold her hands and pry the .45 away from her. *Time* ran a full-page ad in the *New York Times* that showed her holding a rifle beneath the headline "The Girl Who Almost Killed Ford."

On September 11, Sandy Good released a list of seventy governmental and business leaders and companies, saying they were marked for death if they didn't stop polluting the earth. She and a recent convert, Susan "Heather" Murphy, a former nurse, gave a bunch of threat letters to a friend and asked him to mail them. Instead, he turned them over to the FBI.

The FBI, thankfully enough, found that the People's Court of Retribution existed only in Sandy Good's flambent mind. Sandy, on the other hand, claimed that "the International People's Court of Retribution is a wave of assassins of some 2,000 people throughout the world who love the earth, the children and the working people and their own lives. They have been silently watching executives, and chairmen of the boards and their wives of companies and industries that in any way harm the air, water, earth and wildlife of the world." Good also claimed the People's Court had a list of some seventy-five executives of polluting corporations who were, to use an Intelligence phrase, to be "terminated with prejudice." She was happy to release this list in September of 1975 to the Associated Press, but the police found no cause to arrest her just then.

Ruth Ann Morehouse, the famous Ouish and once the lover of the biker they had nicknamed Donkey Dick Dan DeCarlo, was arrested in early October on a four-year-old warrant for the Honolulu dopeburger caper during the Manson trial. When she was to have been sentenced back in April of 1971, she was almost nine months pregnant, and she fled to avoid giving birth in jail. Her sister in Carson City helped her. Later, she married a guy in Reno, had another child and was still wearing at the time of her arrest the bandages from plastic surgery to remove the hideous X on her forehead. She wanted no part of the family and had become, *mirabile dictu*, a stern, doting mom.

On November 26, 1975, a jury in Sacramento found Squeaky guilty of trying to assassinate the president. Squeaky had wanted an assault conviction rather than attempted assassination. She did not testify, and she refused for part of the trial to go into the courtroom, viewing the proceedings in the holding tank over closed-circuit TV. President Ford's testimony was heard by means of a twenty-minute videotape.

Squeaky was sentenced on December 19 to life imprisonment. Later that month, Sandra Good and Susan Murphy were indicted for trying to mail the death threats to the seventy putative polluters.

It was a case that had a hard time a-healin'.

27

Hard Time A-Healin': The Family Splits Up (1976–1988)

1976

In early 1976 Manson turned down *Hustler* magazine for an interview, apparently shocked at the kinky montages in the issues the editor sent him.

In March, Sandra Good and Susan Murphy stood trial for the conspiracy to mail the ecokill letters. Both acted as their own attorneys and both received long sentences.

Late that month, an adaptation of Vincent Bugliosi's *Helter Skelter* was shown as a two-part CBS movie. Squeaky watched it in jail, and she told the *San Diego Union* she found the characterization of Manson "repulsive." Saith she: "I wouldn't have followed the man they showed the American public for ten minutes."

Manson was sent again to the prison psychiatric facility at Vacaville, California, where he was to reside until 1985. Aryan Brotherhood member Kenneth Como and another guy had attacked Charlie in the prison yard, prompting the move.

On July 20, a psychiatric consultant for the California Institute for Women, R. L. Flanagan, M.D., prepared a three-page evaluation of Lesie Van Houten and concluded that "the overall prognosis in terms of her becoming a productive and contributing member in the community is considered to be favorable. From a psychiatric point of view, there are no contraindications for parole consideration."

Three weeks later, Van Houten received a break when a California court of appeal dismissed her conviction. After the trial, the defense had prepared an extensive appeal of the conviction, raising at least sixty-five points the attorneys felt were reversible errors.

The eighty-four-page court of appeal opinion was written by Judge J. Vogel for the three-judge panel. Although Leslie Van Houten's conviction was reversed, Judge Vogel's opinion affirmed the judgments on the other defendants in all respects except that "they were modified to impose a penalty of life imprisonment."

Among the points rejected by the court of appeal was the claim that a change of venue should have been granted because of the adverse publicity. "Even if the venue had been changed," Judge Vogel wrote, "nothing could have prevented the public media from swinging its attention to that place."

Nor did the court of appeal find disturbing the prosecution's premise that communal sexual activities could tend to prep a perp for murder. Judge Vogel: "To amplify the extent of Manson's influence on the family, testimony of certain sexual activities was presented [referring to Manson directing orgies at the Spahn ranch, some of them involving force]. Although the evidence concerning these events was indeed dramatic, it nevertheless reasonably tended to show Manson's leadership of the family, the inference being that if Manson could induce bizarre sexual activities, he could induce homicidal conduct."

And what about Manson's vehement, long-standing desire to be his own attorney? "Manson's contention that he was prejudiced by not being permitted to represent himself," the judge wrote, "is not supported by the record."

In the one part of the appeal accepted, a new trial was ordered for Leslie Van Houten, because the court felt that when her attorney Ron Hughes disappeared and a substitute, Mr. Maxwell Keith, was made just as the trial was coming to a close, Ms. Van Houten should then have been given a new trial separate from the others. Wrote Judge Vogel: "Confronted with these circumstances the trial court should have granted the mistrial. It was not necessary to compel Van Houten to go forward with Keith, however convenient that may have been for the court or respondent. Under our system of justice expedience is never exalted over the interest of fair trial and due process."

Other than the Van Houten reversal, the court of appeal opinion was a vindication of the prosecutorial methods of Bugliosi, Stovitz, Kay and Musich and of the decisions from the bench of Judge Charles Older.

In December, Leslie was brought from the California Insitute for Women at Frontera to the Sybil Brand jail in Los Angeles, in preparation for her retrial.

1977

On January 26, 1977, Lawrence Merrick, producer of *Manson*, the 1970 documentary created by Robert Hendrickson, was shot dead as he entered the offices of his production company and school, the Merrick Studio Academy of Dramatic Arts. The killer was five-foot-eight, midtwenties and heavyset, wearing a yellow knit cap and gold-rimmed sunglasses. The killer got out of there quickly and was never caught. The guy had apparently been hanging around the studio for a two-day period. A student at the school said the suspect had asked about the M Documentary. "He asked me about the movie. He wanted to talk about *Helter Skelter*."

Sharon Tate apparently had once been a pupil at Merrick's film-production and acting school. *Manson* had been nominated for an Academy Award in 1972. It can be found in video stores for those who hunger for a murd-moll breeze of sleaze from 1970.

Things had been going well for Roman Polanski. In 1973 he had directed the very successful movie *Chinatown*, starring Jack Nicholson and Faye Dunaway. Later he had staged Alban Berg's opera *Lulu* at the Festival of Two Worlds in Spoleto, Italy. He made a movie, *Tenant*, that was shown in Cannes in 1976. He applied for French citizenship, on the grounds that he had been born there, and it was granted.

Polanski had also staged *Rigoletto* for the Bavarian

State Opera in Munich. He had a deal for $600,000 to adapt and direct Lawrence Sander's thriller *The First Deadly Sin*, about a publishing executive who becomes a serial killer with an ice axe on the streets of Manhattan.

Mr. Polanski returned to the United States and was in Los Angeles in early 1977. He'd renewed his interest in still photography and had guest-edited the Christmas 1976 issue of *Vogue* of France. Currently he had an assignment to do a photo spread for another magazine.

On March 11, Roman Polanski was arrested for having sex with a thirteen-year-old girl at the home of Jack Nicholson, whose house he had borrowed for a photo session for the magazine assignment. Mr. Nicholson was away and unaware the house was being borrowed. The case created Tate-LaBianca-type headlines, and on August 8, the eighth anniversary of his wife's death, Mr. Polanski pled guilty. The judge he was facing, Lawrence Rittenband, had handled some of the pretrial hearings in the Manson cases. Rittenband ordered Polanski to undergo psychiatric evaluation prior to sentencing at the California Men's Prison at Chino, where Polanski served forty-two unpleasant days during the fall.

The retrial of Leslie Van Houten began in March and lasted four months. Steven Kay was the prosecutor. The jury went out in July and after nine days was deadlocked, seven for first-degree murder, five for manslaughter. A third trial was scheduled.

Ms. Van Houten continued to be held at the Sybil Brand jail in L.A. till December 27, when she was released on $200,000 bail, which was raised by friends and relatives. It looked for a few months like sweet freedom was hers. She worked as a secretary for a lawyer and lived with a female author who was at the time working on a book about her.

Around November 1, Sergeant Bill Gleason was contacted by a lieutenant at the prison in Tracy where Steve Grogan was housed. He said that Clem wanted to talk to them and show them where Shorty Shea's body was. Clem was being denied parole, and he was bidding for a deal.

Gleason and his partner went to Chino and talked with Mr. Grogan and eventually flew him down to Los Angeles. Clem was taken to the barren site of the burned-out Spahn Ranch and showed them where the body was buried, at the base of a steep embankment.

Officers were impressed with Clem's change. And so was I, because of all of the male members of the family (except Watson, Davis and Manson), this young man with the nickname Scramblehead had seemed the most bonkers. It's necessary to allow for human change for the better, and young Mr. Grogan, who had initially become ensnared in the family by virtue of living with his parents near the Spahn Ranch, became rehabilitated and judged suitable for release.

As Gleason recalls, "It's amazing. He went to school in prison and became quite interested in airplanes and got an A-and-E license, which is an airframe and engine mechanics license, because we flew him down to Los Angeles, and he and the pilot were having a great time talking about airplanes."

They waited a month before digging for Shea because they didn't want to put any pressure on Clem in prison for snitching. After thirty days, Gleason and his partner, Barry Jones, went out one afternoon and started digging with shovels. After a couple of hours, they found him. The skeleton was intact, thus severing a key family legend—that Shea was decapitated, sexually assaulted, and dismembered, a tale told over and over in the eery glare of campfires. Gleason thought it "was just a story that they dreamed up to frighten the girls and everybody to keep them from talking."

"Where was it?" I asked. Gleason: "It was between the old road and the railroad tracks. And there was a parking area there where they pulled off the side of the road and killed him and pushed him over the bank."

In addition to the thrill of having a case finally closed, the officers were very glad to find Mr. Shea for a very practical reason: There had always been the faint dread of Shorty Shea showing up. Attorney Paul Fitzgerald: "They really did want to find this body. And they were subject to a lot of kidding and a lot of some good-natured and some not so good-natured ribbing about the fact that they railroaded these Manson people to jail; that this was all fictitious, it was all bullshit; that this Shorty Shea, the flake, would turn up one of these days to the embarrassment of all concerned."

A couple of years later I had dinner with Burton Katz, now Judge Katz, who had prosecuted Clem. Judge Katz told me he felt Clem was rehabilitated and fit for parole. It would take years. Clem's parole date was set in 1983, and he was released in 1985, due in good part to the recommendation of Burt Katz.

In other 1977 news, the sweet-voiced violinist Gypsy Share married Kenneth Como of the Aryan Brotherhood. She was living near Folsom Prison to be near her husband, still in prison for the 1971 Hawthorne shootout. With her was her seven-year-old child, supposedly fathered by Steve Grogan.

Susan Atkins's autobiography, *Child of Satan, Child of God,* tracing her life through the murders to her Christian conversion, was published by a religious press.

1978

In 1978, those who were convicted in 1971 and freed from the death penalty in 1972 were eligible for parole. The average jail term for first-degree murder in California is ten and a half to eleven years, and women tend, on the whole, to serve a lot less time than men when charged with the same crimes.

Just before his sentencing in February, Roman Polanski fled to Paris, afraid of a prison sentence Judge Rittenband had hinted he might impose. Mr. Polanski would stay overseas for over eleven years.

Van Houten's third trial began in March. She hoped for a manslaughter or second-degree murder conviction, which would have allowed for her to be set free on time served. Her attorney was Maxwell Keith; the prosecutors were Dino Fulgoni and the redoubtable Steven Kay. The day after the Fourth of July, Leslie Van Houten was convicted—not of manslaughter, but of first-degree murder. The defense had called four psychiatrists, three of whom concluded that she could be found guilty of manslaughter due to diminished mental capacity caused by mental illness.

Ms. Van Houten freely admitted her part in the killing of Mrs. LaBianca and was remorseful, but there was just no way the defense could overcome the miracle of modern photography.

The prosecution introduced twenty photos of Leno and Rosemary LaBianca and then seven photographs from Sharon Tate's house. Although she was being tried for the LaBianca murders alone, the photos of Cielo Drive were apparently shown to corroborate the testimony of chief witness Linda Kasabian. Most of them were handed to the jury toward the end of the trial.

One juror had been excused early in the trial because of the ghastly photos and the bloody testimony of the coroner, Dr. Thomas Noguchi. The photo of Mr. LaBianca's throat with the knife embedded in it has to be about the most horrifying shot in all the history of photography. The case was appealed, with Ms. Van Houten represented by Paul Fitzgerald, but the conviction was upheld.

A few days later, Patricia Krenwinkel came up for parole. On his own, without instructions from the district attorney, Stephen Kay made an appearance at the July 17 hearing. The board was then called the Community Release Board. Kay had recently refreshed himself on the facts of the case in Van Houten's trial and could therefore deliver a knife-slash-by-knife-slash recitation of the murders—which horrified the Community Release Board. It took Kay about two hours to recount Krenwinkel's part in the murders.

In the hall afterward, he says she swore at him and said something like, "Why'd you do that!?"

Mr. Kay began appearing at virtually all the Manson group's parole hearings. His resume indicates that he was the first district attorney in California to attend a parole hearing to oppose release of a defendant serving a life sentence. Over the next ten years he would attend over thirty-five M group hearings.

Tex Watson's autobiography, *Will you Die for Me?*, was published in 1977. It is a rather tedious read, and from the point of view of clearing up some of the opaque oddnesses of this case, it churns up no new and interesting information.

In the summer and fall, Roman Polanski directed the movie *Tess*, from Thomas Hardy's *Tess of the D'Urbervilles*. The book had been left by his wife in their London bedroom just before she'd sailed on the *Queen Elizabeth II* to New York on the way to Cielo Drive in 1969. It starred the then-unknown Nastassia Kinski, with filming, by necessity as well as by choice, occurring in Europe.

In November the CBS show *60 Minutes* broadcast an interview with Polanski during the shooting of *Tess*. Interviewer Mike Wallace asked him about the themes of despair in his work, to which Polanski answered, "Yes, there is a lot of that in my pictures." "Why?" asked Wallace. Polanski: "I don't think that I have a particular reason for thinking otherwise."

On November 16, Manson came up the first time for parole. He told the Community Release Board he wanted to return to the desert. In denying the parole, one board member noted that the magnitude of M's crimes "eclipses the imagination." It's just difficult for a person to convince his parole board he's a good risk when he has a swastika cut into his forehead. By 1978, Manson had cut the swastika in the correct direction, as opposed to his mirror-image early attempts of 1971.

1979

The question of parole for Ms. Van Houten continued. In January, Dino Fulgoni, who with Stephen Kay had prosecuted the third trial, wrote to the Community Release Board: "I would suggest a period of evaluation of Miss Van Houten by a very practical-minded female professional. The reason for my designating the sex of the evaluator is that she has in my experience proven her ability to charm most men to the extent that they become 'Van Houten advocates.' " The following year Van Houten would be evaluated by a female professional psychologist, who had good things to say.

On January 30, Ms. Van Houten met with the Community Release Board for her first parole hearing. She was turned down.

On February 1, Catherine "Gypsy" Share Como was indicted by a federal grand jury in Sacramento for having jumped bail while making a false statement in a loan application. Gypsy was released on $10,000 bail on February 5, and she failed to appear for her arraignment seven days later.

The summer of 1979 was, of course, the tenth anniversary of the murders, and several interesting articles were written by Tate-LaBianca veteran reporters, including Linda Deutsch of the Associated Press and Bill Farr, then a reporter for the *Los Angeles Times*.

At the time of the tenth anniversary, Krenwinkel, Van Houten and Atkins were all part of the general prison population at the California Institute for Women at Frontera. Atkins, still a born-again Christian, was working as a clerk typist in the psychiatric unit; Krenwinkel was a prison janitor and taking college courses; Van Houten was a medical clerk and editing the prison newspaper while continuing to take correspondence courses with Antioch College.

Linda Kasabian was raising her four children in New England. Tex Watson was preaching the Gospel in the church at the California Men's Colony at San Luis Obispo. Steven Grogan was still in the process of rehabilitation at the prison in Chino.

Manson, on the other hand, was not housed in the "main line" with other prisoners but in a special twenty-one-cell tier, where he had become proficient at the guitar. A prison counselor at Vacaville noted he had broken two guitars and a TV set in fits of rage.

Lynne Fromme was transferred in August from the federal pen in Pleasanton, California, to the maximum-security prison at Alderson, West Virginia, after she apparently went after another prisoner with a hammer.

In October there appeared a widely noted newspaper article by long-time Manson family chronicler Mary Neiswender about a possible alliance between the M group and the Symbionese Liberation Army to raise money for an escape from prison. Neiswender quoted Sacramento police detectives as estimating that Manson family members and SLA associates in jail had accumulated about $1.5 million over the last two years with a sophisticated credit-card scam in California, Oregon, Nevada and Arizona. The SLA, it will be recalled, had been crushed in a fiery burn-out and shoot-out in 1974.

On November 28, Manson was again denied parole by the Community Relations Board. M didn't show, although he sent the Board $200 in Monopoly money and a letter.

1980

A group called Friends of Leslie had its first meeting in January of 1980. Their goal was to set up a favorable climate for the release of Leslie Van Houten. Friends of Leslie held weekly gatherings, with membership rising to around a hundred people. They began appearing on radio shows and in newspaper articles, urging her release, and extolling her complete recovery from Spahn-Goler armageddon.

Van Houten had a hearing on January 17. There were more than a hundred letters deposited with the parole board, now called the State Board of Prison Terms, from psychiatrists, friends and corrections officials in support of her release.

To them Van Houten was thirty, mature, rehabilitated and prepared. The deputy district attorney Steven Kay, however, was again able to deliver a stab-by-stumble-by-scream account of the killings, which horrified the three members of the board. After the board had denied the parole, Mr. Kay said he felt she should wait until she was at least forty: "I'd feel better releasing a middle-aged, forty-year-old Leslie Van Houten than a thirty-year-old Leslie Van Houten."

In August of 1980, Manson was given a prison gardening job at the Protestant chapel at Vacaville, but he remained an inmate in the prison's Willis Unit, a special security area. It was a humane decision to allow him, after so many years, to be outdoors in the mornings and early afternoons.

In September there was a celebrity auction in L.A. to help pay legal fees for *Times* reporter Bill Farr and the group known as Investigative Reporters and Editors, which had run up a combined legal debt of more than $100,000 fighting Farr's legal problems regarding the publication of the Virginia Graham "celebrity hit list" interview back in October of 1970. More than a hundred celebrities donated items to the auction, among them a date with Burt Reynolds, Debbie Boone's Bible, and Charlton Heston's tennis racquet.

1981

A psychological evaluation for the Board of Prison Terms prepared in late November 1980 for the 1981 calendar by a staff psychologist at Leslie Van Houten's prison noted that "in all the years since 1974, all of the reports have indicated no findings of mental disorder or organic impairment and no present violent or dangerous tendencies, along with favorable parole prognosis. One psychiatrist went so far as to note that the changes that he had observed in Leslie over the years had made him a believer in the process of rehabilitation.

"I would . . . like to repeat in summary that in my clinical opinion, Leslie's personality growth is genuine. I find no contraindications to parole but, rather, many positive attributes and strengths which should serve her well in the future in terms of redeeming herself in the society she has wronged. At this time she has the experiences of herself that are imperative to grounding a person in reality and providing them with their own answers. I believe that should Leslie Van Houten be permitted to re-enter society, she would not again violate its mores."

On April 22, 1981, the parole board again denied Van Houten's release.

Roman Polanski's movie *Tess* opened for a week at the end of December 1980, in New York City, to make it eligible for the Academy Awards. In the credits at film's end there was a dedication, "To Sharon." Columbia Pictures distributed it in the spring of 1981. In the summer Polanski directed Peter Schafer's *Amadeus* in Warsaw, during the time of the Solidarity uprisings.

Manson appeared June 12 on NBC-TV's "Tomorrow Coast to Coast," hosted by Tom Snyder, and Manson's performance proved him an adroit mass-media evilness symbol. It was a jolt of electro-ink for M, which stirred controversy among those who said, Why give air time to a murdering mind? Snyder asked him at one point during the fifty-minute interview what he thought of women, to which M replied, in tones of snitchophobia, "Oh, I like them, yeh, they're nice, they're put together well and everything, and they're soft and spongy—long as they kept their mouths shut and do what they're supposed to do."

When Snyder challenged him on this rather limited view of women, Manson added, "Oh, well, I don't want her snitchin' on me."

On July 12, Pat Krenwinkel was again denied parole. On November 3, ditto for M. "I'm not ready for parole," M told the board. He visualized a very distant release date: "By the time I get out," he told them, "I'll parole to space."

1982

For her release hearing in 1982, Leslie Van Houten had acquired over 900 signatures to a petition seeking her freedom. It looked like she'd be released.

Alarmed by this, deputy district attorney Steven Kay contacted Sharon Tate's mother, Doris. Mrs. Tate recalls Kay saying, "You always said you would help, and I need your help now."

"That's when I began to come out of my shell," she said. Till then, she had gone through a long and painful mourning. She had opened a beauty salon, expanded, and stayed to herself. In 1979 she had been one of the founders of the Los Angeles chapter of a nationwide organization known as Parents of Murdered Children.

"To tell the truth, it took me ten years to get out and say 'I've got to do something about these people.' "

After Mr. Kay's phone call asking for help in keeping Leslie Van Houten in jail, Mrs. Tate became a powerful citizen activist on behalf of the victims and relatives of victims of violent crime. She began work on a cumulative list, must of it compiled in 1983 and 1984, of those opposed to the release of any of the murderers of Cielo Drive or Wavery Place. The list ultimately stood at 352,000 and was sent by the boxload to the parole board.

She also helped in a petition drive to keep Sirhan

Sirhan in jail, after the Community Release Board had set an actual release date of September 1, 1984, for Robert Kennedy's killer.

She campaigned for Proposition 8, the "Victims' Bill of Rights," which was approved by California voters in 1982. Proposition 8 allows a victim to be present and to make a statement to the court at the time of sentencing. It provides for the victim to be given any presentence investigation reports. It allows impact statements by victims and close relatives of victims at parole hearings, and it gives them access to any documentation, including psychiatric reports, which the parole board has before it to guide its review.

Proposition 8 also outlawed plea bargaining for certain offenses—murder, rape, arson and armed robbery.

Something happened around 1982 that clouded for the rest of the decade Mr. Kay's belief that a middle-aged Leslie Van Houten would be suitable for release. Prison policy allows inmates to get married. All the Tate-LaBianca defendants, except Manson and Krenwinkel, have been married at one time or another during their incarcerations. So it was with Leslie Van Houten. She married a man named Bill Cywin, who got into trouble—some bad check charges, and he was caught with a women's prison-guard uniform in his possession.

Van Houten divorced Mr. Cywin, but Mr. Kay thought it revealed bad judgment on her part to have taken up with him in the first place and that she must have known about the stolen guard uniform. In Mr. Kay's mind, she was no longer a proper subject for release. Of course, if decent women were to be judged by the sleazebags they sometimes marry, there would be millions of women maljudged.

At his 1982 parole hearing Manson sported a black T-shirt with a white skull and crossbones. No hope, no redemption, no remorse.

1983

On December 27, 1983, the Beach Boys' Dennis Wilson joined a grim procession of famous rock and roll drummers who passed on many years too soon. He drowned after diving off a friend's boat at Marina Del Rey, near L.A.

1984

On September 25, 1984, Manson was in the hobby shop at the Vacaville psychiatric prison when one Jan Holmstrom doused him with paint thinner and set it on fire. M had reportedly objected to Holmstrom's chanting of the Hare Krishna mantra. Holmstrom, a former member of the Hare Krishna sect, had shotgunned his father, a Pasadena doctor, in 1974. Manson suffered burns over 18 percent of his body, most badly on his face, hands and scalp.

The year 1984 marked the first time survivors and relatives could make impact statements at parole hearings under the strictures of Proposition 8. Doris Tate brought 350,000 signatures with her when she came to Tex Watson's hearing to oppose his release. Throughout the 1980s she testified at the hearings for Atkins and Watson, the ones who had killed her daughter and grandson.

Doris Tate ran for the state assembly as a Democrat in 1984, lost, and shifted her affiliation to the Republican Party in subsequent years.

1985

On March 18, 1985, Sandy Good turned down a conditional release from Alderson Federal Penitentiary in West Virginia, where she had been incarcerated for some ten years after her conviction for the big-business ecokill letters of 1975. She had been given a fifteen-year sentence. She was forty at the time, and she refused to promise she would not associate with the Manson myth.

She also objected to being placed in a halfway house among the good people of Camden, New Jersey.

On May 18, Tex Watson, now the Rev. Watson, was again denied parole. Colonel Paul Tate said at the hearing, "That man should never, never, never be turned out into society."

Also in May, Van Houten was rejected for walking papers.

On July 19, Manson was transferred from the shrink prison in Vacaville, after a nine-year stay, back to San Quentin.

On December 7, Vermont's fine governor, Madeline Kunin, was attending a National Governors Association meeting at Lake Tahoe, Nevada, when reporters gave her the news that Sandy Good was out of the slams and living in a "supervised" house near Burlington, Vermont.

1986

In January of 1986, Sandy Good was spotted at a Pizza Hut in Burlington.

In his parole hearing on February 4, M spoke of ATWA as his new religion—Air, Trees, Water and Animals. "I am Abraxas," he intoned, "the son of God, the son of Darkness, and I stand behind all the courts of the world. Until I get my rights, no one has rights."

Reading the text, one encounters the familiar I-am-a-deity fluent aphasia common to Mansonia. Again he pretended to love the earth with a crazed racism while preaching the subjugation of women. He mentioned he might go to Libya or Iran or "join the revolution down south somewhere and try to save my life on the planet Earth."

Stephen Kay was there, and he spoke of Mr. M as "a caged, vicious, wild animal who, if released, would once again be free to prey on innocent victims." It was M's sixth parole hearing. His long gray hair, beard, glasses, and a swastika on his forehead gave evidence that the click-track of time was bearing him toward old age. The next hearing was set for 1989, three years thence.

Charlie Rose interviewed Manson for *Nightwatch* around the time of the 1986 parole hearing. Manson let forth a little more anti-Semitism in the footage than usual, saying that the children of the 1960s had "their minds set by your Jews' media" and how he had "got to seeing the Jews do run everything."

On July 11, Leslie Van Houten, now thirty-six, was again denied parole. The hearing lasted six hours, and the board was once again given a reminder lecture on the details of the murders by deputy district attorney Kay, which helped one of the board members to comment that the savagery of the murders "goes beyond description."

1987

Manson continued his role as America's death-cult hate target, a couch-potato's mild version of Bernard Marx in Orwell's *1984*. He's easy to understand, and viewers from TV chaises across the land can deliver now and then a few shudders of revulsed fascination, as when in January he was interviewed by NBC's *Today Show*.

On December 23, Squeaky Fromme was reported missing at bed check in the penitentiary at Alderson, West Virginia. She had learned that Manson might have testicular cancer and was hastening to the only "old man" she had ever had.

The front page of the *New York Post* blazed the headline "Prez Ford Assailant Flees Jail."

Ms. Fromme had been corresponding with M for about five years. She had been refusing parole hearings since becoming eligible in September of 1985—apparently satisfying the formula "my love's in jail, I'm in jail."

As in previous years, she was feeling depressed. Manson wrote to some friends in Ava, Missouri, that he had testicular cancer. He also wrote around the same time to Squeaky, describing a hunger strike he was staging but not mentioning the cancer. On the day of her escape, Fromme placed a collect call to the people in Missouri, who mentioned M's illness. Shortly thereafter, Squeaky fled the prison, apparently scaling an eight-foot perimeter fence. It was front-page news all over America.

On Christmas day she was discovered two miles from the fence.

1988

On May 9, 1988, Manson grabbed great electro-ink when NBC ran the show "Geraldo Rivera Live from Death Row." Mr. Rivera played on M's penchant for deviltry: "There's people who say you're the devil!"

Mason was ready. "Okay," he said, "I'll play. I'll be the devil." In the midst of trading insults with Mr. Rivera, Manson undertook a series of frantic gyrations of the hands. Cult experts speculated that Manson was utilizing satanic hand-jive in order to communicate with the devil crowd on the outside, calling for Mr. Rivera's demise.

Or maybe it was bullshit.

On May 13, Bruce Davis was denied parole for the eighth time. Davis, it will be recalled, is serving two life terms for the Hinman-Shea murders. The parole board felt that Davis, according to psychological profiles, harbored deep-seated anger and could still be dangerous.

In June, Squeaky Fromme was transferred from Alderson, West Virginia, to a more secure federal facility at Lexington, Kentucky. She had been sentenced to an additional fifteen months for her December break-out.

On September 9, ABC television aired a program on the Death Row, "Class of '72," referring to the year capital punishment was swept away for a while in California. Of the 106 men and women on the Row at the time, forty had subsequently been freed. Most changed their names, married and had jobs. But six were returned to prison, one after a brutal rape.

In October Tex Watson won a ruling from the U.S. 9th Circuit Court of Appeals that stated that prisoners with indeterminate sentences are entitled to have annual parole reviews. The period of review had been changed from annual to triannual. The court ruled that Watson had been promised at the beginning of his sentence an annual review once he were up for parole, and the promise couldn't retrospectively be taken away.

On October 24, the two-hour Geraldo Rivera special "Devil Worship: Exposing Satan's Underground" was one of the most watched in television history. Manson's hand-jive the previous spring had apparently helped inspire the program.

On November 8, forty-year-old Patricia Krenwinkel was denied parole for the seventh time. A recent psychological evaluation had alleged that Krenwinkel was no longer a threat to society, but the board felt that more counseling was required. "This degree of barbaric, violent behavior has no equal," Commissioner Rudolph Caspro said after a two-hour hearing. Stephen Kay held a news conference before the hearing, in which he remarked, "She's probably the most cold-blooded murderess I've ever met in my twenty-one years in the D.A.'s office. This is a person without a heart and without a soul." Kay was accompanied by Doris Tate, on hand to support Proposition 89, a referendum item that would grant the governor the power to overturn decisions made by the Board of Prison Terms.

Mrs. Tate was successful. Proposition 89 passed in the fall of 1988.

Meanwhile, on February 9, 1989, the parole board rejected M's bid for the seventh time. Charles did not appear in person, because apparently they were insisting on bringing him to the hearing in shackles.

It is a case that won't go away.

28

Where Are They Now? The Case That Won't Go Away

A few days before Christmas in 1988, the Christmas cards began piling up on my writing desk next to the computer on which I am writing this chapter. I thought I would take a few minutes to savor the fresh good wishes, the benevolent images of friendship and winter cheer, so I began opening them and placing them face out on the wooden mantle of the fireplace.

In the middle of the pile was a postcard in Christmas greens and reds. I picked it up to scan the cheer. It was a nineteenth-century print of the devil, and the writing was from Charles Manson. It wasn't friendly.

I had written him asking if I could come to San Quentin for an interview. He was apparently less than satisfied with his depiction in this book, and his anger was all over the back of the card in his scrawly handwriting. I noticed that he had drawn a swastika upon the devil's dangling red tongue.

I wrote back to Manson and basically told him to chill out. If he didn't want an interview, let's do it by mail. I typed some questions and sent them to him, adding, "It's true I'm not a fan of yours, but you should really calm down about everybody you feel has wronged you. Maybe you should try to amplify the Christian components of your personality and be more forgiving."

A few days later, I flew out to L.A. to find out what

was going on twenty years after the family's crimes. I had not paid much attention to the Manson group in about fifteen years, except to clip and file what I saw in the newspapers. In my pocket was another postcard from Charles Manson. He'd taken my suggestion and chilled out. He even semi-answered one of my questions! I had inquired about some of the groups he had said he'd met at the Spiral Staircase, the house in which he'd first stayed in Topanga when he came to L.A. in the black bus back in 1967.

In Los Angeles I stayed with Larry and Toni Larsen. During the nineteen years since we began working together researching this book, Larry Larsen had become one of the foremost private investigators in Los Angeles. He is a kind of New Age Philip Marlowe—relentlessly polite, yet politely relentless, a sleuth's sleuth who eschews violence and concentrates on "knowing the new facts early." He gets legendary results. He is an expert at finding fleeing assets. In one famous case, he located a well-hidden ten million dollars in the fiscal collapse of a shady San Diego financier.

He is also one of the foremost time-trackers. After the hideous 1980 MGM Grand Hotel fire in Las Vegas, Larsen created an exhaustive time track of the fire for a chemical company that manufactured the glue that held the ceiling tiles in place, which proved that his client's product did not contribute to the death and destruction.

I've long studied the theory of time-tracking, so I asked him about the MGM fire. "We did a time track that had time designations. We had a plus or minus in minutes as to our estimate of its accuracy. So if we said some event occurred at nine o'clock we either gave a plus or minus zero, five minutes, ten minutes, fifteen minutes, whatever the case was.

"We had times. There were people that were checking in and checking out of the hotel. There were parking-lot time stickers—those things would be time stamped. There were the phone calls and responses to both the Clark County fire department and the Las Vegas fire department; when they arrived. When radio transmissions were made by their fire fighters, they were time logged. Anywhere . . . we could find in the testimony or any of our interviews some mention of time.

"We concluded that the fire spread so rapidly from the time that open flame occurred until the time it reached the front doors of the casinos—and you're talking about just a couple of minutes—that one, if you were in the rear of the casino where the fire broke out, no one made it out. They couldn't make it out running. There wasn't enough time."

Larsen was a deputy county supervisor in Los Angeles from 1975 to 1980. In recent years he returned to the world of private investigation, at first as an associate of well-known P.I. George Barnes. Then he went out on his own and now heads up what's described on his card as "Larry J. Larsen, Trial Preparations and Investigations," which has a staff of five full-time investigators and a support staff of three. One of his daughters has become a licensed P.I. and works on her own, and the younger one is now in training. Another staff member could be classified as a rock and roll detective: She works by day for Larsen and by night she's a rock singer with a powerful voice whose band plays places like the Troubador and the Roxy.

Larsen monitors his staff with hundreds of calls from his car phone as he aches over accuracy. And it's not all compu-sleuthing. Some of his current cases reside in the moil of dirt, land grabs, and midnight stake-outs.

So it was not surprising that the very second I was brought from the airport to the Larsen house I was swooped out late in the evening in the chilly, hydrocarbonish L.A. winter air to a windy, lonely surveillance post, not in the most elegant part of town, with the air corridor overhead festooned with the landing lights of LAX-bound planes. I didn't even have time to brush my teeth, so eager was Larry Larsen to return to the surv-post, where two opposing sets of security guards were vying for control of the same deserted grocery store.

One set of guards under the command of Larsen was protecting the interests of the supermarket corporation against a putative owner who was trying to tear the building down. By mistake, a certificate of title had been delivered to the potential purchaser, who filed it and brought in bulldozers.

One was treated to the remarkable sight of Larry Larsen,

P.I., holding a quart-sized coffee container, standing in a service station across from the disputed supermarket, asking the opposing security guard, a skinny type with slightly curled upper lip, to read at 11:00 P.M. a fairly complicated legal document spread out on the coffee counter, which traced the history of the conflict.

I used Larry Larsen's private-investigation headquarters as my home base in Los Angeles. Through his help I located police officers I hadn't spoken with in seventeen years and found the current addresses of former Manson family personnel, an impossible task without the skills of the modern compu-sleuth. As in the past, he was the gentle nudge, always pointing out the piece of data I should really reach out of my way to acquire. It was advice that always brought results. My thanks to a sleuth's sleuth.

I had heard and read about Doris Tate's activities in the victims' rights movement. During the 1980s she had become a political power in California. She was willing to see me, so I drove to her hillside home in Palos Verdes to spend the afternoon. It's the same house she and her husband, Colonel Paul Tate, now retired, had purchased in 1965 and where in 1969 she had been helping her daughter prepare for the baby.

On her desk was a photo of the beautiful Sharon as she was in the flowerful 1960s.

Doris Tate has a wide, friendly face with full eyes and sad, down-turned lines at the corners of her mouth. Her voice has the tones of the mid South, and as she talked I could see it was one of the instruments of her empowerment.

I had come for the sole purpose of learning about the victims' rights movement. I was not prepared to think or to talk about the murders. As we began our interview, it was obvious that Mrs. Tate is not satisfied with the official explanation of her daughter's death. For example, Helter Skelter does not seem to fulfill in her mind the category of motive.

I interrupted to say that never in a thousand years would I have brought up the subject, but she assured me it was all right to talk about it. Nothing can undo what is done, she said, and she is convinced that Sharon's soul is alive and eternal.

So our discussion was drawn intensely to the crime scene.

She believes that the Manson group had advance word that Sharon Tate was not going to be at the house that night. Back in 1971, Larry Larsen had interviewed Jay Sebring's business partner, from whom we learned Sharon had intended to spend the night with a friend. Mrs. Tate verified that during my visit.

Vern Plumlee had said that he'd heard the family thought she wouldn't be there. My recollection was that at one point during the trial, Krenwinkel had hinted to one of the attorneys that Sharon wasn't supposed to be there.

She believes that someone might have tipped the family off. Doris Tate wondered if someone saw that Sharon's red Ferrari was gone (it was in the repair shop) and called Manson, and then the attack began.

Where was the caretaker during the murder? To this day, Pat Krenwinkel remembers entering the caretaker's house but finding no one there. Yet the caretaker swore he was there all night, listening to records, smoking pot and sleeping. Mrs. Tate has doubts.

It's a mystery she would like cleared up.

She gave me a sheet listing her activities in victim advocacy. She is a trustee of Parents of Murdered Children, a board member of Justice for Homicide Victims and Believe the Children, and the founder of the Coalition on Victims' Equal Rights, among other organizations. She has been very visible on television talk shows—Donahue, Merv Griffin, and the Today Show—as well as numerous news specials.

She is on the California State Advisory Committee on Correctional Services, to represent the viewpoint of victims, which gives her detailed access to current events in the prison system. This committee meets in different prisons each month, and from this vantage point Mrs. Tate collects great amounts of information about what's going on in the system. She has the private numbers of wardens and knows many current details about Watson, Manson, Atkins, Davis, Beausoleil, Van Houten and Krenwinkel.

Just two weeks before my visit, Mrs. Tate made an impact statement at Susan Atkins's most recent parole hearing. She told me she delivered the following remarks: "This woman is guilty of eight murders, which means that she cannot live in an unsuspecting society. I feel very sorry that these people chose this way of life. But, after eight convictions of murder, there's no turning back. And society has been kind to Ms. Atkins by overturning the death penalty, and that is more concern than she gave to my daughter."

Atkins wept during the proceedings, and Mrs. Tate said to her afterwards, "You're an excellent actress. The greatest job since Sarah Bernhardt." Ironically, it was a statement similar to the one the prosecutor had uttered eighteen years ago, when Atkins had seemed to feign illness in order stall the trial.

Mrs. Tate only testifies at the parole hearings of those who actually killed her daughter—Atkins and Watson. She said Atkins had married a twenty-five-year-old guy and then was divorced.

I had not known that prisoners could have intimate conjugal visits, so I later called the California Institute for Men at San Luis Obispo to get the rules. The rules for men's prisons and women's prisons are the same.

The policy began in the early 1980s. There are eight trailers for over 6,000 inmates at CIW, a good many of whom are married, so demand for trailers is intense. Visits last two days and are not limited just to spouses; close family members—mothers and fathers—are also permitted overnight visits. But not girl friends.

During the overnight visitations, relatives have to bring their own food, which is checked for contraband. Mrs. Tate has no objections as a victims' rights advocate, except she thinks they should be forced to use contraceptives.

Under this program, Tex Watson has married and has two children, with a third on the way as this is being typed onto the computer.

She recounted what she had said at Watson's most recent hearing. "I told him that when he entered my daughter's home—that his statement 'I'm the devil and here to do the devil's business,'—I said, 'As far as I am concerned, Mr. Watson, you're still in business.' "

"Watson has never once looked me in the eye," she said. "He can't." Watson, she told me, has recently invited her to visit him, but she is loath to go.

Both Bruce Davis and Mr. Watson are associated with

something called All Loving Ministries and are allowed to preach to the general prison population, a situation she views with suspicion, especially on the issue of "doing the devil's business." My impression was that she regards their ministry as an example of "jailhouse Christianity."

She said that Jay Sebring's parents, who live in Michigan, had recently sent her Sharon's high-school class ring. Sharon must have given it to him when they were engaged. I asked if she were in contact with Roman Polanski. She said she calls him in Paris from time to time and he calls her, although she had not read his autobiography.

Doris Tate was very, very eager to get any new information. I told her I was sending question lists to Manson. She suggested I tell him I'd visited her. Maybe that would jog his memory. She said Manson refers to her as "the old bitch."

She's going to stay on their tail, she said, as long as she is alive. She is the grieving mother, like Demeter of Greek legend, who can never be assuaged.

Larry Larsen and I decided to drive up to Inyo County to visit the high desert dune-buggy haunts of the Manson family. We also set up meetings with law-enforcement officials who had helped bring the family to justice. We drove first to Bishop, about 300 miles north of L.A., the home of several of the officers. Then we rented a four-wheel-drive vehicle and headed toward the Panamint Mountains, on the west side of Death Valley. Our goal was to bounce up rugged Goler Wash to the Barker Ranch to see what it was like after twenty years.

We invited Sergeant James Pursell of the California Highway Patrol to accompany us. Pursell, of course, was the officer who arrested Manson on October 12, 1969, as described in Chapter 23.

After the arrests, James Pursell had been promoted to sergeant and spent two years, 1974–76, in Van Nuys, near Los Angeles, then returned to Inyo County for the rest of his career. He looked remarkably similar to the time nineteen years ago when I watched him testify at the Tate-LaBianca trial. He has a smooth, lean face that knows how to smile, and he wears his short sandy brown hair in such a way that I'd bet he sported a classic 1950s flat top when he was a youth.

The distances are vast in Inyo County. It's 160 miles from Bishop to the mouth of Goler Wash. It's also refreshingly open land—no malls, no condo-manic clusters in the distance—just eye-pleasing naturalness. Ninety-eight percent of Inyo County, Pursell points out, is managed for the public by various agencies—the Forest Service, the military, the U.S. Park Service, the Bureau of Land Management, and the Los Angeles water system.

We drove south out of Bishop along Route 395 through Independence, where Pursell pointed out the Vintage Motel at the south end of town, not far from the Inyo County Courthouse. Squeaky and Sandy had once lived at the motel, doing what would now be called "damage control" prior to Manson being taken to Los Angeles. Even today these clean, Bonnie-and-Clyde cabins are only fifteen dollars a night, with the beautiful snow-topped mountains of the Great Western Divide in the background to the west. We continued to Lone Pine, where we turned east on 136 and twisted down into the salty floor of the Panamint Valley, looking with wonder on all sides at the maroons, the oranges, the grays and the white-grays, the brown-maroon-blacks of the dry and beautiful strewn boulder chaos.

We paused by the steep edge of Crowley Point, where Fillipo Tenerelli's blood-stained car was found in October 1969, another minimystery never to be solved in the equations of this or any other case.

Near the Ballarat ghost town, we whizzed past a sign, "Burro X-ing." It was sad that the Ballarat General Store had closed. Pursell told a humorous anecdote of eating a hideous plate of refried beans at the general store while investigating the case with Ranger Richard Powell back in 1969. Nearby was the fence upon which Deputy Guenther found Shorty Shea's boots impaled. I had memories of visiting the store with attorney Ron Hughes, drinking beer and swapping tales about the family with long-haired miners while the gasoline generator roared in the background, supplying barely working air conditioning.

The entrance to Goler Wash is not apparent until you are almost upon it. Near its mouth we spotted a Bureau of Land Management ranger, who checked his map for us and said it was easy to get up to the Barker Ranch. We paused for photos, with the afternoon sun making gray shadows across the narrow, twisting, forbidding, Helter Skelter slitway.

The Wash swung tortuously back and forth for about five miles as we rose from about 1,000 feet above sea level to around 4,500 feet at the Barker Ranch. The high and narrow walls of the Wash were knobbed with thousands upon thousands of barrel cacti.

The axle-cracking bumpity bump of 1969 has been replaced by a more civilized road in 1989, probably because of increased mining activity. I noticed that instead of the wooden claim stakes on the cliffsides, the modern miner uses sections of white PVC pipe.

We paused by the Lotus Mine, located high above us on the steep cliffside, from which the pregnant seventeen-year-old Kitty Lutesinger, so many years ago, testified she had spotted M's stolen command dune buggy roaring past (enabling Inyo County to hold Manson in jail). In 1989 we see a "Keep Out" sign and a notice that it's now being worked by Keystone Mining of Ketchum, Idaho. There's an old red Texaco gas truck by the side of the road, a grader and dump truck, evidence that the aura of aurum is still a powerful lure.

The bumpy turn-off to the Barker Ranch is not so easy to find. After a wrong turn up a twisty creek bed, we find the correct unmarked path. And there it is, the stone-walled and metal-roofed Barker Ranch, surrounded by antiburro fencing.

There are two main buildings. One is the small central, single-story house with walls of small rounded desert boulders and cement, with a metal roof and a front and side porch. The other building is for storage, located just to the left of the house, which is also of rounded stone with a metal roof. Along the front side of the storage building is a walkway covered with an overhanging arbor, probably for grapes. It was along this walkway toward the main house at dusk on an October day in 1969 that James Pursell slid silently to arrest Charles Manson, Bruce Davis, the unfortunate Christopher Zero, Bill Vance, Dianne Lake and others.

We crossed the fence beneath the traditional chi-shaped

Western ranch entrance—two posts with a horizontal beam. There were shriveled and dried pomegranates on the bushes by the walkway. The first thing we look for is the Manson school bus, with the "America—Love It or Leave It" bumper sticker. I had seen fairly recent photos of it in a very smashed condition. It's not there.

Time has not improved the Barker Ranch. In fact, this desolate and battered little house may no longer be the Barker Ranch. A sign on the living-room door reads: "Campers and Desert Rats. You are at the Chespa Mill Site. It is open to all to use. Please don't destroy this beautiful place. The gate is now being left unlocked so unthinking people won't drive through the fence to park a few feet closer. The fence is needed to keep the burros out. They use the water source for a bathroom. They eat the bark and leaves. Please help to protect what we all have. Keep the respect. Chespa."

The small cabin near the Barker house, where the scientologist gold miner Paul Crockett lived, is in fair condition, but the barrels of Mr. Crockett's ore samples are gone.

Pursell remembers the arrest of Manson as a basketball player remembers a championship game.

He points to the hill in back of the ranch house where he and Ranger Richard Powell waited all day long. At dusk, Manson, Davis and Vance arrived. They'd walked the five miles up from the mouth of the wash. Manson had been in Los Angeles.

"We were keeping the place under surveillance, had no idea that they were going to come walk up the road here. Had they glanced up they would have seen us."

After Manson and the others entered the ranch, Jim Pursell came down the hill and positioned himself out of sight by the side of the storage building. He was waiting for Deputy Don Ward to come up behind him. Then he edged along the walkway under the grape arbor to the ranch house's side door beneath the slatted porch. In 1989, the wall of the storage building is collapsed so that the walkway beneath the overarching arbor is littered with boulders and crumbled cement, but it 1969 it was clear and usable.

"When we hit the place, the evening of the twelfth, they were all in here, and the four—Manson and the guys that came in with him—were learning just at that moment what had happened two days before." Many had been arrested on October 10.

Pursell was in full view, edging along the arborway, gun in hand, when Dianne Lake walked out of the cabin. "She'd washed her hair. She had a towel wrapped around her hair, walked right out here in front of me. She had a hell of a cough, barked and coughed a few times, took the towel off, dried her hair. If she had just turned and looked, I was right in plain view. She went into the cabin and I figured, Okay, it's time to go."

Pursell went to the light-green entranceway. "I just shoved the door open, and there was the sink table there, and as I approached, one of the guys was standing with his back to me, and he had a telescope. I told everybody to raise their hands, and—how disappointing—they didn't do a goddamn thing. They just stared at me. So I told them a second time. The guy puts his hands up above his head with the telescope. And I took the telescope, handed it back to Don, and then I got him out and started to cruise the six gals around the table, ordered them out one at a time.

"Once I cleared this room, then I came in and it was dark in here." He spotted a single candle burning inside a mug on the kitchen table. "I picked that up. And, of course, we'd been in here before. I knew where I was going. I just went around the corner and checked out the bathroom.

"We went in there as Pursell continued tracing the arrests. It was a small room, with white plaster covering the stone walls. In 1969 there was a toilet and a sink with a tiny enclosure beneath it. The enclosure had a door and it was closed.

"Oddly enough, not only was it tiny, but there was a little—like a one-by-two brace, probably for a shelf at one time, running across the middle of that little door, which he had to get over.

"I got my little candle, got my revolver in my right hand, and I'm going around with this dumb candle and it just doesn't give light."

"Why'd you go in there?" I asked.

"Just checking it. I had no idea. I come in and put it down." Pursell reenacted how he lowered the candle in the cup to shed light on the compartment beneath the bathroom sink. "And in the glow of that lamp, there's hair sticking out between the cupboard door and the frame.

"We found some wigs a couple of days before. So for an instant I thought, Another wig. Then all of a sudden, fingers started wiggling out of the hair."

It was Manson.

Twenty years later, the little sink and the door beneath it are gone. All that remains is a pipe jutting through the wall about eighteen inches from the floor.

Tex Watson had claimed in his autobiography that Manson had instructed him to hide overnight with a double-barreled shotgun in an atticlike place above the porch of the ranch house. He was to wait for the return of Ranger Powell and Officer Pursell and kill them.

I told Pursell about this, and naturally he was interested in finding the hiding spot. We looked around. Although there's no attic in the Barker ranch, there is a small recessed spot, opening onto the slatted roofway of the side porch, where Watson possibly could have lain in waiting.

"After I got Manson out, then Don Ward and I came in once more to make one more tour through here. Don was carrying the shotgun. I had my revolver still out. And I think he ran into the corner of the table. All of a sudden there's this godawful explosion, and the stuff is raining down on us. Poor old Don had squeezed off his shotgun." It had been pointed downward.

Pursell pointed at the right side of the doorway on the inside. "There was a broom sitting here like this, and a perfect hole as the shot went through the broom into the floor and then shot and concrete went out of the floor and up and was raining down."

Now, almost twenty years later, we pull up a section of the linoleum someone has put down since then and look for the nicks of buckshot in the concrete.

We visited the Myers Ranch about a quarter-mile away. There are several fuzzy-fronded Athol trees, also known as salt cedars, at the entrance. Pursell remarks how much water the salt cedars devour. "If they get a toehold around some spring, they'll dry the spring out." There is an abundance of "Keep Out" signs, and on the swinging fence entrance "Myers Ranch, 1931." In the final desperate weeks of Helter Skelter, Manson had sent a couple of followers to kill the owner and thereby acquire the ranch, a plan, fortunately, which failed. Pursell recalled that the M group didn't spend much time there anyway, because they believed the place was haunted. "The ghost of Grandpa Myers haunted this house, and that's why they didn't come up here, they told us."

It was close to sundown when Jim Pursell, Larry Larsen and I headed back down Goler Wash to the valley. Pursell recounted Manson's final pitch for freedom twenty years ago. "Charlie was telling us on the way down, coloreds were going to take over the world. And we had two strikes against us. Number one, being white, and number two, being cops. And when it occurred we were in the worst possible position, he wanted us to release all of them and for us to take off and hide."

We drove the same 120-mile path the officers in 1969 had taken hauling the rest of the M group to the Inyo county jail in Independence. "It was very fortunate that everything began breaking down in Los Angeles at the time we had them here," said Jim Pursell. "Because, actually, we had nothing to hold them on. We didn't catch one person on or around any stolen vehicle."

In Bishop, we went out to dinner with Pursell and Buck Gibbens, the district attorney of Inyo County. Mr. Gibbens was an assistant D.A. at the time of the M round-up, and he remembers it well. The county still has an extensive collection of knives collected from the family. There are other curios around but apparently no films. There is talk in Inyo County of someday gathering all the Manson family memorabilia and depositing it in the local museum.

In Jack's Waffle Shop in Bishop, we had breakfast with the insightful former Inyo County district attorney Frank Fowles, now in private practice in Bishop. Mr. Fowles was the district attorney from 1967 till 1974. He's a graduate of the University of California at Berkeley, went to Hastings Law School and was the deputy district attorney in Solano County before moving to Inyo County.

Fowles is one of the more bookish men in the Manson case. He visits Berkeley about three times a year to add to his library. Among the various items collected from the Barker Ranch are several books, including Robert Heinlein's *Stranger in a Strange Land* and Gurdjieff's *Meetings with Remarkable Men*, both of which he read hot from the evidence locker. Heinlein, he recalls, was at one time interested in writing a book about the family, apparently after Sandy Good had approached him about it.

Fowles recounted how everybody was afraid in 1969 that Manson would be set free. The evidence to hold Manson in Inyo County was fairly flimsy, and just before Manson was charged with murder, two reporters from Australia—he believes from Rupert Murdoch's publishing empire—came to Independence and asked, "How much is Manson's bail?"

It wasn't very much. "We'll pay it," they said. They wanted to spring him and whisk him to Australia for exclusive interviews. Fowles had to rush to raise the bail to prevent it.

Frank Fowles has two souvenirs of the case. One is the air scoop on Manson's command dune buggy, which was a key piece of evidence enabling Manson to be held until the murder investigation against him was complete. The other is a Mrs. Butterworth's syrup bottle, which was found in the middle of a circle of rocks on the hill behind the Barker Ranch. It was sort of a votive shrine, where the women in the group could meet in privacy to chat.

Like other officials who investigated the family, Fowles was proud of former family member Paul Watkins, who is now very politically active. "He's the unofficial mayor of Tecopah," a town on the western side of Death Valley.

He outlined for Larsen and me the investigation he helped organize into possible connections between the Manson group, an English satanist organization and an international religious group. Also included was an examination of a possible connection between Manson and the Zodiac killer, who terrorized northern California in the late 1960s.

"It wasn't all that formal," he said. "It was the district attorney of Napa County, whom I knew and was a friend of mine, and myself and some others. It was a real loose contact between various law-enforcement agencies." He went to a conference they held; he thinks it may have been in L.A. "We got together just to compare notes and read each other's reports."

I was surprised at the possible link between Zodiac and M. Fowles said he was very interested because the string of Zodiac killings first came to light in Vallejo, California. "I was deputy district attorney in Solano County. The sheriff's investigator in the first Zodiac-Vallejo killing was a good friend of mine." Zodiac made one of his taunting phone calls within line of sight of Frank Fowles's office window.

Manson, said Fowles, "came from the Bay area around the time of Zodiac. There were unsolved murders up in the coastal region up around Mendocino County." And then there was the connection with the English satanic society, which was active in the Bay Area at the time Manson was there, and other connections that, in the words of Mr. Fowles, "made it worth looking into."

For its era, the Manson case was the case of cases. "The one constant that stuck throughout the years," said Frank Fowles, "is that you believe it's over; you believe that some connection is too wild to think about, and then it happens and it's true. I thought this was all through before the attempt on Ford. Who would have thought of that? I mean, from the beginning, starting out with a car-thief ring from Death Valley, who would think that one of the participants in that would make an attempt on the life of the president of the United States? Who would have even thought at that time that Ford would have been president?"

District attorney investigator Jack Gardiner, we were sad to discover, had died. He had been the guardian of Dianne Lake, who Fowles told us had ultimately graduated from Big Pine High School in Inyo County. "Jack was a helluva guy," said Frank Fowles. "He drove a truck, he liked the West, he liked horses, he also collected violins. He was a strange mixture. He collected antique violins and drove a truck, and was a law-enforcement officer and a hell of an investigator."

The Park Rangers and California Highway Patrol officers who investigated the family were scattered. Ranger Richard Powell, who was instrumental in hauling the M group to justice, is now the head of the Regional U.S. Park Service headquarters in Denver. Officer Dave Steuber, a much-admired investigator who made a number of taped interviews that helped prosecute the M group, was with the California Highway Patrol in Fresno, then retired and was in 1989 doing work for a district attorney's office in northern California. Lieutenant Hurlbut of the C.H.P., who was in overall charge of the Manson case in Inyo County, is retired and lives in Bishop. Deputy Don Ward had died of cancer. Doug Manning is now at the Lone Pine C.H.P. station. Al Schneider is now chief ranger at Lassen Volcanic National Park in northern California.

Back in Los Angeles, I spent time with my old friend Paul Fitzgerald, Patricia Krenwinkel's attorney during her trial and who later represented Leslie Van Houten in the appeal of her conviction after her third trial in 1978. He has the best memory of anyone associated with this case.

Fitzgerald is an accomplished artist and sculptor, with much of his Beverly Hills residence given over to easels, works in progress, and walls lined with paintings. In 1974 he was one of the founders and later the president of California Attorneys for Criminal Justice, an organization of criminal defense lawyers, which has grown since then to over 2,000 members. "Its goals," he told me, "are to provide an educational and training function. You know, no one trains new lawyers or journeyman lawyers. We put on seminars, training sessions, demonstrations, that kind of thing.

"One of the reasons that we all got together and formed this organization was that it had become a monologue in our society about crime. And the monologue was sort of directed by police chiefs. We wanted to turn the monologue into a dialogue." As of 1989, the California Attorneys for Criminal Justice is, along with the ACLU, the only organized group that provides information to legislators on pending legislation from the defense perspective.

Fitzgerald has the same scholarly appearance he had during the trial. He's slightly stooped, bespectacled, and with an elegantly battered nose from his days as a Golden Gloves boxer. His practice is still criminal law, but he is happy to report he has no current murder cases. I had learned, when visiting his office over the years, not to look too closely into any open file cabinet, lest my visual field fill up with the file folders of clients, to which grim snapshots of bullet wounds and staring eyes were paper-clipped.

He hesitates not a millisecond to speak out for the parole of Leslie Van Houten. He feels she has completely rehabilitated herself and is ready for a useful life on the outside. He's active in the campaign to give her a chance.

As an insider who experienced the full spectrum of family activities—from smiles, singing, love and bright colors to snarls and threats—Fitzgerald remembers how the love and tenderness were always so painfully intertwined with knife handles and hard times. When I visited his office he gave me a color drawing, signed "Lulu," of a child and her three cats in a field of grass and flowers. It was drawn by Leslie Van Houten in 1971, when she was on Death Row. He had inscribed it on the back, "Let us not forget that wondrous shiny innocence that makes the enigma of the family so painful."

As a scholar of the criminal justice system, Fitzgerald is concerned about the possible gulagization of America through the creation of an imprisoned permaclass. He informed me there are 73,000 in prison in California in 1989, and, grimly, around 84 percent of Californians believe in the death penalty. America would not find it pleasant to face a separate civilization of millions living in cages within itself.

"In terms of present-day body count, Manson was a punk," said Paul Fitzgerald. "There's now a serial killer that admits to killing 250 Right here in Los Angeles County, we've had ten or twelve people who've killed more than ten or fifteen people. But somehow this case had the right ingredients—movie stars, sex, violence, hippies. And somehow it captured the imagination, not only or the American public, but of the public around the world."

Fitzgerald and I visited the grave of Barry Farrell, who covered the Manson case for *Life* magazine and who died, decades too soon, in 1984. Barry was a fine writer and an investigator with the highest standards. After his years with *Life*, he served as the West Coast editor of *Harper's* and wrote memorable articles on the Symbionese Liberation Army, the Patty Hearst trial, L.A. Police Chief Ed Davis, and the Hillside Strangler for *New West*.

* * *

And what about the legendary team of L.A. sheriff's homicide detectives—Paul Whiteley, Charles Guenther and Bill Gleason—the team that more than any brought the Manson group to justice? They have all retired.

Sergeant Whiteley had transferred out of homicide in the 1970s and onto the vice detail. In the summer of 1988 he ruptured a disk in his back while breaking down a door during a raid, and after thirty-two years, he has retired.

Sergeant Gleason retired from the sheriff's office in 1986 and works part time for a district attorney's office in northern California. He teaches homicide investigation to state prison investigators, who work inside the prisons to handle prison assault and murder cases.

Deputy Charles Guenther has also retired, and he wants to keep his memories stored. As one of his brother officers described it: "I think the thing with Guenther is he really wants to forget about this case. He indicated that he didn't want to even talk about it anymore."

I don't really blame him. What a creepy case.

I went to downtown Los Angeles to the Hall of Justice where the trial was held. It's no longer the court building. The eighth floor, where Judge Older ran the Tate-LaBianca trial, is now part of the offices of the sheriff's department, although the lockup on the thirteenth floor where Manson, and before him Sirhan Sirhan, were held, is apparently still in use. The sidewalk outside the Hall of Justice, where the X-heads lived and awaited their avatar, is packed with lunch-hour striders who do not think at all about the crosses.

The district attorney and the courts are now located in a building across the street that was under construction during the 1970 trial. I remember how the hard hats used to yell down friendly comments at the defense attorneys, such as "Hey Hughes! Go get 'em!" The new criminal courts building seems hard, unrelenting and robo-law gaunt. The basement corridors leading from the parking lot are lined with transfiles packed with public records.

I went to deputy district attorney Steven Kay's office on the eighteenth floor to learn about his activities keeping Van Houten, et al., in jail. While I waited to pass through security, I walked over to the office reserved for the press, which I saw was now called the Bill Farr Pressroom, after the Manson case reporter who went to jail rather than reveal his sources. By the door was a brass plaque with a tressure of leaves: "In remembrance of Bill Farr for his dedication to his community and profession, a model of integrity for all to follow. Los Angeles County District Attorney Investigators' Association, April 16, 1987." Farr had suffered a painful death from cancer.

Steven Kay went to Hollywood High, then to Claremont Men's College, and then to law school at U.C. Berkeley. He began work for the Los Angeles district attorney's office in 1967. There was nothing particular about his office to indicate any obsession with the Manson family. It was appointed with pictures of his family and evidence of his duties as a sports enthusiast—autographed baseballs and mementoes of his work in little-league baseball and soccer.

I asked about the story in Vince Bugliosi's book that Kay had once dated Sandy Good. He replied that it wasn't much of a date. Their mothers had arranged a "let's get the kids together" kind of lunch at the Pancake House in San Francisco. Sandy was fourteen and Steven Kay was fifteen. It was a non-contact event, chaperoned by their moms.

I asked a number of questions about the current whereabouts of those one associated with the family. He keeps track of them. He said that George Spahn died in 1980. Spahn had bought a ranch, with his mate Ruby Pearl, in Klamath, Oregon, after the Spahn Ranch had burned down.

I asked why he had changed his mind about Leslie Van Houten getting parole. I read to him his quote in the *Los Angeles Herald Examiner* in January of 1980: "I'd feel better releasing a middle-age forty-year-old Leslie Van Houten than a thirty-year-old Leslie Van Houten." On August 23, 1989, Leslie Van Houten turned forty.

As a reason for the change, Mr. Kay mentioned the incident in 1982 when Leslie's husband, whom she later divorced, had been caught with a stolen female guard's uniform. Kay feels she should have used better judgment than to hook up with such a person and that she might even have known about the uniform.

"She's the only one I could ever see getting parole," he told me. "Possibly some time in the future, but not now."

But none of the others. Before Manson's hearings, Kay calls San Quentin to get a rundown on recent events. It's the era of support groups, and Charlie gets support, he said, from the devil community. "He gets a lot of devil-worshiper-type of fan mail." About four a day. Kay said M makes little paper scorpions and mails them somewhere in Oregon. He asked M about them at one of the hearings and was told, "The scorpion is the symbol of death, and I am the symbol of death."

So much for rehabilitation. Even though Manson will probably never be paroled, what about the others? Will the Rev. Bruce Davis, the Rev. Charles Watson, Susan Atkins and Patricia Krenwinkel ever get out? Maybe at the turn of the millenium; it's difficult to imagine it sooner.

Patricia Krenwinkel is "real antidrug and incredibly anti-Charlie," according to a friend who sees her frequently. She accepts the fact that she may never get out and talks about doing something to alert children and parents about drugs. "She said to me one time, 'I don't think my life would be a total loss, if they took me, even if it was in a cage, and put me in every auditorium in every high school and had the kids come and look at me and say this is what it can do for you, and stay the hell off drugs.' " Krenwinkel's parents have stood by her; her father visits her every other Thursday like clockwork.

And what about Leslie Van Houten's chances for freedom? She too has the support of her family and a continuing network of supporters. Even so, she faces numerous obstacles, the most mountainous of which is the continuing public fascination with the case. It's a data-retentive era, and the public can always be graphically reminded of the horror done to Rosemary LaBianca. She also faces the necessity of becoming her own public spokesperson—not an easy task. And she faces the growing public animosity towards those who have committed violence within a home.

I talked with a number of the attorneys associated with the case. I called Aaron Stovitz, whom I expected to be bitter about Evelle Younger's removal of him from the case in the middle of the Tate-LaBianca trial. The once vehement prosecutor seems to have mellowed over the years. Mr. Stovitz stayed with the district attorney's office and worked his way back up to where, from 1979 to 1981, he was head of special trials at the central office in Los Angeles, handling various murder cases. He retired in 1981. He's in private practice now and serves as a part-time court commissioner in Pasadena, handling traffic, small claims and some civil trials. He also teaches at a college in the San Fernando Valley.

I spoke with Irving Kanarek, Manson's attorney. Mr. Kanarek is still practicing law. I interviewed Daye Shinn, Atkins's attorney, whom I can still vividly recall striding briskly around the Hall of Justice with a thin Muriel air-tip cigar jutting from his mouth in a slightly upward direction. Mr. Shinn still handles cases and recounts with glee how Squeaky and Sandy would come to his house during the trial to work on their huge book—hand drawn and full of photos and stories, which no one would publish.

Prosecutor Vincent Bugliosi now practices law on Wilshire Boulevard in Beverly Hills but spends most of his time writing books. His book *Helter Skelter*, coauthored with Curt Gentry, sold six million copies and was made into a two-part television docudrama. Since *Helter Skelter* he has written three other successful crime books. I spoke with him several times while writing this chapter. Mr. Bugliosi is now working on a book about the John F. Kennedy assassination, in which his thesis is that Oswald acted alone. "And then I have another book," he told me, "which has just sold for the highest amount that Hollywood has ever paid for a TV miniseries. It's about a murder that took place on a South Sea island in 1974." Bugliosi was the attorney for one of the defendants, and he won the case for her.

After *Helter Skelter* was published, his coauthor, Curt Gentry, began a book on former FBI head J. Edgar Hoover, and he has been toiling upon it for the last fifteen years.

Mr. Bugliosi does not keep tabs on the former members of the family, though he is against the release of any of the murderers. He told me that Ronni Howard aka Shelley Nadell, Susan Atkins's cellmate who had helped break the case, had been murdered sometime in the late 1970s. There had been an attempt on her life during the trial when someone fired a rifle into her living-room window. She had also received $12,000 out of the $25,000 reward posted by Roman Polanski's friends. "I remember the conclusion of L.A.P.D.—I think it was L.A.P.D.," said Vince Bugliosi, "is that it was unrelated to the Manson family."

Judge Charles Older, I learned by calling the superior court, retired in September of 1987 after twenty years of transcripts. Judge Burton Katz, who as a young prosecutor had gotten a first-degree murder conviction on Bobby Beausoleil and later was a superior court judge, went into disability retirement, from a bad back, in April of 1987.

Evelle Younger, the L.A. district attorney during the Manson trial, became state attorney general, then ran against Jerry Brown for the governorship and lost. Mr. Younger has retired, living on the double D.A.-A.G. pensions.

Linda Kasabian's attorney, Gary Fleischman, is still in practice in Los Angeles.

As for Roman Polanski, he finally filmed the "costume extravaganza" called *Pirates*, which was less than a success upon its release in 1986. His next movie, *Frantic*, came out in early 1988, starring Harrison Ford and newcomer Emmanuelle Seigner, Polanski's girl friend. The film was released by Warner Brothers. In early 1988, Mr. Polanski played Gregor Samsa, a part that required much time on stage in an entomologic costume due to the bugification of Mr. Samsa, in a stage adaptation of Kafka's *Metamorphosis* in Paris.

In 1989, Mr. Polanski is still facing the 1978 statutory-rape charge in Los Angeles. There has been speculation that he might finally return to face the court, but his attorney wants Polanski to serve no time. Given the climate of law and order in California, the district attorney might insist on a jail term, especially since Mr. Polanski fled rather than face the humiliation of a cell.

And the houses where the murders were committed? I remembered how back in 1970 Phil Ochs and I went into the sealed Gary Hinman house on Old Topanga Canyon Road to look at the grim writing Beausoleil had placed on the wall. We squeezed down a steep embankment at the rear of the house, which served as the wall, and in through a very narrow breech where the roof touched the steepness. Hinman's house lay empty for a number of years, until it was purchased in 1981 and rebuilt, its size expanded by 400 percent.

The Spanish-style home of Rosemary and Leno La-Bianca, once owned by Walt Disney, at 3301 Waverly Drive—what happened to it? It looks about the same. It was owned in 1988 by a dentist and rented out. The street number has been changed, perhaps to throw off the queries of the curious.

And what about the house at 10050 Cielo Drive? The owner, Rudy Altobelli, put it on the market in 1988 for two million dollars. The agent handling the sale was Adam Jakobson, the grandson of comedian Lou Costello and, important to the Manson family saga, the son of Gregg Jakobson, who as a talent scout for Terry Melcher tried to promote the M Family as some sort of Singing Communards, ripe for prime time. Not long after it was put up for sale, Cielo Drive was purchased by a gentleman named Prell, who acquires name estates such as the home of actress Joan Collins, fixes them up, and deals for dough. As for his father, Gregg, Adam said he had not had much contact with him since early childhood but that his father was fine and living in Laguna Beach, California.

And what about the 100-acre site of the burned-down Spahn Ranch? It has been split up into some three parcels, one of which was purchased by Frank Retz, who, the reader will recall, wanted to purchase the ranch back in 1969. The ranch site is now open space. You drive down Santa Susanna Pass Road and there is a field of grass and weeds where once the dune buggies roared, and in the background is a round-topped hill with huge rounded boulders and mounds of clifflike rock. There's talk, said Steven Kay, of building condos there. I hope not, because the native grasses and the natural boulders are a transforming phenomenon for a place that truly needed healing.

And the Yellow Submarine house at 21019 Gresham

Street in Canoga Park, where the family in its premurder configuration had such high hopes of landing a lucrative recording deal? It's gone, replaced by a six-condo project in 1979.

And what about the hard inner circle? Cathy Gillies, Brenda McCann whose true name was Nancy Pitman, Lynne "Squeaky" Fromme, Sandra Good, and Catherine Share Como aka Gypsy?

Gypsy is gone. The police in L.A. seem to have lost track of her. It's not clear where Cathy Gillies is. Sandy Good has disappeared into the fabric of silence. Squeaky was moved to a more secure federal prison after she tried to escape in the fall of 1987.

And Brenda McCann, one of the most fierce of the family, is married and has three kids, I was told. She lives around Napa, California.

I located Bernard Crowe (in whose body a bullet from Manson probably still resides) in San Diego, thanks to the electro-sleuthery of Larry Larsen's staff, but he had moved on before my letter reached him.

And what about Ouish, Ruth Ann Morehouse, once the fourteen-old runaway daughter of a right-wing minister later turned acidhead? Once a lover of the young biker they called Donkey Dick Dan, she's now middle aged, living in the upper Midwest, and she has three children. She was helped by her sister, and later her mother, to escape the past. She does not broadcast to the public that she is the famous Ouish. As one of her friends told me, "She has a problem that is even more compound. She does not have an American cultural background. She didn't go to high school. Not only can't she say that she was with the Manson family, but she can't explain her background at all to anybody."

She was raised in the school of hard hippie.

Dianne Lake, Snake, is the star of family rehabilitation cases. I asked Steven Kay about Dianne. "She's spectacular," he replied. "Basically she's a corporate executive. Went to college, got straight As, dynamic." He protects where she is and what she does. I found out where she lived through compu-sleuthing. She's married and owns a house along the coast. One of the officers with whom I talked said, "The last I heard she was the vice-president of a bank in Los Angeles. She turned out very well."

I talked to the father of Kitty Lutesinger. She had graduated from college, he assured me, and has nothing to do with that part of her past.

According to the best information I have, Steve Grogan, formerly Clem, is a housepainter in the San Fernando Valley and stays out of trouble.

For Mary Brunner, Manson's first convert, the path was brutal, but after a few years in jail for the 1971 Hawthorne shoot-out, she was released on parole. Her family in Wisconsin offered help, and her son with Mason, Pooh Bear or Sunstone or Valentine Michael, was raised there. He's over twenty-one now. And Mary, too, has escaped the past.

Out there somewhere—the more remote and unattended by ink the better—are the scattered handful of foreheads with faint fading X's and those whom Fate hurled together in the torrid 1960s. Like oat husks blown from a threshing machine, they have gone their chaff paths.

For Bill Vance, the veils of silence fly. For the naked kids of the desert, now middle aged and struggling at the end of a brutal century, silence. For T. J. The Terrible, for Soupspoon, for Collie, for Yeller, for Little Larry, for the ghosts of the Spahn Ranch, silence. And I can appreciate more than ever the words of Andrew Marvell:

> But at my back I always hear
> Time's winged chariot hurrying near:
> And yonder all before us lie
> Vast deserts of eternity.

SIGNET (0451)

TRUE-LIFE CRIME

☐ **THE SHOEMAKER: *Anatomy of a Psychotic* by Flora Rheta Schreiber.** The shocking true story of a split personality, Joseph Kallinger, and his horrifying secret life of rape and murder ... "Chilling fascination."—*Library Journal* (160320—$4.95)

☐ **THE UNICORN'S SECRET: *Murder in the Age of Aquarius* by Steven Levy.** The powerful and harrowing tale of Ira Einhorn, a 1960's peacenik and New Age guru who murdered his girlfriend, fled the country, and is still at large. An utterly fascinating portrait of a man who embodied—and betrayed—an era. "A spellbinding sociological/true-crime study."—*Publishers Weekly.* (401662—$4.95)

☐ **BLIND FAITH by Joe McGinniss.** A galvanizing work of investigative journalism that chronicles the shocking murder of a Tom's River, New Jersey woman by her husband, while exposing the horror and growing disillusionment the couple's three sons experienced in the aftermath of the tragedy. "Remarkable ... fascinating ... a relentlessly true picture of social values gone hellishly wrong."—*Newsday* (162188—$5.95)

☐ **TWO OF A KIND: THE HILLSIDE STRANGLERS: by Darcy O'Brien.** With shocking information never before released to the public and 8-pages of chilling photographs, this is the inside story of a series of rapes, tortures, slayings and nightmares in Los Angeles. Kenneth Bianci and his cousin Angelo Buono, in the longest criminal trial in history, very nearly get away with murder.... "Horrifying"—*People* (163028—$4.95)

☐ **RICHIE by Thomas Thompson.** The heart-rending and powerful true crime story of a normal, strong-valued American family whose lives turn tragic when their son is drawn deeper and deeper into the nightmare world of drugs. "A powerful book.... It ought to be read by every parent and teenager."—*Los Angeles Times* (161297—$3.95)

☐ **BAD BLOOD: A Murder in Marin County by Richard M. Levine.** A couple are savagely slain by their 16-year-old daughter and her 20-year-old lover. This is the story of that murder, and the appalling events that caused it. "A frightening, disturbing book that illuminates the breakdown of the suburban American family ..."—*Los Angeles Times* (155033—$4.50)

Prices slightly higher in Canada.

Buy them at your local bookstore or use coupon on next page for ordering.

SIGNET (0451)

SENSATIONAL CRIME STORIES

☐ **FATAL VISION by Joe McGinniss.** The nationwide bestseller that tells the electrifying story of Dr. Jeffrey McDonald, the Princeton-educated Green Beret convicted of slaying his wife and children. "A haunting story told in compelling detail."—*Newsweek* (165667—$5.95)

☐ **THE MORMON MURDERS: *A True Story of Greed, Forgery, Deceit, and Death* by Steven Naifeh and Gregory White Smith.** The Salt Lake City car bomb murders that rocked the foundations of the Mormon Church. Exclusive interviews and secret documents reconstruct the most riveting tale of God and greed ever exposed. "Compelling, un-put-downable ... a first-rate true crime thriller!"—*Detroit Free Press* (401522—$4.95)

☐ **THE ONLY LIVING WITNESS by Stephen G. Michaud and Hugh Aynesworth.** The book that tells all about mass murderer-rapist Ted Bundy—in his own horrifying words from Death Row. With 16 pages of chilling photos. "Terrifying, bizzarely fascinating. . . ."—*Saturday Review* (163729—$4.95)

☐ **THE HILLSIDE STRANGLER: A Murderer's Mind by Ted Schwartz.** In his startling, in-depth portrait of one of the decades' most notorious murders, Schwartz analyzes the two personalities of Ken Bianchi: Ken, the gentle, friendly former cop; and "Steve", an admitted murderer of young women. The book details the arrest and interrogation of Bianchi, while under hypnosis. (154436—$4.50)

☐ **PRESCRIPTION: MURDER by Ann Kurth.** The nightmare true story of the Texas surgeon who murdered his first wife, and possibly four other people—told by his second wife and would-be victim! (163001—$3.95)

☐ **DEADLY INTENTIONS by William Randolph Stevens.** The chilling true crime story of a brilliant young doctor's monstrously depraved plot to murder his ex-wife—told by the prosecuting attorney who fought desperately to put him behind bars. "Gripping, hair-raising, fiendishly clever!" —*Kirkus Reviews* (162552—$4.95)

Prices slightly higher in Canada

Buy them at your local bookstore or use this convenient coupon for ordering.
NEW AMERICAN LIBRARY
P.O. Box 999, Bergenfield, New Jersey 07621

Please send me the books I have checked above. I am enclosing $________ (please add $1.00 to this order to cover postage and handling). Send check or money order—no cash or C.O.D.'s. Prices and numbers are subject to change without notice.

Name____________________

Address____________________

City ________ State ________ Zip Code ________

Allow 4-6 weeks for delivery.
This offer is subject to withdrawal without notice.